Behind the Public Veil

Behind the Public Veil

The Humanness of Martin Luther King, Jr.

Lewis V. Baldwin

Fortress Press
Minneapolis

BEHIND THE PUBLIC VEIL
The Humanness of Martin Luther King, Jr.

Cover image: Civil rights leader Reverend Martin Luther King, Jr. relaxes at home in May 1956 in Montgomery, Alabama. Image used with permission from Michael Ochs Archives/Getty Images.

Cover design: Laurie Ingram

Library of Congress Cataloging-in-Publication Data
Print ISBN: 978-1-5064-0561-2
eBook ISBN: 978-1-5064-0562-9

The paper used in this publication meets the minimum requirements of American National Standard for Information Sciences — Permanence of Paper for Printed Library Materials, ANSI Z329.48-1984.

Manufactured in the U.S.A.

This book was produced using Pressbooks.com, and PDF rendering was done by PrinceXML.

For my precious wife, Jacqueline Loretta Laws,

who shares both my passion for King scholarship

and my hopes and dreams for humanity

Contents

Foreword

Frye Gaillard

As I began reading the pages that follow—Lewis V. Baldwin's meticulous depiction of a fully human Martin Luther King, Jr.—I found myself remembering the moment when I first saw Dr. King in person. It was April 12, 1963, Good Friday morning, and two white policemen were shoving him along a Birmingham sidewalk. They came within three feet of where I was standing, a white teenager on a high school field trip, only dimly aware of events in that citadel of southern segregation. Already, the fire hoses and dogs had been unleashed, and as the protests lagged in uncertainty and fear, King, Jr. decided that he must go to jail himself. Whatever the risks, it was time, he thought, for a personal demonstration of resolve.

As for myself, I had simply stumbled upon the scene, oblivious to history, but deeply moved by the drama of the moment. The policemen, to me, were the embodiment of malice, one grasping the collar of King, Jr.'s denim shirt, and the other pushing him roughly from behind. But it was King, Jr. himself that I'll never forget. I'm not quite sure what I expected—perhaps some flash of anger or defiance, or maybe the fear I was feeling myself. What I saw, instead, in his large, dark eyes was a stoicism that seemed to shade into sadness, a face that was difficult to read, but clearly, not immune to the meanness on such conspicuous display.

That was the memory seared in my mind, and I later learned what happened next—how King, Jr. was taken away to jail and locked in a claustrophobic cell. There, in the gloom of solitary confinement, he brooded over newspaper accounts of eight white ministers in Birmingham—all of them known as racial moderates—who had publicly criticized his movement. They called his demonstrations "ill-timed" and his nonviolent philosophy a fraud, for his purpose, they said, was to provoke a violent response from racists, and to use the publicity to build support for civil rights. King, Jr. was troubled by the critique, and he set out to respond, scribbling notes in newspaper margins that were smuggled from his cell and pieced together by his staff. The result was his "Letter from the Birmingham City Jail"—another elegant demonstration of his ability to frame the public debate.

"I guess it is easy," King, Jr. wrote, "for those who have never felt the stinging darts of segregation to say, 'Wait'." He went on to write: "But when you have seen vicious mobs lynch your mothers and fathers at will and drown your sisters and brothers at whim; when you have seen hate-filled policemen curse, kick, brutalize and even kill your black brothers and sisters with impunity; . . . when you have to concoct an answer to your five-year-old son asking in agonizing pathos: 'Daddy, why do white people treat colored people so mean?'; . . . when you are harried by day and haunted by night by the fact that you are a Negro, living constantly at tip-toe stance, never quite knowing what to expect next. . . ; when you are forever fighting a degenerating sense of 'nobodiness,' then you will understand why we find it difficult to wait."

For me, the transcendent power of King, Jr.'s message was forever linked to the vulnerability I saw in his face, and I discovered that others had similar perceptions. One day in 1977, I met King, Jr.'s oldest daughter, Yolanda, on a movie set in Macon, Georgia. Yolanda, now deceased, was an actress, playing the part of Rosa Parks in a made-for-television movie about her father. I was working on a magazine article about the movie when Yolanda and I sat down to talk at the Georgia motel where she was staying. After a while, the conversation turned to Birmingham, which had been a place for such tragedy and drama, and she recounted a day when she was not yet eight and the telephone rang at the King home in Atlanta, bringing a horrifying piece of news.

On this particular Sunday morning, September 15, 1963, a bomb had exploded at the Sixteenth Street Baptist Church in Birmingham, killing four young girls, and Yolanda remembered her father's very human response. "I had never seen him so depressed," she said. For several hours, Yolanda remembered, King, Jr. seemed almost catatonic, sitting alone in his office, head in his hands, brooding in silence. This was segregation stripped bare, revealing the violence that lay at its heart—and, in a sense, the white ministers who had questioned King, Jr.'s tactics were right. King, Jr. *had* intended to expose that ugly stain, to put it on full and hideous display for all the world to see more clearly. But he had never imagined that this would be the cost—four girls barely older than his daughter killed, precisely because of his movement.

Eventually, Yolanda explained, her father pulled himself together, for he knew he must, and he traveled to Birmingham to preach the eulogy for the girls. "History has proven over and over again," King, Jr. declared, "that unmerited suffering is redemptive. So in spite of the darkness of this hour, we must not despair. We must not become bitter, nor must we harbor the desire to retaliate with violence. We must not lose faith in our white brothers. Somehow we must believe that even the most misguided among them can learn to respect the dignity and worth of all human personalities." Once again, the sheer depth of his human spirit proved indomitable.

Again and again through the years, when I had occasion to write about King, Jr. and his movement, those who knew him best would tell stories juxtaposing his humanity—his frailties, doubts, and vulnerabilities, *and* his delights in the ordinariness of life—with his extraordinary gifts as a leader. R. D. Nesbitt, a deacon at the Dexter Avenue Baptist Church in Montgomery, would remember a visit to

Atlanta in the fall of 1953. Nesbitt had been sent by his own congregation to gauge King, Jr.'s interest in becoming the new minister at Dexter Avenue, and when he arrived at two in the afternoon, he found King, Jr. eating a plate of pork chops. King, Jr. was polite as they talked about the job in Montgomery, but to Nesbitt, at least, he seemed more interested in the food. Nesbitt remembered being puzzled by that, perhaps even a little put off, but on a January Sunday in 1954, King, Jr. came to preach a guest sermon at the church, and the effect was electric. The deacons offered him the job immediately, and King, Jr. accepted for a salary of $5,000 a year.

Later, in Birmingham, a movement foot soldier named Lola Hendricks recounted her impressions when King, Jr. came to town. She would see him sometimes, despite the stream of threats on his life, walking to lunch at the Fraternal Restaurant, locally famous for its fried chicken and greens, its cornbread and pies. "He seemed so small," Mrs. Hendricks said, "just walking down that street by himself. So ordinary, really. He would talk to anyone who came along." But there was also the day, September 28, 1962, that seemed so remarkable to Lola Hendricks that she had trouble believing it was real. She was one of several hundred people in the audience when King, Jr. was speaking in Birmingham, and early in his talk, as he was going through a list of routine announcements, a white man began walking toward the stage. Nobody thought much of it at first, but then, the man, a Nazi sympathizer named Roy James, rushed the podium and began hitting Dr. King in the face. Several of King, Jr.'s lieutenants leapt to his defense, ready, it seemed, to tear James to pieces, until King, Jr. gently cradled the attacker in his arms. Mrs. Hendricks was astonished as James began to weep, and others did too, at this startling, unrehearsed display of nonviolence. "Dr. King was something special," she remarked.

But, for me, personally, the most poignant memory of all came from Andrew Young, King, Jr.'s lieutenant for so many years, who was with him in Memphis in 1968. On the night of April 3, King, Jr. had delivered his "Promised Land" speech—in the opinion of many civil rights scholars, one of the three or four greatest of his career. "I may not get there with you," he proclaimed in that moment of epiphany. "But I have seen the Promised Land." Exhausted at the end of his emotional address, and depressed, some said, about the future of nonviolence in a nation that clearly was becoming angrier daily, King, Jr. had retreated to the Lorraine Motel, and was waiting there the following afternoon for Young to return from a federal court hearing. Young was late, and King, Jr. was worried about an injunction, and when Young finally came in, King, Jr. in mock exasperation threw him down on the motel bed and began to pound him with a pillow. For a few minutes, they were like a group of school kids—King, Jr., Young, Ralph Abernathy, and the others—tussling and flailing away with the pillows until all of them finally collapsed in laughter. Then, it was time for them to go to dinner, and when they stepped to the balcony of the Lorraine Motel, a shot rang out from a nearby building. The bullet tore through Dr. King's neck, leaving the country with yet another martyr, a man who always seemed larger than life, even to those who witnessed his humanity.

Now comes Lewis V. Baldwin to put the pieces together—the vulnerability and the greatness, the heroism and the feet of clay, and Baldwin is uniquely equipped to do it. He has spent much of his distinguished career as a scholar writing about Dr. King—his philosophy, his faith, his culture, his gifts as a leader—and, as an author, he has always tried to keep it real, so to speak. One reason for that may be his own introduction to King, which came in 1965, when Baldwin, too, was an Alabama teenager wandering onto the fringes of history. King, Jr. had come to rural Wilcox County, where Baldwin lived, trying to get black people registered to vote. Baldwin was on the edge of the crowd, as King, Jr. faced off with Sheriff Lummie Jenkins, a white man who had long been a fearsome, intimidating presence. Baldwin noticed how small King, Jr. seemed, barely five-foot-seven, but there was the sheriff shaking King, Jr.'s hand, as the two of them addressed each other politely.

Soon enough, Baldwin came to understand that this seemingly

ordinary moment was a part of the triumph, for King, Jr. and the movement he led so well had confronted segregation's tyranny of fear. To Baldwin, I think, there was never a sharp distinction between the fully human man at the heart of this achievement and a martyr's role on the great stage of history. Thus, does Baldwin understand, more clearly than most, that King has been oddly dehumanized in memory, lionized, his legacy sanitized into stick-figure greatness. In the pages of this book, Baldwin sets out to reclaim the humanity of a flesh-and-blood King, Jr., portraying in clean and graceful prose, with a scholar's unflagging attention to detail, the man who lived at the heart of the myth.

This is an important piece of work that helps give a face to a history more human than most of us know.

Preface

Much of the inspiration to complete this book came through a very memorable experience I had back in early 2003, after being invited to give lectures on Martin Luther King, Jr. at the St. Paul Missionary Baptist Church in Brooklyn, New York, an all-black congregation led by my friend and former seminary classmate, the Reverend Dr. Johnny Ray Youngblood. I had talked about King, Jr. for almost an hour, highlighting his greatness and many achievements over the thirteen-year period of his very public life, and during the Q and A period, an attentive and curious little boy, who could not have been more than ten years old, asked the question that caused everyone present to stop, think, and frame the discussion in more reasonable, realistic, and down-to-earth terms. Referring to King, Jr.'s assassination, the youngster asked me: "Did the man who killed Dr. King think about his children?" It was, in some ways, the most profound question ever put to me about Dr. King during my twenty years of teaching and writing about him. We were all reminded at that point that while King, Jr. was, and remains, a towering figure and a celebrated leader, he was also a regular person, and, like so many other men, a husband and father. This is too often forgotten in a culture in which we have lionized King, Jr., sanitized his image, and made him larger than life.

That little boy, in his own innocent and humble way, confronted me with a greater sense of urgency regarding the need to re-evaluate King, Jr. with an eye toward reconnecting him to his basic humanity. That is what this book is all about. This is not the first book to highlight this need to humanize King, Jr., but it is the first in-depth and highly analytical treatment of King, Jr. from the standpoint of his fundamental "humanness." The King, Jr. presented here is not so much the great leader who led freedom marches, delivered dynamic sermons and speeches, and dominated headline-making activities, but the ordinary human being who grew up saying and doing what little boys said and did, and who loved to eat, appreciated music and dance, enjoyed the company of females and sex, delighted in sports and games, was a mimic and quite playful, and had the gift of wit, humor, and laughter. This is the King, Jr. that we all need to come to terms with and accept if we are to really understand and properly celebrate him. It is about separating the man from the myth, while placing each in its proper context.

Acknowledgments

I initially felt that writing a book about the "humanness" of Martin Luther King, Jr., or the King behind the public persona, would be an audacious, and perhaps even a risky, undertaking because of the ever-present potential for distorted characterizations. Fortunately, I was surrounded by family, friends, and colleagues who thought otherwise, and my decision to bring this book to completion is, in some measure, a testimony to their kind and generous words of encouragement and support.

I accumulated numerous debts while conceptualizing and writing this book. My first debt is to the many students who took my courses on Martin Luther King, Jr. over a period of thirty years. Before retiring in 2013, I had the privilege of teaching King courses at Colgate University, Fisk University, American Baptist College, and, on a much larger scale, Vanderbilt University, and at all of these institutions, I met students who stimulated my thinking with their probing questions and comments. The genesis of this book and other works I have produced on King, Jr. owes much to the exchanges of ideas I had with them.

I am greatly indebted to the late Professor Lawrence N. Jones of the Howard University Divinity School, who first sparked my interest in the more private side of King, Jr.'s life back in the late 1980s. I had a lengthy conversation with Jones in his office at Howard, and he suggested some leading queries that ultimately proved immensely important as I sought to understand the public–private dichotomy in King, Jr.'s life. Professor Susan F. Wiltshire, a former colleague who taught the classics at Vanderbilt University for many years, was also important in this regard. I benefited significantly from talks Susan and I had in the late 1980s about Martin Luther King, Jr.'s actions in the public sphere versus his attention to the concerns of the private, and her wonderful book, *Private and Public in Vergil's Aeneid* (1989), became my guide in thinking through these issues.

I want to acknowledge my deep indebtedness to two of my former colleagues, Professors Victor Anderson and Herbert R. Marbury of Vanderbilt University's Divinity School, for their generosity and support. They were always willing to engage me in civil and substantive discussion and debate, and spirited conversations with them helped me sort through many ideas in the earliest stage of this book. When it comes to my scholarship on King, Jr., Victor and Herbert have long been wise and insightful critics of both substance and style.

The many invigorating conversations I had in 2013 and 2014 with Rufus Burrow, Jr., a friend and fellow King scholar, were equally invaluable to the completion of this book. He listened carefully and eagerly responded to my reflections on the direction I planned to take with the content of this book. Burrow has published a number of solid, first-rate works on King, Jr., and he has always read my work with a sensitive and benevolent, and yet, critical eye. My conversations with him have greatly deepened my appreciation for, and understanding of, my subject matter. Burrow has always been kind and gracious in his praise for my scholarship on King, Jr., and he should know that I am no less appreciative of what he has done to expose King, Jr.'s significance as both a thinker and a Christian social activist.

I appreciate very much the support and encouragement of Frye Galliard, who has shown a special interest in my writings and teaching as a King scholar. Frye and I have shared very human stories about seeing King, Jr. when we were still too young to really understand what he meant to this nation and the world. Frye is the author of numerous works of non-fiction, covering topics from the civil rights movement to country music, to the political and prophetic significance of Jimmy Carter. I know of no one more knowledgeable when it comes to southern history, life, and culture, and this is why I asked him to write the foreword to this book. I am so pleased by his decision to honor that request.

The late John Egerton and my friend George McMillan were most helpful as I outlined and organized this book's chapter on King, Jr., southern cooking, and the social-cultural significance of food and eating. Egerton, a writer who published extensively on southern culture and folkways, and I met in June, 1986 and shared lunch at Swett's Restaurant, a soul food establishment in Nashville, Tennessee, and the conversation we had, in addition to the insights I gleaned from his interesting book, *Southern Food: At Home, on the Road, in History* (1987), proved enormously beneficial and useful. George McMillan, a former seminary classmate, shared both insights and a beautiful film on the history of soul food. Egerton and McMillan deserve special mention and gratitude.

Equally important were the assistance and encouragement of the late Anne Romaine, whom I was also privileged to interview in Nashville in the late 1980s. A folk music performer, historian, and writer, who was also active in the civil rights movement, Romaine offered rich information concerning the historical background of some of King, Jr.'s favorite songs and anthems. I drew on what I learned from Anne as I wrote the chapter on King, Jr.'s appreciation for various forms of music. I acknowledge with deep appreciation what Anne meant to me and to those involved with the Southern Folk Cultural Revival Project, a racially integrated group of traditional artists who toured the South.

I gratefully acknowledge the support I received from the late Mrs. Emma Anderson and Mrs. Sara V. Richardson, who first met Martin Luther King, Jr. when he was a student assistant to their pastor, the late great J. Pius Barbour, at Calvary Baptist Church in Chester, Pennsylvania. Anderson and Richardson were among other members at Calvary who adopted young King, Jr. as a son, and what they shared with me in their homes in the late 1980s, through oral interviews, afforded rich insights into King, Jr.'s personality, and especially, his love for food, play, and sports. I will always cherish the memory of Mrs. Anderson and Mrs. Richardson, who were living embodiments of practical wisdom.

A number of persons who knew, worked with, and spent time with King at different points in his life provided useful information and insights through oral interviews that helped bring this book to fruition. They are the late Philip Lenud, a close friend and confidante of King, Jr.'s during his student days at Morehouse College, Crozer Theological Seminary, and Boston University; Robert S. Graetz, one of the few white ministers who joined King, Jr. and others in Alabama during the Montgomery bus boycott in 1955–56; the late Bernard Lee and Ralph D. Abernathy, who worked closely with King in the Southern Christian Leadership Conference (SCLC) and in civil rights campaigns throughout the South; and Michael E. Haynes, who served with King, Jr. as an apprentice preacher and an assistant to William H. Hester, the pastor of Twelfth Baptist Church in Roxbury, while King, Jr. was pursuing the PhD at Boston University. The chance to meet, talk, and share with all of these nice people in the late 1980s came as an extraordinary gift.

Several persons who still live in Montgomery, Alabama graciously shared their knowledge about Martin Luther King, Jr. and certain people who knew and associated with him during his years (1954–59) in that city. Nelson Malden, who was both an Alabama State College student and a barber during that time, often cut Dr. King's hair, and was thus exposed to King, Jr.'s humorous side as well as his expressions of concern regarding his personal appearance. Mrs. Alma Johnson, the niece of E. D. Nixon, Sr., one of King, Jr.'s fellow activists in the Montgomery bus boycott, revealed important information about King, Jr. and Mrs. Sallie B. Madison, the Dexter Avenue Baptist Church member with whom King, Jr. and his wife lived on Grove Street while the parsonage was being prepared on South Jackson Street in Montgomery. Claire Milligan, who currently does volunteer work at the Rosa Parks Library and Museum on the campus of Troy State University in Montgomery, shared interesting stories about Sallie

Madison and Georgia Gilmore, who occasionally cooked fried chicken for Dr. King. Mrs. Gilmore lived on Dericote Street in Montgomery during those years. In any case, I am very grateful for the contributions that Mr. Malden, Mrs. Johnson, and Mrs. Milligan made to my understanding of King, Jr.'s human side.

I have always received warm courtesy and generous encouragement and assistance from Cynthia Lewis and Elaine Hall, who are staff persons in the library and archives at the Martin Luther King, Jr. Center for Nonviolent Social Change, Inc. in Atlanta, Georgia. More than anyone else, Cynthia and Elaine aided my foray into the King documents there. They have always been ready and willing to locate and make copies of documents for me, thus reminding me, time and again, that writing a book is always a collective enterprise. Cynthia and Elaine helped make *Behind the Public Veil* possible, and for that, I owe them a hearty word of thanks and appreciation.

My warmest gratitude goes to my wife, Jacqueline, who graciously shared some of the burdens of this book from its inception. She has been patient and supportive in this and so many other ventures. Because she has been with me for almost thirty-eight years, sharing so many of my conversations about Dr. King, I felt compelled to dedicate this book to her. Jacqueline's name appears on the dedication page.

Finally, I thank God for the journey that led to this book. I am always amazed that God would choose such an imperfect vessel like me to write so much about one who was, perhaps, the greatest spiritual genius this nation has produced.

Introduction

I have been writing about Martin Luther King, Jr. for more than three decades, focusing primarily on his roots in, and indebtedness to, black cultural and church traditions.[1] Having heard King, Jr. speak at a voting rights rally at the Antioch Baptist Church in my hometown of Camden, Alabama, the heart of the black belt, in early 1966, when I was only a junior in high school,[2] I have felt, at times, that my emergence as a King scholar is somehow providential. A cultural and religious historian by training, I have functioned on the cutting edge of King scholarship, and would like to think that I have contributed in some way to the development of major trends in the field of King studies. Hopefully, the many books and articles I have penned concerning King, Jr., along with the numerous chapters in books and the articles in journals and newspapers, have been useful and helpful to those who wish to understand and view this phenomenal figure in the proper context and perspective. There is simply no other way to come to terms with the little known southern black Baptist preacher who ultimately achieved national and international fame.

Scores of books have been written about the life, thought, and activities of King, Jr. Biographies highlighting the many events in his

---

1. My very first essay on the subject was "Martin Luther King, Jr., the Black Church, and the Black Messianic Vision," *The Journal of the Interdenominational Theological Center*, 12, nos. 1 and 2 (Fall, 1984/Spring, 1985), 93–108. I went on to publish the first book devoted exclusively to treating King's cultural and religious roots in analytical depth. See Lewis V. Baldwin, *There is a Balm in Gilead: The Cultural Roots of Martin Luther King, Jr.* (Minneapolis: Fortress Press, 1991).
2. Maria Gitin, *This Bright Light of Ours: Stories from the Voting Rights Fight* (Tuscaloosa: The University of Alabama Press, 2014), 250–51.

life date back to the late 1950s, and have become far too numerous to recall.[3] Studies of King, Jr.'s ideas, concepts, and intellectual sources and categories have also appeared in abundance over the last two decades, thus establishing his importance and contributions as a theologian, philosopher, and ethicist. We are also witnessing the ever increasing number of works concerning King, Jr.'s civil rights leadership and Christian social activism, which speak to his gifts, talents, and effectiveness as a preacher and as a practitioner of creative nonviolent protest and civil disobedience. Equally evident is that rather recent body of scholarship that compels us to treat King, Jr. *beyond* context, taking into account his meaningfulness and/or relevance for contemporary times.[4] But despite the rich outpourings of literature on the civil rights leader, I felt an almost intense desire and need to write *Behind the Public Veil: The Humanness of Martin Luther King, Jr.*, in part, because so little is known about the King, Jr. who functioned behind the public persona. The King, Jr. who spoke from pulpits in every corner of the globe, who appeared on countless television and radio talk shows, and who graced the headlines of newspapers across this nation and abroad is now a fixture in the public mind and imagination, but not the King, Jr. who retreated at times to the private sphere of family life, friendships and other intimate relationships, and the raising of children.

The lives of great figures are often sorted into categories of "public" and "private," and this is most certainly the case with Martin Luther King, Jr. As I thought of King, Jr. in these terms, I turned to Professor Susan F. Wiltshire, a colleague who taught the classics at Vanderbilt University for many years, and who had authored a superb book

3. The first biographical treatment of King in book form is Lawrence D. Reddick, *Crusader without Violence: A Biography of Martin Luther King, Jr.* (New York: Harper & Brothers, Publishers, 1959). This book reveals much about King's culture and religion, but it is seriously lacking in critical and analytical depth.

4. For examples of this rather recent trend in King scholarship, see Lewis V. Baldwin et al., *The Legacy of Martin Luther King, Jr.: The Boundaries of Law, Politics, and Religion* (Notre Dame, IN: University of Notre Dame Press, 2002); Lewis V. Baldwin and Rufus Burrow, Jr., eds., *The Domestication of Martin Luther King Jr.: Clarence B. Jones, Right-Wing Conservatism, and the Manipulation of the King Legacy* (Eugene, OR: Cascade Books, 2013); and David L. Chappell, *Waking from the Dream: The Struggle for Civil Rights in the Shadow of Martin Luther King, Jr.* (New York: Random House, 2014).

entitled *Public & Private in Vergil's Aeneid* (1989). Professor Wiltshire and I met and talked at times about my work on King, Jr. in the late 1980s, and our conversations, along with her book, heightened my sense of just how difficult it was in our increasingly fragmented society and world for King, Jr. to strike a proper balance between his activities in the public arena and his private concerns and loyalties.[5] Professor Wiltshire rightly contends that "Both public life and private life are required for living well, and to choose one and neglect the other deprives us of integrative structures of meaning on the one hand and the life-giving dramas of particularity on the other."[6] Needless to say, this point triggered so many thoughts and questions in my mind as I studied the life of King, who obviously confronted what Wiltshire calls "the public–private dilemma,"[7] and who was never able to meet the demands of his public life and his private life with equal reverence. King, Jr.'s public and private worlds routinely conflicted. His commitments to the public realm of social activism and politics too often exceeded the time and energy he devoted to the continuities of family, friendships, and other intimate associations[8] that make for the fullness of personhood and of daily life.

Behind the Public Veil is about King, Jr.'s desire and determination to create and sustain a life, a range of experiences, habits, and associations, beyond the public stage. Its content rests on the conviction that we simply need to know more about those private and largely unknown dimensions of King, Jr.'s life and personality. In other words, what was he like when he was not standing before crowds of people or under the glare of the media spotlight? How did he behave in the presence of his small, inner circle of aides, advisors, and confidantes? Was he more prone to "let his hair down," so to speak, when he was among that few and select group of black clergy with

5. I have given fleeting attention to this in Baldwin, *There is a Balm in Gilead*, 134–36; and Lewis V. Baldwin and Amiri YaSin Al-Hadid, *Between Cross and Crescent: Christian and Muslim Perspectives on Malcolm and Martin* (Gainesville, FL: University Press of Florida, 2002), 202–5.
6. Susan Ford Wiltshire, *Public & Private in Vergil's Aeneid* (Amherst: The University of Massachusetts Press, 1989), 3.
7. Ibid.
8. Baldwin, *There is a Balm in Gilead*, 134–36; and Baldwin and Al-Hadid, *Between Cross and Crescent*, 202–5.

whom he was very close? How did he act around close friends and family? What can we say about his attitude and actions as a husband and father? How did he handle being alone? The answers provided in the chapters of this book should reveal much about the lines that divided King, Jr.'s public and private personas.[9]

The need to make a statement about the polarity between the public and private in King, Jr.'s life was not my only rationale for writing this book. There were other reasons, which will become increasingly clear as readers move from chapter to chapter. One is that I wanted to provide a refreshing approach to King, Jr. Obviously, time and past associations with King have spawned a notable variety of images of the man, but I am tired of being a part of publications and public discussions in which King, Jr. is treated as if he was merely concerned about the world of ideas, the religious life, leading nonviolent demonstrations, and engaging in acts of civil disobedience. This makes King, Jr. accessible only to the well-trained, the religiously inclined, and the socially and politically active sectors of society. Clearly, his own approach to life was far more inclusive, in the sense that it also involved festivity, frivolity, and the ability to celebrate with real abandon. In other words, King, Jr. appreciated and had a festive, celebrative, and feeling-oriented approach to life, which Harvey Cox would characterize as "soul" or "soulful."[10] With this in mind, I wanted to write a book about King, Jr. and human life that would be of interest to ordinary people who delight in life's gusto, and not simply to

9. Brief but insightful references to "dichotomy and public-private persona" as this relates to King are made in Stewart Burns, *To the Mountaintop: Martin Luther King Jr.'s Sacred Mission to Save America, 1955-1968* (New York: HarperCollins Publishers, Inc., 2004), 259–60, 264, 346–47. Also writing about King, Richard Lischer comments on "the contradiction between the public mask and the private person." See Richard Lischer, *The Preacher King: Martin Luther King Jr. and the Word that Moved America* (New York: Oxford University Press, 1995), 196.

10. Harvey Cox's reflections on how festivity, frivolity, and joyous celebration are paths to a richer, more human and humane style of life were immensely important as I conceptualized this book about King's private persona. Cox highlights black Americans' amazing capacity for festivity and spontaneous and joyous celebration, and he declares that "the ability to celebrate with real abandon is most often found among people who are no strangers to pain and oppression." Cox goes on to note that "The awakened interest of white people in the black experience has enhanced our appreciation for a more festive and feeling-oriented approach to life. We call it 'soul'." See Harvey Cox, *The Feast of Fools: A Theological Essay on Festivity and Fantasy* (New York: Harper & Row, Publishers, 1969), 18 and 28.

academics, religious elites, and activists. Hopefully, the picture of King, Jr. painted on these pages will unlock fresh ways of viewing, understanding, and relating to him as a person and/or human being, especially for the uninformed reader, who is never present in spaces in which King, Jr.'s life, thought, and activities are seriously studied, discussed, and debated, and who is bombarded with "bigger than life images" of the civil rights leader via social media.

At the same time, I wanted to produce a work that would be of some benefit to scholars and students. While some may question the need for a work that shifts the research focus from King, Jr.'s academic pilgrimage, the usual configuration of the sources of his life and thought, and the essentials of his social justice activism toward a greater appreciation of his private life, there is still something here for academics and scholars who are open to enriching and deepening, and perhaps even rethinking, their understanding of the man who is variously known and celebrated as "the dreamer," "an American Gandhi," and "a drum major for justice."[11] This may apply even more to King scholars, whose interest in King, Jr.'s private life so far has been limited primarily to claims about marital infidelity.[12] *Behind the Public Veil* should push the conversation regarding King, Jr.'s private persona forward, beyond the charges of philandering and also his alleged

11. Lewis V. Baldwin and Paul R. Dekar, eds., *"In an Inescapable Network of Mutuality": Martin Luther King, Jr. and the Globalization of an Ethical Ideal* (Eugene, OR: Cascade Books, 2013), xxi (introduction); and Clayborne Carson and Peter Holloran, eds., *A Knock at Midnight: Inspiration from the Great Sermons of Reverend Martin Luther King, Jr.* (New York: Warner Books, Inc., 1998), xviii–xix (introduction).

12. While I understand the need to tell the story about this side of King private life, especially if we are to get a clearer sense of his "humanness," I am literally baffled by the longevity of the published works concerning his infidelity. Over the last three decades, numerous books about King have devoted pages and even chapters to his private sex life. I have often wondered why so much attention has been devoted over time to King's philandering when, comparatively speaking, we have seen so little in print about the sex lives of great men such as George Washington and Thomas Jefferson, the founding fathers, who reportedly had sex and even fathered children by their slave women. Perhaps this says something about what Calvin Hernton, Nat Hentoff, and others view as our continuing struggle, perhaps unconsciously, with the intertwining myths of race and sex in this country. See Calvin C. Hernton, *Sex and Racism in America* (New York: Grove Press, Inc., 1965), 4–5; David J. Garrow, *Bearing the Cross: Martin Luther King, Jr., and the Southern Christian Leadership Conference* (New York: William Morrow and Company, Inc., 1986), 374–76; Taylor Branch, *Parting the Waters: America in the King Years, 1954–63* (New York: Simon and Shuster, 1988), 239, 242, and 860–62; Rufus Burrow, Jr., *God and Human Dignity: The Personalism, Theology, and Ethics of Martin Luther King, Jr.* (Notre Dame, IN: University of Notre Dame Press, 2006), 8–12; Baldwin and Burrow, eds., *The Domestication of Martin Luther King Jr.*, 120–40; and Chappell, *Waking from the Dream*, 149–74.

intellectual dishonesty, toward broader and more inclusive approaches to the man behind the public image. If this happens, this book could possibly become an indispensable *vade mecum* for future King scholars.

I was compelled, for yet another reason, to write *Behind the Public Veil*. I wanted to separate the man that was Martin Luther King, Jr. from the myth that has been created in the decades since his death. The King, Jr. captured in myth has little or no resemblance to the real person who walked this earth, who had human needs, and who made human choices. To use King, Jr.'s sister Willie Christine King Farris's comment, which were made in reference to one of her own essays on her brother's life, "I hope" what is presented here "will help to demythologize one of our heroes."[13] The national holiday, the 30-foot stature on the National Mall in Washington, DC, and the occasional nominations for sainthood, have stripped King, Jr. of his basic, down-to-earth humanity, and have made the myth much larger than the man himself. The content of *Behind the Public Veil* humanizes King. Absolutely no uncritical adulation of King, Jr. is expressed or intended in the pages that follow. I have also tried to avoid any hint of a hagiographical tone, or any suggestion that King, Jr. was a saint who was literally obsessed with the common, daily problems that beset what he called "the least of these." King the human being should be retrieved, reclaimed, affirmed, and celebrated, and not so much the King who has been transformed to satisfy our obsessive and often unrealistic craving for heroes in this capitalistic society and culture.

This book consists of six chapters. Chapter 1 covers King, Jr.'s childhood and adolescence years—critical time frames that have long received inadequate attention even in the works of major King biographers. The central point here is that King, Jr. was essentially no different from any other boy growing up in the South in the 1930s and 40s, and that his boyhood and adolescence years constitute the appropriate point of departure for any serious assessment of his "humanness," or the quality of his life as a human being. This chapter

---

13. Christine King Farris, "The Young Martin: From Childhood through College," *Ebony*, Vol. XLI, no. 3 (January, 1986), 56.

will reveal the ways in which King, Jr. was quite human as a boy, even as he struggled to better understand what it meant to be human in theoretical terms. Considerable attention is also devoted to King, Jr.'s years at Morehouse College in Atlanta, Georgia (1944–48), Crozer Theological Seminary in Chester, Pennsylvania (1948–51), and Boston University in Boston, Massachusetts (1951–54), and how his studies in these academic settings, along with personal experiences, helped him to mature and to make the transition from childhood and adolescence to adulthood.

Chapter 2 is an attempt to answer, with some specificity, the question that drives this volume: who was this man called Martin Luther King, Jr.?[14] The answer provided is essentially twofold. First, that King, Jr. was endowed with a basic, rich, and genuine "humanness" which determined the direction and quality of his life, and which informed his outreach to both ordinary persons and the elites in our society and world. In more precise terms, according to this chapter, King, Jr.'s "humanness" suggests that he was fully capable of mistakes and weaknesses, which he frequently acknowledged, and yet, a deeply courageous, committed, and sensitive individual who really tried to liberate, uplift, and empower humanity.

Second, this chapter shows that the public realm did not define nor frame all of King, Jr.'s choices in life. Put another way, King, Jr. was not so public in his social mission and goals that be became completely oblivious to the equally compelling demands of his private sphere. Home and family were always on his mind, he devoted "quality time" to the fulfillment of his roles and responsibilities as a husband and father,[15] and friends and comrades in the struggle were never more than a letter or a telephone call away. Thus, the demands of the private side of King's life—however limited by time, commitments,

---

14. Interestingly enough, this question is raised in the interesting biography of Vernon Johns, who preceded King as pastor of the Dexter Avenue Baptist Church in Montgomery, Alabama. See Patrick L. Cooney with Henry W. Powell, *The Life and Times of the Prophet Vernon Johns: Father of the Civil Rights Movement*, unpublished version (1998), http://www.vernonjohns.org/tca1001/vjtofc.html, Chapter 26, 4.
15. Coretta Scott King, *My Life with Martin Luther King, Jr.* (New York: Henry Holt and Company, 1993), 200–201, 257, and 312; and Baldwin, *There is a Balm in Gilead*, 135–36.

circumstances, and other factors—were never entirely lost, even as he was catapulted into the international spotlight.

Chapter 3 explores King, Jr.'s abiding love for southern cooking, and especially soul food, which is one of those largely unplumbed dimensions of his private life that calls for further exploration. This chapter benefited from my conversation with John Egerton, and also, from a reading of Egerton's outstanding book, *Southern Food: At Home, on the Road, in History* (1987). Egerton shares a lot in his book about foodways in the American South,[16] and our exchange of ideas on this subject helped me to write perceptively in this chapter about King, Jr.'s appreciation and enjoyment of soul food in all of its glorious variety, and about how King, Jr., through his sharing of good food with family, loved ones, and friends, was actually participating in a long history and a culture and tradition that claim continuity.[17] Much attention is given to King, Jr.'s eating habits as they developed from childhood to his adult years, to his favorite food and drink, to those times he spent in his kitchen cooking during the first year of his marriage, to his appreciation for family-style dining, and to how he understood and appreciated the social significance of food and eating.[18]

Perhaps more than anything that has been written so far, this chapter captures King, Jr.'s sense of the immeasurable importance of food and eating as essentials of culture, and as a vital force in cementing family ties, in creating a spirit of human community, and in forging bonds and obligations between black people in the midst of oppression. It is not difficult to imagine how all of this took shape in King, Jr.'s consciousness, especially since the ideal of community was not only "the capstone" of his thought, but also, "the organizing principle" of all of his activities.[19]

Chapter 4 focuses on another significant and woefully neglected aspect of culture that figured prominently in King, Jr.'s youth and

---

16. John Egerton, *Southern Food: At Home, on the Road, in History* (New York: Alfred A. Knopf, Inc., 1987), 1–345; and *A Private Interview with John Egerton*, Nashville, Tennessee (27 June 1986).
17. Baldwin Interview with Egerton (27 June 1986).
18. Only fleeting attention is given to these concerns in Baldwin, *There is a Balm in Gilead*, 35.
19. Kenneth L. Smith and Ira G. Zepp, Jr., *Search for the Beloved Community: The Thinking of Martin Luther King, Jr.* (Valley Forge, PA: Judson Press, 1974), 119.

adult life—namely, major forms of sacred and secular music, or what might be called "expressive culture."[20] The main point is that great vocal and instrumental music, which was almost always tied to flexed, fluid bodily positions and movements in black communities, was part of King, Jr.'s cherished family, church, and folk heritage, and thus, central to the narrative of *who* and *what* he was.[21] The development of King, Jr.'s attitude and feelings toward music over time is traced in some detail, and so is his struggle to reconcile certain secular musical and dance forms with both the single-minded moralism of his church culture and his own personal religious values.[22]

This chapter affords a glimpse into the spiritual heart of King, Jr. It is largely a celebration of King's voice and life in song. It establishes, beyond doubt, that King, Jr.'s deep love and appreciation for the spirituals of his slave forebears, for the great hymns of the Christian church, for gospel songs, and for other musical forms, reveal the soul of a man who saw great art as inseparable from labor, from struggle, and indeed, from life. This helps explain why King, Jr. was so instrumental in bringing the rich musical forms and talents present in his family, in the church, and in the larger culture refreshingly to life in the context of the civil rights movement.

Chapter 5 examines King, Jr.'s playful attitude toward and approach to life—a side that remained essentially unknown outside of his circle of relatives and close friends. King, Jr. continued to play, in the sense of displaying a keen and enduring love for fun and frivolity, throughout his life, and not just during his childhood.[23] This chapter concludes that playfulness was one of King, Jr.'s greatest and most attractive

20. This term comes from Lawrence W. Levine, *Black Culture and Black Consciousness: Afro-American Folk Thought from Slavery to Freedom* (New York: Oxford University Press, 1978), 6.

21. Important references to the place of music in King's life and thinking are provided in Baldwin, *There is a Balm in Gilead*, 32–35; Lewis V. Baldwin, *To Make the Wounded Whole: The Cultural Legacy of Martin Luther King, Jr.* (Minneapolis: Fortress Press, 1992), 62–66; and Lewis V. Baldwin, *The Voice of Conscience: The Church in the Mind of Martin Luther King, Jr.* (New York: Oxford University Press, 2010), 103–5.

22. I have noted elsewhere that the young King, Jr. found it difficult to justify his appreciation for secular music and dance "in light of the objections and teachings of the church." See Baldwin and Al-Hadid, *Between Cross and Crescent*, 16.

23. King, *My Life with Martin Luther King, Jr.*, 59, 78, and 89; and "'I Remember Martin': People Close to the Late Civil Rights Leader Recall a Down-to-Earth and Humorous Man," *Ebony*, Vol. 39, no. 6 (April, 1984), 33–34, 36, 38, and 40.

character traits. Serious consideration is given to the ways in which he injected playfulness into his interactions with family and friends, thereby creating stronger bonds of mutual love, respect, and support while also contributing positive emotions to those relationships. It should become clear that for King, Jr., playing was not only personally enriching, gratifying, and fulfilling, but also, a powerful ingredient in enhancing the character of community.

This chapter raises and seeks to answer probing questions about the impact of King, Jr.'s tendency to bring his own, unique playful attitude and actions into the range of his life situations: What did this say about King, Jr.'s sense of himself and his philosophy of life?[24] Did his lifelong spirit of playfulness prove that he was secure, happy, and content? In what precise ways did this enhance the quality of his relationships? Was King, Jr.'s playfulness a source of love, of tenderness, of warmth, and of his connection to others? How did this translate into his robust love for and involvements with sports and sports heroes? How are we to reconcile King, Jr.'s often carefree and playful moods with the more popular image of the serious and responsible crusader, committed to the improvement of the human condition through nonviolent direct action? Was playing King, Jr.'s way of releasing negative energy and coping with life in the midst of all the drama, heartbreak, tension, stress, and threats against his well-being and life? Was being playful his recipe for freeing himself from worry and fear? How did this impact his physical and mental health? The answers afforded in Chapter 5 constitute further evidence that King, Jr. was steeped in black culture, and that his greatness cannot be fully grasped apart from his basic "humanness."

Chapter 6 examines King, Jr.'s genuine and enduring appreciation for folk wit, humor, and laughter, which means, in part, that the

---

24. While writing this chapter, I came across one of James Evans's most recent books, which explains playing as a key to the recreation of the self. Evans discusses playing as frivolous, but declares that "it is really the pulse of life itself." Evans's insights were quite helpful as I sought to frame my thoughts about King's playful attitude and approach to life. See James H. Evans, Jr., *Playing: Christian Explorations of Daily Living* (Minneapolis: Fortress Press, 2010), 2–4. For a very early, but equally important work on the subject, see Karl Groos, *The Play of Man* (New York: D. Appleton, 1916), 2–3.

relaxed and playful side of his personality will be explored in greater depth. Here, the focus is on King, Jr.'s respect for his people's ability to perceive, to express themselves, and to act in an ingeniously humorous manner, and also on King, Jr.'s humor as a form of playfulness. King, Jr.'s image as a good-natured and humorous person who delighted in the gift and power of folk wit and who told jokes to experience greater joy and laughter, and to amuse and lift the spirits of others, is highlighted. Attention is also given to some of the many comic anecdotes King, Jr. knew and shared freely concerning preachers, the church, ordinary people, and daily life itself.[25] Equally important in this chapter are the ways in which King, Jr. poked fun at white bigots, at the system of Jim Crow, and also at himself, relatives, friends, and others with whom he interacted and worked on a day-to-day basis. The conclusion is that the many personal and social problems and challenges King, Jr. faced never eroded his predisposition to play, wit, humor, and laughter.

As this last chapter in this books shows, folk wit, humor, and laughter are social and cultural phenomena that tell a lot about a people's spirit and philosophy of life. This was most certainly the case with Martin Luther King, Jr. and the black South that produced and nurtured him. King, Jr. shared his people's capacity to laugh even in the midst of adversity and pain, and this begs the question: Why? To answer this and other questions about King, Jr.'s love and need for fun and laughter, I read parts of John Morreall, ed., *The Philosophy of Laughter and Humor* (1987), Lawrence Levine's *Black Culture and Black Consciousness* (1978), and Howard Clinebell's *Well Being: A Personal Plan for Exploring and Enriching the Seven Dimensions of Life* (1992).

The Morreall volume, which includes selections from philosophers, appraises the value of traditional theories of wit, humor, and laughter, giving special attention to Plato and Aristotle's view of laughter as an expression of an attitude of superiority over another person, Immanuel Kant and Arthur Schopenhauer's sense of laughter as a human reaction to the perception of some incongruity, and Herbert Spencer and

25. Some of these jokes are discussed in Baldwin, *There is a Balm in Gilead*, 303–10.

Sigmund Freud's idea that laughter is about releasing superfluous nervous energy.[26] I found insights here that proved useful in explaining King, Jr.'s keen sense of humor and his wonderful capacity for hearty laughter, but the Levine book proved more beneficial, especially since the author treats folk wit, humor, and laughter in the context of black history, life, and culture. Levine's insights build substantially on what James Weldon Johnson, Claude McKay, W. E. B. DuBois, Jessie Fauset, and others said about the Negro's capacity to rise above the pain, ambiguities, uncertainties, and ironies of life through "the gift of laughter."[27] Casually dismissing the stereotypical view that black laughter is an indication of a "vacuous, happy-go-lucky" personality, which harks back to slavery, Levine, a cultural historian, concludes that laughter has long been a compensating mechanism which enabled black people to transcend the ironies and contradictions of life, to confront oppression and hardship without bowing to insanity and genocide, and to exert some degree of control over their environment.[28] King, Jr.'s humor, which found its fullest expression in his own familial circles, among close friends and associates, and in black church settings, increasingly made sense as I engaged Levine's reflections on "the economy of laughter," and on humor as "an interactive process" among people "who share a sense of commonality of experience and situation."[29]

Clinebell, an authority in pastoral psychology and counseling, provided yet another angle from which King, Jr.'s humorous side is

---

26. See John Morreall, ed., *The Philosophy of Laughter and Humor* (Albany: State University of New York Press, 1987), 1–7 and 9–126.

27. See Levine, *Black Culture and Black Consciousness*, 298–366.

28. Ibid., 298–366 and 488n1. The Jewish scholar Lawrence Levine actually draws on the insights of Claude McKay, James Weldon Johnson, W. E. B. DuBois, Jessie Fauset, Thomas Talley, and other black and white thinkers who made significant references to the unique ability of black people to laugh in the face of misfortune, and who struggled to know more about the philosophy of laughter as it related to people of African descent in the United States. Also see Jessie Fauset, "The Gift of Laughter," in Alain Locke, ed., *The New Negro: An Interpretation* (New York: Albert and Charles Boni, 1925), 161–67 and 214–15; James Weldon Johnson, *Along This Way: The Autobiography of James Weldon Johnson* (New York: The Viking Press, 1933), 118–20; W. E. B. DuBois, *Dusk of Dawn: An Essay toward an Autobiography of a Race Concept* (New York: Schocken Books, 1971; originally published in 1940), 148–49; and Thomas Talley, *Negro Folk Rhymes* (Port Washington, NY: Kennikat Press, 1968; originally published in 1922), 244–45.

29. Baldwin, *There is a Balm in Gilead*, 303–10; and Levine, *Black Culture and Black Consciousness*, 320–21 and 358–59.

examined and explained in this book. Clinebell asserts that experiencing "the healing energy of playfulness and laughter" is an "important and joyful way" to "health" or "wellness." "Laughing at yourself and the absurdities of life, and with others," he adds, "is an inexpensive, easily available, drug-free form of stress reduction that certainly can add life to your years and probably some years to your life. It's one of the simplest, healthiest, and most liberating health gifts you can give your mind, body, and spirit."[30] Such observations are quite relevant to any discussion of the ways in which King, Jr. employed humor, especially since, as stated earlier, he often laughed at life and at himself—at the way he looked, dressed, and ate.[31] This book will reveal that the healing effects of this kind of humor and laughter are difficult to exaggerate, especially for a widely known and celebrated public figure such as King, Jr., who constantly lived under the threat of death. The findings and insights of Clinebell, Levine, Morreall, and other scholars came together in my consciousness as I examined the needs and uses of wit, humor, and laughter for King, Jr.

The picture of King, Jr. coursing through chapters 5 and 6 of *Behind the Public Veil* contrasts sharply with the characterizations projected in even the most respected, innovative, and celebrated works on this colorful figure. Apparently drawing on a different body of evidence, some of the most reputable King scholars have described King, Jr. as a man who was "always worried," "tortured," "torn up on the inside," chronically "self-critical," plagued by mounting "inner tension" and "self-doubts," and haunted by "consuming guilt" and "the menacing threat of despair." They have also written in touching language about King, Jr.'s "underlying loneliness," his "growing pessimism," his "deep" and "nearly incapacitating depression," his "persistent despondency, confusion, and doubt," the difficulties he faced "persevering" and living "comfortably," and how he "drank more" in the final days of

---

30. Howard Clinebell, *Well Being: A Personal Plan for Exploring and Enriching the Seven Dimensions of Life—Mind, Body, Spirit, Love, Work, Play, the Earth* (New York: HarperCollins Publishers, 1992), 159. Clinebell also make a fleeting but important reference to "the healing energy of laughter" in Howard Clinebell, *Basic Types of Pastoral Care & Counseling: Resources for the Ministry of Healing and Growth* (Nashville: Abingdon Press, 2011), 344.
31. Baldwin, *There is a Balm in Gilead*, 309.

his life.[32] The purpose of *Behind the Public Veil* is not to question nor refute this seemingly one-dimensional view of King, but, rather, to call the reader's attention to that side of King, Jr.'s life and personality which has gotten lost in all of the aforementioned claims made by King, Jr. scholars—that side that had to do with unfettered festivity, enjoying and celebrating the many pleasures of life in the moment without worrying unnecessarily, the ability to sing, dance, play, and laugh, and the capacity "to see the humor in even the most difficult situations."[33] King, Jr.'s voracious appetite for soul food; his deep and lasting appreciation for different kinds of music; his strong and abiding love for play and sports; his keen sense of the power of folk wit, humor, and laughter; his amazing, lifelong openness to merrymaking and a celebrative and feeling-oriented approach to life and living—these are vital and amply attested elements of King, Jr.'s "humanness," which accounts about his personal defects and struggles should not be permitted to overshadow.

Behind the Public Veil was never designed to provide a complete portrait of Martin Luther King, Jr., and nor is it an attempt at a revisionist use of King, Jr. The book is simply an effort to humanize King, Jr. and to bring to light that largely unknown side of *who* and *what* he was. It reclaims the man who smiled, laughed, and cried, and who, by the power of his presence and personality, made others smile, laugh, and cry. It refocuses attention on a man who identified with ordinary people, who did the kinds of things they did, and who simply wanted to

---

32. Burns, *To the Mountaintop*, 225–27, 260–61, 265, 280, 287, 345–47, 355, 377–78, 394, 403, 406–7, 421–22, 427, 429–30, and 435–37; David J. Garrow, *The FBI and Martin Luther King, Jr.: From "Solo" to Memphis* (New York: W. W. Norton & Company, 1981), 216–19; Baldwin and Burrow, *The Domestication of Martin Luther King Jr.*, 126–27, 131, and 137; Garrow, *Bearing the Cross*, 114–15 and 603–4; Branch, *Parting the Waters*, 702; Lischer, *The Preacher King*, 167–72; Chappell, *Waking from the Dream*, 13, 186n7, 187n12, and 188n26–27; and Taylor Branch, *At Canaan's Edge: America in the King Years, 1965–68* (New York: Simon & Schuster, 2006), 194–95 and 641. Interestingly enough, even Coretta Scott King characterized her husband as guilt-ridden. See King, *My Life with Martin Luther King, Jr.*, 169–70. I have taken issue with this limited view of King in Baldwin, *There is a Balm in Gilead*, 309–10. Rufus Burrow appears to challenge the claims about King's growing pessimism. See Rufus Burrow, Jr., *Extremist for Love: Martin Luther King Jr., Man of Ideas and Nonviolent Social Action*. (Minneapolis: Fortress Press, 2014), 309.
33. King, *My Life with Martin Luther King, Jr.*, 89; Baldwin, *There is a Balm in Gilead*, 303–10; and "'I Remember Martin,'" 33–40.

be seen and treated as a human being. Strangely, this man remains "an enigma"[34] for all too many in our nation and world.

It is not excessive to suggest that humanizing King, Jr. makes him more, and not less, heroic. In fact, it is in his humanity that we discover the sheer quality of his character, life, soul, and spirit. Here lies the essence of his heroism and greatness.

34. "'I Remember Martin,'" 33.

1

"A Regular Fella": The Boy Named M. L. King, Jr.

Children will grow up substantially what they are by nature—and only that.
  –Harriet Beecher Stowe[1]

What has not been emphasized enough is that Martin was once a boy. He, like others, developed gradually. He was funny. He was curious. He liked to play. He was a regular "fella."
  –Christine King Farris[2]

Martin Luther King, Jr.'s life and adventures as a child have seldom been taken seriously in works about him. It is too often forgotten that King, Jr. was an ordinary boy before he became a great man. In the rare cases in which his childhood has been seriously considered, it is used primarily to further highlight what Frederick L. Downing calls his "mythic and heroic trajectory."[3] Consequently, we get embellished portrayals of the gifted child who grew up to become a great hero, but

---

1. Quoted in Charles Noel Douglas, comp., *Forty Thousand Sublime and Beautiful Thoughts: Gathered from the Roses, Clover Blossoms, Geraniums, Violets, Morning Glories, and Pansies of Literature* (New York: Louis Klopsch, 1904), 257.
2. Christine King Farris, *My Brother Martin: A Sister Remembers Growing Up with the Rev. Dr. Martin Luther King, Jr.* (New York: Simon & Schuster Books for Young Readers, 2003), 39.

not images of an average boy who looked, thought, and acted like a child before becoming a genuinely human and down-to-earth man.[4]

This first chapter reclaims King, Jr.'s childhood as foundational for understanding his essential "humanness." It begins with a focus on a boy who not only participated in a variety of rough-and-tumble play, as children typically do, but who, like so many other youngsters in his day, was also quite sensitive, curious, attentive, unusually mature in mental aptitude, and prone to a questioning attitude toward life.[5] Attention is also devoted to the human side of King, Jr., as revealed through the lens of his everyday life and interactions at Morehouse College in Atlanta, Georgia; Crozer Theological Seminary in Chester, Pennsylvania; and Boston University in Boston, Massachusetts. King, Jr.'s Boston years—1951 to 1954—are treated as the terminal point for the content of this chapter because it was during this time frame that King, Jr.'s transition from boyhood to manhood, particularly at the level of his values and choices, first became most pronounced and evident.

A. To Be Young, Curious, and Black: King, Jr.'s Childhood Years

In an article about Martin Luther King, Jr.'s childhood years, Willie Christine King Farris has noted that "my brother was no saint, ordained as such at birth." She went on to describe little M. L or Mike, as King, Jr. was affectionately called in those early years, as an average and ordinary boy who absolutely delighted in doing the kinds of things boys usually did.[6] An "extraordinarily healthy child" from birth, he

3. Frederick L. Downing, *To See the Promised Land: The Faith Pilgrimage of Martin Luther King, Jr.* (Macon, GA: Mercer University Press, 1986), 11.
4. Christine King Farris, "The Young Martin: From Childhood through College," *Ebony*, Vol. XLI, no. 3 (January, 1986), 56; Alberta King, "Dr. Martin Luther King, Jr.: Birth to Twelve Years Old by His Mother," a recording, Ebenezer Baptist Church (18 January 1973), Library and Archives of The Martin Luther King, Jr. Center for Nonviolent Social Change, Inc., Atlanta, Georgia; and "'I Remember Martin': People Close to the Late Civil Rights Leader Recall a Down-to-earth and Humorous Man," *Ebony*, Vol. 39, no. 6 (April, 1984), 3–34, 36, 38, and 40.
5. Clayborne Carson, ed., *The Autobiography of Martin Luther King, Jr.* (New York: Warner Books, Inc., 1998), 1–12; Martin Luther King, Sr., *Daddy King: An Autobiography*, with Clayton Riley (New York: William Morrow & Company, 1980), 107–28; and Christine King Farris, *Through It All: Reflections on My Life, My Family, and My Faith* (New York: Atria Books, 2009), 16–27.
6. Farris, "The Young Martin," 56.

found great pleasure in climbing, jumping, and sticking his head out of the back door windows of parked cars.[7] King, Jr. also enjoyed playing different games with his older sister, Christine, and his baby brother, A. D. The King home at 501 Auburn Avenue Northeast in Atlanta, Georgia—comprising also the children's parents, King, Sr. and Alberta Williams King; their maternal grandmother, Jennie C. Parks Williams; their great aunt, Ida Worthem; and their uncle Joel King[8]—was often the scene of spirited activity, as King, Jr., Christine, and A. D. did their share of running, tussling, and tumbling, in addition to playing "hide and seek" and "tag" and locking themselves in the hall cabinet, almost breaking the door at one point.[9] Christine "was often teased by her more rambunctious younger brothers," and the play did get a little too rough at times, but King, Jr., unlike A. D., was never known in his neighborhood for toughness or for antagonizing other children.[10] However, this did not mean that the youngster was totally incapable of the kind of genuine fighting to which boys commonly resorted. On one occasion, when A. D. antagonized Christine, King, Jr. "conked his battling brother over the head with a telephone, leaving him dazed and wobbly on his feet." After determining that A. D. was not seriously injured, M. L., Sr. and Alberta Williams King, the children's parents, found some humor in the incident and laughed mildly, sensing that little A. D. had gotten a taste of his own medicine.[11]

But King, Jr., who inherited his "single-minded determination, faith

7. Clayborne Carson, et al., eds., *The Papers of Martin Luther King, Jr., Volume I. Called to Serve, January 1929-June 1951* (Berkeley: University of California Press, 1992), 359; Farris, "The Young Martin," 56; Farris, *Through It All*, 21–22; and King, "Dr. Martin Luther King, Jr.: Birth to Twelve Years Old."
8. This type of family fabric made all the more possible the transmission of cultural and spiritual values across generations, dating back to the slave quarters. King, Sr. was a Baptist pastor; his wife, Alberta, an accomplished musician; Mama Jennie, a widely sought-after speaker; Aunt Ida (Grandma Jennie's sister), a teacher; and Uncle Joel, a preacher. All were deeply rooted in southern black Baptist Protestantism, and were exemplary in their faith. See Farris, *Through It All*, 31; Farris, "The Young Martin," 56; and Lewis V. Baldwin, *There is a Balm in Gilead: The Cultural Roots of Martin Luther King, Jr.* (Minneapolis: Fortress Press, 1991), 91–126.
9. Carson, et al., eds., *King Papers*, I, 359; Farris, "The Young Martin," 56; Farris, *Through It All*, 21–23; King, "Dr. Martin Luther King, Jr.: Birth to Twelve Years Old"; and Frederick L. Downing, *To See the Promised Land*, 43–44.
10. King, *Daddy King*, 126.
11. Christine recalls that despite "being the baby, A. D. never acted it." From the beginning, she added, "he was the bravest and most 'devilishly creative' of us all." Philip Lenud, one of King, Jr.'s boyhood friends, reported that as a teenager, A. D., perhaps spoiled because he was the youngest of the trio, had conflicts with even M. L., Sr., and his daddy threatened to put him out of the house

and forthrightness" from his father, fondly called Daddy King, did not have the temper of the elder King, who allegedly got physical on one occasion with a preacher who owed him money and refused to pay the debt.[12] When it came to matters of temperament, King, Jr. tended to be more like his mother, Alberta, from whom he "got his love, compassion and ability to listen to others." Mother Dear, as King, Jr. and his siblings called her, "was the strong pacifist in the family," and King, Jr. "got that from her."[13] King, Jr. himself recalled that he was never "one" to "retaliate" or "to hit back too much," that this "was a part of my native structure so to speak. . . ."[14] Daddy King, also weighing in on the question of his son's manner of thinking and behaving as a child, noted that King, Jr. "was always a little sensitive in his responses to even the most casual matters, and he was always one to negotiate a dispute instead of losing his temper."[15] King, Jr.'s mother Alberta agreed wholeheartedly, declaring: "No, he didn't fight at all. He didn't fight like a lot of little boys, guns or anything."[16]

At a time when boys took pride in and virtually glorified their pistol and holster sets, King, Jr. absolutely refused to play with guns.[17] This tendency on the child's part owed much to the teachings and example of not only his mother, but also Grandma Jennie and Aunt Ida—all of whom shared, to some degree, Daddy King's idea of a "morally strict,"

on a few occasions. See Farris, *Through It All*, 22; King, *Daddy King*, 126–27; and A Private Interview with Philip Lenud, Vanderbilt Divinity School, Nashville, Tennessee (7 April 1987).
12. Farris, "The Young Martin," 57; and Baldwin Interview with Lenud (7 April 1987).
13. Farris, "The Young Martin," 57; Baldwin Interview with Lenud (7 April 1987); King, "Dr. Martin Luther King, Jr.: Birth to Twelve Years Old"; Downing, *To See the Promised Land*, 43–44; Coretta Scott King, *My Life with Martin Luther King, Jr.* (New York: Henry Holt and Company, Inc., 1993; originally published in 1969), 77; and Baldwin Interview with Lenud (7 April 1987).
14. King made these comments in the context of an interview in which he declared that he was never apt to retaliate against whites who verbally and physically assaulted him when he was a child, and this included the white woman who "slapped me" in "one of the downtown stores of Atlanta" "when I was about eight years old." See "Face to Face: Dr. Martin Luther King, Jr. and John Freeman," U. K. (London?), recorded from transmission and aired (29 October 1961), King Center Library and Archives, 4–5.
15. King, *Daddy King*, 126.
16. Alberta elaborated further, noting that this tendency toward nonviolence "came up" in King, Jr., and that "that was a part of him when he got to be a man." She went on to say: "And that was why when he wanted to get things done and make things better for all of us, he wanted to do it without a lot of fussing and fighting. He wanted to do it another way. And he did." See King, "Dr. Martin Luther King, Jr.: Birth to Twelve Years Old"; and Downing, *To See the Promised Land*, 43.
17. King, "Dr. Martin Luther King, Jr.: Birth to Twelve Years Old"; and Downing, *To See the Promised Land*, 43.

somewhat "provincial," and "rather regimented" upbringing for his children. In conformity with the King family's house rules, King, Jr. not only went to bed early, arrived at school on time, returned home immediately after school, did his homework, and attended Sunday School and Church,[18] but also limited himself, for the most part, to toys that were considered safe and enjoyable as well as educational for youngsters. King, Jr.'s toys "included a train, building blocks, skates, and a bicycle," with "a swing, a slide, and a basketball goal" in the backyard. The youngster played hard and "perhaps with some abandon," and on a few occasions, was either frightened, grazed, or slightly struck by a car as he chased balls or rode his bicycle in the streets. Constant warnings from his parents about playing in the streets were not always heeded. In any case, King, Jr. "had a good time when he was a little boy,"[19] and he never got into the kind of trouble that required the attention and involvement of his principals, teachers, the police, or other authority figures outside the family. Undoubtedly, young King, Jr.'s "congenial home situation," in which his parents "always lived together very intimately" and hardly "ever argued,"[20] was more significant than anything else in the shaping of this side of his personality.

Despite King, Jr.'s generally peaceful childhood demeanor, he nevertheless had a strong inclination toward the kind of mischief that caused discomfiture in others, including his own sister, Christine. He and A. D. beheaded a number of Christine's dolls and "scattered their body parts throughout the house" and "in the backyard in the weeds near the fence." Needless to say, such behavior was always most annoying for Christine, who "liked playing with dolls. . . ."[21] At times, King, Jr. joined both of his siblings in frightening people with their

---

18. It is reported that King, Jr. left for school at 8:00 a.m. and returned home by 3:00 p.m. At Sunday School, and at the meetings of the Baptist Youth Training Union, the boy heard Bible stories that he memorized. See King, "Dr. Martin Luther King, Jr.: Birth to Twelve Years Old"; and Downing, *To See the Promised Land*, 45–46.
19. King, "Dr. Martin Luther King, Jr.: Birth to Twelve Years Old"; and Downing, *To See the Promised Land*, 43–44.
20. Carson, et al., eds., *King Papers*, I, 360; and Carson, ed., *The Autobiography of Martin Luther King, Jr.*, 4–5.
21. Farris, *Through It All*, 22.

21

Grandma Jennie's "old fox fur," which was "complete with head and glass eyes." The youngsters would "tie the fox fur to a long stick," hide behind shrubbery in their front yard, and take turns wiggling and dangling the fox as unsuspecting folk approached, thus scaring them "as they walked by on the sidewalk." This prank was particularly effective with women, who "would scream and clutch their husbands by the arm." The "great commotion" that followed proved gratifying for King, Jr. and his siblings, who likely responded with a lot of giggling and high-pitched noises. The "little prank went on for quite a while," but ended abruptly when neighbors informed Daddy King of what his children were doing.[22]

King, Jr. was viewed in certain family circles as a "bullheaded" boy who always preferred to lead, rather than follow.[23] But, interestingly enough, he usually played the role of teaser and prankster without becoming overly aggressive, and was never seriously agitated when his classmates and playmates teased, played mischievous tricks, or poked fun at him. At times, he was called names that corresponded with a particular aspect of his personality or behavior. When King, Jr.'s mother, Alberta purchased him a brown tweed suit for his sixth-grade graduation from Atlanta's David T. Howard Elementary School, the boy wore the suit so much until his friends jokingly called him "Tweed," a "name that stuck with him for the next several years." King, Jr. apparently took all of the teasing and laughter in stride.[24] Strangely, the youngster's love for that "tweed" or "draped suit," which was "tight at the ankles and baggy in the legs,"[25] was actually suggestive of what would become a lifelong fascination with and appreciation for nice, fancy, and stylish clothes.[26]

The ordinary routines of child's play constituted the source of much of King, Jr.'s fun, happiness, and sense of security in those early years.

22. Ibid., 22–23.
23. Ibid., 21.
24. Farris, "The Young Martin," 57; and Farris, Through It All, 27.
25. Farris, "The Young Martin," 57.
26. King, Jr.'s sister Christine recalls that their parents taught them "to dress properly and appropriately at all times." Daddy King was known to wear a necktie everyday, even "if he had his sleeves rolled up." See Farris, Through It All, 18.

His experiences with playing were important for his own growth and emotional well-being, and they helped him to relate in generally positive ways to nature and the physical world, to better understand self and others, to develop strong interactive skills, and to build solid social relationships. It is difficult to imagine a better background, especially for one who would grow up to become a major participant in types of community formation.[27] But there were also experiences that were not as enriching and empowering—though nonetheless educational for King, Jr. A case in point was the youngster's relationship with two white boys whose father owned a store in the King family's neighborhood. The boys became King, Jr.'s "inseparable playmates" for a few years. They "played ball" and "climbed trees" together, but when King, Jr. was about six years old, his white playmates told him that their "father had demanded" that they not "play childhood games" with him any longer, obviously because he was colored.[28] Shocked, confused, and utterly devastated, little King, Jr. turned to his mother for an explanation:

> My mother took me on her lap and began by telling me about slavery and how it had ended with the Civil War. She tried to explain the divided system of the South—the segregated schools, restaurants, theaters, housing; the white and colored signs on drinking fountains, waiting rooms, lavatories—as a social condition rather than a natural order. Then she said the words that every Negro hears before he can yet understand the injustice that makes them necessary: "You are as good as anyone."[29]

27. It could be safely argued that one has to begin with King, Jr.'s childhood experiences in order to comprehend what would become his life long quest for community, or the truly integrated society and world. This point was first made in the most emphatic and sophisticated terms in Walter E. Fluker, *They Looked for a City: A Comparative Analysis of the Ideal of Community in the Thought of Howard Thurman and Martin Luther King, Jr.* (Lanham, MD: University Press of America, 1989), 82; and Baldwin, *There is a Balm in Gilead*, 16–63.
28. "Face to Face: Dr. Martin Luther King, Jr. and John Freeman," 2–3; Carson, et al., eds., *King Papers*, I, 362; Martin Luther King, Jr., *Stride toward Freedom: The Montgomery Story* (New York: Harper & Row, Publishers, 1958), 19; King, *Daddy King*, 130; and Carson, ed., *The Autobiography of Martin Luther King, Jr.*, 3–4. King's sister, Christine corroborates much of this account, reporting that she, King, Jr., and their brother A. D. "could often be found in the backyard playing with other neighborhood kids, two of whom were little white boys. . . ." See Farris, *Through It All*, 24–25.
29. King, *Stride toward Freedom*, 18–19; "Face to Face: Dr. Martin Luther King, Jr. and John Freeman," 3; and Farris, *Through It All*, 25. At another point, King recalled that "We were at the dinner table when the situation" with the two white boys "was discussed." See Carson, et. al., eds., *King Papers*, I, 362.

King, Jr. went on to recall that "this was really the first time" that he became conscious "of the existence of a race problem," and, "from that moment on," he was "determined to hate every white person."[30] This incident with the two white boys clearly created a context for a teaching moment, and it, in King, Jr.'s case, also provided a foundation for creative learning, for the boy's parents, who embodied wisdom gleaned through generations of painful experiences, taught him that it was his "duty as a Christian" to love and not hate white people.[31] The impact of such teaching on King, Jr.'s life is probably impossible to measure, but evidently, it gave him a set of values that would guide and sustain him in the arenas of interpersonal and intergroup relations, and it helps explain, to some extent at least, why he would later emerge as one of the nation's and the world's foremost advocates and practitioners of the *agape* love ethic.

Although King, Jr. continued to immerse himself in the amusement, games, sports, and other recreational activities that he literally enjoyed as a child, his early experiences with white supremacist values and folkways, with the day-to-day realities in the Jim Crow South, whetted his curiosity and inspired in him a tendency to question virtually everything. "He was," according to Daddy King, "a curious youngster who really did wonder constantly about this peculiar world he saw all around him."[32] The boy simply could not understand why white people were so full of hatred, why they readily and eagerly accepted the common stereotypes and handy caricatures associated with Negroes as a whole, why they were guilty of ruthless and even savage behavior toward all people of color, why they were capable of such a callous, emotional detachment from the suffering of their black victims, and why they so casually perverted the very system of justice that they had often sworn to uphold. King, Jr. wondered why a full grown white woman would slap an eight-year-old black child and refer to him as "that nigger" in a downtown Atlanta store for essentially no

---

30. "Face to Face: Dr. Martin Luther King, Jr. and John Freeman," 3; and Carson, et al., eds., *King Papers*, I, 362.
31. Carson, et al., eds., *King Papers*, I, 362.
32. King, *Daddy King*, 130.

reason at all.[33] He was intrigued by the segregated schools, swimming pools, public parks, rest rooms, restaurants, theaters, and lunch counters, and he remembered that the "first time" he was "seated behind a curtain in a dining car," it was as if "the curtain had been dropped on my selfhood."[34] It was impossible for King, Jr. to make sense of the monstrous evil that was the Ku Klux Klan and its full-blown campaigns of terror against innocent black victims. He learned about "police brutality" and the barbaric lynchings and beatings to which his people were subjected, but in his own young searching mind, found no logical explanations for the continuing cycles of devastating and senseless violence.[35]

King, Jr.'s childhood curiosity and questioning attitude toward the established order of things were reinforced as he learned black history lessons and developed a growing sensitivity to the vulnerability of his parents under Jim Crow. Due largely to the teachings of his mother, Alberta, who had been an elementary school teacher in Atlanta; to the reminiscences of his daddy, King, Sr.; to the "interesting stories" of his maternal grandmother, Jennie; and to the readings of his aunt Ida "from newspapers, books and encyclopedias," King, Jr. was aware of the heritage of slavery and sharecropping on the maternal and paternal sides of his family,[36] and this alone made it possible for him,

33. "Face to Face: Dr. Martin Luther King, Jr. and John Freeman," 4–5; King, *Daddy King*, 130; Carson, ed., *The Autobiography of Martin Luther King, Jr.*, 7–12; Carson, et al., eds., *King* Papers, I, 362; and Baldwin, *There is a Balm in Gilead*, 21–22.
34. "Face to Face: Dr. Martin Luther King, Jr. and John Freeman," 4–5; and King, *Stride toward Freedom*, 20–21.
35. "Face to Face: Dr. Martin Luther King, Jr. and John Freeman," 4–5; and King, *Stride toward Freedom*, 18–20.
36. Farris, "The Young Martin," 56; "Face to Face: Dr. Martin Luther King, Jr. and John Freeman," 3; King, *Daddy King*, 130; Carson, et al., eds., *King Papers*, I, 359; Farris, *Through It All*, 16 and 25; and King, *Stride toward Freedom*, 19. The teachings King received in those early childhood years undoubtedly accounted for some of the rich and probing insights he would later bring to his analyses of slavery and the essentials of slave culture. See, for example, Martin Luther King, Jr., "The Meaning of Hope," unpublished version of sermon, delivered at the Dexter Avenue Baptist Church, Montgomery, Alabama (10 December 1967), King Center Library and Archives, 14; Martin Luther King, Jr., "Field of Education a Battleground," a speech before The United Federation of Teachers, New York, New York (14 March 1964), King Center Library and Archives, 2; Martin Luther King, Jr., *Where Do We Go from Here: Chaos or Community?* (Boston: Beacon Press, 1968; originally published in 1967), 122–24; Baldwin, *There is a Balm in Gilead*, 58, 61, 85, 95, 102, and 117; and Lewis V. Baldwin, *To Make the Wounded Whole: The Cultural Legacy of Martin Luther King, Jr.* (Minneapolis: Fortress Press, 1992), 64–66.

even at such a young age, to easily identify with a world that was larger and more complex than anything he knew or imagined on the playgrounds of Auburn Avenue. There was always that world within but apart from the white South that was most appealing to King, Jr.—one of color with its own values, traditions, and institutions.[37] Within that world, the youngster was made to understand why Daddy King responded so indignantly to white policemen who called him "a boy," and also why the elder King refused to accept service at segregated business establishments.[38] Although King, Jr. "became very frightened" and "seemed ready to cry" on at least one occasion when Daddy King reacted angrily to a white bigot and stormed out of a store that practiced segregation, the youngster appreciated his father's pledge that he would "be fighting against" the "stupidity and cruelty of segregation" as "long as there was breath" in him, and he also assured Daddy King that "he would help" him "all he could." "He was such a little fellow then," Daddy King recounted, "but M. L. seemed so thoughtful and determined on this matter that I felt certain he wouldn't forget his promise to help."[39]

Subjected to a classic best of times, worst of times experience in the Jim Crow South, it was virtually impossible for a boy such as King, Jr., who was "sensitive" and "somewhat precocious, both physically and mentally,"[40] to grow up and survive unscathed. Although the youngster was being raised in a nurturing, rather secure, and affectionate environment in which he enjoyed the best creature comfort by the standards of the 1930s and early 40s, he was, by his own admission, conflicted because he could not escape that larger white world that seemed so determined to reduce him to something less than human. "As I look back over those early days," he said on one occasion, "I did have something of an inner tension. On the one hand my mother taught me that I should feel a sense of somebodiness. . . . On the other hand, I had to go out and face the system, which stared me in the

---

37. Baldwin, *There is a Balm in Gilead*, 16–63.
38. King, *Daddy King*, 108–9; and King, *Stride toward Freedom*, 19–20.
39. King, *Daddy King*, 108–9.
40. Ibid., 108–9 and 127; and Carson, et al., eds., *King Papers*, I, 359.

face everyday saying, 'you are less than,' 'you are not equal to'. So this was a real tension within."[41] Fortunately, King, Jr. was part of a household comprised of three generations of family members[42] who nurtured his social-emotional development, who constantly reminded him that nothing could obscure his innate beauty as a creature shaped in God's image, and who instilled in him a core of strong spiritual values. This proved to be a compensating mechanism which enabled the child to deal with the inner tension or the conflicting impulses that raged within him without losing his self-esteem. The Ebenezer Baptist Church in Atlanta, with Daddy King as pastor, was also a sphere of influence in this regard for King, Jr.[43]

This is why images of the King family and Ebenezer Church were inseparable in King, Jr.'s consciousness from a very early age. This is evident from some of the letters the youngster wrote to his parents when they were out of town, or when he was away from them for a short time for some reason. Those letters, written when the boy was between ten and fifteen years of age, reveal that he rarely thought of family without also thinking of Ebenezer, and that he knew that he would be disciplined if he acted or behaved in such a way as to displease the folks on both sides.[44] Small wonder that young King, Jr. was so obedient and respectful when in the presence of his parents and other elders. That attitude on the youngster's part was cultivated largely by Daddy King, who "found that a switch was usually quicker and more persuasive" when dealing with his boys. On one occasion, when Daddy King was attending some church-related event, King, Jr. wrote him a nice letter, telling him "I am being a good boy while you

---

41. "Face to Face: Dr. Martin Luther King, Jr. and John Freeman," 3.
42. Farris, *Through It All*, 31; Farris, "The Young Martin," 56; and Baldwin, *There is a Balm in Gilead*, 91–126.
43. "Face to Face: Dr. Martin Luther King, Jr. and John Freeman," 9; William D. Watley, *Roots of Resistance: The Nonviolent Ethic of Martin Luther King, Jr.* (Valley Forge, PA: Judson Press, 1985), 33–36; and Baldwin, *There is a Balm in Gilead*, 159–206.
44. King, Jr. grew up in an era when black children were required and expected to respect their elders. It was not unusual for authority figures (i.e. teachers, etc.) and elders from Ebenezer Baptist Church and the larger neighborhood or community to chastise children "who acted up," so to speak. See Carson, et al., *King Papers*, I, 101–17; Farris, *Through It All*, 31; King, *Daddy King*, 130–31; Lawrence D. Reddick, *Crusader without Violence: A Biography of Martin Luther King, Jr.* (New York: Harper & Brothers, Publishers, 1959), 5; and Lewis V. Baldwin, *The Voice of Conscience: The Church in the Mind of Martin Luther King, Jr.* (New York: Oxford University Press, 2010), 15–16.

are away."[45] "Whippings must not be so bad," King, Jr. said once as he reflected on his childhood years, "for I received them until I was fifteen."[46] Daddy King "had a temper," and King, Jr. saw that "With his fearless honesty and his robust, dynamic presence, his words commanded attention." The youngster had a healthy respect for his father that may have bordered on fear during those very early years, but it is a bit of a stretch to interpret this in terms of an Oedipus complex.[47]

It is known that King, Jr. was far more at ease when relating to the other most important elders in his family—namely, his mother, Alberta; his Aunt Ida; and her sister, Mama Jennie. King, Jr. would remember Alberta as "soft-spoken and easy-going," as "a very devout person with a deep commitment to the Christian faith," and as one operating "behind the scene setting forth those motherly cares, the lack of which leaves a missing link in life." "Although possessed of a rather recessive personality," he once wrote, "she is warm and easily approachable."[48] Although King, Jr. had far less to say publicly and in his writings about his Aunt Ida, she too impacted his early life in positive ways, for she, through hours of reading to the boy, "whetted his curiosity about the world around him" and "helped him develop into an inquisitive child and an avid reader."[49] Mama Jennie, whom King, Jr. called "a saintly grandmother," nurtured her grandson's social-emotional development in profound ways through her unconditional love and care-giving routines. Whenever Daddy King whipped little King, Jr., she was always there with "a hug, kiss or kind word to help the hurt go away." She frequently told her son-in-law that

---

45. Carson, et al., eds., *King Papers*, I, 107.
46. King, *Daddy King*, 131; Reddick, *Crusader without Violence*, 5; Farris, *Through It All*, 31; and Downing, *To See the Promised Land*, 182.
47. King, *Daddy King*, 130–31; and King, *Stride toward Freedom*, 19. Interestingly enough, one source declares that Daddy King "ruled his household as an old-fashioned disciplinarian," and that when it came to his relationship with his son King, Jr., there was "evidence of an Oedipal struggle that should delight Freudians." See Eugene D. Genovese, *The Southern Front: History and Politics in the Cultural War* (Columbia: University of Missouri Press, 1995), 160.
48. Carson, ed., *The Autobiography of Martin Luther King, Jr.*, 3.
49. Farris, "The Young Martin," 56. Aunt Ida must have meant a lot to King, Jr., for he mentioned her in one of his childhood letters to Daddy King. See Carson, et al., eds., *King Papers*, I, 107. Strangely, however, her name does not appear in his "Autobiography of Religious Development." See Ibid., 359–63.

"she hated to see him spank" King, Jr. "because 'the child looked so pitiful' when he did."[50] In the mind of a child, this kind of love is always unquestioned, and indeed, unquestionable.

King, Jr. and his grandmother "were extremely close," and out of his deep affection and respect for her, he is said to have "attempted suicide" twice before reaching age thirteen.[51] The first attempt allegedly occurred one day in the winter of 1941, when King, Jr. and his brother, A. D. were playing in the upstairs part of their home. A. D. slid down the banister to the first floor and accidentally knocked Mama Jennie down. Thinking that he and A. D.'s horseplay had killed their grandmother, King, Jr. "ran to the upstairs window and jumped." The youngster refused to get up until he heard that Mama Jennie "was all right." A few months later, on May 18, 1941, Mama Jennie suffered a heart attack in a church and died, and this supposedly led to King, Jr.'s second suicide attempt.[52] Apparently, the youngster had disobeyed his father's orders and snuck downtown Atlanta to see a parade, instead of doing his homework, and he felt that Mama Jennie's death was somehow God's punishment for his act of disobedience. Once again, King, Jr. "ran upstairs and leaped from the window," convinced that he would "follow his grandmother to another world."[53] The boy was shaken, but not seriously hurt. "He cried off and on for several days," according to Daddy King, "and was unable to sleep at night."[54] King, Jr. himself would recall years later that it was after his grandmother's

---

50. Carson, et al., eds., *King Papers*, I, 359; and Farris, "The Young Martin," 56. It has been reported that when King, Jr. "stood in front of his father to be punished, he would take that punishment with tears rolling down his face." However, the boy never gave "in to the emotional urge to cry in an uncontrolled fashion." Daddy King saw this as "very peculiar and never forgot the scene or that trait in his son." See Downing, *To See the Promised Land*, 46; and Lerone Bennett, Jr., *What Manner of Man: A Biography of Martin Luther King, Jr.* (Chicago: Johnson Publishing Company, 1964), 24.

51. Farris, "The Young Martin," 56; and Downing, *To See the Promised Land*, 98.

52. Downing, *To See the Promised Land*, 98–99; Farris, *Through It All*, 12; and King, *Daddy King*, 109. Mama Jennie died before she was to give a speech in a church one Sunday evening. Strangely, her daughter, King, Jr.'s mother Alberta, also died in church, but at the hands of a deranged assassin. No one in the King family, including King, Jr. himself, ever mentioned a suicide attempt after Mama Jennie's death in their autobiographical accounts. See "Mrs. Williams to be Funeralized this Afternoon," *Atlanta Daily World* (21 May 1941), 1; "Funeral Notices," *Atlanta Daily World* (19 May 1941), 6; "Funeral Wednesday," *Atlanta Daily World* (20 May 1941), 1; Baldwin, *The Voice of Conscience*, 26 and 265n49; and Carson, et. al., eds., *King Papers*, I, 34.

53. Downing, *To See the Promised Land*, 98–99.

54. King, *Daddy King*, 109.

sudden death that he "talked at any length" for the first time "on the doctrine of immortality." "My parents attempted to explain it to me and I was assured that somehow my grandmother still lived," he remembered.[55] This eased the pain of King, Jr.'s loss. The explanation of his parents could have been provided by any of his elders at Ebenezer, and indeed, across the South, because the belief in the surviving spirits of ancestors, which maintain an interest in the affairs of the living, extended back to slavery and was indicative of continuing African influences among blacks.[56]

Widely accepted psychosocial theories, which allege suicide attempts, are grossly inadequate for explaining young King, Jr.'s highly emotional response to his grandmother's unexpected death.[57] Explanations that are culturally based are far more reliable. King, Jr. spent his childhood years in a black culture in which "respect for age" was "the basis of much of black African culture and the principal inspiration for its art," and grandmothers, in particular, were held in the highest esteem because they were, among other things, the pillars of family strength, great nurturers, strong spiritual forces, the cement that kept generations together, and repositories "of the accumulated lore" of their folk.[58] In that culture, "the sacred domain of the ancestors and those soon to be ancestors" was never to be violated or dishonored in any fashion.[59] That respect for ancestors and elders was deeply felt by King, Jr., and the death of the boy's grandmother, along with his audacity in disobeying his father, compelled him to discipline himself.

55. Carson, et al., eds., *King Papers*, I, 362.
56. See Sterling Stuckey, *Slave Culture: Nationalist Theory and the Foundations of Black America* (New York: Oxford University Press, 1987), 333; and Lewis V. Baldwin and Amiri YaSin Al-Hadid, *Between Cross and Crescent: Christian and Muslim Perspectives on Malcolm and Martin* (Gainesville, FL: University Press of Florida, 2002), 12–13.
57. Frederick L. Downing has taken this approach, using the psychosocial theories of Erik H. Erikson and the "stages of faith" advanced by James W. Fowler. I have learned so much from reading this book, but wonder about the applicability of Erikson and Fowler's theoretical frameworks for understanding a black boy who grew up in the Jim Crow South in the 1930s and 40s. See Downing, *To See the Promised Land*, 3–293.
58. Stuckey, *Slave Culture*, 333–34. For some of the most brilliant insights on the importance of the black grandmother during slavery, see E. Franklin Frazier, *The Negro Family in the United States* (Chicago: The University of Chicago Press, 1968), 114–16. Also see Baldwin, *There is a Balm in Gilead*, 108–11.
59. Stuckey, *Slave Culture*, 333–34.

After this experience, a number of family members and friends of the Kings were amazed with the changes in King Jr.'s personality, noting that "he seemed to have grown more mature."[60]

Perhaps one of the most glaring changes involved King, Jr.'s continuing and growing tendency toward a questioning attitude toward life. It was probably in the midst of his personal struggle with Mama Jennie's death that the twelve-year-old "shocked his Sunday school class by denying the bodily resurrection of Jesus." The subjects of personal immortality, the afterlife, and the spirit world had come up quite a bit in family discussions about that time, and the possibility that the youngster made some connection between his grandmother's death and surviving spirit and the question of the death and physical resurrection of Jesus should not be casually dismissed. In the mind of a perceptive child such as King, Jr., such a connection would have made perfect sense. In any case, King, Jr. remembered that "Doubts began to spring forth unrelentingly."[61]

The same might be said of the youngster's increasing capacity for critical and analytical thinking. King, Jr. matured much as a thinker in the three years following the loss of Mama Jennie, particularly as he focused a critical eye on slavery and racism, social evils that his mother Alberta had told him about when he was only six years old. In his most important childhood speech on record, "The Negro and the Constitution," delivered at an oratorical contest at the First Baptist Church in Dublin, Georgia, soon after he turned fifteen, King, Jr. alluded to the irony of a nation born in freedom while, at the same time, denying her Negro citizens the most basic of civil and human rights. "Slavery has been a strange paradox in a nation founded on the principles that all men are created free and equal," he declared. A junior at Atlanta's Booker T. Washington High School at the time, the youngster went on to identify those glaring social ills that kept

60. Farris, *Through It All*, 12.
61. Carson, ed., *The Autobiography of Martin Luther King, Jr.*, 6–7; Carson, et al., eds., *King Papers*, I, 362–63; King, *Daddy King*, 109; King, *My Life with Martin Luther King, Jr.*, 81; Baldwin, *There is a Balm in Gilead*, 166; and Martin Luther King, Jr., *Strength to Love* (Philadelphia: Fortress Press, 1981; originally published in 1963), 147.

America from being "an enlightened democracy," and that prevented her citizens from becoming a "truly Christian people."[62] These words must have taken on an even more powerful meaning for King, Jr. personally, as he, on the trip from Dublin back to Atlanta after the speech, was forced to surrender his bus seat to a white passenger—an incident that had some of the earmarks of another situation that would catapult King, Jr. to a position of leadership in the Montgomery bus boycott more than a decade later.[63]

"The Negro and the Constitution" was perhaps the defining moment in King, Jr.'s childhood, because it provided some clues about the path his life would take from that point into his adult years. The speech offered a glimpse into the mind of a young man who apparently appreciated the beauty of language and the power of ideas and concepts, and, perhaps more importantly, it contained the central theme of what would later become King, Jr.'s most consistent and enduring message to the American people—namely, the need to overcome slavery, racism, and segregation as "strange paradoxes in a nation founded on the principle that all men are created equal."[64]

There was much palpable in those early years, aside from "The Negro and the Constitution," for which he won the oratorical contest, that suggested that King, Jr. might emerge as a leader among his people. The youngster had a fascination for great preachers and preaching, which was quite unusual for boys his age. King, Sr. recalled

---

62. Carson, et al., eds., *King Papers*, I, 109–10; and Carson, *The Autobiography of Martin Luther King, Jr.*, 8–9.

63. There are different accounts of this incident. One claims that it occurred during the trip to Dublin from Atlanta, and the other, that it happened during the trip from Dublin back to Atlanta. At any rate, King, Jr. and his teacher, Sarah Grace Bradley, were instructed by the bus driver to give up "their seats to newly boarding white passengers." Young King initially resisted, but was finally persuaded by his teacher to "leave the seat." See Carson, ed., *The Autobiography of Martin Luther King, Jr.*, 8–10; Carson, et al., eds., *King Papers*, I, 108–11; and Baldwin, *There is a Balm in Gilead*, 22 and 24. King, Jr.'s best recollection of the incident is recorded in James M. Washington, ed., *A Testament of Hope: The Essential Writings and Speeches of Martin Luther King, Jr.* (New York: HarperCollins Publishers, 1986), 342–43.

64. The dichotomy of freedom versus un-freedom, captured so poignantly in King, Jr.'s "The Negro and the Constitution," would also constitute the point of departure for the young man's developing intellectual approach to the New South ideal. See Lewis V. Baldwin, et. al., *The Legacy of Martin Luther King, Jr.: The Boundaries of Law, Politics, and Religion* (Notre Dame, IN: University of Notre Dame Press, 2002), 1–51; Martin Luther King, Jr., "The Negro Speaks—The Negro is the Most Glaring Evidence of White America's Hypocrisy," *St. Louis Post Dispatch* (25 August 1963), 1 and 3; and "Bold Design for a New South" in Washington, ed., *A Testament of Hope*, 112–16.

that his son enjoyed listening "to good preachers before he was old enough to understand them," and that "If he heard that some outstanding man was going to speak, he would ask me to take him." The elder King remembered "after one such occasion" when King, Jr. "was only about ten, he said, 'That man had some big words Daddy. When I grow up I'm going to get me some big words'."[65] If this was not telling enough, one only had to consider the boy's deep love for the church and its traditions, ceremonies, and ritual, and especially, his "intimate knowledge of Baptist life, including such details as congregational governance, ward meetings, church finances, and social events."[66] Thus, it was not surprising that King, Jr.'s elders saw something very special about him, and some had begun to sense that he was somehow a child of destiny.

But there was always that other side of King, Jr.'s personality during those early adolescent years that appeared, at least on the surface, to be so much at odds with the rapidly maturing, thoughtful, inquisitive, and seemingly no-nonsense image. King, Jr. enjoyed roaming "up and down 'Sweet Auburn'" with "Mole," "Rooster," "Sack," and other friends, undoubtedly playing and engaging in child's talk. Much of the money he made on his newspaper route was spent on nice clothes and patent leather shoes, and he was always interested in girls. King, Jr. was "just about the best jitterbug in town," and it is said that he "kept flitting from chick to chick."[67] He tried smoking cigarettes, and was always ready for a party. Frederick L. Downing has concluded that King, Jr. was actually "two persons" during those early teenage years. There was, on the one hand, the serious and "mild-mannered, though often moody, young student who deferred to his elders," and, on the other, "the smooth-talking teenager" who charmed the girls, flirted with a few bad habits, and "danced to every tune."[68] As is the case with every human being, King, Jr. would never overcome the

---

65. King, *My life with Martin Luther King, Jr.*, 78.
66. King, *Daddy King*, 127; Carson, et al., eds., *King Papers*, I, 30; and King, *My Life with Martin Luther King, Jr.*, 58.
67. The claim that King, Jr. "changed girl friends almost as often as the dark suits" may be a bit too harsh. See Downing, *To See the Promised Land*, 126.
68. Farris, "The Young Martin," 56–58; and Downing, *To See the Promised Land*, 126.

conflicting tendencies that seemed to be at war within his person—a kind of "twoness"[69] which would find different modes of expression as King, Jr. moved through adolescence into full adulthood.

B. Moving on Up a Little Higher: The Morehouse, Crozer, and Boston Years

Martin Luther King, Jr. was only fifteen when he began his studies at Atlanta's Morehouse College, a historically black male institution, in the fall of 1944.[70] Having skipped his senior year in high school, his decision to enroll early arose out of a desire not "to be outdone" by his sister, Christine, who had finished high school and was entering Atlanta's Spelman College. That "competitive streak," as Christine called it, had always been there. King, Jr., by his own admission, had actually joined the family's church at age five one Sunday morning because he did not want Christine, who was the first to rise and go down to the altar, to "get ahead of me."[71] Sibling rivalry aside, there were questions about whether or not King, Jr. was ready for the challenges and demands of college life, especially since he "had to overcome a comparatively weak high school background." Despite his rather impressive critical-analytical skills, he "was still reading at only an eighth grade level" and had some problems with writing and spelling.[72] Furthermore, there were concerns among family members and friends that he was not mature enough to interact with a student population that tended, on the average, to be three to five years older

69. W. E. B. DuBois actually coined this word "twoness" in explaining the "double-consciousness" of the American Negro—the "two souls, two thoughts, two un-reconciled strivings; two warring ideals in one dark body"—but he obviously had in mind something quite different from what Downing and I are saying here about King, Jr. See W. E. B. DuBois, *The Souls of Black Folk* in *Three Negro Classics* (New York: Avon Books, 1965), 215; and Downing, *To See the Promised Land*, 126.

70. King, Jr.'s father and maternal grandfather, the Reverend A. D. Williams, also graduated from Morehouse, so that institution was actually a part of the Kings's extended family. In other words, one has to think in terms of the intertwining significance of family, church, and Morehouse College as formative influences in King, Jr.'s early life. See Carson, *The Autobiography of Martin Luther King, Jr.*, 13; and Farris, *Through It All*, 36–37.

71. King, *Daddy King*, 139; Farris, *Through It All*, 37–38; and Carson, et al., eds., *King Papers*, I, 361.

72. This is not surprising because Booker T. Washington High School in Atlanta, Georgia was among the most highly segregated public schools, and such institutions were, compared to the white ones, so ill-equipped in terms of resources and facilities. See King, *Daddy King*, 139; Carson, et al., eds., *King Papers*, I, 156; and Carson, ed., *The Autobiography of Martin Luther King, Jr.*, 13.

than him. But the strong will and determination of King, Jr. prevailed over any doubts or objections those close to him may have had, especially after the youngster passed "a new test" that allowed "successful rising juniors to be admitted directly into college."[73]

King, Jr. had advantages in relation to Morehouse that made it possible for him to adjust with relative ease. The institution was located in his hometown, which meant that he remained close to family, the Ebenezer Baptist Church, friends, and others who constituted his primary base of support.[74] Also, administrative staff persons and professors at Morehouse—such as the president, Benjamin E. Mays; the religion professors George D. Kelsey and Lucius M. Tobin; and the philosophy professor Samuel Williams—had known the King family for years before King, Jr. was born, and these men were among that illustrious group of Baptist preachers who had a long and close association with Daddy King in the National Baptist Convention (NBC). Having grown up as part of a large and thriving black middle class in Atlanta, King, Jr. was also surrounded by physicians, dentists, morticians, contractors, insurance executives, bankers, businesspersons, and real estate agents, and these "symbols of success and progress" were there to inspire and remind the youngster that he, in conformity with the Morehouse motto, should be the very best in whatever course he took "in this hostile world."[75] It is difficult to imagine a richer and more attractive environment for King, Jr., especially since Morehouse existed at the center of the nation's Mecca of black education, which also included Atlanta University, Clark University, Morris Brown College, and Spelman College.

Morehouse men typically exuded the aura of the aristocrat, or a keen sense of being a part of the elite, but King, Jr. quickly became known as a plainspoken, down-to-earth young fellow with a kind and generous spirit. Those who knew him best spoke of his "very pleasing

73. Farris, *Through It All*, 37–38.
74. King, *Daddy King*, 139.
75. Fluker, *They Looked for a City*, 85; Baldwin, *There is a Balm in Gilead*, 25; and Linda Williams, "Molding Men: At Morehouse College, Middle Class Blacks are Taught to Lead," *The Wall Street Journal* (5 May 1987), 1 and 25.

personality," of his "friendly and courteous" manner, and of his ability to "get along well with people."[76] Fellow students found him "to be a quiet and reserved young man," or "just a regular student." Some of the Morehouse professors who knew King, Jr. saw him as "well-disciplined," "quiet," "humble," introspective," and "very much introverted," and still others remembered his "good integrity" and his "mental ability," "moral stamina," and "apparent sincerity."[77] And there was a romantic quality about King, Jr. that attracted the beautiful young ladies, some of whom were older than him. He loved music and poetry, the world of nature with its change of seasons, the fun-filled night life, and, as he reached his late teens, wore either "fancy" sport coats or the stylish, double-breasted suits, almost always with shirt, tie, handkerchief, and wide-brimmed hats,[78] but never overly ornate in appearance. Interestingly enough, King, Jr.'s dress, perhaps more than anything else, "made him a recognizable figure on campus."[79]

Although King, Jr. valued the material things of life, there were nonetheless an eagerness and adventuresomeness about him that led to choices that would have been frowned upon by the most elitist-minded students at Morehouse. Having a "growing social consciousness," King, Jr. wanted, for an example, "to learn at firsthand what life was like for really underprivileged people—to learn their problems and feel their feelings," a desire not entirely surprising since he, as he himself put it, "could never get out of my mind the economic insecurity of many of my playmates and the tragic poverty of those living around me."[80] Thus, he decided not to take summer jobs at the "white collar black businesses," but, instead, "to do hard manual labor." The summer before enrolling at Morehouse, the youngster worked in the tobacco fields of Simsbury, Connecticut. King, Jr. spent other summer vacations in Atlanta, "handling baggage for the Railway

76. Carson, et al., eds., King Papers, I, 151–55.
77. David J. Garrow, Bearing the Cross: Martin Luther King, Jr., and the Southern Christian Leadership Conference (New York: William Morrow and Company, 1986), 37; and Carson, et al., eds., King Papers, I, 151–55.
78. Farris, Through It All, 29–30; and King, My life with Martin Luther King, Jr., 55.
79. Garrow, Bearing the Cross, 37.
80. King, My Life with Martin Luther King, Jr., 82; King, Stride toward Freedom, 90; Carson, et al., eds., King Papers, I, 360; Farris, Through It All, 38; Farris, "The Young Martin," 58; and King, Daddy King, 145.

Express Agency" and working "on the loading platform of the Southern Bedspring Mattress Company." Needless to say, the work "was exhausting for him physically," and King, Jr. also "suffered almost daily humiliation" while working for the white boss of the Railway Express Agency, who routinely "addressed the black workers as 'niggers'."[81] The youngster had grown up on "Sweet Auburn" Avenue in Atlanta, referred to as "the richest Negro street in the world,"[82] but he chose nonetheless to live in a different world. Perhaps he chose to do so because he, as has been suggested, felt guilty about his privileged background.[83]

Despite having a range of other personal concerns, King, Jr. went to Morehouse with a deep and growing "interest in intellectual matters," "a strong social consciousness," and "a normal youthful rebellion against tradition." At first glance, this seemed to be a perfect fit for the youngster because Morehouse had long provided a stimulating environment, intellectually and spiritually, for black men such as King, Jr., who thought in terms of serving humanity and particularly their own people.[84] There were highly respected black and white faculty there who were devoted to educating the offsprings of ex-slaves and sharecroppers. In this respect, Morehouse, like the King family's home, Ebenezer Baptist Church, and the larger black community of Atlanta,

81. Farris, *Through It All*, 24–25 and 38. Coretta Scott King claims that the "circumstances of " King, Jr.'s life protected him from the worst of the suffering of segregation. . . ." This point should be made with some qualifications. Although King, Jr. grew up in a middle class home, the evidence shows that this did not exempt him from the kind of verbal and physical abuses that victimized the poorest of blacks in the South. Race or skin color clearly outweighed all considerations of class in the minds of southern white bigots, though the two were closely intertwined and interrelated. See King, *My Life with Martin Luther King, Jr.*, 79; "Face to Face: Dr. Martin Luther King, Jr. and John Freeman," 2–7; King, *Stride toward Freedom*, 19–21; King, *Daddy King*, 108–9 and 130; Carson, ed., *The Autobiography of Martin Luther King, Jr.*, 8–12; and Baldwin, *There is a Balm in Gilead*, 20–24.

82. Farris, *Through It All*, 25.

83. Coretta Scott King reported that her husband "felt that having been born into what was a middle class African American family was a privilege he had not earned. . . ." Thus, he constantly examined "himself to determine if he was becoming corrupted," or "if he was accepting honors too easily." Be that as it may, it seems logical that King, Jr. accepted certain jobs during his Morehouse years because he really wanted to feel connected with common laborers. The personal responsibility principle also figured into his decisions. In other words, King, Jr. was determined "to pay some of his expenses on his own, rather than always having to call on his daddy." Frederick Downing rightly reports that the elders along "Sweet Auburn" Avenue viewed actions of this nature by young King, Jr. "as an exercise in self-reliance and in the mastery of finances." See King, *My life with Martin Luther King, Jr.*, 59 and 82; and Downing, *To See the Promised Land*, 126.

84. Williams, "Molding Men," 1 and 25; and King, *My Life with Martin Luther King, Jr.*, 81.

became a ray of light in an otherwise unfriendly and frightening world. The institution fostered an atmosphere that valued liberal arts education, but, strangely enough, King, Jr. did not respond well to the academic demands, especially from the outset. Melvin Kennedy, his freshman advisor and history professor, remembered that the youngster "was 'not particularly impressive' when he first arrived at Morehouse." Apparently, King, Jr. "'had a tendency to be withdrawn and not to participate'" in student discussions, and he "always sat in the back of classrooms."[85] In all probability, he felt intimidated by his older and generally more intelligent classmates. Professor Gladstone L. Chandler, his English professor at Morehouse, "found King to be a C–B– student" whose "grades could have been higher had he mastered spelling and elementary grammar."[86]

But King, Jr. always had a rare capacity to grow and mature, personally and intellectually, especially when he felt deeply passionate about something. He routinely "took copious notes"[87] in his classes, and by the time he completed his sophomore year, had begun to express openly and publicly his views on even the most controversial issues. In August, 1946, King, Jr., perhaps reacting "to the racially motivated murders of two black couples" in rural Georgia, sent a letter to the *Atlanta Constitution*, the local newspaper, declaring that "We want and are entitled to the basic rights and opportunities of American citizens," including "the right to earn a living at work," "the right to vote," "equality before the law," and "the right" to basic necessities such as education, health, and recreation. The young man went on to assert, in a statement overflowing with passion, that the call for just treatment "for the Negro" had nothing to do with "social mingling and intermarriage"—as "a certain class" of white people suggested. "We aren't eager to marry white girls," King, Jr. wrote, "and we would

---

85. See Garrow, *Bearing the Cross*, 37.
86. Baldwin, *There is a Balm in Gilead*, 26 and 29; and Garrow, *Bearing the Cross*, 37. Morehouse College had developed a strong academic tradition by the time King, Jr. arrived there, so King, Jr.'s struggles at such a young age would not have been surprising. See Lawrence E. Carter, Sr., ed., *Walking Integrity: Benjamin Elijah Mays, Mentor to Martin Luther King Jr.* (Macon, GA: Mercer University Press, 1998), 353–76.
87. Garrow, *Bearing the Cross*, 37.

like to have our own girls left alone by both white toughs and white aristocrats."[88]

Evidently, the youngster had been inspired, in part, by the uncensored atmosphere of academic freedom at Morehouse, in which he had had his "first frank discussion on race," and in which his professors encouraged him "in a positive quest for a solution to racial ills."[89] He was already feeling "a strong love for the people and a very strong sympathy for the underdog," for what he called "the masses,"[90] and he had also begun to consider possible avenues toward a more genuine, inclusive, and enduring model of human freedom and community. But there was little tangible during those Morehouse years to indicate that King, Jr. would become a major proponent of racial integration, unless it was his work with interracial student organizations which, incidentally, helped him to overcome that bitterness he had felt toward whites since age six; unless, possibly, it was his reading and rereading of Henry David Thoreau's treatise on civil disobedience, which often reminded him of the role whites might assume in the continuing struggle against racial injustice.[91] Whatever the case, King, Jr.'s letter to the *Atlanta Constitution*, which "received widespread and favorable comment," further convinced his parents of his "developing greatness."[92]

During his junior year at Morehouse, King, Jr. wrote two essays on "The Purpose of Education," which afforded added proof of his expanding and maturing mind. In these essays, which were published in the *Maroon Tiger*, the campus newspaper, King, Jr. insisted that the purpose of education was not to endow persons "with the proper

88. Garrow, *Bearing the Cross*, 37. King, Jr. apparently understood, even as a teenager, the hypocrisy of southern white males who preached segregation during the daytime and practiced miscegenation at night. See Carson, et al., eds., *King Papers*, I, 121.
89. King, Jr. recounted that Morehouse provided "a free atmosphere" because "The professors were not caught up in the clutches of state funds and could teach what they wanted with academic freedom." Here, we see, in the case of young King, Jr., the beginnings of a regional consciousness shaped by the politics of racial injustice and racial separatism. See Carson, ed., *The Autobiography of Martin Luther King, Jr.*, 13.
90. King, *My Life with Martin Luther King, Jr.*, 58.
91. Carson, et al., eds., *King Papers*, I, 363; Baldwin, *There is a Balm in Gilead*, 28; and Carson, ed., *The Autobiography of Martin Luther King, Jr.*, 14.
92. Carson, et al., eds., *King Papers*, I, 121; and King, *Daddy King*, 127.

instruments of exploitation so that they can forever trample over the masses," but, rather, to "equip us with the power to think effectively and objectively," to "discipline the mind for sustained and persistent speculation," to instill "intelligence plus character," to provide a path "beyond the horizon of legions of half truth, prejudices and propaganda," to "integrate human life around central, focusing ideals," and to "achieve with increasing facility the legitimate goals" of life. "It is not enough to know truth," King, Jr. added, "but we must love truth and sacrifice for it."[93] These words would ultimately define important dimensions of both his public and private life.

Although King, Jr. majored in sociology, perhaps his greatest intellectual struggle at Morehouse centered on religion and the role of the church and its ministry in the world—concerns that always evoked the strongest emotions in people of his background at that time. He said that his first two years at Morehouse "brought many doubts" into his mind, and that "the shackles of fundamentalism were removed" from his body. He had difficulty reconciling what he "had learned in Sunday School" at Ebenezer Baptist Church with what he "was learning in college," and his studies made him "skeptical," especially since he failed to see "how many of the facts of science could be squared with religion."[94] Moreover, King, Jr. frowned upon the excessive emotionalism, hypermoralism, and anti-intellectualism that pervaded much of black church life, and he wondered if religion could be both "intellectually respectable" and "emotionally satisfying," and if it "could serve as a vehicle to modern thinking."[95] Although the youngster came to reject the biblical literalism of his father and his Sunday School teachers, he continued to affirm the authority of the Bible, believing that "behind the legends and myths of the Book were many profound truths which one could not escape."[96] This was a very

93. See Carson, et al., eds., *King Papers*, I, 122–24.
94. Carson, ed., *The Autobiography of Martin Luther King, Jr.*, 6 and 15; and Carson, et al., eds., *King Papers*, I, 362–63.
95. Carson, et al., eds., *King Papers*, I, 362–63; and Carson, ed., *The Autobiography of Martin Luther King, Jr.*, 15.
96. Carson, ed., *The Autobiography of Martin Luther King, Jr.*, 6 and 15; Carson, et al., eds., *King Papers*, I, 361–62; and Lee E. Dirks, " 'The Essence is Love': The Theology of Martin Luther King, Jr.," *National Observer* (30 December 1963), 1 and 12.

positive sign for Daddy King, who was concerned that his son's growing biblical and theological liberalism, and more particularly, his questioning attitude toward the established order of things, might make it all the more unlikely that King, Jr. would follow him as the pastor of Ebenezer Baptist Church.[97]

King, Jr. actually "felt the urge to enter the ministry" when he was still in high school, "but accumulated doubts somewhat blocked the urge." He "began to feel an insistent call" while working in the tobacco fields of Simsbury, Connecticut, where he led devotions for his friends and co-workers.[98] Although King, Jr. "was guided by admirable motivations," he "suffered good-natured ribbing" from some of his classmates, who teasingly asserted that "it was not the Lord but the hot sun of the tobacco fields that 'called him' into the ministry."[99] In any case, King, Jr. finally accepted the call to preach during his senior year at Morehouse, and was ordained at Ebenezer Baptist Church in February, 1948, despite making it known, in response to a question from his ordination committee, that he did not believe that "Jesus was born of a virgin."[100] Initially, the young man wanted to be either a physician or a lawyer, thinking that he could do more for "the black masses" in "a profession outside the ministry." But there were powerful influences, including King, Sr. himself,[101] who had steered

---

97. Daddy King remembered that King, Jr. said "very little about preaching" while growing up, and that that made him believe through King, Jr.'s "earliest years" that the youngster "would evolve more naturally than A. D. to take a place in the pastorate of Ebenezer." According to the elder King, A. D. "was determined from his earliest days not to be what his father was." "At times" A. D. "got so dramatic about it," said Daddy King, "that we had a few run-ins over the matter, even while he was still very young." But, interestingly enough, A. D. would one day join Daddy King and his brother King, Jr. as a co-pastor at Ebenezer. See King, *Daddy King*, 127–28, 143, and 147; and Baldwin, *There is a Balm in Gilead*, 276–79.

98. Carson, ed., *The Autobiography of Martin Luther King, Jr.*, 16; and King, *My Life with Martin Luther King, Jr.*, 82–83.

99. Farris, "The Young Martin," 58.

100. King, Jr.'s ordination committee consisted of Daddy King, Benjamin Mays, Paul Anderson, Samuel Williams, Lucius M. Tobin, and several other Baptist ministers. Keith Miller concludes that the ministers on the committee decided to ordain King, Jr. despite his views on the Virgin Birth because "unlike fundamentalists, they did not regard Biblical literalism as a litmus test of true Christianity." The committee actually consisted of both fundamentalists and more liberal ministers, and it is highly likely that King's views were not acceptable to some of them. The young man was ultimately ordained, first and foremost, because he was the son of Martin Luther King, Sr., one of the most prominent ministers in the entire South. See Keith D. Miller, *Voice of Deliverance: The Language of Martin Luther King, Jr., and Its Sources* (New York: The Free Press, 1992), 40; and Baldwin, *The Voice of Conscience*, 46.

King, Jr. in the direction of ministry from his earliest childhood. The elders around whom he had grown up were "church-going" and exemplary in their piety, and his childhood playmates had attended Sunday School regularly.[102] This kind of robust religious culture, in and of itself, not only minimized any negative influences that King, Jr. might otherwise have encountered, but also reinforced and sustained his sense of and commitment to the church and to spiritual values. Although the young man had come to see "unlettered" preachers prone to a shallow and unenlightened piety as the standard, he also met preacher-intellectuals at Morehouse, such as Benjamin Mays and George Kelsey, who combined learning and a spiritually enriching ministry with a deep social consciousness and a keen sense of social obligation.[103] Thus, King, Jr. was able to overcome any reluctance he had about pursuing ministry as a life vocation. He made it clear before leaving Morehouse that he understood the call to preach in terms of service to God and humanity.[104]

King, Jr. graduated from Morehouse College in June 1948, and after sharing pulpit duties with his father at Ebenezer Baptist Church for much of that summer, moved to Chester, Pennsylvania to begin his studies at Crozer Theological Seminary. Family members, friends, and professors, who recommended him to Crozer, spoke of his "good integrity" and ability to "adjust well interracially," and they described him as "a little above average in scholarship" and "serious about the ministry."[105] But King, Jr. was only nineteen and, despite showing great "promise for the ministry in personality and ability," he had not surrendered his seemingly insatiable appetite for girls and the party scene. Needless to say, Daddy King was quite concerned and fully convinced that his son needed to be under the supervision of some

---

101. King, *My Life with Martin Luther King, Jr.*, 81.
102. Carson, et al., eds., *King Papers*, I, 360; and Carson, ed., *The Autobiography of Martin Luther King, Jr.*, 6.
103. Speaking of Mays and Kelsey, King, Jr. noted that "I could see in their lives the ideal of what I wanted a minister to be." The young man called Mays his "spiritual mentor." See Carson, ed., *The Autobiography of Martin Luther King, Jr.*, 15; and King, *My Life with Martin Luther King, Jr.*, 83.
104. Martin Luther King, Jr., "My Call to Preach," stated before the American Baptist Convention (7 August 1959), King Center Library and Archives, 1; Carson, ed., *The Autobiography of Martin Luther King, Jr.*, 14; and Carson, et al., eds., *King Papers*, I, 363.
105. Carson, et al., eds., *King Papers*, I, 151–53 and 155–56; and Garrow, *Bearing the Cross*, 38–39.

well-established black pastor and church family that would make sure that he studied hard, behaved himself, and maintained a sense of values, especially in a northern city with which he was so unfamiliar.[106]

King, Jr.'s adjustment to the Crozer environment and culture was another consideration, because the youngster was committing himself to an extensive period of study at an essentially white academic institution, with its very different "social and theological climate," for the very first time.[107] King, Sr. contacted J. Pius Barbour, the pastor of Chester's Calvary Baptist Church and a long-time friend and associate in the National Baptist Convention, and Barbour (Crozer's first black graduate, who first recommended that institution to King, Jr.) agreed to take King, Jr. under his care, to use his services as a youth minister, and to monitor his studies and activities at the seminary.[108] King, Jr. became "a son of Calvary," and yet another chapter in his young but exciting and seemingly productive life began to take shape.[109]

King, Jr. functioned in essentially two different worlds in Chester, one of which was white and the other black, each with its own values, challenges, demands, and expectations. That white world consisted largely of Crozer, a liberal American Baptist seminary, with its all-white male faculty and administration, its predominantly white student body, and a curriculum that was completely dominated by Euro-American theological content and interests. At any rate, King, Jr. began "a serious intellectual quest," immersing himself in the social gospelism of Walter Rauschenbusch, the Christian realism of Reinhold Niebuhr, the ethical idealism and socio-political activism of Mohandas K. Gandhi, the economic determinism of Karl Marx, and "the social and ethical theories" of Plato, Aristotle, Jean-Jacques Rousseau, Thomas

---

106. Carson, et al., eds., *King Papers*, I, 151; King, *Daddy King*, 144–45; Farris, *Through It All*, 45; and Downing, *To See the Promised Land*, 151.

107. Downing, *To See the Promised Land*, 151 and 155; and King, *Daddy King*, 145.

108. Miller, *Voice of Deliverance*, 44; Garrow, *Bearing the Cross*, 39; Baldwin, *There is a Balm in Gilead*, 125 and 282; Downing, *To See the Promised Land*, 154–55; Farris, *Through It All*, 49; A Private Interview with Emma Anderson, Chester, Pennsylvania (29 May 1987); and A Private Interview with Sara Richardson, Chester, Pennsylvania (29 May 1987).

109. Baldwin Interview with Richardson (29 May 1987); Baldwin Interview with Anderson (29 May 1987); Baldwin, *There is a Balm in Gilead*, 125, 167, and 282; and "History of the Calvary Baptist Church," in *Program Booklet of the Calvary Baptist Church Centennial Celebration, 1879-1979* (Chester, PA: Linder Printing Company, 1979), 25.

Hobbes, Jeremy Bentham, John Stuart Mill, Friedrich Wilhelm Nietzsche, John Locke, and other great philosophers.[110] "I never go anywhere much but in these books," King, Jr. declared in a letter to his mother.[111] The young man admitted that he "was occasionally shocked when" his "intellectual journey carried" him "through new and sometimes complex doctrinal lands, but the pilgrimage was always stimulating," gave him "a new appreciation for objective appraisal and critical analysis, and knocked" him "out of" his "dogmatic slumber."[112] Despite a heavy and demanding course load, King, Jr.'s academic record at Crozer was considerably better than that at Morehouse. Interestingly enough, he made Cs in two public speaking courses his first year, but made gradual and consistent progress, and ended up with nothing lower than a B in his second year and straight As in his third and last year.[113] Crozer's Dean Charles E. Batten praised King, Jr. as "one of our most outstanding students," noting particularly how he exhibited "fine preparation, an excellent mind, and a thorough grasp of the material." Some of Crozer's faculty members were equally impressed with the youngster. The biblical scholar Morton Scott Enslin described King, Jr. as "a very competent student" with "more than usual insight,"[114] and the liberal Christian theologian and ethicist George W. Davis, with whom King, Jr. completed 34 of his 110 course hours, pointed especially to the young man's "exceptional intellectual ability" and "discriminating mind."[115]

Despite distinguishing himself by his impressive academic performance, King, Jr. could not escape the curse that the society ascribed to black skin. He encountered attitudes among whites daily that caused him to reconsider long-held assumptions about race

110. Carson, ed., *The Autobiography of Martin Luther King, Jr.*, 17–29; King, *Stride toward Freedom*, 91–99; King, *Strength to Love*, 150–51; King, *Daddy King*, 144–45; and Downing, *To See the Promised Land*, 155.
111. Carson, et al., eds., *King Papers*, I, 161.
112. King, Jr., *Strength to Love*, 147; Carson, ed., *The Autobiography of Martin Luther King, Jr.*, 17–29; and Downing, *To See the Promised Land*, 155.
113. Carson, et al., eds., *King Papers*, I, 382 and 390; and Garrow, *Bearing the Cross*, 39, 41, and 43.
114. Carson, et al., eds., *King Papers*, I, 382 and 390–91; Clayborne Carson, "Martin Luther King, Jr.: The Crozer Years," *The Journal of Blacks in Higher Education* (Summer, 1997), 123; and Garrow, *Bearing the Cross*, 38–40.
115. Carson, et al., eds., *King Papers*, I, 382; and Garrow, *Bearing the Cross*, 41.

relations in the North.[116] Years earlier, while working on that tobacco farm in Connecticut, King, Jr. had noted in letters to his mother, Alberta that "Negroes and whites go to the same church," and that there "was no discrimination at all" because "the white people here are very nice,"[117] but his experiences during his Crozer years reminded him that white supremacy knew no boundaries.

King, Jr., through no fault of his own, was at the center of several potentially violent incidents involving race while at Crozer. On one occasion, a white Crozer student named Lucius Z. Hall, Jr., from North Carolina, mistakenly identified King, Jr. as the prankster who "rearranged his room" and threatened him with a gun.[118] On another occasion, King, Jr. accompanied Dupree Jordan, another white Crozer student, to a white-owned restaurant in nearby Philadelphia, and after demanding and receiving service, discovered sand in his food.[119] On yet another occasion, King, Jr., his black classmate Walter McCall, and their dates were refused service and threatened with a gun by the white proprietor at a restaurant in nearby Camden, New Jersey. The case ended up in court, but charges were dropped after three white student witnesses from the University of Pennsylvania decided not to testify on King, Jr. and his friends' behalf.[120] Reinhold Niebuhr's insights concerning group morality and the kind of collective egoistic impulses that drive white supremacy must have been reinforced in King, Jr.'s thinking at that point. In any case, in all of these incidents, King, Jr. remained quiet and graceful, and refused to create a scene.[121] His actions became a metaphor for how he would respond years later, when confronted by racist mobs in the context of civil rights demonstrations.

116. Downing, *To See the Promised Land*, 153.
117. Carson, et al., eds., *King Papers*, I, 112; King, *Daddy King*, 145; Farris, *Through It All*, 38; and Farris, "The Young Martin," 58.
118. For a more complete account of this incident, see Downing, *To See the Promised Land*, 153–54; and Garrow, *Bearing the Cross*, 40.
119. Garrow, *Bearing the Cross*, 40.
120. See "Statement on Behalf or Ernest Nichols, *State of New Jersey vs. Ernest Nichols*," by W. Thomas McGann in Carson, et al., eds., *King Papers*, I, 327–29; Downing, *To See the Promised Land*, 153; and Garrow, *Bearing the Cross*, 40.
121. John J. Ansbro, *Martin Luther King, Jr.: The Making of a Mind* (Maryknoll, NY: Orbis Books, 1982), 152–53; Garrow, *Bearing the Cross*, 40; and Downing, *To See the Promised Land*, 153–54.

There were continuing patterns of segregation and discrimination in Chester, and Crozer was no exception. The fact that its student body was "largely Southern in constitution"[122] undoubtedly explained some of its limitations around the question of race. Although King, Jr. became friends with a few of his white classmates, such as Dupree Jordan and Francis Steward, both of whom were from Georgia, and while he was eventually elected Crozer's student body president, supposedly because of his strong academic record, emotional maturity, and calmness of spirit,[123] the youngster would have found it much more difficult to adjust had he not been thoroughly grounded in a healthy sense of self and his culture,[124] and had he not worked with interracial student organizations during his time at Morehouse College.[125] Even so, King, Jr. was always conscious of being black at Crozer, and was also very much on guard when in the presence of whites. Professor Kenneth L. Smith, from whom King, Jr. took courses on social Christianity, recalled that King, Jr. had "a certain reserve about him, which made him difficult to get close to"[126]—a demeanor that most certainly owed much to what he knew about white people and their conception of the place of blacks in society. Keenly aware of the ways in which whites, even the intellectual elite, stereotyped black people, King, Jr. reported that "I was grimly serious for a time. I had a tendency to overdress, to keep my room spotless, my shoes perfectly shined and my clothes immaculately pressed." "If I were a minute late to class," he added, "I was almost morbidly conscious of it and sure that everyone noticed it."[127]

But there was always that black world within but apart from that

---

122. Carson, et al., eds., *King Papers*, I, 382.
123. Downing, *To See the Promised Land*, 153–54; Garrow, *Bearing the Cross*, 40; and Carson, et al., eds., *King Papers*, I, 382 and 391.
124. King actually wrote what would become perhaps his most extensive and penetrating account of his cultural roots while at Crozer, focusing on family, church, and the larger black community of Atlanta, Georgia. In my judgment, this paper is the most important source for getting at King's most decisive formative influences. See Carson, et. al., eds., *King Papers*, I, 359–79.
125. Interestingly enough, King, Sr. had initially opposed his son's decision to work with white students in the Intercollegiate Council, declaring that "You don't need to risk any betrayals from them, and that's mainly what you'll get...." See King, *Daddy King*, 141; and Carson, et al., eds., *King Papers*, I, 363.
126. Quoted in Garrow, *Bearing the Cross*, 41.
127. William Peters, "Our Weapon Is Love," *Redbook* (August, 1956), 72.

of whites in Chester, in which King, Jr. could relax and be himself, so to speak, and to which he could turn for support and reinforcement. That world included the ten other black students who, along with King, Jr., constituted a small percentage of the slightly less than one hundred students at Crozer. King, Jr. was especially close to Horace "Ed" Whitaker, an older black classmate, and Walter McCall, who had also been his classmate and one of his closest friends at Morehouse. The three often dated girls, attended church services, and frequented parties and other social functions together, had a lot of fun bowling and playing billiards and card games, and at times, teased each other and argued about race and politics.[128]

There was also that larger black community of Chester, including Calvary Baptist Church, which was made up of migrants from various parts of the South and their descendants. Having lived among southern blacks virtually all of his life, King, Jr. had absolutely no problem fitting in. That some of these people, such as Calvary's pastor J. Pius Barbour and his wife, Olee Littlejohn Barbour, were long-time friends of the King family contributed to King, Jr.'s sense of solidarity with them. According to Sara Richardson, an active member of Calvary for decades, King, Jr., commonly referred to as "Mike" in and around Chester, was actually adopted by the Barbours, and Reverend Barbour and the young man enjoyed a kind of "father-son relationship." "Mike was very fond of Reverend Barbour and Reverend Barbour was also fond of him," said Emma Anderson, another long-time member of Calvary.[129] King, Jr. could often be found relaxing, listening to the radio, or eating at the Barbour's home, and sometimes, he and Pastor Barbour engaged in heavy theological and philosophical discussions. "He is full of fun, and he has one of the best minds of anybody I have ever met," said King, Jr. of Barbour in a letter to his mother, Alberta.[130] At other

128. Farris, *Through It All*, 45 and 47–48; Garrow, *Bearing the Cross*, 39; and Downing, *To See the Promised Land*, 152–53.
129. Barbour "was like a father" to all of the black students at Crozer. See Baldwin Interview with Richardson (29 May 1987); Baldwin Interview with Anderson (29 May 1987); and Garrow, *Bearing the Cross*, 39. Interestingly enough, King, Sr. mentions King, Jr.'s decision to matriculate at Crozer, but says essentially nothing about Reverend Barbour in his autobiography. This is difficult to understand in view of what had been a rather close relationship between the two men for many years. See King, *Daddy King*, 144–45.

times, King, Jr. accompanied Barbour in visiting and praying with church members who were ill or otherwise confined to their homes, or simply sat around listening to the singing of Mrs. Barbour. King, Jr. also occasionally preached for Pastor Barbour and assisted him with the ministry to youth at Calvary.[131]

King, Jr.'s sense of the extended family, which had served him so well in Atlanta, was recreated in Chester. "He was very fond of the Talley family who attended our church," Sara Richardson recalled, "and he called Esther Talley 'mother'." "I would always leave my house key under a brick when I was away," Mrs. Richardson continued, "and he would come here and cook and eat with his friends. With his head in his hand, he always seemed in deep thought, but he also had a very human side."[132] Emma Anderson remembered that King, Jr. "made you feel comfortable around him" and "was very easy to meet." Mrs. Anderson also found the young man to be "very interested in elderly people," primarily because of the rich reservoir of experience and wisdom he knew they had to share with him.[133] Others who became very close to King, Jr. in Chester recalled a young man who exuded quiet nobility, a vital capacity for religious feeling, bold mannerisms of speech and language, an eloquence of style, a gentle spirit, and a fun-loving, down-to-earth approach to life.[134] Pastor William E. Gardner and some of his members at the First Baptist Church of East Elmhurst in Queens, New York, where King, Jr. also served as a ministerial assistant bimonthly in the fall of 1950, had a more mixed view of King, Jr. While Mrs. Matilda Sims found the youngster to be "marvelous" and "brilliant," Pastor Gardner criticized his "pulpit ability," accusing him of "an attitude of aloofness, disdain and possibly snobbishness which prevent his coming to grips with the rank and file of ordinary people," and of "a smugness that refuses to adapt itself to the demands of ministering effectively to

130. Farris, *Through It All*, 49; Carson, et al., eds., *King Papers*, I, 47, 161, 330, and 332; Baldwin Interview with Richardson (29 May 1987); and Baldwin Interview with Anderson (29 May 1987).
131. Baldwin Interview with Richardson (29 May 1987); Baldwin Interview with Anderson (29 May 1987); and Baldwin, *There is a Balm in Gilead*, 282.
132. Baldwin Interview with Richardson (29 May 1987).
133. Baldwin Interview with Anderson (29 May 1987); and Baldwin, *There is a Balm in Gilead*, 37–38.
134. Baldwin, *There is a Balm in Gilead*, 37.

the average Negro congregation."[135] The best that can be derived from these different perspectives is that King, Jr. was as complex as he was human in personality and demeanor.

Frederick L. Downing suggests that the Crozer experience changed King, Jr. in the sense that it separated him "from his family of origin" and afforded the opportunity he needed "to project himself toward his first life structure as an adult."[136] Although King, Jr. did become increasingly independent in his thinking and behavior over time, his correspondence files and family records reveal that he remained very close to both his immediate and extended family structures. He often wrote, called, or visited with his sister Christine, who was studying at New York's Columbia University.[137] Also, King, Jr. was constantly in touch with his parents via the mail or telephone, and they traveled from Atlanta to Chester at times to see him. "I often tell the boys around the campus I have the best mother in the world," King, Jr. commented in a letter to his mother, Alberta. "You will never know how I appreciate the many kind things you and daddy are doing for me." King, Jr. was also known to address letters to the entire Ebenezer Baptist Church family in Atlanta, updating them on his progress as a student and expressing gratitude for the congregation's enduring support.[138]

King, Sr. had no problem with his son's attitude toward family or anyone else, for that matter, but there was some concern about what has been described as King, Jr.'s "rather busy night life," and especially, his relationships with young ladies. Known as quite a ladies' man before he arrived at Crozer, King, Jr. was never able to outlive that kind of reputation. During his first year at Crozer, he dated Juanita Sellers, the daughter of a prominent Atlanta mortician, whom he had known in high school, and who was then pursuing graduate work at Columbia University along with his sister, Christine. He occasionally visited with Gloria Royster, an old girlfriend from Atlanta's Spelman College, who

---

135. Garrow, *Bearing the Cross*, 42; and Carson, et al., eds., *King Papers*, I, 380–81.
136. Downing, *To See the Promised Land*, 163.
137. Farris, *Through It All*, 45 and 47–48.
138. Carson, et al., eds., *King Papers*, I, 161; and Baldwin, *There is a Balm in Gilead*, 125–26.

was studying at Temple University in Philadelphia. On one occasion, he wrote his mother, Alberta about yet another young lady, noting that "I met a fine chick in Phila who has gone wild over the old boy." King, Jr. went on to say that "Since Barbour told the members of his church that my family was rich, the girls are running me down." And as if to put his parents' minds at ease, the young man quickly added: "Of course, I don't ever think about them—I am too busy studying."[139] On the day King, Jr. graduated from Crozer in 1951, several young ladies who did not know each other showed up, each in anticipation that she would win the young man's heart, and perhaps, ultimately become Mrs. Martin Luther King, Jr.[140]

King, Jr.'s friends never really questioned nor interfered with his dating habits, except when he became romantically involved with a white girl, the daughter of a German immigrant woman who worked in the Crozer cafeteria. Those closest to King, Jr. made "jokes about whose theological and racial liberalism was being most sorely tested" and, when King, Jr. and the young lady began to discuss marriage, these concerned friends joined Reverend Barbour in reminding King, Jr. of the difficulties of an interracial relationship, especially for a young preacher of color who planned to return to the Negro church in the South. Also, King, Jr. wondered what his parents and other family members might think and say. In any case, the couple amicably agreed to end their relationship after six months, and the girls' parents removed her from the Crozer environment.[141] If King, Jr.'s relationship with the white girl indicated anything at all, it showed that he had possibly undergone a revolution in terms of his thinking concerning

139. Downing, *To See the Promised Land*, 126 and 154; David L. Lewis, *King: A Critical Biography* (New York: Praeger Publishers, 1970), 32; Carson, et al., eds., *King Papers*, I, 161; and Farris, *Through It All*, 45 and 47–48.
140. Downing, *To See the Promised Land*, 154; and Lewis, *King*, 32.
141. Downing, *To See the Promised Land*, 154–55; and Garrow, *Bearing the Cross*, 40–41. I have found no record of what King, Jr.'s parents thought about this interracial relationship, but, given Daddy King's own expressions of distrust of white people at that time, one can safely assume that he was anything but happy. See Taylor Branch, *Parting the Waters: America in the King Years, 1954–63* (New York: Simon & Schuster, 1988), 89.

white people, and especially, interracial marriage.[142] But there is no evidence that he ever dated a white girl after that experience.

As was always the case, the more serious and conscientious side of King, Jr. prevailed over any inclination he had toward risky behavior and a fun-filled life, and he completed his training at Crozer with both a superb academic record and an image of high repute. King, Jr. drew high praise for "his moral character," and for being "held universally in high regard by faculty, staff, and students," and one of his professors, Morton Scott Enslin, predicted that "he will go far in his profession." George W. Davis, King, Jr.'s favorite professor at Crozer, commended King, Jr. for being "very personable" and for making "a good impression in public speaking and discussion," and he expressed certainty that the young man would "make an excellent minister or teacher." King, Jr. actually became the valedictorian of his graduating class, and he also won the Pearl Ruth Plafkner Award for outstanding scholarship and the Lewis Crozer Fellowship for graduate studies. The glowing evaluations and awards King, Jr. received meant as much or more than the green Chevrolet his daddy bought him as a graduation gift.[143] He had engaged in "a serious intellectual quest for a method to eliminate social evil" at Crozer, but, by the time of his graduation, he was also interested in achieving the best that the academic life had to offer for its own sake. Thus, he turned his attention to the PhD program in systematic theology at Boston University and began his studies in the fall of 1951.[144]

In Boston, Massachusetts, the small collegial climate of Crozer was "replaced by the mass bustle of a large urban university," but King, Jr. continued, nonetheless, to live in basically two worlds.[145] There was the serious-minded, hardworking, and productive student who functioned primarily in a predominantly white academic setting, and also, the playful and fun-loving young minister who found a special home and

142. Before entering Morehouse College, King, Jr. had essentially denied any desire at all on the part of black men to marry white women. See Carson, et al., eds., *King Papers*, I, 121.
143. Farris, *Through It All*, 50; Downing, *To See the Promised Land*, 164; Carson, et al., eds., *King Papers*, I, 382 and 391–92; and Garrow, *Bearing the Cross*, 41.
144. Carson, et al., eds., *King Papers*, I, 382 and 390–92; and King, *Stride toward Freedom*, 91.
145. Branch, *Parting the Waters*, 92.

a sense of an extended family in Boston's black community. At Boston, King, Jr. was able to effectively combine his scholarly interests with his continuing search for an answer to social evil, because Dean Walter Muelder and theology and ethics professors such as Allen Knight Chalmers, Edgar S. Brightman, and L. Harold DeWolf were not only polished and accomplished academics, but also had "a passion for social justice" and "a deep sympathy for pacifism." King, Jr. studied personalistic philosophy under Brightman and DeWolf, and this provided "a metaphysical and philosophical grounding" for his belief in "the idea of a personal God" and "the dignity and worth of all human personality"—concepts to which he was first exposed at home, at Atlanta's Ebenezer Baptist Church, and in other black church circles in the South.[146] King, Jr. also read the works of great philosophers such as Georg Wilhelm Friedrich Hegel and Immanuel Kant, and in his PhD dissertation, entitled, *A Comparison of the Conceptions of God in the Thinking of Paul Tillich and Henry Nelson Wieman* (1955), insights from two traditions, the European-American academy and the Negro church, were brought together, perhaps almost unconsciously during the last two years of his graduate work.[147]

Boston, like Chester, must have reminded King, Jr. of the South in some ways. Not only was there segregation, but whites at all levels, including some among the intellectual elite, who never seriously doubted nor questioned theories of the superiority of Anglo-Saxon blood, of the innate inequality of the races, and of the dire necessity of maintaining white racial purity. Although King, Jr. experienced some "intimacy between faculty and students" at Boston University,[148] he survived primarily because he drew strength from a black community comprising largely of migrants from the South who had recreated the essentials of their own culture in their new environment, especially in the Roxbury area of Boston, where Twelfth Baptist Church, under

---

146. King, *Stride toward Freedom*, 100; Watley, *Roots of Resistance*, 31–45; and Baldwin, *There is a Balm in Gilead*, 168–72.
147. King, *Stride toward Freedom*, 100–101; and Clayborne Carson, et al., eds., *The Papers of Martin Luther King, Jr., Volume II: Rediscovering Precious Values, July 1951–November 1955* (Berkeley: University of California Press, 1994), 339–548.
148. Carson, et al., eds., *King Papers*, II, 59.

the leadership of Daddy King's close friend William H. Hester, was located.[149] By affiliating with and becoming a preaching assistant at Twelfth Baptist, which had served a century earlier as a sanctuary for free Africans and slaves as well as an antislavery meetinghouse, King, Jr. virtually assured that he would remain at the center of that culture. The young man became "an adopted son" at Twelfth Baptist and Twelfth Baptist became his "preaching station, his fellowship station, his feeding trough, and his home away from home."[150] King, Jr.'s dealings with Pastor Hester and his wife, Beulah mirrored what had been his relationship to Pastor Barbour and his wife, Olee Littlejohn back in Chester, for the Hesters became his guardians, and also, his link to that larger black community to which he could turn for spiritual sustenance, social networking, support, and reinforcement.

King, Jr. made a lot of friends and acquaintances in Boston's black community, but was quite close to Philip Lenud and Michael E. Haynes. Lenud, an Alabama-born Baptist minister, fellow Morehouse graduate, and student at Tufts University, became King, Jr.'s roommate in Boston, and the two organized twelve students into a philosophy club that met on weekends, and they also had a lot of fun double dating, shopping, dining together, and "horsing around," so to speak.[151] Lenud recognized in King, Jr. a serious student and a dear friend who also possessed the very best in terms of human qualities:

> We were like brothers. This is the only man I have lived around or with, and never had a quarrel with him. Martin and I were very much alike, I suppose, in some areas—in terms of grasping and seeking for knowledge, and a craving to make a difference in the world for people. He was totally passive. He was just a born pacifist. People would just take advantage of him because he was so good-natured. People would come by and want him to do things or drive them places, not realizing that Martin had to

---

149. Martin Luther King, Sr. did acknowledge Hester's importance during King, Jr.'s Boston years, a consideration he, as stated previously, did not give to J. Pius Barbour in relation to his son's Crozer experience. See King, *Daddy King*, 147–49; and Baldwin, *There is a Balm in Gilead*, 125 and 283.
150. *One Hundred and Five Years By Faith: A History of the Twelfth Baptist Church, 1840–1945* (Boston: Twelfth Baptist Church, 1946), 11 and 17–18; *Three-Fold Celebration Year: Souvenir Journal, Twelfth Baptist Church*, (May, 1985), 19; and A Private Interview with Reverend Michael E. Haynes, Twelfth Baptist Church, Boston, Massachusetts (25 June 1987).
151. King, *Daddy King*, 148–49 and 151; Farris, *Through It All*, 74; King, *My Life with Martin Luther King, Jr.*, 55 and 89; Baldwin, *There is a Balm in Gilead*, 39–40; and Downing, *To See the Promised Land*, 169.

study. They put so much work on him at Boston. He would come home sometimes with twelve to fifteen books to read, and he really didn't have time to be doing things for people. But he was always willing to do what he could to help people.[152]

Michael Haynes, who served with King, Jr. as an apprentice preacher at Twelfth Baptist Church, offered a somewhat similar assessment of King, Jr.'s personality, noting also that "he carried himself with dignity, but yet with humility and a sense of humor." "For a guy who was distinctly middle class and bourgeois, comparatively speaking, and better off than many of the guys who were here," declared Haynes, "Martin carried himself in a very, very humble manner. He made me feel completely at ease, although we were in two different theological and intellectual worlds."[153]

The nice guy image solidified King, Jr.'s rising popularity among blacks and whites in Boston, but the demands of the PhD program were such that the young man could not sustain the kind of active social life he had known in Atlanta and Chester. Boston clearly had so much more to offer in this regard, and King, Jr., only in his early twenties, was not yet mature enough to resist the many temptations that shimmered before him. "Where are the girls that would set my heart on fire?," he asked Michael Haynes soon after settling in Boston.[154] King, Jr. and Philip Lenud occasionally joined friends for an evening of fun at the Totem Pole and other night spots in Roxbury, where beautiful young ladies often showed up in considerable numbers, and where jazz and other secular music sometimes swelled and overflowed into vigorous dance routines.[155] King, Jr. dated quite a bit and usually had more than one girlfriend at a time. "Reverend and Mrs. Hester were always concerned with what Martin and all of the other single guys at Twelfth

---

152. Baldwin Interview with Lenud (7 April 1987); Baldwin, *There is a Balm in Gilead*, 39–40; and King, *My life with Martin Luther King, Jr.*, 55 and 87.
153. Baldwin Interview with Haynes (25 June 1987); and Baldwin, *There is a Balm in Gilead*, 39.
154. "MLK After 40 Years: A Fraternal Memoir," radioopensource.org/mlk-jr.-after-40-years-a-fraternal-memoir/-36k-(26 January 2008), 1. For the most brilliant use of psychosocial theory to explain much of King, Jr.'s attitude and behavior toward young women during those years, see Downing, *To See the Promised Land*, 126, 154, and 169–70.
155. Downing, *To See the Promised Land*, 169; Baldwin, *There is a Balm in Gilead*, 40; Stephen B. Oates, *Let the Trumpet Sound: The Life of Martin Luther King, Jr.* (New York: Harper & Row, Publishers, 1982), 41; and Baldwin Interview with Lenud (7 April 1987).

Baptist were doing with the girls with whom they were going out," Michael Haynes recounted. "It was like a family kind of thing."[156] Horace Whitaker, an old classmate from Crozer, was equally concerned. "Apparently you are still meeting these girls who are one-time wreckers," he jokingly asserted in a letter to King, Jr. "Watch the Doctor and don't let one catch you with your shoes off."[157] W. T. Handy, Jr., a student at Boston during King, Jr.'s first year there, also sent King, Jr. a letter, obviously teasing him about his dating habits and cautioning him against taking this too far:

> I know you are now married? Which one was it? No, I know you are still gallivanting around Boston, the most eligible and popular bachelor in town. I wonder how you are progressing with my steadying influence gone. Remember M. L., "we are expecting great things from you." The only element to restrain our expectations from bearing fruit will be M. L. himself. However, I know he will not allow himself or influences to bring failure about him or embarrassment to his beloved father and Mother.[158]

King, Jr.'s search for that very special young lady essentially ended in February 1952, when Mary Powell, wife of the nephew of the Morehouse College President Benjamin Mays, introduced the young man to Coretta Scott, an Alabama native, a proud member of the African Methodist Episcopal Zion Church (AMEZ), and a student at the New England Conservatory of Music in Boston.[159] Initially, King, Jr. seemed so "short" and looked so "unimpressive" to Coretta, but the young man "had a way with words" when it came to women, and the more he talked, the more he "radiated charm" and "grew in stature." Coretta also sensed that King, Jr., unlike so many ministers she had known, was not "overly pious" and "very narrow" in his "thinking"—that he was, in fact, genuinely sincere and quite intelligent

---

156. Downing, *To See the Promised Land*, 169; Farris, *Through It All*, 74; and Baldwin Interview with Haynes (25 June 1987).
157. Carson, et al., eds., *King Papers*, II, 159.
158. Ibid., 163.
159. King, Jr.'s friend Michael Haynes recalls that Mary Powell, the Reverend Hester's secretary at Twelfth Baptist Church, "thought she had all of these familial rights to Martin, and she didn't want him running around with all kinds of girls. So she deliberately plotted to bring him and Coretta together." See Baldwin Interview with Haynes (25 June 1987); King, *My Life with Martin Luther King, Jr.*, 49–51, 54, 57, and 61–64; and Baldwin, *There is a Balm in Gilead*, 284–85.

and eloquent in mind and manner. Coretta remembered that King, Jr. spoke "so strongly and convincingly," and that he, "with a very masculine self-possession," seemed "to know exactly where he was going and how he was going to get there."[160] In a short period, the two became very serious about each other, feelings reinforced by their shared southern sense of place, particularly their sensibilities regarding religion, music, food, and other aspects of culture, and also, by their common desire to eventually return to the South and contribute in some way to the betterment of its racial situation.[161] King, Jr. had always had a preference primarily for southern black women, and it was widely assumed in family circles that some highly educated and progressive-minded young lady from the South would, one day, become his wife.

The relationship between King, Jr. and Coretta blossomed and the couple became engaged only months after meeting each other. The nature of the relationship was graphically expressed in a letter King, Jr. wrote to Coretta in July 1952, shortly after they had apparently argued about something. Referring to Coretta as "my darling" and apologizing for going "off on such a poetical and romantic flight," the young man noted that his love for Coretta "was based on such a solid foundation that the stormy winds of anger cannot blow it asunder." "My life without you is like a year without a spring time which comes to give illumination and heat to the atmosphere which has been saturated by the dark cold breeze of winter," King, Jr. stated further. He went on to make references to his reading of Edward Bellamy's novel, *Looking Backward* (1888), to his thoughts about communism, socialism, and capitalism, to his hope for "a warless world," and to a range of other social, political, and economic concerns, thus suggesting that he and Coretta were perhaps as interested at that time in learning and thinking through world problems as they were in each other.[162]

160. King, *My Life with Martin Luther King, Jr.*, 50–53; Farris, *Through It All*, 72–73; and Edythe Scott Bagley, *Desert Rose: The Life and Legacy of Coretta Scott King* (Tuscaloosa: The University of Alabama Press, 2012), 95–99.
161. King, *My Life with Martin Luther King, Jr.*, 18, 50–67, and 90–91; King, *Stride toward Freedom*, 21–22; Downing, *To See the Promised Land*, 171; and Baldwin, *There is a Balm in Gilead*, 41.

King, Jr.'s decision to marry Coretta was well-received by friends and family members, with the exception, of course, of Daddy King, who became very concerned when informed that his son had been in the company of this "extremely attractive young lady" on two occasions when he preached at Twelfth Baptist Church. The elder King actually visited King, Jr. in Boston and discovered that this particular young lady was Coretta, the music student and aspiring concert singer, and that the two were very much in love. Up to that point, King, Sr. was certain that his son would marry the daughter of one of the "fine, solid Atlanta families, folks we've known for many years, people we respect, and whose feelings we'd never trample on."[163] He simply could not understand King, Jr.'s willingness to unite in matrimony with a young lady who "was planning a career on the concert stage"—a move he felt was quite inappropriate for "a young man from a strict Baptist upbringing and background."[164] King, Jr. had always respected and listened to his father before making major decisions in life, but in this case, his independence of heart and mind triumphed over Daddy King's insistence that he marry some "Atlanta girl with social connections" within his own circle of close acquaintances.[165] In any event, King, Jr. and Coretta exchanged vows on June 18, 1953 at Coretta's childhood home in Marion, Alabama, and King, Sr., interestingly enough, performed the ceremony. From that point, King, Jr. and Coretta struggled to be the ideal husband and wife even as they also sought to grow spiritually and to complete their academic studies in Boston.[166]

King, Jr. was only twenty-four when he and Coretta resolved to become one flesh, so to speak, and there were questions among friends

---

162. Clayborne Carson, et al., eds., *The Papers of Martin Luther King, Jr., Volume VI: Advocate of the Social Gospel, September 1948–March 1963* (Berkeley: University of California Press, 2007), 123–26.

163. King, *Daddy King*, 147–50; Farris, *Through It All*, 73–74; and King, *My Life with Martin Luther King, Jr.*, 65.

164. King, *Daddy King*, 149.

165. According to Coretta King, King, Jr. "was amazingly respectful, thoughtful, and considerate of Daddy King's feelings." King, Jr.'s friend Philip Lenud agreed, claiming that King, Jr. "found such awesome security in his father because his father was such a strong man, like my father was." See King, *My Life with Martin Luther King, Jr.*, 66; Baldwin Interview with Lenud (7 April 1987); Baldwin, *There is a Balm in Gilead*, 126; Downing, *To See the Promised Land*, 169; and Farris, *Through It All*, 74.

166. King, *My Life with Martin Luther King, Jr.*, 67–87; Bagley, *Desert Rose*, 102–3; and Farris, *Through It All*, 76–77.

and family about the extent to which married life would change him. His disposition to seek out activities that were enjoyable and amusing declined somewhat over time, but never really ended, and those closest to him, who also knew his weaknesses, still felt the need at times to remind him of the necessity of remaining morally upright and steadfast, especially since he was a young man of the cloth. A year after the wedding, King, Sr. sent a letter to King, Jr. about the importance of maintaining a clean personal life. "You are becoming very popular," the elder King wrote. "As I told you, you must be in prayer," for persons "like yourself are the ones the devil turns all his forces aloose to destroy."[167]

There was also some concern, especially on King, Sr.'s part, about how his son's PhD studies might impact him personally and from the standpoint of his ideas and values. The hope was that King, Jr. would not become arrogant—which was the case with all too many academics in those days—and that he would not become excessively liberal or too radical in terms of his theology, his approach to the Bible, and his political outlook. King, Jr.'s essential good nature, humility, and charitable spirit never faded, but Daddy King had mixed feelings about where his son was headed at the level of ideas and values. "I admired his mind's receptivity and the genuine passion he had for learning," Daddy King declared, and his "arguments, theological or not, were precisely constructed and convincing." "Politically, he often seemed to be drifting away from the basics of capitalism and Western democracy that I felt very strongly about," the elder King added. "There were some sharp exchanges," and "I may even have raised my voice a few times."[168] King, Jr. himself admitted repeatedly that he differed substantially with his father theologically and politically, but that that admiration for a real father never wavered. Moreover, the young man was always influenced by the noble moral and ethical principles and ideals his parents instilled in him.[169]

"The Boston years," writes Frederick L. Downing, "represented a

---

167. Carson, et al., eds., *King Papers*, II, 320.
168. King, *Daddy King*, 147.
169. Carson, et al., eds., *King Papers*, I, 363.

continuation and a refinement of King's vocational quest," for he had actually decided at Morehouse that he would devote his life to "some form of ministry." But there remained "some ambiguity" in his thinking about whether he would pastor a church like his father, teach like his mother, Alberta and sister, Christine, or pursue a career in either medicine or law.[170] When King, Jr. completed the residential requirements for the PhD with impeccable academic credentials in 1954, job offers poured in from various parts of the country. Churches in the northeast and the South sought his services as pastor, and colleges, universities, and seminaries offered him administrative positions and professorships.[171] Imbued with a deep sense of regional identity and regional responsibility in a southern context, King, Jr. soon accepted "the Call of Destiny," and he and his wife Coretta became the pastor and first lady of the Dexter Avenue Baptist Church in Montgomery, Alabama.[172] It was here, in the heart of Dixie, that the competing claims of public life and private life began to frustrate King, Jr.'s capacity to give adequate attention to long-time friends, family, and other special attachments. Exactly how this occurred is the subject of the next chapter.

170. Downing, *To See the Promised Land*, 166–67.
171. Carson, et al., eds., *King Papers*, II, 160 and 211; Baldwin, *There is a Balm in Gilead*, 41–42; and Baldwin, *The Voice of Conscience*, 68–69.
172. Farris, *Through It All*, 77; King, *My Life with Martin Luther King, Jr.*, 93–99; and Baldwin, *There is a Balm in Gilead*, 30–42.

2

"The Measure of a Man": Who was Martin Luther King, Jr.?

The true test of civilization is, not the census, nor the size of cities, nor the crops—no, but the kind of man the country turns out.
–Ralph Waldo Emerson[1]

The worth of an individual does not lie in the measure of his intellect, his racial origin or his social position. Human worth lies in relatedness to God.
–Martin Luther King, Jr.[2]

In one version of his celebrated sermon, "The Three Dimensions of a Complete Life," delivered at a church in Pasadena, California in February 1960,[3] Martin Luther King, Jr. reminded his listeners that "in the final analysis, everything that you see in this universe is a shadow

---

1. John Bartlett, ed., *The Shorter Bartlett's Familiar Quotations: A Collection of Passages, Phrases, and Proverbs Traced to their Sources in Ancient and Modern Literature*, ed. by Christopher Morley and Louella D. Everett (New York: Pocket Books, Inc., 1964), 122.
2. Martin Luther King, Jr., *Where Do We Go from Here: Chaos or Community?* (Boston: Beacon Press, 1968; originally published in 1967), 97; Martin Luther King, Jr., *The Measure of a Man* (Philadelphia: Fortress Press, 1988; originally published in 1959), 1-31; and Martin Luther King, Jr., "What is Man?," unpublished version of a sermon on "Sunday with Martin Luther King, Jr.," WAAF—AM, Chicago, Illinois (17 April 1966), Library and Archives of The Martin Luther King, Jr. Center for Nonviolent Social Change, Inc. Atlanta, Georgia, 1.
3. The title of this chapter came from King, Jr. *The Measure of a Man*.

cast by that which you do not see." King, Jr. went on to illustrate the point in these terms: "You don't see Martin Luther King; you see my body. You can never see my mind; you can never see my personality. You can never see the me which makes me me."[4] Although King, Jr. was making a metaphysical distinction concerning the difference between mind and body, or what is ontological or real and what is phenomenal, his essential point, among other considerations, was that there is a side to every person that the human eye and consciousness cannot detect nor grasp. King, Jr. knew that some considered him, first and foremost, a preacher; others regarded him as essentially a civil rights leader; and still others saw him as a profound thinker and intellectual who put the power of ideas to the service of nonviolent direct action, but that these images did not constitute the essence of who and what he actually was. In short, King, Jr. was speaking in his sermon about the King who was a human being—the King who existed and functioned behind the public persona.

This second chapter is an attempt to answer the question, "Who was Martin Luther King, Jr.?" Much of the stress is on the King who personified natural human tendencies even as he was crowned by his most loyal followers and supporters with messianic qualities.[5] King, Jr.'s years as a pastor, civil rights leader, and social activist are considered, especially, in terms of how he negotiated the demands of the private realm inside the bonds of friendship and other associations, including his roles as husband and father. It will become evident that the public and the private often conflicted with one another in King's life. In other words, King usually acted in the public to the neglect of concerns in the private arena, and his failure to achieve a proper and necessary balance between the two worlds actually prevented him from living what he himself defined and envisioned as a genuinely meaningful and complete life.[6]

4. Clayborne Carson, et al., eds., *The Papers of Martin Luther King, Jr., Volume VI: Advocate of the Social Gospel, September 1948-March 1963* (Berkeley: University of California Press, 2007), 402–3.
5. For some of the most brilliant insights on this subject, see Frederick L. Downing, *To See the Promised Land: The Faith Pilgrimage of Martin Luther King, Jr.* (Macon, GA: Mercer University Press, 1986), 9–14. Also See Lewis V. Baldwin, *There is a Balm in Gilead: The Cultural Roots of Martin Luther King, Jr.* (Minneapolis: Fortress Press, 1991), 243–52.

A. To Be Man and Messiah: King, Jr.'s Divided Persona

Martin Luther King, Jr. arrived in Montgomery, Alabama in the spring of 1954, and there, he soon found direction for his life and ministry. His image and role as the senior pastor at Dexter Avenue Baptist Church ultimately allowed him to establish his place as both a religious leader and community leader. He was quite young, well-educated, and marvelously gifted, but also a virtually unknown and rather ordinary human being, not likely to attract attention outside the confines of his own congregation and community. Even at Dexter Church, there were a few long-time and well-established members who found young King to be unimpressive and possibly immature, and wondered if he was up to the task of church leadership. Dr. Zelia S. Evans, a professor of Education at Montgomery's Alabama State College, was the only member at Dexter to vote against King, Jr. for pastor because she felt he was simply too youthful and inexperienced.[7] When Mary Fair Burks, another Dexter member and Alabama State professor, first saw King, Jr., she said, "You mean that little boy is my pastor. He looks like he ought to be home with his mamma."[8] Some of the most important local black male leaders in Montgomery also agreed that King, Jr. looked "more like a boy than a man," but age and looks would prove to be poor and unreliable indicators of King, Jr.'s readiness to meet the challenges that confronted him as a leader.[9]

---

6. This observation draws on the insight of Susan Wiltshire, who wisely and persistently reminds us that "Both public life and private life are required for living well, and to choose one and neglect the other deprives us of integrative structures of meaning on the one hand and the life-giving dramas of particularity on the other." See Susan Ford Wiltshire, *Public & Private in Vergil's Aeneid* (Amherst: The University of Massachusetts Press, 1989), 3.
7. Zelia Evans later regretted and preferred to forget her decision to vote against King for obvious reasons. A long-time member of Dexter and one of the organizers of that congregation's "strong and dynamic Women's Council," she also became one of its most important historians. See Zelia S. Evans and J. T. Alexander, eds., *Dexter Avenue Baptist Church, 1877-1977: One Hundred Year History of a Famous Religious Institution* (Montgomery: Dexter Avenue Baptist Church, 1978); Clayborne Carson, et al., eds., *The Papers of Martin Luther King, Jr., Volume II: Rediscovering Precious Values, July 1951-November 1955* (Berkeley: University of California Press, 1994), 290-91; and A Telephone Interview with Nelson Malden (15 March 2014).
8. Coretta Scott King, *My Life with Martin Luther King, Jr.* (New York: Henry Holt and Company, 1993; originally published in 1969), 94-95.
9. David J. Garrow, *Bearing the Cross: Martin Luther King, Jr., and the Southern Christian Leadership Conference* (New York: William Morrow & Company, Inc., 1986), 20.

Undoubtedly, the quality of King, Jr.'s life as a human being would be significantly impacted in Montgomery. The path that led him to prominence, and ultimately, fame and notoriety began with the Montgomery bus boycott in 1955, an event precipitated by Rosa L. Parks's arrest for refusing to surrender her bus seat to a white male passenger.[10] King, Jr. became president of the new Montgomery Improvement Association (MIA), organized to spearhead the boycott, and he began his practical quest to bring the principle of the beloved community, or the completely integrated society, to vivid life through nonviolent resistance and protest.[11] His activism in Montgomery was complimented by dynamic sermons and mass meeting speeches that, with his distinctive and always engaging panache, enlightened the minds and stirred the consciences of people, and also, motivated them to act courageously in the interest of justice and the common good.[12] In time, King, Jr. became a fixture in the public consciousness and his role actually assumed mythic and messianic significance among many of his own people in the South, who variously and respectfully referred to him as "the Alabama Moses," "just like Jesus," "De Lawd," and the person whom "God has gloriously called" to "lead and liberate his people."[13] Coretta Scott King noted that "it was very difficult" for

10. Martin Luther King, Jr., *Stride toward Freedom: The Montgomery Story* (New York: Harper & Row, Publishers, 1958), 43–70; and Clayborne Carson, ed., *The Autobiography of Martin Luther King, Jr.* (New York: Warner Books, Inc., 1998), 50–62.

11. King, *Stride toward Freedom*, 57 and 73–74.

12. Clayborne Carson and Peter Holloran, eds., *A Knock at Midnight: Inspiration from the Great Sermons of Reverend Martin Luther King, Jr.* (New York: Warner Books, Inc., 1998), 159–62. According to Richard Lischer, "After the boycott commenced, King's Sunday morning sermons found a new purpose and vitality. The specificity of race...now sharpened the point of his biblical interpretation and preaching." See Richard Lischer, *The Preacher King: Martin Luther King Jr. and the Word that Moved America* (New York: Oxford University Press, 1995), 85.

13. Theodore Silver, "Rev. M. L. King: Alabama Moses," *The American Negro*, I (June, 1956), 13; Downing, *To See the Promised Land*, 9; A Telephone Interview with James M. Lawson, Jr. (11 June 2013); John A. Ricks, "'De Lawd' Descends and is Crucified: Martin Luther King, Jr. in Albany, Georgia," *Journal of Southwest Georgia History*, Vol. 2 (Fall, 1984), 3–14; and Clayborne Carson, et al., eds., *The Papers of Martin Luther King, Jr., Volume IV: Symbol of the Movement, January 1957–December 1958* (Berkeley: University of California Press, 2000), 499. Shortly after being convicted of "violating Alabama's anti-boycott law" in March, 1956, King was greeted by thousands at Montgomery's Holt Street Baptist Church "amid thundering cheers" and the voice of a platform speaker who declared that "he who was nailed to the cross for us this afternoon approaches," and some in the crowd asserted that "He's next to Jesus himself." See Clayborne Carson, et al., eds., *The Papers of Martin Luther King, Jr., Volume III: Birth of a New Age, December 1955–December 1956* (Berkeley: University of California Press, 1997), 199; and Baldwin, *There is a Balm in Gilead*, 243–52. During the Albany Movement in 1961–62, King was referred to as "the Moses of the twentieth century" by both his friend

her husband "to keep from being worshiped by the black masses."[14] In a larger sense, King the man became thoroughly intertwined with King the celebrated hero and messianic figure.[15] The amazing changes that occurred in connection with King's "symbolic leadership role," as King, Jr. himself put it, "happened so quickly that I had no time to think through the implications of such leadership."[16]

King, Jr. became widely known nationally and internationally during the Montgomery protest. This was due, largely, to images of him created and projected by the national news media which, like the earliest biographies of King, Jr. by scholars, tended "to promote the mythic status of a rising young national leader."[17] King, Jr. increasingly became both "a media magnet" and "a media target,"[18] and other black leaders inside and outside of Montgomery felt that he was receiving too much attention and personal publicity to the neglect of others whose contributions to the struggle were no less, and in some cases greater, than his own. Although King, Jr. knew that he was on a march toward greatness that seemed providentially ordained, and that he had to accept "the symbolic role that history had thrust upon me," he never really sought nor embraced the mythic and messianic mold that many of his admirers created for him, and nor was he to blame for the immense media attention and coverage visited upon him.[19] In fact, King, Jr. never really sought a place among the leadership of the Montgomery bus boycott, and when he was first nominated to head

Ralph Abernathy and Dr. William G. Anderson, the leader of the Albany Movement. See Clayborne Carson, et al., eds., *The Papers of Martin Luther King, Jr., Volume VII: To Save the Soul of America, January 1961–August 1962* (Berkeley: University of California Press, 2015), 518n1 and 523n2.

14. King, *My Life with Martin Luther King, Jr.*, 165.

15. Downing, *To See the Promised Land*, 9–11; and Baldwin, *There is a Balm in Gilead*, 243–52.

16. Downing, *To See the Promised Land*, 9; and Clayborne Carson, et al., eds., *The Papers of Martin Luther King, Jr., Volume V: Threshold of a New Decade, January 1959–December 1960* (Berkeley: University of California Press, 2005), 329.

17. Ibid., 22. Also see Richard Lentz, *Symbols, the News Magazines, and Martin Luther King, Jr.* (Baton Rouge: Louisiana State University Press, 1990), 27–33.

18. Richard Lischer concludes that King's preaching made him "a media magnet," and this is quite true, but King's nonviolent activism was also important in this regard. See Lischer, *The Preacher King*, 191.

19. According to Coretta King, her husband never "took on the pretentious qualities of the leader of a large movement," that he never felt "the need to have people at his beck and call," and that "he refused" to allow even his own staff "make him a person of importance who should have all sorts of attention paid him." "He would much rather drive a Ford car than a Cadillac," she added. See King, *My Life with Martin Luther King, Jr.*, 165.

the MIA, he, being new to the city of Montgomery, was reluctant to accept because he felt that one of the local, more established black leaders would, perhaps, be better suited for the position.[20] King, Jr. was described by those closest to him in Montgomery as "the opposite of an egotist," as displaying an "almost touching modesty," and he became most emphatic in saying that "I have no Messiah complex."[21] He struggled primarily for acceptance and not necessarily for recognition, praise, and laudatory accolades, and was always highly honored and gracious when an admirer asked for an autograph or to take a photograph with him. But the very idea of anyone crowning his picture with some sort of angelic halo must have been most uncomfortable for him.[22] Thus, King, Jr. was unlike all too "many men who rise in the world," and he was most critical of black preachers who typically had an egotistical need for status and recognition.[23] "Publicity is evanescent," he wrote, in response to those who accused him of "bigness" in Montgomery. "It is here today and gone tomorrow." He insisted that "only the shallow-minded are excited about publicity," and that the person who "falls in love with publicity is not fit to have it and will end up in misery."[24]

Although King, Jr. was not a publicity seeker, by any stretch of the imagination, he was quite interested in, and sometimes overly concerned about, how he was perceived by others, and especially those who looked to him for spiritual and moral leadership in that period

20. Martin Luther King, Sr., *Daddy King: An Autobiography*, with Clayton Riley (New York: William Morrow & Company, Inc., 1980), 177; Carson, ed., *The Autobiography of Martin Luther King, Jr.*, 105 and 136–37; Carson, et al., eds., *King Papers*, V, 328–29; Downing, *To See the Promised Land*, 9–10 and 22 King, *My Life with Martin Luther King, Jr.*, 165; Christine King Farris, *Through It All: Reflections on My Life, My Family, and My Faith* (New York: Atria Books, 2009), 85; and Garrow, *Bearing the Cross*, 88.
21. Lawrence D. Reddick, *Crusader without Violence: A Biography of Martin Luther King, Jr.* (New York: Harper & Brothers, Publishers, 1959), 7; and Carson, et al., eds., *King Papers*, V, 477. Coretta King noted that her husband simply wanted "to be a good servant of his Lord and Master, who was crucified on Good Friday," but he apparently never felt that one could achieve the messianic status of the man from Nazareth. See King, *My Life with Martin Luther King, Jr.*, 206–7.
22. King, *My Life with Martin Luther King, Jr.*, 59; and James M. Washington, ed., *I Have a Dream: Writings and Speeches that Changed the World* (New York: HarperCollins Publishers, 1992), 191–92.
23. King, *My Life with Martin Luther King, Jr.*, 165; Martin Luther King, Jr., "Answer to a Perplexing Question," unpublished version of a sermon, Ebenezer Baptist Church, Atlanta, Georgia (3 March 1963), King Center Library and Archives, 7–8; and Martin Luther King, Jr., *Strength to Love* (Philadelphia: Fortress Press, 1981; originally published in 1963), 59.
24. King, *Stride toward Freedom*, 155–56; King, *My Life with Martin Luther King, Jr.*, 59; and King, *Strength to Love*, 59.

of epic change. King, Jr. was never fully satisfied with the way he looked, thinking, according to his friend Philip Lenud, that he was not tall enough and not particularly handsome.[25] He closely resembled his mother, Alberta and inherited her short build, high forehead, and full lips and nose, and his complexion was brown, his voice strong, clear, and precise. He was about five feet seven inches tall, "carrying a heavy chested one hundred and eighty-five pounds."[26] Though King, Jr. was rather slight in stature, it is difficult, in hindsight, to think of him as having been small in any way, particularly in these times of hero worship and a burgeoning social media.

In any case, King, Jr. took special steps to improve his personal appearance and hygiene, beginning each day with a shower or bath, the brushing of his teeth, and the use of "Magic Shave" and after shave lotion or cologne. Although he almost never got eight hours of sleep, was known to smoke cigarettes and consume alcohol in moderation, sometimes failed to follow doctors' orders, and occasionally, showed a stunning disregard for his personal well-being and safety, he ate well, was quite healthy, and was only hospitalized a few times for high fever, nervous stomach, exhaustion, respiratory problems, and a few other minor ailments between 1954 and 1968.[27] King, Jr.'s habit of dressing in dark suits and immaculately shined shoes for public appearances, which was first cultivated in his childhood, never changed.[28] According to his close associate Ralph Abernathy, King, Jr.'s procedure of getting cleaned up and dressed each day was so meticulous and time-consuming that "it was the one reason he was always late" for appointments and meetings.[29]

25. A Private Interview with Philip Lenud, Vanderbilt Divinity School, Nashville, Tennessee (7 April 1987).
26. Baldwin, *There is a Balm in Gilead*, 107; Downing, *To See the Promised Land*, 127; and King, *My Life with Martin Luther King, Jr.*, 52 and 94–95.
27. Ralph D. Abernathy, *And the Walls Came Tumbling Down: An Autobiography* (New York: Harper & Row, Publishers, 1989), 323, 382, 438, 440, and 491–92; Carson, et al., eds., *King Papers*, III, 312; Carson, et al., eds., *King Papers*, IV, 113, 289, 316, and 519; Carson, et al., *King Papers*, V, 101; and Dora McDonald, *Secretary to a King: My Years with Martin Luther King, Jr., the Civil Rights Movement, and Beyond* (Montgomery, AL: New South Books, 2012), 71 and 74–75.
28. King apparently "had a favorite shoeshine man at the airport" in Atlanta, where he "would always stop to get his shoes shined." After King was assassinated, his aide Bernard Lee took his "burial shoes to the airport so that man could shine them for the last time" on April 9, 1968. See McDonald, *Secretary to a King*, 45–46 and 111.

King, Jr. tended to be very apologetic whenever he felt improperly dressed. In June, 1966, when offering remarks at the funeral of Armistead Phelps, one of the movement's supporters, in Enid, Mississippi, he apologized profusely for being in public on Sunday "without a tie or without the proper ministerial attire."[30] After spending time with his wife, Coretta in India, "the land of Gandhi," back in 1959, King—impressed with Gandhi's ascetic lifestyle or his ideal of the "simplicity of living"—actually entertained the thought "of changing his style of dress to a simpler one," but "decided that since his main purpose was to attract people to the Cause, unusual dress might even tend to alienate followers." After all, "Dress was really a superficial form rather than the spiritual quality" King "was aiming for."[31] Also, while he admired and respected Gandhi for wearing the garments of the untouchables, the lowest and most scorned Hindu caste in India, King understood that any decision on his part to shift to a much more simple and unusual dress style, for the sake of identifying more with the poor and outcast, would not have been well-received in the culture of the black church, in which ministers were strongly encouraged and expected to wear the very best clothes and the finest jewelry. King looked for other ways, aside from dress styles, to share with the poor "the kind of life that was imposed upon them daily by the system." A case in point was his decision to rent and live in a slum apartment in Lawndale, a section of the Chicago ghetto, during his campaign against poverty and slum conditions in Chicago in 1966.[32] Be that as it may, it was always evident, and at times, amazing to King, Jr. that "the measure of a man" for all too many people had to do, first

---

29. Abernathy reported that most of King's time getting ready for his daily routines was devoted to shaving with "Magic Shave," the "worst smelling stuff anyone ever rubbed on his face," because his "skin was so tender that he couldn't use a razor." See Abernathy, *And the Walls Came Tumbling Down*, 438; and Farris, *Through It All*, 106.
30. Martin Luther King, Jr., "Remarks at the Funeral of Armistead Phelps," Enid, Mississippi (12 June 1966), King Center Library and Archives, 1.
31. King, *My Life with Martin Luther King, Jr.*, 162–64.
32. See King's Palm Sunday sermon on Gandhi in Carson, et al., eds., *King Papers*, V, 152 and 154–55. Also see King, *My Life with Martin Luther King, Jr.*, 162–65 and 257; William D. Watley, *Roots of Resistance: The Nonviolent Ethic of Martin Luther King, Jr.* (Valley Forge, PA: Judson Press, 1985), 94; and James R. Ralph, Jr., *Northern Protest: Martin Luther King, Jr., Chicago, and the Civil Rights Movement* (Cambridge, MA: Harvard University Press, 1993), 55.

and foremost, with outward appearances and not with what resided within.[33]

As King, Jr. grew in stature, he also became more and more careful about his demeanor or the way he conducted himself as a leader. High integrity and impeccable character were always the ideal for him, even in those moments when he somehow fell short of the mark. Sensitive to how wealth, materialistic ingredients, and power had corrupted even religious leaders, King, Jr. cared little for money and never really desired fine cars, expensive jewelry, and luxurious homes.[34] Here, he chose the anti-capitalist ethic of his mother, Alberta over the strong capitalist leanings of his father, King, Sr.[35] As president of the SCLC, he only accepted one dollar a year for tax and insurance purposes, and the $54,000 he received as part of the Nobel Peace Prize in 1964 were donated to the SCLC and other civil rights organizations.[36] King, Jr. never wanted to be involved, in any way, in a controversy about money because he so resented attacks on his personal honesty and integrity. "Though I am not perfect," he asserted, "If I have any virtues, the one of which I am most proud is my honesty where money is concerned." When a Montgomery grand jury indicted King, Jr. on a charge of "falsifying his Alabama State income-tax returns for 1956 and 1958," an accusation that "was utterly false," he was nonetheless devastated because, as he put it, "Many people will think I am guilty."[37]

33. King, *The Measure of a Man*, 15–16.
34. King said in January, 1965, in an interview with *Playboy Magazine*, that "If I have any weaknesses, they are not in the area of coveting wealth." Shortly thereafter, he declared that he was "sick and tired of seeing Negro preachers riding around in big cars and living in big houses and not concerned about the problems of the people who made it possible for them to get these things." King called this "Jumboism," or an unhealthy obsession with "bigness." See King, *Strength to Love*, 59; Martin Luther King, Jr., "Transformed Nonconformist," unpublished version of sermon, Ebenezer Baptist Church, Atlanta, Georgia (16 January 1966), King Center Library and Archives, 8–9; Carson, et al., eds., *King Papers*, VI, 134; and Lewis V. Baldwin, *The Voice of Conscience: The Church in the Mind of Martin Luther King, Jr.* (New York: Oxford University Press, 2010), 135–36 and 227. King's wife Coretta once commented that she and her husband "never had serious differences" over "economics," but King reported that she did question his tendency to "overdo it" in terms of giving at times. See King, *My Life with Martin Luther King, Jr.*, 56 and 59; James M. Washington, ed., *A Testament of Hope: The Essential Writings and Speeches of Martin Luther King, Jr.* (New York: HarperCollins Publishers, 1991), 371; and Garrow, *Bearing the Cross*, 421.
35. Baldwin Interview with Lenud (7 April 1987); King, *Daddy King*, 147; and Baldwin, *There is a Balm in Gilead*, 122–23. King referred to Daddy King as "a thoroughgoing capitalist." See King, *My Life with Martin Luther King, Jr.*, 56 and 76.
36. King, *My Life with Martin Luther King, Jr.*, 3; and Garrow, *Bearing the Cross*, 368.

Clearly, what bothered King, Jr. most was not so much how he was judged and condemned by the media and in judicial and political circles, nor how he was perceived and judged in the court of public opinion, but, rather, how he was understood and viewed by those who considered and embraced him as the model of moral and spiritual leadership.[38]

At times, when attacked by his critics and enemies, King, Jr. got angry and spoke loudly and clearly, but almost always in a thoughtful, measured, and charitable way. His words were always wisely and cleverly chosen, and his capacity to forgive unwavering. Lingering resentment and bitterness toward others were foreign to him. This is why he could so easily forgive Izola Curry, the demented woman who stabbed him with a letter opener in a Harlem department store in 1958, and the Reverend Joseph H. Jackson, who falsely accused him of masterminding an invasion of the National Baptist Convention floor that led to the accidental death of the Reverend Arthur G. Wright, a fellow clergyman, three years later.[39] King, Jr. knew that if he was to be truly effective as a moral leader among faithful and freedom-loving people, he himself had to be an example of how to respond to evil and hatred without violence, vengeance, and recrimination. Thus, he developed that internal sense of spiritual security that nothing he experienced in external reality could remove. There was, for him, little or no room for worrying unnecessarily, and for wallowing in anger, self-pity, and self-doubt.[40] King, Jr. saw himself for who and what he really was, and he was never afraid or hesitant to question himself or to engage in "private self-examination" and public "self-criticism."[41] This

---

37. Coretta King recounted that her husband's "sense of morality was so offended," but he was ultimately found "Not guilty." See King, *My Life with Martin Luther King, Jr.*, 170–71. King's secretary, Dora McDonald suggested that King's concern about his public image explained his insistence on transparency and also his flair for even "minor details." "Dr. King often said that our freedom struggle must be conducted in a spirit of openness," she wrote, "because we had nothing to hide." See McDonald, *Secretary to a King*, 34 and 79–80.

38. King, *My Life with Martin Luther King, Jr.*, 170–71.

39. Carson, et al., eds., *King Papers*, IV, 513; King, *My Life with Martin Luther King, Jr.*, 154–57; Baldwin, *There is a Balm in Gilead*, 218–20; and Sherman Roosevelt Tribble, *Images of a Preacher: A Study of the Reverend Joseph Harrison Jackson* (Nashville, TN: Townsend Press, 2008), 133–34, 147, and 155–56.

40. Carson, et al., eds., *King Papers*, IV, 504; and King, *My Life with Martin Luther King, Jr.*, 169–71.

41. King actually found in Gandhi a unique capacity for both private self-examination and public self-criticism, and this, in his view, explained to a great degree Gandhi's importance as a model of

was a critical and enduring part of the meaning of his life. In short, it constituted the very essence of who he was as a human being.

King, Jr. led and participated in numerous campaigns and crusades for basic civil and/or constitutional rights, political enfranchisement, economic justice, and international peace, always sacrificing his well-being and risking his life. Over a thirteen-year period, from 1955 to 1968, he moved from Montgomery to Washington, D. C. to Memphis and beyond, simultaneously attracting loyal supporters and fierce adversaries. He was admired and celebrated worldwide and received more than four hundred awards, including a Nobel Peace Prize, which he refused to accept only on his own behalf.[42] King, Jr. gave himself to a cause he felt was greater than himself, and by his own admission, actually ran the risk of losing himself. "I am conscious of two Martin Luther Kings," he told his old friend and mentor J. Pius Barbour. "I am a wonder to myself. . . . I am mystified at my own career. The Martin Luther King that the people talk about seems to me somebody foreign to me. There is a kind of dualism in my life." King, Jr. "couldn't understand his career, all the publicity and things he'd gotten . . . with no effort on his own," Barbour reminisced. "He always said that that Martin Luther King the famous man was a kind of stranger to him."[43] Coretta King explained the issue with her husband in these terms:

He felt that having been born into what was a middle-class African-American family was a privilege he had not earned, just as he felt the many honors heaped on him in the later years were not his alone. He would constantly examine himself to determine if he was

saintly virtues. See Carson, et al., eds., *King Papers*, IV, 504 and 541. King declared that "One of the sure signs of maturity is the ability to rise to the point of self-criticism." See Carson, et al., eds., *King Papers*, V, 284; King, *My Life with Martin Luther King, Jr.*, 158 and 255; David J. Garrow, *The FBI and Martin Luther King, Jr.: From "Solo" to Memphis* (New York: W. W. Norton & Company, 1981), 217; and Carson, et al., eds., *King Papers*, VI, 94–97.

42. Carson and Holloran, eds., *A Knock at Midnight*, 185. King accepted the Nobel Award on behalf of all involved in the civil rights program, irrespective of race, class, or gender, a gesture that spoke to the quality of his magnanimous spirit. See Washington, ed., *A Testament of Hope*, 224; King, *My Life with Martin Luther King, Jr.*, 3–4; and Martin Luther King, Jr., "What the Nobel Peace Prize Means to Me," *New York Amsterdam News* (28 November 1964), 1–2.

43. In some of his sermons, King declared that "each of us is something of a schizophrenic personality. We're split and divided against ourselves. There is something of a civil war going on within all our lives." See Carson, et al., eds., *King Papers*, VI, 95–96; and Garrow, *Bearing the Cross*, 101 and 289.

becoming corrupted, if he was accepting honors too easily. He was very sensitive about having people do things for him because of his position. He was extremely grateful for any help he got. He was truly a humble man and never felt that he was adequate to his positions.[44]

"King's naturalness" was evident to all who came "face to face with him." "To meet him is to enter an atmosphere of simplicity, free of pretense or posing," wrote Lawrence Reddick, who knew King, Jr. from the beginning of his public pilgrimage in Montgomery. Reddick went on to share the following about King, Jr.: "He smiles and shakes hands easily. He is unhurried. He never seems to respond impulsively or impatiently. This delayed and calm reaction has helped him out of many an explosive situation."[45] But King, Jr. brought so much more, in terms of personality, gifts, and resources, to his public role and outreach, not the least among which were the power of oratory, spiritual-moral vitality, unfailing gallantry and courage, the ability to engage issues with a sharp eye and keen sensibilities, high quality leadership, a rare capacity to draw out the theological and ethical implications of an issue, an affinity for ordinary people, a rare kind of empathy for people, a clarity of social vision and analysis, and tireless advocacy and efforts on behalf of the oppressed. Appealing to the wisdom of his forebears, gleaned through centuries of suffering and sorrow, King, Jr. not only found the right mixture of spirituality and social activism, but also, put justice and the common good to the forefront of his consciousness and the fruit of his profound thinking to the service of direct social action.

The public stage increasingly became King, Jr.'s home away from home. He was constantly on the move, often meeting with the staff of his Southern Christian Leadership Conference (SCLC), speaking at academic institutions or to groups of clergy and grassroots activists, preaching at churches of various denominations, or traveling to some foreign land to solidify connections between the civil rights struggle in America and other movements of the oppressed. In moments of quiet

44. King, *My Life with Martin Luther King, Jr.*, 59; King, *Stride toward Freedom*, 156; and Michael G. Long, *Martin Luther King Jr. on Creative Living* (St. Louis, MO: Chalice Press, 2004), 1.
45. Reddick, *Crusader without Violence*, 6.

and serious reflection, King, Jr. complained of being "faced with the responsibility of trying to do as one man what five or six people ought to be doing," and of finding himself "in a position" he "could not get out of." "My whole life seems to be centered around giving something out and only rarely taking something in," he said in a letter to a friend in April 1960. "If the situation is not changed," said he on another occasion, "I will be a physical and psychological wreck." King, Jr. was convinced that he could not "continue to go at this pace."[46] All of the planning, traveling, and public appearances and commitments would have emotionally paralyzed or perhaps even broken a less healthy, spiritual, and dedicated man.

The many pressing demands, the crowded schedules of activities, and the deep tensions of the movement resulted, at times, in both mental and physical fatigue for King, Jr. There was less and less time for rest and relaxation and for thinking through the range of future obligations and challenges that stood before him. There was, at times, a painful emptiness in King, Jr. that all of his honors and awards could not fill,[47] and he sometimes expressed a need to quietly get away from it all. "I must admit that at times I have felt that I could no longer bear such a heavy burden," he explained in the spring of 1960, "and was tempted to retreat to a more quiet and serene life." "But every time such a temptation appeared," he added, "something came to strengthen and sustain my determination."[48]

King, Jr.'s ethic of "self-love" and 'self-acceptance" was such that he occasionally demanded and even insisted on a brief respite and some temporary refuge from the rigors of his own public life and involvements.[49] He wanted to be an ordinary human being behind all the headlines. Frustrated over what had long seemed an "inability to retreat, concentrate, and reflect," King, Jr., by the mid-1960s, had begun to seek idyllic spots "for resting, meditation, and reflection."

46. Quoted in Garrow, *Bearing the Cross*, 125 and 135; and Carson, et al., eds., *King Papers*, V, 436.
47. King, *My Life with Martin Luther King, Jr.*, 59.
48. Quoted in Garrow, *Bearing the Cross*, 135; and Carson, et al., eds., *King Papers*, V, 436.
49. There are still questions about whether or not King stressed *agape* or altruistic love, or an unselfish and unconditional love for others, to the neglect of self love, especially since he did not always take the best care of himself. See Carson, et al., eds., *King Papers*, VI, 307 and 398.

Before receiving the Nobel Peace Prize in December 1964, he, at the urging of Congressman Adam Clayton Powell, went to Bimini in the Bahamas, where there were "great fishing, no telephones in the hotel rooms, great beaches."[50] Also, King, Jr. periodically took "a self-imposed day of silence," during which he escaped to some tranquil retreat or some sacred space to restore his energy and revive his soul. On such days, he usually checked into a hotel room unannounced and abstained from radio, television, telephone, and other distractions of daily life, and instead, turned to prayer, meditation, and "a rigorous discipline of 'think time'."[51] During quiet moments at night, King, Jr. sometimes retreated to his pastor's study, closed the door, and sat in silence and prayed. Jail cells afforded less attractive, but also, at times, equally important settings for him to nurture his spiritual life through silent prayer and meditation. Family members reported that King, Jr. "hated being alone,"[52] especially when he was in jail, but he actually needed time to be with and by himself.[53] Apparently, the problem for King, Jr. was not being alone, but loneliness—which he felt at times even in the presence of his family, friends, and most trusted aides.[54] Those closest to him most certainly shared his company, but they were not in a position to share his state of mind or to know and experience what was actually going on inside him. As King, Jr. expanded his commitments over time and increasingly came under the glare of the national and global spotlight, both his private life and his public life were, to a large extent, compromised.[55]

---

50. McDonald, *Secretary to a King*, 75–76.
51. Garrow, *Bearing the Cross*, 134; Lewis V. Baldwin, *Never to Leave Us Alone: The Prayer Life of Martin Luther King Jr.* (Minneapolis: Fortress Press, 2010), vii (Foreword); From Wyatt Tee Walker to Lewis V. Baldwin (30 April 2009); and Lewis V. Baldwin, ed., *"Thou, Dear God": Prayers that Open Hearts and Spirits—The Reverend Dr. Martin Luther King, Jr.* (Boston: Beacon Press, 2012), xi–xxii (introduction).
52. King, *My Life with Martin Luther King, Jr.*, 179; King, *Daddy King*, 174–75; and Carson and Holloran, eds., *A Knock at Midnight*, 162. The idea of "a self-imposed day of silence" was apparently suggested to King by Allan Knight Chalmers, one of King's professors at Boston University. See Carson, et al., eds., *Papers*, V, 436.
53. King, Sr. said that his son "was never comfortable in isolation." "He enjoyed people too much," continued the elder King, "to be cut off from others without suffering enormous anxiety." See King, *Daddy King*, 174–75; and King, *My Life with Martin Luther King, Jr.*, 179. For other perspectives, see Downing, *To See the Promised Land*, 130; and Garrow, *Bearing the Cross*, 289.
54. Garrow writes about King's "underlying loneliness." See Garrow, *Bearing the Cross*, 603.
55. Baldwin, *There is a Balm in Gilead*, 134–35; Lischer, *The Preacher King*, 169; and Garrow, *Bearing the Cross*, 125, 135, and 421.

B. Conflicting Loyalties of Public and Private Life: King's Friendships

At every stage in his life, from childhood to adulthood, Martin Luther King, Jr. developed close personal relationships which stood the test of time. He not only took friendship very seriously, but always had a high regard for the friends he made and was fortunate, for the most part, to retain their personal affection and loyalty. Friendships characterized by unfailing affection and indefatigable loyalty were what he longed for and sought to develop, and he literally enjoyed traveling and making new friends and acquaintances. The search for genuine and lasting friendship networks came naturally for King, Jr., especially since he was so heartily rejected, hated, and maligned by his adversaries and enemies.

King, Jr. needed human contact because he himself was fundamentally human. "When the burdens of his leadership role kept him unsettled and awake with worry, Martin needed people close to him," said Andrew Young, one of King's closest aides in the SCLC. Dorothy F. Cotton, who worked with King, Jr.'s staff as education director, heartily agreed, noting that

> We felt he was our best friend. He needed us as friends as well as coworkers to help him bear the incredibly heavy burden of leading this powerful social change movement in which we were involved. A few of us knew all the various aspects of his personality and of his life and he needed us close to him in just this way. The world may stand in awe of him, but he needed us to help him.[56]

More often than not, the person closest to King, Jr. was Ralph Abernathy.[57] The friendship between the two dated back to Montgomery, where both served as pastors of Baptist Churches and participated in the bus boycott, and they were sometimes called "the civil rights twins." Whenever King, Jr. spoke in terms of "abiding

---

56. Andrew Young, *An Easy Burden: The Civil Rights Movement and the Transformation of America* (New York: HarperCollins Publishers, 1996), 176; and Dorothy F. Cotton, *If Your Back's Not Bent: The Role of the Citizenship Education Program in the Civil Rights Movement* (New York: Atria Books, 2012), 188–89.
57. Young, *An Easy Burden*, 176.

friends," Abernathy came to mind.[58] Abernathy reported that he and King, Jr. were actually friends before they were civil rights leaders, and that that friendship was later strengthened in the confines of their united efforts to win freedom for their people:

> From the beginning, Martin and I shared so much, but never without a price. Our homes in Montgomery—and my church—were bombed. When he went to jail, I went with him. (Most of the time we shared the same cell). When he marched in Birmingham and Selma and Chicago, I marched beside him. When he faced the dogs and the tear gas, I faced them, too. When he worried over a problem at some cheap motel in a strange and hostile city, I worried with him. And when he was gunned down in Memphis, I was the one who rode with him in the ambulance; and after the doctors had given up on him, it was I, not Jesse Jackson, who cradled him in my arms until he died.[59]

Dorothy Cotton recounted that King, Jr. and Abernathy "had the kind of friendship that I don't believe could ever have been broken." Elaborating further on the bond between the two leaders, she added:

> I've never seen anyone so willing to lay down his life for a friend as Ralph was willing to do for and with Martin. I believe Ralph would have taken that bullet for him if he had had such a choice. I say this as I was regularly with them and observed how Martin and Ralph's friendship was displayed when we debated various actions SCLC should take. Always these discussions and debates took place in the awareness that arrests and jailings and even worse were inevitable. Ralph was ready to walk with him anywhere, anytime.[60]

The friendship between King, Jr. and Abernathy endured the test of time even as most of the personal fame and accolades went to King, Jr.,[61] and the two men had a kind of unspoken agreement to stand

58. A Private Interview with Ralph D. Abernathy, Atlanta, Georgia (17 March 1987); A Private Interview with Ralph D. Abernathy, Atlanta, Georgia (7 May 1987); Carson, et al., eds., *King Papers*, IV, 513; King, *Stride toward Freedom*, 45 and 175; King, *My Life with Martin Luther King, Jr.*, 97; and Baldwin, *There is a Balm in Gilead*, 330–31.
59. Ralph David Abernathy, "My Old Friend Martin," *The Tennessean: USA Weekend* (12–14 January 1990), 6–7.
60. Cotton, *If Your Back's Not Bent*, 191–92.
61. Young, *An Easy Burden*, 176. Dorothy Cotton does not deny Abernathy's jealousy of King as King grew in popularity. "I also recognized his jealousy or perhaps resentment as Martin's star shone brighter and brighter," she declared, "the world recognizing his powerful leadership for the freedom of oppressed peoples everywhere." "It seemed that Ralph could not help feeling

together and to not criticize nor disagree with each other publicly. Abernathy unintentionally violated this agreement one night by disagreeing with King, Jr. at a meeting of the MIA, and the board voted with him against King, Jr. King, Jr. was so angry until he hurried home, "took a tranquilizer, and went to bed." When Abernathy tried to "straighten things out," King, Jr. bluntly stated, "You can have anything you want, but please don't disagree with me in public." Abernathy promised never to do this again, and the two forgot the incident and moved on.[62]

A number of other ministers figured prominently within King, Jr.'s small circle of friends, including his brother, A. D. King, Bernard S. Lee, Joseph E. Lowery, C. T. Vivian, Andrew Young, Hosea Williams, James Bevel, and Wyatt Tee Walker. All of these men were involved with the SCLC and in King, Jr.'s major civil rights campaigns. After marches and demonstrations in the South, the ministers routinely sat around in hotel rooms or the homes of other ministers and discussed movement strategy. In the more private hotel settings, they ate and drank, told jokes, teased each other, had pillow fights, and laughed a lot.[63] Such meetings were almost never open to laypersons, women, and whites, for obvious reasons. In any case, King, Jr. was always so comfortable, free-spirited, and candid in his expressions when fellowshipping in these private spaces with his minister friends.[64] In such settings, he found emotional and spiritual support, and men who listened when he needed to voice his disappointments and release his anger and pent-up frustrations. In a few instances, King, Jr. was said to have shed tears in the presence of this small cadre of clergymen. Tears of joy occasionally

somewhat slighted," she continued. "After all, he was indeed always at Martin's side and ready to play any role that called for his skills." See Cotton, If Your Back's Not Bent, 191–92.

62. Abernathy, And the Walls Came Tumbling Down, 439; and Baldwin, There is a Balm in Gilead, 303.

63. A Private Interview with Bernard S. Lee, Washington, DC (9 July 1986); Baldwin Interview with Abernathy (17 March 1987); Baldwin Interview with Abernathy (7 May 1987); Abernathy, And the Walls Came Tumbling Down, 468–70; Young, An Easy Burden, 328–29 and 463–64; Andrew Young, A Way Out of No Way: The Spiritual Memoirs of Andrew Young (Nashville: Thomas Nelson Publishers, 1994), 75 and 101; Baldwin, There is a Balm in Gilead, 302–5; and Martin Luther King, Jr., "Why We Must Go to Washington," unpublished version of a speech, SCLC Retreat, Ebenezer Baptist Church, Atlanta, Georgia (15 January 1968), King Center Library and Archives, 5.

64. Abernathy, And the Walls Came Tumbling Down, 468–70; Young, An Easy Burden, 328–29; and Young, A Way Out of No Way, 75 and 101.

flowed after some great success in the movement, and there were also tears of pain, as was the case when he was preparing his eulogy for those four little girls in Birmingham in 1963.[65] But this was not likely to happen in the presence of ordinary foot soldiers in the movement, who needed to see, in King, Jr., an image of unwavering courage, strength of character, and a bold and resilient spirit.

There was that wider circle of long-time friends that also consisted largely of fellow male clergy—some of whom King, Jr. had known since his childhood. After becoming prominent, King, Jr. maintained some level of contact up to a point, usually by letter or telephone, with Philip Lenud and Walter McCall, who had been students with him at Morehouse, and with Horace "Ed" Whitaker, who, also like McCall, had been rather close to him at Crozer.[66] King, Jr. also counted among his friends some of the most popular and dynamic preachers in the country, among whom were William Holmes Borders, Caesar Clark, Kelly Miller Smith, Sr., C. L. Franklin, William H. Gray, James B. Cayce, Fred Shuttlesworth, Samuel D. Proctor, Theodore J. Jemison, and Samuel Billy Kyles. Benjamin E. Mays, Melvin H. Watson, J. Pius Barbour, William H. Hester, Mordecai W. Johnson, Vernon Johns, Howard W. Thurman, Sandy D. Ray, and Gardner C. Taylor were not only King, Jr.'s friends, but trusted counselors as well.[67]

But King, Jr.'s increasing involvements in the public realm of politics and social activism, especially in the 1960s, actually framed his choices in terms of those friends with whom he spent the most and the least time, and he rarely saw and associated in person with many of these and other friends who were not heavily involved in his daily life and

---

65. Young, *An Easy Burden*, 176; and *Eyes on the Prize: America's Civil Rights Years, 1954-1965* (New York: Viking Penguin, Inc., 1987), 278. King's eulogy "was one of the few times" he "was ever seen weeping openly in public." See Tavis Smiley, *Death of a King: The Real Story of Dr. Martin Luther King Jr.'s Final Year*, with David Ritz (New York: Little, Brown and Company, 2014), 48, 166, and 218. Dora McDonald felt that King "was thinking of his two little daughters at home" when he eulogized the girls in Birmingham. She recalls that King "was deeply affected" and "moved to tears." See McDonald, *Secretary to a King*, 53-54.
66. Baldwin Interview with Lenud (7 April 1987); and Carson, et al., eds., *King Papers*, IV, 449-50 and 581-82.
67. See Baldwin Interview with Abernathy (17 March 1987); Baldwin Interview with Lenud (7 April 1987); Evans and Alexander, eds., *The Dexter Avenue Baptist Church*, 109-12 and 126; and Baldwin, *There is a Balm in Gilead*, 302-3.

activities. The ever-growing demands on King, Jr.'s time and the sheer magnitude of his public commitments meant that he had fewer and fewer opportunities to visit and sit and talk at length with those friends who were not a part of his SCLC staff, including those with whom he had studied in the academy and those in Ebenezer Baptist Church and his hometown of Atlanta. Ironically, this occurred during the period in King, Jr.'s life when he attached perhaps the highest value to, and stood in the greatest need of, close friendships. He needed the tender touch and the caring words and embrace of friends to help ease the burden of the cross he was bearing. "Every morning when I brush my teeth, I have to stare at this cross and realize that this day could be my last," said King, Jr. to his dearest friends "from time to time."[68] And even when King, Jr.'s interests were most directed at the public good, he never ceased to stress the need to "cultivate genuine and abiding friendships" with a select few which, in his mind, were so essential to one's personal health and well-being.[69]

Both clergy and non-clergy persons who were quite close to King, Jr. in the 1960s spoke of his rich and genuine "humanness," of that down-home, folksy demeanor that added to his commanding presence and endeared him to so many of the ordinary, fleshly people he met daily. Dorothy Cotton, who served as education director for King, Jr.'s SCLC, noted that King, Jr. "really liked people and appreciated friendships." "There was a special kind of joy just being around him, and we felt appreciated as both friends and staff," she recounted. "And he really was a lot of fun to be with. He could be the life of the party, and more often than not he was." "Although Dr. King was one of the greatest Americans ever born, he had a down-to earth personality and never felt or acted as if he were as great as he actually was," said Theodore J. Jemison, who was an advisor to and an associate with King, Jr. in the National Baptist Convention. Jemison went on to say:

He was humble in spirit, patient in judgment, and strong in wisdom.

---

68. McDonald, *Secretary to a King*, 29.
69. Baldwin Interview with Abernathy (17 March 1987); Baldwin Interview with Abernathy (7 May 1987); Carson, et al., eds., *King Papers*, IV, 504; Young, *An Easy Burden*, 176; and Cotton, *If Your Back's Not Bent*, 188–92.

I shared many light moments with him, and some heavy ones as well. I remember that he sometimes loved to compliment attractive people. He'd say, "When the history of fine-looking people is recorded, you'll be page one, paragraph one, line one." That was one of his favorite statements.[70]

Others close to King, Jr. were equally emphatic in identifying King's most human qualities. "Dr. King was a very warm, lively person who really loved life," according to Samuel Kyles. "We do a disservice when we try to make a saint of him, because he wasn't." Willie Barrow described King, Jr. as "so human," especially in terms of his "unusual and unique patience":

I remember on several occasions, during retreats and staff meetings, there would be strong personalities such as Wyatt tee Walker and Jesse Jackson and Hosea Williams and Dorothy Cotton. We'd get into some heated arguments. Even though Dr. King was chairing the meetings, he'd just sit for hours and listen and make notes mentally. He never did use much script. Then, after everyone finished, he'd summarize everything we'd said and then he'd chastise and criticize us, but he never interrupted or told us to quiet down.[71]

It was not always easy for a man of King, Jr.'s ability, stature, and popularity to enjoy genuine and lasting friendships. All of the personal publicity, praise, honors, and awards he received led some who had been his friends earlier in life to become jealous and to turn against him.[72] Even in King, Jr.'s hometown of Atlanta, people whom he knew well and admired in his neighborhood and church, driven by "a degree

70. "'I Remember Martin': People Close to the Late Civil Rights Leader Recall a Down-to-Earth and Humorous Man," *Ebony*, 39, no. 6 (April 1984), 34 and 36; and McDonald, *Secretary to a King*, 71.
71. "'I Remember Martin,'" 34 and 38. Bernard Lee agreed with this assessment of King's way of handling the "reindeer personalities" and the "ego-clashes and arguments" at SCLC meetings. Lee said that King had a way of smoothing out all the chaos and bringing "it into focus—into perspective." "That was part of his genius," Lee added. "That pastoral ability would just come out." Dora McDonald essentially agreed with this assessment, noting particularly King's "hands-off" style of leadership. See Baldwin Interview with Lee (9 July 1986); and McDonald, *Secretary to a King*, 55, 91, and 99.
72. Interestingly enough, years after King's death, beginning in 1983, when he was honored with a national holiday and obviously became a national icon, some of these same ministers began to boast about having been Dr. King's friend and having marched with him. See "Negro Pastor Urges King to Leave Town," *The Plain Dealer*, Cleveland, Ohio (20 April 1967), 14; King, *Daddy King*, 177; Baldwin, *There is a Balm in Gilead*, 207–24; Baldwin, *The Voice of Conscience*, 137–38; and Peter J. Ling, *Martin Luther King, Jr.* (New York: Routledge, 2002), 224.

of jealousy," insisted that the publicity and fame he claimed were undeserved.[73] E. D. Nixon, Sr., who loomed large in the Montgomery bus boycott, befriended King, Jr. and strongly supported him to head the MIA, but resentment later surfaced and spilled over into outright conflict, essentially because of "the considerable personal fame that had come to King...." The rift between King, Jr. and Nixon never really healed, despite King, Jr.'s efforts at reconciliation.[74]

Another case in point was the Reverend Joseph H. Jackson, president of the historically black and powerful National Baptist Convention, consisting of roughly five million members. Jackson had been a strong supporter of King, Jr. and the MIA during the Montgomery bus boycott in 1955–56,[75] but soon after the boycott, he, sensing that King, Jr. posed a threat to his own "popularity and leadership," began to criticize King, Jr.'s civil disobedience tactics and actually removed King, Jr. from his position as vice president of the convention's Sunday School and Baptist Training Union Congress in 1961. It was quite obvious to the friends and supporters of both King, Jr. and Jackson that the problem was a combination of jealousy on Jackson's part and Jackson's fear that King, Jr. was being groomed to take over the presidency of the NBC. Jackson ultimately became King, Jr.'s most powerful enemy in black church circles.[76] When King, Jr. and his SCLC arrived in Chicago in January, 1966 to participate in the Chicago Freedom Movement, Jackson and a number of other black ministers, some of whom had studied with King, Jr. at Morehouse College and had marched with

73. King, *Daddy King*, 177.
74. Garrow, *Bearing the Cross*, 88; Wally G. Vaughn and Richard W. Wills, eds., *Reflections on Our Pastor: Dr. Martin Luther King, Jr., at Dexter Avenue Baptist Church, 1954-1960* (Dover, Massachusetts: The Majority Press, Inc., 1999), 5–6, 9, 98–99, 107, 124–25, and 143–44; and Lewis V. Baldwin and Aprille V. Woodson, *Freedom is Never Free: A Biographical Portrait of E. D. Nixon, Sr.* (Nashville: United Parcel Service Branch, 1992), 59–68 and 83–115. King offered a very positive and even glowing description of Nixon's importance to the struggle in Montgomery and the entire state of Alabama in King, *Stride toward Freedom*, 34, 38–39, 44–46, 55–57, 72, 140, 160, and 173.
75. From Joseph H. Jackson to Martin Luther King, Jr. (28 September 1955), King Center Library and Archives, The Martin Luther King, Jr. Papers, Mugar Memorial Library, Boston University, Boston, Massachusetts, 1; Carson, et al., eds., *King Papers*, III, 162–63; and Baldwin, *There is a Balm in Gilead*, 208–9.
76. Charles H. King, "Quest and Conflict: The Untold Story of the Power Struggle Between King and Jackson," *Negro Digest* (May 1967), 6–9 and 71–79; Joseph H. Jackson, *A Story of Christian Activism: The History of the National Baptist Convention, USA, Inc.* (Nashville: Townsend Press, 1980), 281–82, 424, and 483–86; and Baldwin, *There is a Balm in Gilead*, 206–24.

him in the South, joined the city's mayor, Richard J. Daley, in insisting that King, Jr.'s activities were not needed. According to Jesse Jackson, King, Jr. had depended and actually counted on the friendship of these ministers as he shifted to the North with his nonviolent strategy and tactics, and the reception he received "really broke his heart."[77]

King, Jr.'s comradeship with some of his white friends also brought a mixture of rich and rewarding experiences and bitter disappointments. He attracted the friendship and support of a considerable number of liberal whites from the time of the Montgomery bus protest in the mid-1950s up to the Memphis sanitation strike and the Poor People's Campaign, his last crusades, in 1967–68. Robert S. Graetz, a white Lutheran pastor who served a black congregation in Montgomery, supported the Montgomery bus boycott and was counted, along with Glenn Smiley, who taught King, Jr. a lot about Gandhian nonviolence, among King, Jr.'s first white friends in the movement. There were also Clifford and Virginia Durr, Aubrey Williams, and the outspoken Juliette Morgan, who was "completely ostracized" by the white community and driven to suicide after praising the Montgomery protest and comparing it to Gandhi's crusade in India.[78] In the 1960s, Stanley Levison, the Jewish lawyer, became a friend and legal advisor to King, Jr., and King, Jr. also enjoyed friendships with clergypersons such as his former professor L. Harold DeWolf and Rabbi Abraham J. Heschel, and with white liberals and New South advocates such as Harris Wofford, Anne Braden, Lillian Smith, and Ralph McGill.[79] King, Jr. considered a number of his white supporters to be both personal friends and friends of the movement, especially since they stuck by him and "paid

---

77. Jackson, *A History of Christian Activism*, 424; Ralph, *Northern Protest*, 78–79; and Baldwin, *There is a Balm in Gilead*, 215–24.

78. King, *Stride toward Freedom*, 74, 163, and 173; King, *My Life with Martin Luther King, Jr.*, 127–28; A Private Interview with Robert S. Graetz, Cincinnati, Ohio (26 July 1988); and Washington, ed., *A Testament of Hope*, 462. For an account of Graetz's role in Montgomery and beyond, see Robert S. Graetz, *Montgomery: A White Preacher's Memoir* (Minneapolis: Fortress Press, 1991), 1–132; and Robert S. Graetz, Jr., *A White Preacher's Message on Race and Reconciliation: Based on His Experiences Beginning with the Montgomery Bus Boycott* (Montgomery: New South Books, 2006), 9–272.

79. Washington, ed., *A Testament of Hope*, 93; From Ralph McGill to Martin Luther King, Jr. (1 May 1967), King Center Library and Archives, 1; From Anne Braden to Martin Luther King, Jr. (1 December 1962), King Center Library and Archives, 1–3; and Lewis V. Baldwin, et al., *The Legacy of Martin Luther King, Jr.: The Boundaries of Law, Politics, and Religion* (Notre Dame, IN: University of Notre Dame Press, 2002), 11–36.

dearly" for their efforts. He was often criticized by Malcolm X and other nationalists and black power advocates for relying too much on the resources of his phony "white liberal friends,"[80] but King, Jr. sought authentic friendships with his white allies and supporters and never thought in terms of simply using them for his own personal benefit or for the advancement of the civil rights cause. When it came to the movement, King, Jr.'s rich and genuine humanity informed his friendships with both ordinary citizens and the elite of society, irrespective of race.

But as King, Jr. increasingly called, during his final years, for a radical redistribution of economic power, and as he became more forceful in his assault on capitalism and the US adventure in Vietnam, some of his white friends abandoned him. Those friendships appeared safe and enduring whenever King, Jr. spoke of integration in terms of rubbing shoulders and elbows, but they turned into rejection and outright opposition as King, Jr. increasingly defined the beloved community as involving shared power, and as he more forcefully linked capitalism and Vietnam to the nation's epidemic of poverty and economic injustice. Ralph McGill spoke for some of these whites in 1967, when he, after scolding King, Jr. for urging young men to file as "conscientious objectors," assured the civil rights leader that he had lost their "full confidence and unbounded admiration," and that "we are obliged to part company with you."[81]

Life, for King, Jr., became even more of a recurring cycle of partings, as many of those he loved separated from him due to differences over economic, political, and global peace issues. With these partings came not only frustration, but more and more loneliness for King. These feelings were reinforced by the fact that his own father, Martin Luther King, Sr., and friends in high positions of civil rights and government leadership, such as Roy Wilkins of the National Association for the

---

80. King, *My Life with Martin Luther King, Jr.*, 127; Kenneth B. Clark, *King, Malcolm, Baldwin: Three Interviews* (Middletown, CT: Wesleyan University Press, 1985; originally published in 1963), 42–43; and C. Eric Lincoln, *The Black Muslims in America* (Trenton, NJ: William B. Eerdmans Publishing Company and Africa World Press, Inc., 1994; originally published in 1961), 134.
81. McGill to King (1 May 1967), 1–2; and Baldwin, et al., *The Legacy of Martin Luther King, Jr.*, 35–36.

Advancement of Colored People (NAACP), Whitney M. Young of the National Urban League, Senator Edward Brooke of Massachusetts, and the U. N. Undersecretary Ralph Bunche, were questioning and attacking his decision to bring capitalism and Vietnam within the sphere of his moral critique and social justice activism.[82]

Evidently, being a widely famous and highly celebrated and controversial public figure taught King, Jr. a lot about the good, efficacious, beneficial, and priceless qualities of friendship, but he was also repeatedly reminded that friendships are about making choices, that they are challenging and can often be too demanding, fragile, and short-lived. Having so little time to share with his dearest friends, and seeing friends turn into opponents and even bitter enemies, had to be taxing and must have troubled King, Jr.'s very soul, especially since he was so sensitive and caring in spirit. His frequent allusions to both the virtues and the potential burdens of friendship in sermons and speeches revealed much about his own desire for acceptance and affirmation, about the tension that existed between his longing for companionship in his private life and his need to fulfill core obligations in the public realm, and about his larger search for human reconciliation and community. For King, Jr., forging strong and enduring friendships was absolutely essential to both personal fulfillment and the advancement of the larger communitarian ideal. Building close and enduring family relations, he believed, was equally important in this regard.

C. Negotiating Public and Private Spaces:
King, Jr. as Husband and Father

Martin Luther King, Jr. had no plans to become thoroughly immersed in public life when he and Coretta Scott united in holy matrimony in June 1953. The couple chose not to have "a traditional honeymoon" and spent that summer with King, Sr. and Alberta King in Atlanta, but actually resided in Boston during most of that first year of marriage.

---

82. Lewis V. Baldwin, *To Make the Wounded Whole: The Cultural Legacy of Martin Luther King, Jr.* (Minneapolis: Fortress Press, 1992), 276–77.

At that point, King, Jr. was merely thinking in terms of completing the requirements for his PhD at Boston University, and Coretta, her musical education at the New England Conservatory of Music.[83] He and Coretta also looked ahead to what they thought would be a full but relatively quiet and peaceful life as pastor and first lady of some black Baptist congregation in the South. Although they had thoughts of contributing in some way to the improvement of race relations in their native South,[84] the couple never imagined the many public demands, responsibilities, and challenges that awaited them, and that would, in time, alter, define, and even threaten the peace, comfort, and vitality of their private lives as husband and wife.

But the balance between the public and private dimensions of King, Jr.'s life was never really at risk during that first year of marriage. While he studied hard and became quite popular as he preached at black churches in and around Boston, he spent a lot of time with Coretta, whom he affectionately called "Corey," at their small apartment in the city. This was the only period in King, Jr.'s adult life when he consistently took on a range of household chores. The couple "did the weekly shopping for groceries together" on Saturdays, and King, Jr. always cooked a southern-style dinner on Thursday nights when Coretta was in her music class. He also did "all the heavy cleaning and even the washing," which left much to be desired because the clothes always "looked like the 'before' on TV commercials." "I was always very appreciative," Coretta recalled, "but I would wish to myself that he had let me do the job." In any case, all of the domestic work at that time seems to have been inspired by genuine love and a desire on King, Jr.'s part to be the ideal husband, and it did not make King, Jr. "self-conscious" because he "was too sure of his manhood."[85]

King, Jr.'s sense of the proper role of a husband and wife in the

---

83. King, *My Life with Martin Luther King, Jr.*, 72 and 85; and Baldwin, *There is a Balm in Gilead*, 130.
84. Baldwin, *There is a Balm in Gilead*, 130; King, *My Life with Martin Luther King, Jr.*, 56, 58, 81, and 90–91; and King, *Stride toward Freedom*, 21–22.
85. Unfortunately, very little has been written about King and Coretta's first year of marriage, the only period during which they actually enjoyed anything approaching the full benefits of their relationship. See King, *My Life with Martin Luther King, Jr.*, 86–87; Baldwin, *There is a Balm in Gilead*, 132; and Cotton, *If Your Back's Not Bent*, 313.

context of both marriage and family life was apparently shared by Coretta from the beginning of their relationship. At the couple's request, King, Jr.'s father had actually "left out the bride's promise to obey" before pronouncing "them man and wife."[86] King, Jr.'s consent to this change in the marriage vow was most interesting since he, like his parents and generations of his forebears, had grown up in the Negro church and in a culture in which women were considered subordinate or subservient to men.[87] As King, Jr.'s sister, Christine put it, women "were expected to tend to their families, raise the children, cook, clean, sew, and make few waves."[88] King, Jr. was never able to fully escape the impact of this culture, and this is why he "had, all through his life," according to Coretta, "an ambivalent attitude toward the role of women." "On the one hand," Coretta wrote, "he believed that women are just as intelligent and capable as men and that they should hold positions of authority and influence," but in his own case, "he thought in terms of his wife being a homemaker and a mother for his children." In other words, King, Jr., according to one of his friends, believed that "Biologically and aesthetically women are more suitable than men for keeping house."[89] King, Jr. "was very definite," said Coretta, that he expected "whomever he married to be home waiting for him."[90] After the two married, King, Jr. repeatedly reminded Coretta, "I don't want a wife I can't communicate with," and at other times, he teasingly informed her that "I want my wife to respect me as the head of the family" because "I am the head of the family." The couple would then "laugh together" at the "slightly pompous" remark, and King, Jr. would quickly back down, declaring, "I

---

86. King, *My Life with Martin Luther King, Jr.*, 71; King, *Daddy King*, 151; and Farris, *Through It All*, 75–76.

87. The same can be said of Coretta, which explained her willingness to live her life primarily in accordance with her husband's plans and goals in life. See King, *My Life with Martin Luther King, Jr.*, 88 and 91; and Octavia Vivian, *Coretta: The Story of Coretta Scott King*, Commemorative Edition (Minneapolis: Fortress Press, 2006), 46–47.

88. Christine says that their maternal grandmother, Jennie C. Parks Williams, "was a bold exception to this formula." Mama Jennie's attitude was another example of the spirit of resistance to practices of human inequality that was rooted deeply in King family traditions. See Farris, *Through It All*, 10.

89. King, *My Life with Martin Luther King, Jr.*, 57–58; Abernathy, "My Old Friend Martin," 6; and Baldwin, *There is a Balm in Gilead*, 132–35.

90. Redding, *Crusader without Violence*, 5.

don't mean that. I think marriage should be a shared relationship." But Coretta was convinced that "he really did mean it."[91]

It is misleading to suggest that King, Jr. was essentially no different from the average man from the South and nationwide in the 1950s when it came to the subordination of women to men in the confines of marital relationships. He was sexist, but not, like all too many men, misogynistic.[92] King, Jr. was quite clear in saying that "I must have a wife who is as dedicated as I am"—"that I will be the pastor of a large black church in the South" and "want the kind of wife who will fit into that kind of situation" and "adjust to 'Aunt Jane,'"[93] but he was equally emphatic in noting, as he did in 1955 in a sermon on "The Crisis in the Modern Family," "that the day has passed when the man can stand over the wife with an iron rod asserting his authority as boss." "This does not mean that women no longer respect masculinity," King, Jr. explained, but that "there is no boss in the home" or "no Lord-servant relationship," that enlightened minds could no longer tolerate a culture in which "women will be trampled over and treated as some slave subject to the dictates of a despotic husband." "Women must be treated as human beings and not treated as mere means," King, Jr. added. He went on to suggest that marriage should be "a cooperative enterprise" with husband and wife "working together for a common goal."[94]

This idea of marriage as "a cooperative enterprise" took on a special meaning when King, Jr. became the full-time, senior pastor at the

---

91. King, *My Life with Martin Luther King, Jr.*, 58 and 88.
92. James Cone is right in saying that King was "sexist" and, like "most blacks," did not see "sexism as a major problem connected with and as evil as racism," but he wrongly implies that King was as committed as the typical male of his times to the ethic of female subordination when it came to marriage. See James H. Cone, *Martin & Malcolm & America: A Dream or a Nightmare* (Maryknoll, NY: Orbis Books, 1991), 274.
93. By "Aunt Jane," King "meant the good but uneducated parishioner who does not know the difference between, as he put it, 'you does' and 'you don't'." See King, *My Life with Martin Luther King, Jr.*, 58 and 90–91; Vivian, *Coretta*, 46–47; Baldwin, *There is a Balm in Gilead*, 132–33; and King, *Stride toward Freedom*, 21–22.
94. This point shows that King was ahead of his time in affirming, at least in principle if not in practice, the equality of a man and a woman in a marital situation, and it actually reflects the influence of the Personalism (personal idealism) to which King had been exposed as a PhD student at Boston University. Aside from the idea of the personal God of love and reason, Personalism upheld the concept of the dignity and worth of all human personality. See Carson, et al., eds., *King Papers*, VI, 212.

Dexter Avenue Baptist Church in Montgomery in 1954. As the years passed, he found himself busier than ever before, as he divided most of his time between church duties and obligations he felt toward the larger black community in Montgomery. Coretta remembered that "I hardly saw him as he rushed in and out of our home." In 1958, *Jet* magazine described King, Jr. as the "Man on the Go," and reported that he traveled 780,000 miles while delivering 208 speeches.[95] In his absence, he urged Coretta "to be active outside the home" and was "very pleased" when she "had ideas" of her own or even when she "could fill in for him," but, as Coretta herself realized, "it was the female role he was most anxious for me to play." "That was an adjustment I had to make," Coretta declared, "and I believe I made it very well."[96] Apparently, she was not "liberated"—as that term would be used by a later generation. That is to say, she did not put her own career and self-interests above or against those of her husband. In fact, many of the plans she had with respect to her music career were put on hold. The image of the supportive wife would essentially define Coretta's role in the marriage and the movement. She also evoked the co-worker and partnership models in describing her relationship to her husband. "As Martin was being made ready to be the leader and the symbol of the black Movement," Coretta maintained, "so I was being prepared to be his wife and partner."[97]

But King, Jr. supported the idea of Coretta teaching or giving concerts if she "wanted to" in order to "be independent" in some way. She did "work over the years" when King, Jr. "was involved in the struggle," and the money she earned helped tremendously. But King, Jr. himself "wanted the major responsibility" in the marriage. "I am supposed to earn enough money to take care of you and the family," he would often say to Coretta, especially after the birth of Yolanda, their first child, in November 1955. There were echoes here of Daddy King,

95. King, *My Life with Martin Luther King, Jr.*, 148. Paul Garber adequately describes King as "literally a theologian on the run," contending that the man spent "more time in airports and aboard planes" than at home. See Paul R. Garber, "Too Much Taming of Martin Luther King?," *The Christian Century* (5 June 1974), 616; and Baldwin, *To Make the Wounded Whole*, 60n9.

96. King, *My life with Martin Luther King, Jr.*, 58 and 88; and Baldwin, *There is a Balm in Gilead*, 133.

97. King, *My Life with Martin Luther King, Jr.*, 92.

King's father, who strongly believed in separate spheres of activity for men and women, and who epitomized this concept of the man as the head of the family and household.[98] But, apparently, King, Jr.'s point about taking on the primary responsibility as breadwinner did not strike Coretta as a sign of male insecurity or egoism. In her judgment, her husband had none "of the psychological insecurities" that seemed "to beset so many men in white America." "He always made me feel like a real woman because he was a real man in every respect," she asserted. "I always said that if I had not married a strong man, I would have 'worn the pants,'" she stated further. "Martin was such a very strong man, there was never any chance for that to happen." Coretta went on to point out that King, Jr. "imparted this quality not only to me but also to other people who met him. This was particularly true of men, who seemed to derive strength from their association with him and were drawn to him for it."[99]

King, Jr.'s concern was to not only be the best husband he could possibly be, but also, to properly groom Coretta for her role as the wife of a black Baptist minister. From the time of their courtship, the two had talked a lot about clothes and the matter of personal appearance, and this continued on a much larger scale during their years in Montgomery and as King, Jr. rose to national and international fame. Though there was really no need for King, Jr. to polish Coretta's manners and graces, he often reminded her about the need to always comb her hair carefully, to put on lipstick and make-up, and about buying and wearing beautiful coats and dresses. Such advice was sometimes greeted with mixed feelings by Coretta, who, by her own admission, had been "indoctrinated" in the attitude that "clothes don't matter," and who had never taken "great pains" about her appearance. As if to model what he had in mind, King, Jr., as always, "was very fastidious about his appearance," especially in public.[100]

98. King, *Daddy King*, 98 and 128; Farris, *Through It All*, 16 and 23; Baldwin, *There is a Balm in Gilead*, 112–13; and Carson, ed., *The Autobiography of Martin Luther King, Jr.*, 5.

99. King, *My Life with Martin Luther King, Jr.*, 87–88; and Baldwin, *There is a Balm in Gilead*, 133.

100. Lawrence Reddick, one of King's friends in Montgomery, reported that King's "habit of giving attention to personal appearance goes back to his youth." It is known that his maternal grandmother, Jennie C. Parks Williams, with whom King, Jr. was very close, dressed well and had

Member after member of Montgomery's Dexter Avenue Baptist Church recalled a young man who "was well-dressed" and "always very neat and in style," and some spoke specifically about "those nice hats," "fine suits," and "carefully polished shoes" King, Jr. routinely wore. At the same time, the general impression was that King, Jr. "was not ostentatious"—that he was well-dressed "in a simple way" or in "an English style, nothing flashy."[101] At any rate, King, Jr., from all indications, believed that one's personal appearance said a lot about not only one's view of self, but also one's perception of others and attitude toward life generally. He wanted Coretta to better understand this, and also, how important personal appearance really was in the life and culture of the black church,[102] and she ultimately took the lessons to heart and lived accordingly. Her ability to adjust and become the ideal minister's wife owed much to cultural and familial influences as well as her own upbringing in the black church in the South.[103]

For King, Jr., personal appearance at its best also included a warm and pleasing personality, and he, in subtle and not so subtle ways, repeatedly talked to Coretta about this, especially since she was known in family circles to have a temper.[104] Here again, King, Jr. sought to teach by example. In Montgomery, King, Jr. became known as the preacher who was "small in physical stature," but robust in personality. Many of his church members saw him as "so human," and felt that his "human qualities endeared him to the people." Dr.

an "impeccable sense of style." "She loved shoes, gloves, hats, and her black purse." Dressing "properly and appropriate at all times" was a lesson taught to King, Jr. and his siblings. See King, *My Life with Martin Luther King, Jr.*, 60; Reddick, *Crusader without Violence*, 3, 55, and 130; Farris, *Through It All*, 11 and 18; Farris, "The Young Martin," 57; and Downing, *To See the Promised Land*, 126.

101. Photographs of King from those years confirm these reports. Words like "immaculate" and "impeccable" were also used by Dexter's members to describe King's manner of dress. See Vaughn and Wills, eds., *Reflections on Our Pastor*, 39, 57, 66, 70, 94, and 116; and Telephone Interview with Malden (15 March 2014). Also see photographs in King, *Stride toward Freedom*, 65–68 and 165–68; King, *My Life with Martin Luther King, Jr.*, between 144 and 145; and Donnie Williams, *The Thunder of Angels: The Montgomery Bus Boycott and the People Who Broke the Back of Jim Crow*, with Wayne Greenhaw (Chicago: Lawrence Hill Books, 2006), between 134 and 135.

102. Being the dialectical thinker he was, in terms of taking a "both-and" rather than an "either-or" approach to reasoning, King also spoke of dress as "a superficial form" that does not equate with "spiritual quality." See King, *My Life with Martin Luther King, Jr.*, 164.

103. Baldwin, *There is a Balm in Gilead*, 127–58.

104. King, *Daddy King*, 150; and King, *My Life with Martin Luther King, Jr.*, 65 and 71.

Ralph Brison recalled that King, Jr. "had the persona that went with a charismatic leader—warmth, intellect, compassion and understanding." Others said that King, Jr. "was a saint," but most remembered "an ordinary, down-to-earth Christian gentleman" who was also "truthful," "authentic and simple," "patient," "always pleasant to talk to," "never boasted," "friendly but reserved," "an ambivert." Still others saw King, Jr. as "a person" who "was full of life," who "ruled by love and with the Bible," and who "made you feel at ease."[105] Coretta had heard about and seen these qualities in her husband as far back as the Boston years, and she, seemingly without any hesitation at all, viewed him as setting the standard for how she was supposed to act or behave, especially in black church circles.[106] Thus, King, Jr. was not only Coretta's husband and partner, but also, her spiritual leader and teacher, and the two were evidently quite comfortable with such an arrangement.

King, Jr. himself was humble, gracious, and charitable enough to acknowledge that the lessons learned were not one-sided in terms of their benefit, especially when it came to the human struggle, and that he learned as much or perhaps even more from Coretta than Coretta learned from him. Speaking at one point about Coretta's importance to the civil rights movement, King, Jr. conceded that "I think at many points she educated me." "When I first met her," King, Jr. added, "she was very concerned about all of the things we're trying to do now. I never will forget that the first discussion we had when we met was

---

105. Vaughn and Wills, eds., *Reflections on Our Pastor*, 37, 53, 73, 81, 90, 94, 111, 117, 119, 143, 148–49, 152–53, and 155; Reddick, *Crusader without Violence*, 6; and Telephone interview with Malden (15 March 2014).
106. To the perceptive critic, it seems as if Coretta was bowing to the structures of patriarchal domination that pervaded so much of black church life and culture in the 1950s and 60s. Interestingly enough, she was known to complain about the society's attack on "black manhood," and, more specifically, about "black men" not being able "to take their natural place as the heads of households and the protectors of their families." This would explain her primary emphasis on learning from her husband instead of the two necessarily learning from each other. It is important to note, however, that Coretta became a staunch advocate of women's rights before her death in 2006, and there is every reason to believe that she would have made a different point at that time affirming gender equality and the need for husband and wife to respect and learn from one another. See King, *My Life with Martin Luther King, Jr.*, 53–54, 58, 60, 87, and 91; Coretta Scott King, "U. S. Needs More Willing Women Participants in Foreign Policy," *The Tennessean* (1 March 1988), 9A; Coretta Scott King, "Empowering Women Will Benefit Nation," *The Tennessean* (13 November 1990), 9A; Vivian, *Coretta*, 120; and Baldwin, *To Make the Wounded Whole*, 311–12.

the whole question of racial injustice, economic injustice, and peace." King, Jr. further noted that Coretta "had been actively engaged in movements dealing with these problems" while a student at Antioch College." "I wish I could say, to satisfy my male ego, that I led her down this path," King, Jr. admitted, "but I must say that we went down together."[107] This shared commitment to the human struggle to overcome oppression had been part of the magnetic pull between King, Jr. and Coretta from the very first time they met.

Coretta was King, Jr.'s most loving critic and she also taught him rich, powerful, and enduring lessons in courage and about the indomitability of the human spirit. In the midst of the nasty and threatening telephone calls that mostly came late at night, the bombing of their home in Montgomery, the threats made against King, Jr. and other members of the family, and the daily verbal and physical assaults on her husband, Coretta stood steadfast and remained what King, Jr. himself called "a real soldier."[108] Her intimate companionship and nurturing care was essential to King, Jr.'s happiness, and unarguably, to his health and survival as well. King, Jr. was particularly amazed at times at how Coretta adjusted to the possibility that he would be seriously injured or assassinated, and this too was a source of instruction and inspiration to him. Noting that Coretta had adjusted to such frightening possibilities by being "realistic" and by "looking at it philosophically," King, Jr. quickly added that "this does not stop her in her commitment in going about her daily work."[109] For King, Jr.,

107. "Martin Luther King, Jr.: A Personal Portrait," a videotaped interview (Goldsboro, NC: Distributed by Carroll's Marketing and Management Service, 1966–67); King, *My Life with Martin Luther King, Jr.*, 56; Baldwin, *There is a Balm in Gilead*, 144–45; and John H. Britton, "Women Stay in the Shadows, But Give Men Strength to Fight," *Jet*, Vol. XXV, no. 17 (13 February 1964), 22–24.

108. King, *My Life with Martin Luther King, Jr.*, 122; "Martin Luther King, Jr.: A Personal Portrait," a videotaped interview; Baldwin, *There is a Balm in Gilead*, 145; and Angela Shelf Medearis, *Dare to Dream: Coretta Scott King and the Civil Rights Movement*, illustrated by Anna Rich (New York: Puffin Books, 1994), 29–31.

109. "Martin Luther King, Jr.: A Personal Portrait," a videotaped interview; King, *My Life with Martin Luther King, Jr.*, 1, 4, 113–14, and 122; Baldwin, *There is a Balm in Gilead*, 145–46; Vaughn and Wills, eds., *Reflections on Our Pastor*, 121; Roger Simon, "To Her, Rev. King was Simply Dad," *Los Angeles Times* (14 January 1985) and *Chicago Tribune* (14 January 1985); and "King's Daughter Recalls Father's Message," *Chicago Tribune* (19 January 2002). Even King's co-workers witnessed and spoke constantly about Coretta's importance to her husband's work. King's secretary, Dora McDonald insisted that "Dr. King found a strong-spirited wife, partner and helpmate in Coretta. . . ." McDonald went on to recount how Coretta, upon receiving the news of her husband's death

Coretta "was a most outstanding wife, who has given me consolation when I needed it most," and he also described her as "an excellent minister's wife."[110] Little has been said about those moments during which Coretta brightened his life. She was his vital and indispensable co-worker in the movement, and their shared determination largely explained the difference between success and failure in King-led civil rights campaigns. It is not insignificant that King, Jr. dedicated his very first book, *Stride toward Freedom: The Montgomery Story* (1958), to "Coretta, my beloved wife and co-worker."[111] Consequently, understanding King, Jr. and his wife's relationship requires looking beyond media images of what appeared to be the perfect picture of the celebrity and the glamorous supportive wife.

The relationship between King, Sr. and Alberta King, King's parents, became a metaphor for how King, Jr. related to his own wife, Coretta. King, Jr. always showered Coretta with kind words, praise, and affection, and occasionally, sent flowers to her.[112] The sheer depth of the love and respect he had for her was quite apparent even when the two engaged in conversation and prayed together.[113] Oftentimes, King, Jr. showed his love and affection by teasing, being playful, and laughing heartily with Coretta—a habit he had developed from the beginning of their courtship. While acknowledging that her husband "was remarkably mature" and could be "so serious, so deeply sincere," Coretta declared that "he was also so alive and funny, and so much fun to be with." "He was a great tease," Coretta continued, and "how he loved to tease me when we were courting by pretending to like

on April 4, 1968, "was stoic, calm, resigned, regal, and composed." And at the funeral, writes McDonald, "Mrs. King was the epitome of poise and grace as she looked upon her husband's face for the last time." See McDonald, *Secretary to a King*, 110 and 113.

110. "Martin Luther King, Jr.: A Personal Portrait," a videotaped interview; and Carson, et al., eds., *King Papers*, II, 336.

111. King, *Stride toward Freedom*, dedication page; and Baldwin, *There is a Balm in Gilead*, 145.

112. Strangely enough, the very last flowers King had delivered to his wife, on the eve of his assassination, were "beautiful red carnations" and they were also "artificial flowers." Coretta recalled that this was the first time this had happened in "all the years" they had "been together." King told Coretta: "I wanted to give you something that you could always keep." "Somehow, in some strange way," Coretta concluded, "he seemed to know how long they would have to last." See King, *My Life with Martin Luther King, Jr.*, 284; Farris, *Through It All*, 72; and Baldwin, *There is a Balm in Gilead*, 103.

113. King, *Stride toward Freedom*, 21; and Carson, et al., eds., *King Papers*, IV, 488.

some other girl until I rose to the bait, my eyes spitting fire. How he would laugh at me then!" In his most playful moments, King, Jr. teased Coretta about a lot of things. He used to say that she married him to escape the cotton fields in Marion, Alabama, where Coretta had grown up while earning the reputation as "a very good cotton-picker." "If you hadn't met me," King, Jr. joked, "you'd still be down there picking cotton." At other times, he reminded Coretta about them having to spend the night with Mr. and Mrs. Robert E. Tubbs, friends of theirs who were also undertakers, immediately after their wedding in Marion because hotels were segregated. "Do you know we spent our honeymoon at a funeral parlor," he said jokingly, and the couple would laugh heartily.[114]

Good-natured ribbing about Coretta's personality and proper place as a wife was never beyond the pale for King, Jr., for he was always cautious and measured and he instinctively knew what was off limits when it came to teasing and joking. From the time of their courtship through their fifteen years of marriage, he joked mildly on occasions about her temper, about whether or not she passed the test in her cooking, about the importance of her being subordinate to him, about the need for her to always be waiting for him when he arrived at home, and about deserting and leaving him alone when he needed her most.[115] All of the teasing, playfulness, and laughter were always in good taste, and this mellowed Coretta over time, and apparently, helped make her more patient, more at ease, and less temperamental.

King, Jr. was, on the whole, a good, caring, and devoted husband, but he had habits and views that must have been annoying to Coretta at times. From the time he first met Coretta, he had a tendency to be "so slow" and sometimes late for dates, in part because he devoted so much time to getting dressed. King, Jr. was also known for driving fast, and he was occasionally pulled over by police offers or state troopers and given tickets. Coretta would drive at times when it was clear to her that he might fall asleep at the wheel.[116] The fact that King, Jr. was

---

114. King, *My Life with Martin Luther King, Jr.*, 24, 52, 54–55, 59, and 72; and Redding, *Crusader without Violence*, 105.

115. King, *My Life with Martin Luther King, Jr.*, 65, 67, 71, 88, and 124.

away from home so much eventually took its toll, prompting Coretta to sometimes complain. Coretta also had some difficulty, initially, accepting the loss of privacy that came with King, Jr.'s rising public stature, popularity, and the increasing media attention, and there were occasional marital differences, as time passed, over King, Jr.'s decision to donate all of his Nobel Prize money to civil rights organizations, his insistence that his family live as modestly as possible, and his feeling that Coretta should remain at home and raise their children while he was away on movement business.[117] But Coretta was convinced that she was married to "such a very good man," one whose "conscience was a formidable thing that kept him on the path he thought was right."[118]

This picture of the ideal husband sharply contrasted with reports that extramarital affairs were the proverbial Achilles' heel of King, Jr.'s private life.[119] It is doubtful that King, Jr. was the serial adulterer he is said to have been,[120] but he was apparently guilty of some level of philandering and marital infidelity. Exactly when the problem began is questionable, but it has been suggested that King, Jr.'s infidelities dated "back to his tenure in Montgomery."[121] During that time, he

116. Farris, *Through It All*, 71 and 74–75; King, *My Life with Martin Luther King, Jr.*, 59, 71, and 115; Abernathy, *And the Walls Came Tumbling Down*, 438; Baldwin Interview with Lee (9 July 1986); and Baldwin Interview with Abernathy (17 March 1987).

117. David Garrow is right in saying that there were "serious marital differences," but any suggestion that the marriage was put at risk is difficult to sustain in view of Coretta's own claims about their relationship. See Garrow, *Bearing the Cross*, 374; King, *My Life with Martin Luther King, Jr.*, 59; and Vivian, *Coretta*, 19–54.

118. King, *My Life with Martin Luther King, Jr.*, 59.

119. Stewart Burns, *To the Mountaintop: Martin Luther King Jr.'s Sacred Mission to Save America, 1955–1968* (New York: HarperCollins Publishers, Inc., 2004), 265.

120. Garrow writes about King's "compulsive sexual athleticism," Dyson about King's "sexual excesses," and Chappell about the chaos of King's private life and "his frequent and sometimes careless extramarital sex." Although these scholars have written excellent works on King, and are on track in terms of their delineation of certain traits in his personality, their conclusions about the extent of his philandering are questionable and indeed debatable. Clayborne Carson, another King scholar, has noted that his examination of FBI files indicates, for example, that "the evidence was not as definitive," as Garrow's account of King's sex life suggests. This point applies to some extent to Dyson's and Chappell's accounts as well, especially since they draw substantially on Garrow. See Garrow, *Bearing the Cross*, 375; Michael Eric Dyson, *I May Not Get There with You: The True Martin Luther King, Jr.* (New York: The Free Press, 2000), 159, 161–62, and 167; David L. Chappell, *Waking from the Dream: The Struggle for Civil Rights in the Shadow of Martin Luther King, Jr.* (New York: Random House, 2014), 153 and 155; and Clayborne Carson, *Martin's Dream: My Journey and the Legacy of Martin Luther King, Jr.—A Memoir* (New York: Palgrave Macmillan, 2013), 117–18.

121. Taylor Branch, *Parting the Waters: America in the King Years, 1954–63* (New York: Simon and Schuster, 1988), 238–39. Branch himself implies that this claim is not based on solid and reliable evidence, and it, of course, was challenged by one of the deacons at the Dexter Avenue Baptist Church in

became a media celebrity and "America's most scrutinized citizen," which meant that not only his words, but also his public and private life, would be consistently dissected. The sheer longevity and severity of the claims and charges swirling around King, Jr.'s sex life boggle the mind,[122] but perhaps, this is to be expected in the case of a man who was a clergyman, the moral leader of his nation, and a spiritual advisor and counselor who offered advice on the virtues of virginity, marital fidelity, and honest communication in marriage while also embracing the ideal of the monogamous family life. It is difficult to explain King, Jr.'s sexual involvements with women other than his wife in light of his professed convictions concerning sexuality, and also, his broader sense of morality and ethics.[123] If he was, as Coretta claimed, determined to stay on the right path in life, then why did he turn to sexual practices that were universally prohibited and roundly condemned at that time by the Christian faith?[124]

Explanations vary and have not come easily. One is that King, Jr.'s

Montgomery, who recounted that he "was with Pastor King in some close places where women did everything they could to tempt him and he handled himself as a perfect gentleman." No one can pinpoint with certainty when King's womanizing problem began. See Vaughn and Wills, eds., *Reflections on Our Pastor*, 111.

122. For almost three decades now, books and articles treating aspects of King's sex life have been published, and attention to the subject, or lack thereof, has frequently been a consideration in determining whether or not books on King are accepted for publication. I have no quarrel with scholars who raise the issue of King's marital infidelity, but I have often wished, for the sake of scholarly integrity and objectivity, that they would treat the white supremacy and white privilege that sought to emasculate King with the same levels of analytical depth and intensity. Rufus Burrow raises this issue, noting that there are things much worse than "extramarital sex between *consenting* adults that do not even seem to disturb some of the most vocal critics of King's sexual ethic and behavior. Racism is one such thing." Burrow goes on to assert that "The racist critic of King, for example, does not easily acknowledge his own racism or his unearned privilege." Burrow critiques those King scholars who have "earned huge book royalties, in part, for focusing heavily on the alleged sex tapes and files," and he wonders "about the racist element embedded in the tendency (especially among white male scholars) to devote so much attention to King's personal moral shortcomings." See Farris, *Through It All*, 109; Lewis V. Baldwin and Rufus Burrow, Jr., eds., *The Domestication of Martin Luther King Jr.: Clarence B. Jones, Right-Wing Conservatism, and the Manipulation of the King Legacy* (Eugene, Oregon: Cascade Books, 2013), 121; and Rufus Burrow, Jr., *God and Human Dignity: The Personalism, Theology, and Ethics of Martin Luther King, Jr.* (Notre Dame, IN: University of Notre Dame Press, 2006), 11. Also see my critique of David Garrow and others in Baldwin, *To Make the Wounded Whole*, 295–96.

123. Carson, et al., eds., *King Papers*, IV, 268–69, 306, 327–28, 393, 402, 444, 459, and 504; and Reddick, *Crusader without Violence*, 5.

124. Interestingly enough, Rufus Burrow suggests that Christian moral standards may not be the best avenue for challenging King's womanizing. He depends more on "the philosophical point in personalism and its emphasis on human dignity," which seems perfectly logical in light of King's study of personalism. See Rufus Burrow, Jr., "Behind the Public Veil—Comments," unpublished (7 February 2015), 6.

"sexual habits grew out of a subculture of promiscuity" that "was rampart" in the black church and "among clergy and religious figures in every faith."[125] Some activists who associated with King, Jr. held that such habits were "typical of the overall movement," especially for a figure such as King, Jr., who was away from home a lot and whose opportunities with women were virtually unlimited. The view that King, Jr. was simply reacting as a *real* man to the many women who flirted with and threw themselves at him seemed logical enough to many of those around him, especially the men. There was the impression also that King, Jr. needed a type of companionship and affection that he was not finding at home. The feeling that King, Jr. was rebelling, perhaps unconsciously, against the saintly image so many sought to attach to him probably never registered well, even in the thinking of those who knew the most about his affairs with women.[126] The idea that King, Jr.'s womanizing was somehow the product of a deeply ingrained sexism would not have been entertained to any serious degree in that era.[127] In fact, since King, Jr. lived in an age when reporting on the sex lives of famous religious figures was considered taboo, few actually knew or cared about his philandering and his public image never really suffered on those grounds.[128]

Rigid and high-minded moralistic and hyper-moralistic perspectives on King, Jr.'s philandering and marital infidelity have become the norm for his critics, but they tell us essentially nothing about *why* and *how* King, Jr. could engage in such behavior. Moral judgments by human

125. Dyson, *I May Not Get There with You*, 160; and Garrow, *Bearing the Cross*, 375. For a womanist perspective on this matter, see Cheryl Kirk-Duggan's essay in Baldwin and Burrow, eds., *The Domestication of Martin Luther King Jr.*, 107–9. Extramarital affairs on the part of clergy in this country dated back to frontier times, and were not a problem unique to black clergy or clergy who were actively involved in civil rights. The Reverend James Bevel, who was active in King's SCLC, reported that "many of the ministers attached" to that organization were "burdened by the guilt of extramarital affairs." See Smiley, *Death of a King*, 154.
126. Garrow, *Bearing the Cross*, 374–75 and 586–87.
127. This position would be advanced decades later by certain black male and female liberation, womanist, and feminist theologians and ethicists. See Cone, *Martin & Malcolm & America*, 273–80; Cheryl J. Sanders, *Empowerment Ethics for a Liberated People—A Path to African American Social Transformation* (Minneapolis: Fortress Press, 1995), 97–102; and Burrow, *God and Human Dignity*, 10–15; Traci West, "Gendered Legacies of Martin Luther King Jr.'s Leadership," *Theology Today*, Vol. 65, no. 1 (2008), 41–45. Also see the chapters by Rufus Burrow and Cheryl A. Kirk-Duggan in Baldwin and Burrow, eds., *The Domestication of Martin Luther King Jr.*, 100–140.
128. Chappell, *Walking from the Dream*, 150.

beings are always provisional, and those who use them in framing arguments about King, Jr.'s sexual escapades and disregard for the sanctity of marriage run the risk of playing God, who is, in fact, the final judge. The best that can be said is that King, Jr.'s infidelities, and the guilt that came with them, revealed his fundamental and genuine "humanness."[129] Close associates who viewed King, Jr.'s sexual delights "as a humanizing revelation that bonded them even closer to him and his public purpose," or "as 'a natural human concomitant' of the tense, fast-paced life" he led,[130] were being remarkably realistic. King, Jr. was a man fully capable of human mistakes and weaknesses, and was never oblivious to his own brokenness. He understood himself to be an imperfect creature living in an imperfect world.

Having studied the Apostle Paul, Plato, Thomas Carlyle, Reinhold Niebuhr, and other great thinkers, who affirmed both good and evil as natural tendencies in the human spirit, and who said so much about the paradoxical or dialectical nature of humanity,[131] King, Jr. must have been able to make some sense of his extramarital affairs, theologically and philosophically, even as he struggled with them morally. For him, every human being amounts to "two selves" or "two personalities," and he spoke more specifically in terms of the "higher" or "good self" and the "lower" or "evil self." The "great burden of life," then, is "to always try to keep that higher self in command," which is not always possible due to the glaring reality and potential for human sin and evil.[132] In other words, every human life is a study in contradictions.

129. Since the 1980s, when reports of King's sex life first received major attention, this point has been repeatedly made by King scholars, but too often without extensive commentary. What is needed in King scholarship is a more pragmatic approach to King's private life as it relates to sex. This requires a change in tone but not necessarily values. See Garrow, *Bearing the Cross*, 375; Branch, *Parting the Waters*, 860; Baldwin, *There is a Balm in Gilead*, 155; and Baldwin and Burrow, eds., *The Domestication of Martin Luther King Jr.*, 121.

130. Branch, *Parting the Waters*, 860; Garrow, *Bearing the Cross*, 375; and Abernathy, *And the Walls Came Tumbling Down*, 470–71.

131. John J. Ansbro, *Martin Luther King, Jr.: The Making of a Mind* (Maryknoll, NY: Orbis Books, 1982), 90–92; and Kenneth L. Smith and Ira G. Zepp, Jr., *Search for the Beloved Community: The Thinking of Martin Luther King, Jr.* (Valley Forge, PA: Judson Press, 1998; originally published in 1974), 73–83.

132. Interestingly, King spoke to this dualism in the self in sermons and prayers. In one sermon, King declared that the Prodigal Son was not "his real self" or "whole self" when he abandoned the love and security of home and ventured into some far, unknown country, and one can only imagine how King saw this in terms of his own sex life. See Carson, et al., eds., *King Papers*, VI, 95–97; Martin Luther King, Jr., "The Prodigal Son," unpublished version of sermon, Ebenezer Baptist Church,

King, Jr.'s "best" or "higher self" yearned for moral purity, and perhaps, even "sainthood," but his "worst" or "lower self" succumbed at times to the "demon delights" of his private sex life.[133] He clearly saw that "strange dualism" or "dichotomy," which Paul, Plato, Carlyle, Niebuhr, and so many others had identified at the very core of human nature, at work in his own life experiences. The shady side of King, Jr.'s humanity exposed a tendency toward adulterous behavior,[134] but he still faithfully surrendered to God's call and healed more wounds than he inflicted, and his ministry was a composite of what God can do through an imperfect human vessel that is nonetheless committed to a life of faithful service.[135] This is not so much an attempt to condone King, Jr.'s behavior with women other than his wife, but, rather, to place it in a human context.

The argument that "King's humanity" has become "the generally accepted response for deflecting attention from his actions" as an adulterer may hold some validity,[136] but no one can logically deny that such actions were those of a flawed but yet sensitive and committed human being.[137] It is equally logical to consider the possibility that the relentless assault on King, Jr.'s sexual habits in certain academic and conservative Christian circles has become the widely accepted way of diverting attention from the racist attitudes and structures

Atlanta, Georgia (4 September 1966), King Center Library and Archives, 4; Dyson, *I May Not get There with You*, 162; and Baldwin, ed., *"Thou, Dear God,"* 11, 47, 73.

133. "Like all religious leaders," said King on one occasion, "I have the desire to reach the majestic heights of sainthood." But King knew he was not a saint, and he spoke to the difficulty of living up to such high standards, noting that even the man who became St. Augustine had committed adultery and cried out, "Lord make me pure but not yet." King identified with such piercing, audible language of the heart. Augustine's prayer was in some sense his own prayer, and this is why King quoted it repeatedly. King prayed that his "best" or "higher self" would be in control as he went about his civil rights activities, "even if it will mean assassination, even if it will mean crucifixion," which King also called "the high way." See "Martin Luther King, Jr.: A Personal Portrait," a videotaped interview; King, "The Prodigal Son," 4; Martin Luther King, Jr., "We Would See Jesus," unpublished version of sermon, Ebenezer Baptist Church, Atlanta, Georgia (7 May 1967), King Center Library and Archives, 7; Baldwin, *"Thou, Dear God,"* 47; Carson, et al., eds., *King Papers*, VI, 95–97; Baldwin, *There is a Balm in Gilead*, 135; Branch, *Parting the Waters*, 860; and Smiley, *Death of a King*, 154–56, 162, and 182.

134. King himself is said to have "admitted that his two major weaknesses were women and food." See Downing, *To See the Promised Land*, 126.

135. Ansbro, *Martin Luther King, Jr.*, 91–92; Burrow, *God and Human Dignity*, 11; and Baldwin, *There is a Balm in Gilead*, 155.

136. Chappell, *Waking from the Dream*, 159.

137. Baldwin, *There is a Balm in Gilead*, 155.

that exploited and oppressed black people, that made King, Jr.'s social activism necessary, and that led to his persecution, and ultimately, his assassination. This, too, speaks to the intertwining dynamics of race and sex in the history and culture of the society. But King, Jr. was killed not because of sexual transgressions, but because he was a black man who challenged white power and sought to transform society in the interest of the poor, the marginalized, and the oppressed. In other words, he was murdered for being a good human being.

The concern here is not only about what King, Jr.'s failures in the private sexual sphere of his life did to his own image as a husband and father, but also, how this impacted his wife and his children, and indeed, his family as a whole. One view, which highlights King, Jr.'s own personalism, and especially, "his doctrine of human dignity," is that "King's affairs violated Mrs. King's human right to be respected and treated with dignity."[138] Another is that King, Jr. "betrayed his wife and children," and "committed a grave disservice to the family, especially the black family."[139] These seem to be solid claims and they are rooted to some degree in moral considerations, but they should be made with more analytical depth and are nevertheless debatable. Unquestionably, King, Jr.'s philandering revealed his selfishness, which is also a natural human tendency, but it did not necessarily mean that he was an unloving husband and father, and the impact on his wife and children cannot be determined on the basis of Christian-moral standards which are increasingly being challenged around issues of human sexuality. Coretta King once hinted that she knew nothing of her husband's extramarital affairs, but she, upon hearing about them years later, "acknowledged that the sexual allegations bothered her." But she never addressed the issue nor expressed her feelings publicly.[140] Coretta's image of her husband was not that of an adulterer

---

138. Rufus Burrow, a personalist himself by training and by his own admission, is the only King scholar who has consistently advanced this argument. Burrow apparently has "some sympathy with the fact that King's sexual escapades involved choices made by consenting adults," but he hastens to add that "the fact remains that as one who was married," King "owed the obligation of fidelity to his wife." See Baldwin and Burrow, eds., *The Domestication of Martin Luther King Jr.*, 139–40; and Burrow, *God and Human Dignity*, 14, 140, 145, and 147.

139. Chappell, *Waking from the Dream*, 160.

140. Carson, *Martin's Dream*, 118. In a recent book, Tavis Smiley notes that King confessed to Coretta

and philanderer, but of a caring husband and father, and also, a man of considerable unselfishness and bravery whose "refusal to be beaten down" was real and unshakeable.[141]

The view that King, Jr. was able to manage his and Coretta's "emotional relationship, forming a tricky balance between love, devotion, responsibility, and guilt," makes sense when the couple's marriage is put in proper perspective. Apparently, that "delicate balance" was upset in January 1968, when King, Jr. was informed that Coretta required "surgery for a stomach tumor." The very "thought of losing his wife" filled King, Jr. "with fear," and he canceled "all engagements" and remained "by her side and in deep prayer" until the tumor was declared benign and successfully removed. King, Jr. rejoiced at the outcome.[142] Clearly, his devotion to his wife in that time of crisis was noble, but it must be considered against the background of the many queries raised about his private sex life.

The ways in which King, Jr. met the challenges and demands of fatherhood also raise some questions, but here again, the record reveals a man who meant well and wanted to do what was right. King, Jr. loved children and he and Coretta, from the time they decided to get married, looked forward to the responsibilities and pleasures of being parents.[143] King, Jr. initially wanted eight children, but the couple compromised and agreed to have four. Although King, Jr., in conformity with family traditions regarding childbearing and naming,

that he had had "an adulterous relationship," which, if true, speaks volumes about King's decency as a human being. "Having heard rumors of Doc's affairs," writes Smiley, "Coretta isn't shocked by his admission, but she is nonetheless hurt and angry." In any case, King, according to Smiley, promised his wife that he would "cut off this relationship" and, from that point, would "walk the straight and narrow." See Smiley, *Death of a King*, 155–56.

141. King, *My Life with Martin Luther King, Jr.*, 58–59, 88, and 90–91; and Baldwin, *There is a Balm in Gilead*, 136–38. This portrait of King is all the more believable since he reportedly confessed to Coretta that he had "had an adulterous relationship," a confession that understandably hurt and angered her. But there was a measure of honesty here on King's part. See Smiley, *Death of a King*, 155–56.

142. Smiley, *Death of a King*, 155.

143. As far back as his Boston years, King expressed a deep interest in the kind of ministry that involved working closely with children, and he "related well to children" as the pastor of the Dexter Avenue Baptist Church in Montgomery. He also had a very interesting and attractive way of reaching out to youngsters he encountered in different cities during civil rights campaigns, even those associated with gangs. See A Private Interview with Michael E. Haynes, Boston, Massachusetts (25 June 1987); King, *My Life with Martin Luther King, Jr.*, 98; Vaughn and Wills, eds., *Reflections on Our Pastor*, 36; and Cotton, *If Your Back's Not Bent*, 262.

wanted a boy who carried his name as their first child, he was nonetheless quite pleased when their daughter, Yolanda Denise, nicknamed Yoki, was born in November 1955. Two sons and a daughter followed. They included Martin Luther King, III, called Marty, in October 1957; Dexter Scott, named after the only church King served as a full-time pastor and for Coretta's side of the family, in January 1961; and Bernice Albertine, named after her two grandmothers and nicknamed Bunny, in March 1963.[144] King, Jr. gave them all "names of affection," such as "'Yoki-poky," "Marty-bopy," "Dexter-wexter," and "Bunny-bopy."[145]

King, Jr. tended to be "very attentive and concerned" during Coretta's pregnancies, and there were never any serious disagreements concerning the importance of voluntary family planning and strong and responsible parenthood as a means of training, nurturing, raising, and molding their children. The deep love the two had for each other was always evident to their children, as their son Dexter pointed out:

> My parents were always very loving. I think the best word for their marriage is partnership. It wasn't like one parent was dominant over the other. You felt shared responsibility. When we would sit around the table, they both would have input in the drift of the conversation. My mom gave my father respect, as man of the house. I never heard them argue. Maybe they were good at keeping it from us, since the married couple doesn't exist that hasn't had arguments.[146]

King, Jr. felt that the integrated and "congenial home situation" not only demanded that he and Coretta live together intimately, but that they be the most important influence in the cultivation of those higher qualities of the intellectual, moral, spiritual, cultural, and artistic in

144. King, *My Life with Martin Luther King, Jr.*, 20, 97–99, 149, 189, 204, and 318–19; Farris, *Through It All*, 20–21, 87–88, and 93; King, *Daddy King*, 181–82; Vivian, *Coretta*, 55–64; and Baldwin, *There is a Balm in Gilead*, 134.

145. Dexter Scott King, *Growing Up King: An Intimate Memoir*, with Ralph Wiley (New York: Warner Books, Inc., 2003), 25. For interesting reflections on naming and names in the King familial circles, and how this reflected long-established and cherished traditions, see Baldwin, *There is a Balm in Gilead*, 133–34.

146. King, *Growing Up King*, 43. King said the same about his parents, King, Sr. and Alberta, years earlier. See Carson, ed., *The Autobiography of Martin Luther King, Jr.*, 2–3; and Clayborne Carson, et. al., eds., *The Papers of Martin Luther King, Jr., Volume I: Called to Serve, January 1929–June 1951* (Berkeley: University of California Press, 1992), 360.

their children.[147] He also believed that their children should be highly respected and "raised moderately, neither overly inhibited nor allowed to run wild," and he, much like his own father King, Sr., approved of corporeal punishment, but only as a last resort.[148] The children, King, Jr. insisted, were expected to always respond to him and Coretta with respect, obedience, and, whenever possible, a sense of personal and family responsibility. Here, he insisted on the cooperative model of family life, or the idea of family as "a partnership" or "a cooperative enterprise,"[149] which had been the norm for his own parents, and which, for him, constituted the ideal. This could not have been more important in view of King, Jr.'s conviction that strong, cohesive, stable, and secure families are the foundation of a strong and prosperous people and also of that larger human communitarian ideal to which he devoted so much of his life. He repeatedly gave expression to this conviction in not only his sermons, speeches, and interviews, but in his writings as well.[150]

It has long been said that a man who really devotes himself to a

147. King, *My Life with Martin Luther King, Jr.*, 77 and 98. King grew up around books and preferred the same for his children as one way of educating them while instilling certain kinds of values and priorities. He had found a model for this in his Aunt Ida Worthem, who had read books to him in his childhood. Also see Carson, et al., eds., *King Papers*, IV, 327, 350, 374, and 402; Carson, et al., eds., *King Papers*, VI, 212; Reddick, *Crusader without Violence*, 5–6; and Baldwin, *There is a Balm in Gilead*, 156–57.

148. According to King's youngest son Dexter, "My mother always said that Daddy didn't believe in spanking, but she also said if he had spent more time around us, he might have changed his mind." But King apparently did believe in using the belt, but he almost never did. King, *Growing Up King*, 38.

149. Reddick, *Crusader without Violence*, 5–6; King, *Daddy King*, 130; Carson, et al., eds., *King Papers*, VI, 212; Ervin Smith, *The Ethics of Martin Luther King, Jr.* (Lewiston, NY: The Edwin Mellen Press, 1981), 94–98; King, *My Life with Martin Luther King, Jr.*, 65–66, 76, 82, and 88; King, *Growing Up King*, 43; and Farris, *Through It All*, 16–51.

150. For a sense of how King related an integrated and harmonious family life to the larger ideal of community, including what he termed "the great world house," see Martin Luther King, Jr. to the Student Body of Jesse Crowell School, Albion, Michigan (1 December 1960), King Center Library and Archives, 1–2; James R. Wood to Mr. L. F. Palmer, Jr., dictated by Martin Luther King, Jr. (23 February 1961), King Center Library and Archives, 1–2; Martin Luther King, Jr., "What a Mother Should Tell Her Child," unpublished version of sermon, Ebenezer Baptist Church, Atlanta, Georgia (12 May 1963), King Center Library and Archives, 1–14; Martin Luther King, Jr., "Training Your Child in Love," unpublished version of sermon, Ebenezer Baptist Church, Atlanta, Georgia (8 May 1966), King Center Library and Archives, 1–11; Martin Luther King, Jr., "The Negro Family," unpublished version of an address, University of Chicago, Chicago, Illinois (27 January 1966), King Center Library and Archives, 1–28; Martin Luther King, Jr., "The Dignity of Family Life," unpublished version of an address, Abbott House, Westchester County, New York (29 October 1965), King Center Library and Archives, 1–11; and Baldwin, *There is a Balm in Gilead*, 91–158.

social cause has no place or need for a family,[151] but this was not the case with Martin Luther King, Jr. King, Jr. always said that his oldest child "came at a time in his life when he needed something to take his mind off the tremendous pressures" that weighed heavily upon him. Yoki "was there cooing and cuddly and trustful and loving" whenever her father came home "from the stress and turmoil" of his daily activities, and the experience could not have been more refreshing and reassuring, especially since the Montgomery bus boycott started only two weeks after she was born. Yoki was so "close to his heart" during the boycott, literally "the darling of my life," King, Jr. declared, and King, Jr. never forgot how he was comforted "night after night" by "that little gentle smile."[152] "My father was my first buddy," Yoki would later declare, "and we shared such a loving connection."[153]

When Marty, Dexter, and Bunny came along, King, Jr. was even more deeply involved in civil rights activism, and also, increasingly overstressed. The very presence of his children was renewing for him because they positively impacted his emotional and spiritual well-being. "There was a spiritual quality that one could feel and sense in Martin's relationship with Yoki, Marty, and the others," declared Bernard Lee, an SCLC activist who frequently dined with the family. "Spirituality was always present, even when Martin disciplined his children. Things were often said about him by others that would

---

151. King himself once said this to Coretta, who was perhaps shocked but not hurt by the statement. See King, *My Life with Martin Luther King, Jr.*, 165; and Baldwin, *There is a Balm in Gilead*, 145 and 148.
152. King, *My Life with Martin Luther King, Jr.*, 98–99; Carson and Holloran, eds., *A Knock at Midnight*, 161; "Martin Luther King, Jr.: A Personal Portrait," a videotaped interview; and Baldwin Interview with Lee (9 July 1986).
153. Yolanda frequently referred to her father as "my buddy" or "a buddy-daddy." See Yolanda King and Wanda Marie, *Embracing Your Power in 30 Days: A Journey of Self-Discovery and Personal Freedom* (Culver City, CA: Higher Ground Publications, 2005), 14; and Simon, "To Her, Rev. King was Simply Dad." Yolanda's private memories of her father are supposedly set forth at great length in *The Content of My Character* (Emmaus, PA: Rodale Press /Books, 2002), 1–256. Strangely enough, an exhaustive search for this book on the worldwide web proved unsuccessful. This author was informed via email, by a representative simply called Jessica of Rodale Books, that the book was actually issued in published form in January, 1990, but the only publication date shown is 2002. See Corinne Nelson's review of the book, in "New Books by African-American Authors," *The Black Collegian* (First Semester Super Issue, 2002), 126; and Email Message from Customer Service of Rodale Books to Lewis V. Baldwin (21 May 2015), 1.

normally break up a family unit, but that spirituality would exude and just take over."[154]

King, Jr. had looked forward to spending much time with his wife and children, but the problem was that he, aside from being a husband and father, was also the pastor of a church, the leader of a movement, and a very popular world figure, with equal commitments in all directions. As King, Jr. grew in popularity and fame, and expanded his commitments over time, his relationship to his wife and children, and with his family as a whole, became almost like the proverbial ship passing into the night. Although he had earned a reputation as "very much a family man" while in Montgomery, he found himself increasingly choosing the struggle over his wife and children.[155] The job of finding good schools in Atlanta and getting the children registered, even in integrated schools in 1965, was left to Coretta. When Marty and Dexter had their tonsils removed at the same time later that same year, King, Jr. was "at the signing of the Voting Rights Bill" in Washington, DC[156] He was seldom at home when his children were celebrating birthdays and other special occasions, raising questions, thirsting for comforting words after bad dreams, and crying out for that love, security, and sense of belonging that only a father could provide, and this was "very difficult" for him, often causing agonizing guilt on his part. "This is one of the most frustrating aspects of my life," King, Jr. maintained. "I have to be away from home a great deal. I have to be out of town more than I am in town, and this takes

154. Baldwin Interview with Lee (9 July 1986).
155. J. Raymond Henderson, King's friend and a fellow clergyman, wrote King as early as September, 1958, with several questions about his divided commitments and loyalties: "How much does a leader owe his people? How much is he called on to suffer for them? How fair is it to his wife and family to continue them over-long in a situation fraught with constant danger, tension, and the possibility of future neuroses, especially for the children?" These and other questions must have confronted King with increasing frequency as his public commitments collided with his private world. See Carson, et al., eds., *King Papers*, IV, 498; Reddick, *Crusader without Violence*, 5; King, *My Life with Martin Luther King, Jr.*, 165, 233–34, 257, and 312; "Martin Luther King, Jr.: A Personal Portrait," a videotaped interview; and Baldwin, *There is a Balm in Gilead*, 134.
156. Coretta noted that "At times like this, when I had to take care of the children by myself, I generally did not mind. Only occasionally would I think about the fact that I was there by myself." See King, *My Life with Martin Luther King, Jr.*, 165, 233–35, 257, and 312; "Martin Luther King, Jr.: A Personal Portrait," a videotaped interview; Baldwin, *There is a Balm in Gilead*, 134–35; Lischer, *The Preacher King*, 167; and Garrow, *Bearing the Cross*, 577.

away from the family so much. It is just impossible to carry out the responsibilities of a father and a husband when you have these kinds of demands."[157] It is also evident that King, Jr. lost so much time during which he himself would have found more love, satisfaction, fulfillment, and positive reinforcement as a husband and father.

Like Mohandas K. Gandhi before him, King, Jr. witnessed firsthand just how difficult it was to find a proper and acceptable balance between the public realm of politics and social involvement and the private realm of family, intimate relationships, and the raising of children. He saw and actually experienced firsthand how families so often suffer in the public sphere. Being media superstars, King, Jr. and Coretta were always in the public eye, and their children were often sought out and questioned by classmates and other curious persons. The children also had to deal with the knowledge "that their father was in danger," with the "threats and attempted bombings," with their father frequently being in jail, and with other kids who called them "niggers" and disparagingly referred to their father as "a liar," "a jail bird," "a Communist," "a troublemaker," or "an Uncle Tom."[158] Coretta explained that she and her husband learned "to accept the loss of privacy as part of the price we had to pay in the work we were trying to do," and that "we always tried to protect the children from that kind of public focus,"[159] but they were never able to completely resolve the public versus private dilemma which defined their lives and existence.

King, Jr. and Coretta tried to teach their children why their father's frequent absences and all of the publicity were necessary. Yoki, Marty, Dexter, and Bunny were taught that they should never be ashamed or fearful to call their father's name or to speak proudly of his work, that "daddy is doing God's work," that "this is the cross that we must

---

157. "Martin Luther King, Jr.: A Personal Portrait," a videotaped interview; Vivian, *Coretta*, 46–47; King, *My Life with Martin Luther King, Jr.*, 165, 200, 233–34, and 256–57; and Baldwin, *There is a Balm in Gilead*, 83 and 134.
158. King, *My Life with Martin Luther King, Jr.*, 4, 175, 196–97, and 235; Simon, "To Her, Rev. King was Simply Dad"; and King and Marie, *Embracing Your Power in 30 Days*, 22, 50, and 98.
159. King, *My Life with Martin Luther King, Jr.*, 4, 175, 196–97, and 235; and Baldwin, *There is a Balm in Gilead*, 134–35. King's son Dexter reported that "my father was protective of us at home, didn't let reporters or photographers in." There were a few exceptions, however. See King, *Growing Up King*, 25.

bear," that his jail-going was part of his effort "to help people," and therefore, "a badge of honor," and that he would be coming back to see them on certain occasions. Yoki would cry at times when she heard the news on radio or TV that her father was in jail, and she expressed the desire to be there with him. She wept profusely when he was arrested in early December 1961, thinking that he perhaps would not be home for Christmas, and Marty consoled his sister, reminding her that their Daddy had "to help some more people" and that "he will be back." Sometimes, shades of humor surfaced in such painful situations. On one occasion, as Coretta was explaining to Yoki how her father's jail-going would make it possible for "colored children" such as her to go to Atlanta's Funtown, "a sort of miniature Disneyland with mechanical rides," the child innocently responded: "Well, that's fine Mommy. Tell him to stay in jail until I can go to Funtown."[160]

King, Jr. was convinced that "in some ways" his children understood his need to be away from home so much, "even though" it was "pretty hard on them." The children clearly missed their father, but they were never alone because, aside from Coretta, Daddy King and Alberta King, a number of aunts and uncles, and other members of the extended family were always there to fill in and to help meet their many physical, emotional, and material needs. The vital supportive role assumed by King, Jr.'s and Coretta's extended family members in this case was immeasurable, even as some of them constantly urged King, Jr. to get out of the movement. Many of the conversations King, Jr. had with his father, after the two had quietly retreated to the pastor's study at Atlanta's Ebenezer Baptist Church, were about Yoki, Marty, Dexter, and Bunny. Though Coretta "wanted to go to jail" or to participate more actively in other kinds of civil rights activities at times, King, Jr. never wanted her to do so "while the children were so young." As the threats against his life mounted, he was especially concerned about

---

160. King, *My Life with Martin Luther King, Jr.*, 4, 175–76, 195–96, 227–28, 256, and 303; "Martin Luther King, Jr.: A Personal Portrait," a videotaped interview; Baldwin, *There is a Balm in Gilead*, 142 and 147–49; Simon, "To Her, Rev. King Was Simply Dad"; and Carson, ed., *The Autobiography of Martin Luther King, Jr.*, 146. King, like his father King, Sr., also believed that a preacher of the gospel is "called for life," and this necessarily meant that the families of those called had to make special sacrifices, including adjustments to their frequent absences. See King, *Daddy King*, 185.

his wife working with him in the more dangerous areas of the South, where white supremacist attitudes and structures were pervasive, and where circumstances could have easily led to his assassination. Also, for the protection and well-being of their children, the couple agreed never to travel by airplane together, except in rare and "unusual circumstances," and King, Jr., from the time of the Montgomery bus protest, always insured "himself heavily" when flying.[161] But in the minds of children, none of this would have fully explained a father's need to be away from home so much. King, Jr.'s frequent absences, in conjunction with his attitude toward money and decision not to own a lot of material things, must have always been perplexing to his children.[162]

Although King, Jr. was at home only about ten percent of the time, especially after he received the Nobel Peace Prize in December 1964, his wife and children were almost always on his mind. He was not so consumed by his public mission and goals that he became totally oblivious to the equally compelling demands of his private life and relationships. He occasionally spoke to his children by phone and looked forward to those times when they could talk, play, eat, and sing together. "He wanted so badly to share with the children more," Coretta declared, "and he made sure that the time he spent with them was *quality time.*" "He wanted to be like his father," she added, "always by his children's side." This is actually what King, Jr. appreciated most

---

161. "Martin Luther King, Jr.: A Personal Portrait," a videotaped interview; Baldwin Interview with Lee (9 July 1986); King, *My Life with Martin Luther King, Jr.,* 4 and 176; Baldwin, *There is a Balm in Gilead,* 140, 147, and 149–51; McDonald, *Secretary to a King,* 77; and King, *Daddy King,* 169. Dorothy Cotton recalled that en route to Oslo, Norway to receive the Nobel Peace Prize, King and his wife rode on separate planes as "a safety measure." See Cotton, *If Your Back's Not Bent,* 12–13 and 233. King insured himself to the tune of $50,000 when "flying north and south" and $100,000 on east and west flights, when he has to cross over the mountains." "His wife and children, he says, deserve to be well taken care of." See Reddick, *Crusader without Violence,* 5.

162. King's attitude toward the idolatry of money has been well-established in this and other sources. See Reddick, *Crusader without Violence,* 5, 7, and 179; Vaughn and Wills, *Reflections on Our Pastor,* 154–55; Garrow, *Bearing the Cross,* 421; and Washington, ed., *A Testament of Hope,* 371. King understood "that people who have been oppressed often have the need to live luxuriously as a sort of compensation," or what some sociologists would call "conspicuous consumption," and he wanted to avoid this tendency while hoping that his self-sacrificial devotion would become a standard for others in the struggle. See King, *My Life with Martin Luther King, Jr.,* 59, 148, and 162–63; Baldwin, *There is a Balm in Gilead,* 53–54; Martin Luther King, Jr., "Speech at a Mass Meeting," unpublished version, Selma, Alabama (16 February 1968), King Center Library and Archives, 8; and King, *Where Do We Go from Here?,* 132.

in the realm of the private, because he always had the feeling that he would not live very long.[163] Thus, he insisted on creating some self-distance from the public square from time to time for the sake of his children.

When King, Jr. "was home it was something special," Coretta recalled, for "he was wonderful with his children, and they adored him." Occasionally, when Coretta was out shopping, at the hairdresser, meeting with female friends, or attending some church function, her husband would baby-sit, and he and the children would have "a wild time together," with them roughhousing and jumping on top of him in the bed. "I might come into my bedroom and find all our family on top of him," said Coretta. "I must admit that I occasionally got cross about things being thrown helter-skelter in the room and the house almost being dismantled, but Martin would appear to be so surprised at my annoyance, which always completely disarmed me." There were many occasions on which the King home was literally turned into a playground or a basketball court. "Occasionally, on rainy days, when Martin was in town and happened to be at home," Coretta remembered, "you could hear me saying over and over, 'Martin, please don't play ball in the house'." On sunny days, King, Jr. took time to teach his children how to swim and ride a bike. At other times, he took them to playgrounds and amusement parks, and enjoyed with them the swings, rides, games, and other forms of entertainment. When Funtown in Atlanta "quietly desegregated" in 1963, he and his children went and "had a glorious time," as they "went on all the rides." King, Jr. was described as "boyishly happy" on that occasion.[164]

King, Jr. invented a number of games for the amusement of his children and to satisfy his own need for play. One was called "the

163. Works that claim that King somehow "betrayed" or "committed a grave disservice" to his family need to study and devote more attention to the systemic white supremacy that made his frequent absences, struggles, and sacrifices necessary. See King, *My Life with Martin Luther King, Jr.*, 232, 243, 247, 257, 280, 284, 290, 292, and 301; Coretta Scott King, "Address at the National Conference on Civil Rights," Nashville, Tennessee (5 April 1986); Baldwin, *There is a Balm in Gilead*, 135–36; and Chappell, *Waking from the Dream*, 160.
164. King, *My Life with Martin Luther King, Jr.*, 78, 198, and 200; Simon, "To Her, Rev. King was Simply Dad"; King and Marie, *Embracing Your Power in 30 Days*, 14; and Baldwin, *There is a Balm in Gilead*, 136–37.

refrigerator game," which King, Jr. came up with when his daughter Yoki was still quite young. King, Jr. would sit Yoki on top of the refrigerator and "tell her to jump," and he would then "catch her in his arms." The game was also played with Marty, Dexter, and Bunny, and they all literally enjoyed it. Recalling such playful moments, Yoki later described her father as "such a fun-loving person" who tended to "cut up" or to "let his hair down when he was with us." "He'd get down on the floor and rock with us and roll around, much to the concern of my mother, who was always afraid we'd break something," she recounted. Coretta would often intervene, telling her husband to "Stop, stop!" "And then we'd stop for a few minutes until she left and then he'd roll around with us again," Yoki reported. "He was as much a kid at heart as we were."[165] King, Jr.'s "kissing game" with his youngest child Bunny revealed both his incredibly playful tendencies and his genuine "humanness" in ways that were only known to his family and closest associates at that time. As soon as King, Jr. arrived at home from one of his many trips, "Bunny would run and swing into his arms." Coretta described King, Jr.'s response and the rest of the game in these terms:

He would stoop to lift her up and say, "Give me some good old sugar." With her arms around his neck, she would smack him on the mouth. He had previously taught her where the sugar spot was for each person in the family. He would then say, "I bet you don't know where Yoki's sugar is!" She would smack him on the right side of his mouth. "Where is Dexter's sugar?" Then she kissed him on the right cheek. Next he would say, "I know you don't know where Marty's sugar is!" She would quickly kiss him on the forehead. "I just know you've forgotten where Mommy's sugar is!" She would kiss him in the center of his mouth. Finally, he would say, "And Bunny doesn't have any sugar." "Yes, I do." And with a loud smack, she would kiss him on the right cheek. When she found all of the designated sugar spots, which she always did quickly, the game ended.[166]

165. King, *My Life with Martin Luther King, Jr.*, 78, 198, and 200–201; "'I Remember Martin,'" 38; and King, "Address at the National Conference on Civil Rights" (5 April 1986). For another interesting account of King's roughhousing games with his children, see Vivian, *Coretta*, 59; and Simon, "To Her, Rev. King was Simply Dad."

166. King, Jr.'s son Dexter reported that he and all of his siblings, and not just Bernice, participated in "the Kissing Game." See King, *My Life with Martin Luther King, Jr.*, 200–201; Baldwin, *There is a Balm in Gilead*, 137–38; King, *Growing Up King*, 22; Baldwin Interview with Lee (9 July 1986); and Vivian, *Coretta*, 59.

King, Jr.'s love for all four of his children ran deep and was unquestionable for those who knew the family well, but Bunny touched him in a special way and was seemingly a spoiled child by any standard. According to Coretta, "Martin never could resist Bernice's wishes," for "she was the greatest charmer of them all, full of affection and joyful spirit and an extra large dose of her father's ability to persuade people." King, Jr. often said that he wished he could have frozen the child just the way she was—"so cute, so full of innocence and sweetness." Coretta delighted in watching the two together, "playing their games" and "loving each other." She "would have the most painful consciousness of how much Bernice," being the youngest of the four children, "needed her daddy," and she prayed fervently "that nothing would happen" to her husband.[167]

It was a longing for a certain kind of companionship that pulled King, Jr. in the direction of his children. He was able to enter his children's world of laughter and play in which the vive was youthful, exciting, and energetic, and where there was a basic civility about life. Spending time with his children provided opportunities for King, Jr. to be playful, and this added tenderness, warmth, and positive emotions to their relationship while also deepening the intimacy and forging stronger bonds of love and respect between him and them. Playing with his children also afforded opportunities for both teaching and learning about life and human obligations toward other humans, and it brought much-needed relaxation, a reduction in stress levels, and some light into what were too often chaos and gloom in his own world. "I knew that, being the kind of man he was, Martin needed us," Coretta declared, referring to the importance of the children and her self in King, Jr.'s life. "He functioned better with a wife and children," she continued, "because he needed the warmth we gave him, and from the standpoint of the Cause, having us gave him a kind of humanness which brought him closer to the mass of the people."[168] In appreciation

---

167. King, *My Life with Martin Luther King, Jr.*, 263 and 267; King, "Address at the National Conference on Civil Rights" (5 April 1986); Baldwin, *There is a Balm in Gilead*, 134, 137–38, 141, 147, and 149; Baldwin Interview with Lee (9 July 1986); Vivian, *Coretta*, 59; "'I Remember Martin,'" 38; and Farris, *Through It All*, 91.

for their enduring love and support, King, Jr. dedicated his book, *Why We Can't Wait* (1963), "To my children—Yolanda, Martin III, Dexter, Bernice—for whom I dream that one day soon they will no longer be judged by the color of their skin but by the content of their character."[169]

Always concerned about his children's growth and well-being from an educational, spiritual, moral, emotional, and economic standpoint, King, Jr., aside from the care-free and playful attitude and approach, had other ways of teaching and instilling values in his children. Yolanda remembered "the simple and honest way" in which her father told "me and my older brother about the birds and the bees." King, Jr. spent "a few quiet evenings" telling his children stories and reading to them "from their favorite books." He also shared with them lessons and values to which he had been exposed as a child. The children were given a sense of the moral order and of religious principles, and of the intrinsic sacredness of their own personhood and that of other humans as well. They were taught that all people share a common humanity, that hatred stemmed from ignorance, that love is the most powerful and durable force in the universe, how to live their most lofty and cherished dreams, that the ethical life is the best life, that freedom always has a price, that they should always strive for excellence in their chosen fields of endeavor, that the quality of life exists not in how long one lives but how well one lives, and other empowering lessons. King, Jr. and Coretta also repeatedly reminded their children of the significance of taking seriously the more mundane concerns of daily life, such as respecting the wishes of their parents and teachers, getting up early every morning, studying and being on time for school, doing household chores, and saving and sharing with others.[170] One of

---

168. King, *My Life with Martin Luther King, Jr.*, 165; and King, "Address at the National Conference on Civil Rights" (5 April 1986).

169. Martin Luther King, Jr., *Why We Can't Wait* (New York: The New American Library, Inc., 1963), dedication page; Baldwin, *There is a Balm in Gilead*, 148–49; and Baldwin Interview with Lee (9 July 1986).

170. King, *My Life with Martin Luther King, Jr.*, 195–97, 201, 256, 260, 263, and 312; Simon, "To Her, Rev. King was Simply Dad"; and Baldwin, *There is a Balm in Gilead*, 140–41. Abundant evidence of King's impact on the lives and value systems of his children can be found in sources such as Bernice A. King, *Hard Questions, Heart Answers: Speeches and Sermons* (New York: Broadway Books, 1996), 3–175;

the most interesting lessons were imparted through what King, Jr. and Coretta called the children's "sacrificial Christmas," during which Yoki, Marty, Dexter, and Bunny would "accept just one gift" so the family could also share with poor children and families.[171]

Although King, Jr. was not a heavy-handed disciplinarian like his father, he was known on rare occasions to spank his children when they disobeyed his teachings and wishes, engaged in mischief, or misbehaved in other ways. On one occasion, he spanked Yoki and Marty for pouring water in his ear while he slept, an experience the children never forgot.[172] On another occasion, when Yolanda and Dexter plotted to steal their father's cigarettes, King, Jr. "hit the ceiling when they were not where he had left them." Although he did not spank the children, the look on his face was enough of a lesson for them. "I think that was the first time, probably," Dexter wrote, "all of us saw him truly upset, where he was obviously angry." King, Jr.'s hope was that his children would grow up to be thoughtful, disciplined, prosperous, trustworthy, and respectable human beings, and his preference was to always talk to and with his children about matters ranging from sex to education to how they should plan for their futures.[173] Remembering those times with his daddy, Dexter would later comment:

This and other lessons stuck with me. He was very much a talker, he would talk about subjects with us, was intimate in his feelings, in terms of our being able to understand the subject and his feelings. You felt like his equal, almost, like he was bringing you up in the world to his level, not like he was coming down to you. He was soothing to listen to, authoritative

King, *Growing Up King*, 7–308; King and Marie, *Embracing Your Power in 30 Days*, 14, 18–19, 22, 32, 50, 92, 94, 98, 108, 122, and 149; Yolanda King and Elodia Tate, *Open My Eyes, Open My Soul: Celebrating Our Common Humanity* (New York: McGraw-Hill, 2004), 13–22; Lynn Norment, "The King Family: Keepers of the Dream," *Ebony*, Vol. XLII, no. 3 (January, 1987), 25–26, 28, 30, 32, and 34; and Lynn Norment, "New Generation of Kings Take Over," *Ebony*, Vol. L, no. 3 (January, 1995), 25–26, 28, 30, 32, and 34.

171. Vivian, *Coretta*, 58; Baldwin Interview with Lee (9 July 1986); and King, "Address at the National Conference on Civil Rights" (5 April 1986).

172. In one account, Yolanda recounted that this incident involved her and her brother Marty, and in another she said that it involved "My sister and I." Even so, there is no reason to doubt the validity of the account. See Baldwin Interview with Lee (9 July 1986); King, *Daddy King*, 130; Farris, *Through It All*, 31; Simon, "To Her, Rev. King was Simply Dad"; and Reddick, *Crusader without Violence*, 5.

173. King, *Growing Up King*, 37–38.

you knew, because he was Daddy, but also deliberate, precise; when he spoke, you listened.[174]

Perhaps King, Jr.'s greatest lessons for his children came through the example he set as a leader in the struggle for justice, equal opportunity, human dignity, and peace. He not only talked to Yoki, Marty, Dexter, and Bunny about the civil rights movement, he also shared with them its values through the prism of stories and songs, and even allowed them all to march with him at one time or another for the cause.[175] The idea was that the children should also have some exposure to and involvement in the daily, practical realities of the human struggle, and that they should always understand that the goal of the movement was the creation of the beloved community. This is why King, Jr. taught his children to use the titles of "Uncle" and "Aunt" when referring not only to blood kin, but to movement activists such as Andrew Young, Ralph Abernathy, Harry Belafonte, and Dorothy Cotton, all of whom were very close to King, Jr.[176] The kids' earliest conception of community, then, occurred in the context of that kind of extended familial arrangement.

Toward the end of his life, King, Jr. was torn more and more between his pressing need to spend more time with family and his commitments to a social movement that was expanding daily. "I'm tired of all this traveling I have to do," he stated emphatically in August, 1967, only months before his death. "I'm killing myself and killing my health, and am always away from my children and my family." "I'm tired now," said he, a short time later. "I've been in this thing thirteen years now and I'm really tired."[177] Reports that King, Jr. was increasingly plagued by self-doubts, deeply depressed, and prone to excessive drink are apparently exaggerated, but it was obvious that he felt that he needed a break from all of the drama and turmoil that

---

174. Ibid., 36. One might compare Dexter's image with that projected of King by his daughter Yolanda. See "'I Remember Martin,'" 38.
175. King, *My Life with Martin Luther King, Jr.*, 195–98, 255–57, 263–64, 278, and 283; and Baldwin, *There is a Balm in Gilead*, 148.
176. King, *Growing Up King*, 23 and 52–53; and McDonald, *Secretary to a King*, 37.
177. Quoted in Lischer, *The Preacher King*, 167; and Garrow, *Bearing the Cross*, 577.

surrounded his days, and that kept him from living up to his fullest potential as a husband and father.[178]

King, Jr.'s attitude toward and dealings with his wife and children further highlighted the ways in which his private life conflicted with his public persona, and yet, he understood that both a public life and a private life were essential for being human and living well in his time. His activities and involvements in the public sphere on the one hand and his longing for self-distance and solitude on the other often divided his loyalties and pulled him in different directions, but because King, Jr.'s life and career were aimed at both his own personal liberation and empowerment and the liberation and empowerment of others, he was able, at least on some levels, to bridge those private and public worlds.[179] The next chapter, which discusses King, Jr.'s habits as they relate to cooking, food, and eating, offers additional insights into how this bridging process actually occurred.

178. Carson and Holloran, eds., *A Knock at Midnight*, 164; and Martin Luther King, Jr., "Ingratitude," unpublished version of sermon (18 June 1967), King Center Library and Archives, 9. Dora McDonald recalled those times when King was frustrated, disappointed, and even depressed, and how he was able to ease himself out of such bad moods "by the sheer force of plunging into the work at hand." See McDonald, *Secretary to a King*, 29, 55–56, 71, 75–76, 82–83, 97–99, 101–2, and 104.

179. These insights developed out of my many conversations with Susan Wiltshire, and also out of my reading of Wiltshire, *Public & Private in Vergil's Aeneid*, 3–143.

3

"Let Us Break Bread Together": Martin Luther King, Jr., Southern Cooking, and the Socio-Cultural Significance of Food and Eating

Let us break bread together on our knees;
Let us break bread together on our knees.
When I fall on my knees,
With my face to the rising sun,
O Lord, have mercy on me.
    –Negro Spiritual[1]

It may be true that man cannot live by bread alone, but the mere fact that Jesus added the "alone" means that man cannot live without bread.
    –Martin Luther King, Jr.[2]

---

1. Christa K. Dixon, *Negro Spirituals from Bible to Folksong* (Philadelphia: Fortress Press, 1976), 61; and *Songs of Zion: Supplemental Worship Resources 12* (Nashville: Abingdon Press, 1981), 88.
2. Martin Luther King, Jr., *The Measure of a Man* (Philadelphia: Fortress Press, 1988; originally published in 1959), 14; and Martin Luther King, Jr., "Why a Movement," unpublished version of a speech (28 November 1967), Library and Archives of The Martin Luther King, Jr. Center for Nonviolent Social Change, Inc., Atlanta, Georgia, 1.

Martin Luther King, Jr. was steeped in the values and traditions of what has been called "a food-conscious culture," or a culture known for its long, rich, and varied food history.[3] Southern cooking, food, and eating figured prominently in the narrative whole of his life, and these essentials provide yet another angle from which to examine his basic "humanness." King, Jr.'s entire life unfolded in a social climate and culture in which the principal staples of southern cuisine and the consumption of large quantities of soul food were intimately linked to family reunions, weddings, funerals, revivals and other church activities, and to more informal gatherings with relatives, friends, visitors, and neighbors. Food and eating had long assumed ritualistic value and were very much a part of the religious heritage of black folk in the South, as evidenced by the slaves' practice of putting food on the graves of ancestors, by the innumerable pictorial references to "that land overflowing with milk and honey" in folk sermons, and by spirituals such as "Let Us Break Bread Together," "Dwelling in Beulah Land," and "I'm Gonna Sit at the Welcome Table One of these Days."[4]

This chapter explores King, Jr.'s lifelong attitude toward southern culinary customs, foods, and eating, particularly as it progressed from his childhood through his years as a seminary and graduate student, pastor, civil rights leader, and world figure. Much consideration is given to King, Jr.'s eating habits as they developed in the context of family and church life, to lessons he learned at mealtime around the family table, to his own very limited but meaningful experiences as a cook during his years as a student in the northeast, and to how he ultimately understood cooking, food, and eating in relation to the movement, life, and the more general quest for human community. What all of this reveals about King the private man and King the public figure is equally important in this chapter.

---

3. John Egerton, *Southern Food: At Home, on the Road, in History* (New York: Alfred A. Knopf, Inc., 1987), 35.
4. Lewis V. Baldwin, *There is a Balm in Gilead: The Cultural Roots of Martin Luther King, Jr.* (Minneapolis: Fortress Press, 1991), 34–35.

A. Sitting at the Welcome Table:
Food, Faith, Family, Friends, and Fun

The Atlanta in which Martin Luther King, Jr. was born and raised was a city brimming with southern charm, and perhaps more importantly, known for its mouth-watering selections of delicious, home-cooked food. In the 1920s and 30s, when King, Jr. was a small child, the strikingly picturesque ways of life in Atlanta's black community could not have been more evident, as restaurants and homes emitted the sharp smell of fried fish and barbecued ribs, fruits and vegetables were temptingly displayed in parking lots and on street corners, and overly zealous street preachers proclaimed the coming judgment while peddling food and drink along with religious objects and tracts. Food and eating were a mainstay in the daily lives of the folk. But there was also another side to life in Atlanta and the South as a whole that caught King's Jr.'s attention before he was old enough to enroll in elementary school, and that was the economic crises resulting from the Great Depression. "I was much too young to remember the beginning of this depression," wrote King, Jr. at age twenty-one, "but I do recall how I questioned my parents about the numerous people standing in breadlines when I was about five years of age." The young man went on to assert that "I can see the effects of this early childhood experience on my present anti-capitalistic feelings."[5] That being the case, it is also not unreasonable to conclude that what King, Jr. witnessed during the Depression led to, perhaps, his earliest understanding of the relationship of culinary practices, food, and eating to the meaning and quality of human life.

The Kings's neighborhood on Auburn Avenue in Atlanta was located up the hill from a poor black ghetto, where blacks "lived squalidly" in "ramshackle wooden shanties" and "crowded rooming houses" marked

5. *Atlanta: A City of the Modern South*, compiled by The Works of the Writer's Program of The Work Projects Administration in the State of Georgia (New York: Smith and Durrell, 1942), 5; A Private Interview with Philip Lenud, Vanderbilt Divinity School, Nashville, Tennessee (7 April 1987); Clayborne Carson, et. al., eds., *The Papers of Martin Luther King, Jr., Volume I: Called to Serve, January 1929-June 1951* (Berkeley: University of California Press, 1992), 359; and Baldwin, *There is a Balm in Gilead*, 19-20.

by the noisy "cries of little ragged brown children," but "the family suffered no privation even in the worst years of the Depression."[6] King, Jr., most commonly called M.L., had three meals a day and dined sufficiently throughout the Depression years, and was always taught to offer thanks to God before eating. King, Sr. boasted that "I'd become a prosperous young pastor, a husband and father whose family had never lived in a rented house or driven a car on which a payment was ever made late." "We dressed well, we ate well, we enjoyed great respect among the people of our community," the elder King declared.[7] Daddy King was serving as pastor of a number of small churches in rural Georgia when the stock market crashed in October 1929, nine months after King, Jr. was born, and the members were generous despite the hardships they themselves faced. "When things grew worse for my congregations," Daddy King reported, "they'd do like good country people do and bring food to services to share with the preacher" and his family.[8] When King, Sr. succeeded his father-in-law and King, Jr.'s maternal grandfather A. D. Williams as the pastor of Atlanta's Ebenezer Baptist Church in 1931, that same spirit of generosity found expression. Such actions on the part of church folk must have impacted little King, Jr. in profound ways, for he, even as a child, sensed the need for black unity, especially in a region in which blacks were not only heavily exploited economically on a daily basis, but also subjected to the worst in terms of verbal insults and physical abuse.[9]

Among King, Jr.'s favorite foods as a child, according to his mother, Alberta, were chicken, ice cream, and chocolate cake. The youngster

6. *Atlanta: A City of the Modern South*, 5; David J. Garrow, *Bearing the Cross: Martin Luther King, Jr., and the Southern Christian Leadership Conference* (New York: William Morrow and Company, Inc., 1986), 33; and Baldwin, *There is a Balm in Gilead*, 19 and 105.

7. Martin Luther King, Sr., *Daddy King: An Autobiography*, with Clayton Riley (New York: William Morrow and Company, Inc., 1980), 98; Carson, et. al., eds., *King Papers*, I, 360; Clayborne Carson, ed., *The Autobiography of Martin Luther King, Jr.* (New York: Warner Books, Inc., 1998), 5; James Baldwin, "The Dangerous Road before Martin Luther King, Jr.," *Harper's Magazine* (February, 1961), 37; Baldwin Interview with Lenud (7 April 1987); A Private Interview with Ralph D. Abernathy, West Hunter Baptist Church, Atlanta, Georgia (17 March 1987); and Baldwin, *There is a Balm in Gilead*, 105.

8. King, *Daddy King*, 89.

9. Carson, et. al., eds., *King Papers*, I, 121; and Baldwin, *There is a Balm in Gilead*, 30–31.

also loved watermelon and very early developed a special taste for succulent fried chicken, ham, black-eyed peas, and other highly seasoned soul foods which were most common in the South among blacks and also many whites in that period.[10] King, Jr. always looked forward to eating his mother's delicious tea cakes on Saturday mornings, which were routinely shared with other kids in the neighborhood,[11] and his maternal grandmother, Jennie C. Parks Williams, and great aunt, Ida Worthem, were also among his favorite cooks. "Cooking and the loving preparation of family meals were a big part of" Big Mama Jennie's life, especially on Sundays, and King, Jr. recounted the times when he and his siblings, Christine and A. D., would run around Auburn Avenue telling their playmates about the great biscuits prepared by their grandmother.[12] King, Jr.'s own eagerness to express his feelings about his favorite foods actually put him in a difficult situation on one occasion, when he was only five years old. The boy was still too young for school but, being so close to his sister Christine and having "always competed with" her "in everything," "begged" his mother Alberta "to let him go along." Alberta "finally relented" and King, Jr. was allowed to go and enroll, but his "initial stint in grade school" ended when the teacher overheard him "boasting to some of the other kids about his birthday cake and the

10. Alberta King, "Dr. Martin Luther King, Jr.: Birth to Twelve Years Old by His Mother," a recording, Ebenezer Baptist Church, Atlanta, Georgia (18 January 1973), King Center Library and Archives; Baldwin Interview with Lenud (7 April 1987); Frederick L. Downing, *To See the Promised Land: The Faith Pilgrimage of Martin Luther King, Jr.* (Macon, GA: Mercer University Press, 1986), 42 and 126; and Stephen B. Oates, *Let the Trumpet Sound: The Life of Martin Luther King, Jr.* (New York: Harper & Row, Publishers, 1982), 4. Daddy King also loved fried chicken, which was typical of black preachers in the South, who often joked about being hooked on "the gospel bird." See Christine King Farris, *Through It All: Reflections on My Life, My Family, and My Faith* (New York: Atria Books, 2009), 164.
11. Baldwin Interview with Lenud (7 April 1987). Mrs. Alberta King continued to share her tea cakes with neighborhood kids long after her own children had become adults and moved on. David Leon Baldwin, the brother of this author, witnessed this when he served as a math tutor for children at the Community of Hope Lutheran Church, a storefront church, off Wellington Avenue in Atlanta, Georgia in 1973. He remembers Mrs. King driving over in a white Chevrolet Impala on Wednesdays with tea cakes for the kids, who always waited eagerly for the treat. David and I have talked about this on numerous occasions, especially during our many conversations about Martin Luther King, Jr., his family, and his eating habits. A Telephone Interview with David L. Baldwin (17 April 2015).
12. Farris, *Through It All*, 5 and 11; Martin Luther King, Jr., "Prelude to Tomorrow," unpublished version of an address, SCLC's Operation Breadbasket Meeting, Chicago, Illinois (6 January 1968), King Center Library and Archives, 4–5; Baldwin Interview with Lenud (7 April 1987); and Baldwin, *There is a Balm in Gilead*, 109.

121

'five big candles on it'." The child's "true age was confirmed" and "he was sent home until he reached the required age" of six.[13]

Apparently, the problem for King, Jr. during those very early years was not consuming the large helpings of food put on his plate, but, rather, the fact that he, Christine, and A. D. were required to do the dishes after meals. "Like most children," Christine recalled, "M. L. never liked doing household chores. He was forever able to come up with excuses for why he was unable to do the dishes when it was his turn." "Most often," Christine added, "he simply claimed he had to use the bathroom when it came his time to clean the kitchen."[14] "Kitchen duty" was also most often "the prescribed punishment" when King, Jr. and his siblings disobeyed Daddy King or failed to return home by his curfew, as was the case one night when the trio returned home from a party much too late. To avoid helping with the kitchen work, King, Jr. "went into a bathroom" and A. D. fell "asleep on the ironing board." Daddy King appeared suddenly and quietly to discover his sons goofing-off, and he furiously spanked A. D. Hearing "the commotion," King, Jr. "started moving around very noisily—flushing the toilet, turning on every faucet he could find, anything he could do to make noise to prove he was cleaning."[15]

Mealtimes in the King home always brought members of the extended family together at the dining room table, especially on Sundays. Because Sundays were so busy in the King household, the food was usually cooked the night before, and on "those late Saturday nights," after other family members "had gone to bed," King, Jr., who appreciated the magic that routinely happened in the kitchens of southern black women, "would stay up and talk to his mother as she prepared those meals for Sunday."[16] Apparently, "sit-down dinners were not optional" but "*mandatory*." They were a vital part of the

13. Farris, *Through It All*, 26–27; and Christine King Farris, "The Young Martin: From Childhood through College," *Ebony*, Vol. XLI, no. 3 (January, 1986), 57.
14. Farris, "The Young Martin," 56.
15. Farris, *Through It All*, 30–33. Such actions were obviously inconsistent with the image of King, Jr. as a child "who seemed to care about the approval of his parents." See King, "Dr. Martin Luther King, Jr.: Birth to Twelve Years Old"; and Downing, *To See the Promised Land*, 43.
16. King, "Dr. Martin Luther King, Jr.: Birth to Twelve Years Old"; and Downing, *To See the Promised Land*, 44.

family's binding credo. Daddy King always "sat at the head of the table," Alberta at the opposite end facing him, with Big Mama Jennie, Aunt Ida, and Uncle Joel to his left, and King, Jr. and his siblings to his right. King, Jr. vividly remembered being "required to learn Scriptural verses for recitation at evening meals."[17] During such times, and especially during family reunions, the table overflowed "with fresh greens from the garden, baked macaroni and cheese, fried chicken, glazed ham, smothered pork chops, corn on the cob," and "cakes and pies, bread pudding, and various cobblers,"[18] along with tea, lemonade, water, soft drinks, or milk, and the eating and drinking always took on deep social and cultural qualities.[19] In other words, mealtimes allowed for a special dose of both socialization and acculturation, as familial bonds were strengthened and an already stable family life reinforced. The meals were always filled with a lot of "laughter and joy" and King, Jr., Christine, and A. D. were allowed to fully express themselves, but they were also taught "important lessons." The children were taught their history as "descendants of African slaves," that Jim Crow was "not in keeping" with their "social and religious beliefs," that they "were as good as anybody," and that they should "speak out against hatred and bigotry" and "stand up for what was right."[20] Interestingly enough, King, Jr.'s painful loss of his two white playmates at age six, highlighted earlier in Chapter 1, was actually "discussed at the dinner table," and "for the first time," the child "was made aware of the existence of a race problem."[21] Such experiences underscored the significance of the

---

17. Farris, *Through It All*, 16; Farris, "The Young Martin," 56–57; and Zelia S. Evans and J. T. Alexander, eds., *The Dexter Avenue Baptist Church, 1877-1977* (Montgomery: Dexter Avenue Baptist Church, 1978), 69.
18. Farris, *Through It All*, 11 and 213–14.
19. There is evidence that Daddy King and Alberta King attached much importance to family reunions. See "Rev. and Mrs. King Return to Atlanta," *Atlanta Daily World*, Atlanta, Georgia (7 July 1948), 3; and Farris, *Through It All*, 16–19.
20. This type of socialization within the realm of any culture is always a very powerful phenomenon. See Farris, *Through It All*, 16–17; Farris, "The Young Martin," 56; and Carson et al., eds., *King Papers*, I, 362.
21. As noted in Chapter one, this issue was also addressed at length as King, Jr. sat on his mother Alberta's lap. See Carson, et al., eds., *King Papers*, I, 362; King, *Daddy King*, 130; Martin Luther King, Jr., *Stride toward Freedom: The Montgomery Story* (New York: Harper & Row, Publishers, 1958), 19; Carson, ed., *The Autobiography of Martin Luther King, Jr.*, 3 and 7; Farris, *Through It All*, 25; Farris, "The Young Martin," 57; and "Face to Face: Dr. Martin Luther King, Jr. and John Freeman," U.

King family as both an educational agency and a vital socio-cultural phenomenon.

There were other lessons that were not so much of a political nature, but nonetheless important for King, Jr. and his sister and brother. They were taught "respect" for their "elders," the importance of sharing with others, the need "to stand upright" in "the presence of others," "to look people directly in the eye" when they "spoke to them," to always "dress properly," and to attach the highest value to education. "We would talk about our day at school and the night's homework assignment, right there at the dinner table," Christine recalled. "Math and English lessons had to be recited," "grammar corrections were made," and the proper "use of the English language" discussed.[22] Food and eating had symbolic meanings associated with love, comfort, and family unity, which must have been most evident at those times to King, Jr., who was known to be "somewhat precocious" and always "curious" about virtually everything that occurred around and about him.[23]

Members of Ebenezer Baptist Church and friends and neighbors from the larger black community of Atlanta and surrounding areas frequently found seats around the table at the King's home, which, on some Sundays after worship services and on holidays, literally turned into a temporary dining hall or restaurant. Among the most "frequent visitors" were also Baptist preachers such as Melvin Watson of Atlanta and Sandy Ray of Brooklyn, New York's Cornerstone Baptist Church, a friend of Daddy King who often spoke at Ebenezer. The guests always "contributed to the stimulating atmosphere and conversation as well."[24] Eating at such times was not simply about black folk forging physical links to a particular place or each other, or the consumption of food and drink to sustain life and to fulfill the body's fundamental needs for growth, development, and activity. These were occasions

K. (London?), recorded for transmission and aired (29 October 1961), King Center Library and Archives, 2–3.

22. Farris, *Through It All*, 17–18 and 24; and Farris, "The Young Martin," 56.

23. Carson, et al., eds., *King Papers*, I, 359; King, *Daddy King*, 130; and Carson, ed., *The Autobiography of Martin Luther King, Jr.*, 2.

24. Farris, *Through It All*, 18–19.

for feasting, spiritual revival and celebration, sharing and giving, and historical remembrance, and the prayers, Bible readings, and singing mingled easily with the storytelling, good humor, laughter, spirited greetings, and home-style cooking.[25] Food and eating heightened the spirit of community and racial solidarity. The sharing of food allowed the Kings and their guests to more fully participate in community life. They undoubtedly shared with each other stories of their hardships under Jim Crow, found inspiration in communion with each other, celebrated their common joy in God's acceptance of them, and gave voice to their unwavering faith in God's power to deliver. The gathering of relatives and friends without the spreading of a feast of southern food and drink was unimaginable for the Kings in those times. King, Jr. always delighted in the pleasures of such occasions as a child, and the sociocultural significance of food and eating was central to his identity and also to his earliest sense of place and of human community.[26]

The image of the Ebenezer Baptist Church was equally significant in the shaping of King, Jr.'s earliest understanding of cooking, food, and eating as not only a social activity and a cultural experience, but also as something quite sacred. The large, elaborately prepared meals were a common feature at Ebenezer during revivals, church anniversaries, picnics, fund-raising drives, and other church-related events,[27] and the female members, including King, Jr.'s mother, maternal grandmother, and great aunt, always undertook the burdensome task of preparing the large quantities of soul food. Even before King, Jr. was born, his father King, Sr. associated Ebenezer with a "sense of family" and with "plenty of good food among very warm, affectionate people." In the 1920s and 30s, as so many suffered the effects of the great economic downturn, Ebenezer "poured money back into the community to make food available to the hungry."[28] These people were spiritually

---

25. Farris, "The Young Martin," 56; and Downing, *To See the Promised Land*, 44–45.
26. Farris, "The Young Martin," 56–58; Farris, *Through It All*, 11 and 16–19; King, *Daddy King*, 71 and 89; and Baldwin, *There is a Balm in Gilead*, 34–35.
27. King, *Daddy King*, 71 and 89; and Baldwin Interview with Lenud (7 April 1987).
28. King, *Daddy King*, 71 and 89. The name "Ebenezer," according to Daddy King, was taken from the Bible, and specifically Samuel 7:12, and it means "stone of help." See Murray M. Silver, *Daddy King*

connected to food because they saw it as a gift from God, they prayed for and sang about it, for they knew that so many across the South, and indeed, throughout America had no sense of what would be the source of their next meal. Food and eating in this environment and context was also identified with a zest for life and living, despite the forces that consistently threatened black existence. This was the church culture to which King, Jr. was exposed in his childhood years. Associated with Ebenezer from the time he was born, he grew up knowing the congregation's best cooks and claiming his share of the variety of delicious dishes served in the fellowship hall in the basement of the church. King, Jr. had this and much more in mind when he spoke of the church as "a second home for me."[29]

When King, Jr. reached his teens, he had already become known for his hearty appetite, especially for southern cooking. Whenever Alberta King missed her son "from the house and yard" on Auburn Avenue, she knew to look for him down at the home of his friend Alfonzo Johnson, whose "mother was an excellent cook and may have been responsible for Martin's fondness for collard greens and black-eyed peas."[30] Although he occasionally ate at his friends' homes and at black restaurants and other businesses that served soul food in Atlanta, he always had a preference for his mother's cooking. In the summer of 1944, King, Jr. took a job on a tobacco farm in Connecticut and ended up working in the kitchen, where there was "very good food,"[31] and as much as he wanted, but he still wrote his mother on at least one occasion, asking her to send some of her fried chicken and rolls.[32] The fact that King, Jr. had also eaten at some of the "finest" restaurants

& Me: Memories of the Forgotten Father of the Civil Rights Movement (Savannah, GA: Continental Shelf Publishing, LLC, 2009), 25–26.

29. Carson, et al., eds., King Papers, I, 361; Carson, ed., The Autobiography of Martin Luther King, Jr., 6; Baldwin, There is a Balm in Gilead, 160–165; Lewis V. Baldwin, The Voice of Conscience: The Church in the Mind of Martin Luther King, Jr. (New York: Oxford University Press, 2010), 13–45; and Baldwin Interview with Lenud (7 April 1987).

30. L. D. Reddick, Crusader without Violence: A Biography of Martin Luther King, Jr. (New York: Harper & Brothers Publishers, 1959), 52–53. King, Jr. most certainly had this and other experiences in mind when he spoke of the black community of his childhood as "characterized with" a kind "of unsophisticated simplicity." See Carson, et al., eds., King Papers, I, 360.

31. King, Daddy King, 145; Farris, Through It All, 38; Farris, "The Young Martin," 58; and Carson, et al., King Papers, I, 111–17.

32. Carson, et al., eds., King Papers, I, 112 and 115–16; Farris, Through It All, 40; and Coretta Scott King,

in the City of Hartford, Connecticut at that time made his request all the more interesting. Even while pursuing his undergraduate degree at Morehouse College from 1944 to 1948, the youngster chose to live with his parents and not on campus,[33] partly because of what he had to look forward to in terms of the glorious variety of rich and tasty soul food and old-fashioned, family-style dining. King, Jr. moved to Chester, Pennsylvania in the fall of 1948 to begin what turned out to be six years of academic studies in the northeast, but, despite what life had to offer regarding culinary customs and food choices in that part of the country, the food of the black South remained his consuming passion.

B. Soul Kitchen: Cooking, Food, and Eating Beyond Dixie

Martin Luther King, Jr. was zealous about experiencing and understanding as much as possible about his new environment and circumstances in Chester. Although he was there to focus primarily on academic pursuits at Crozer Theological Seminary, a predominantly white institution, he wasted no time exploring the town, and especially the black community, in search of warm fellowship and the best places to satisfy his dietary habits and needs. One of King, Jr.'s black classmates "had an aunt who lived there and prepared the collard greens that both of them relished," but it was the historic Calvary Baptist Church in the black, blue-collar area of Chester, at which King, Jr. served as a Sunday School teacher and youth minister, that provided his primary connection to good cooking, delicious food, and delightful, genuine, and enduring companionship.[34] He and other black male students from Crozer "enjoyed frequent dinners" at the home of the

My Life with Martin Luther King, Jr. (New York: Henry Holt and Company, 1993; originally published in 1969), 82–83.
33. Carson, et al., eds., King Papers, I, 38; Baldwin Interview with Lenud (7 April 1987); and King, Daddy King, 139.
34. Calvary was the oldest black Baptist church in Chester, and King was called "a son of Calvary." See Glen Justice, "Remembering Mentor to a Generation of Young Black Preachers: Among His Interns was the Rev. Dr. Martin Luther King Jr.," Philly.Com, posted 7 August 1994, http://articles.philly.com/1994-08-07/news/25841616_1_oldest-black-church-senior-pastor-interns (19 May 2014), 2; David L. Lewis, King: A Critical Biography (New York: Praeger Publishers, 1970), 27; and The Centennial Yearbook of the Calvary Baptist Church, 1879-1979 (Chester, PA: Calvary Baptist Church, 1979), 25–26.

pastor, J. Pius Barbour, and his wife, Olee Littlejohn Barbour, and "the sumptuous home-cooked meals" of Mrs. Barbour, who hailed from Spartanburg, South Carolina, were always followed by a lot of joking, laughter, and "bull sessions" concerning religious topics.[35] Mrs. Barbour's "specialty was a steak simmered in a spicy brown sauce," and she recalled that King, Jr. "could eat more than any little man you ever saw in your life."[36] King, Jr. himself reported that Pastor Barbour's house "was like a second home to him,"[37] and he, at times, mentioned Mrs. Barbour's great dinners in letters to his mother Alberta. King, Jr. also noted that Pastor Barbour, who was from Texas, was "one of the single most influential forces in his life."[38] The Barbours would always remember King, Jr. as the youngster with the big heart, an inquisitive mind, a love for lofty and complicated ideas, a rare eagerness to engage in serious theological and philosophical debate, and a voracious appetite for southern home-cooked meals.

King, Jr. also found southern-style food in the homes of some of Calvary's members, who, like the folk he knew back home at Atlanta's Ebenezer Baptist Church, modeled the spirit of brotherly and sisterly love. These were primarily ordinary church-going women, such as Emma Anderson, Sara V. Richardson, and Mother Esther Talley, whose families had migrated from the South, and who approached the art of food preparation with the same sincerity, caring spirit, and sense of

---

35. Some sources refer to "the 'soul food' relief of Mrs. Olee Barbour," and describe her dinners as "feasts of some renown." See *The Centennial Yearbook of Calvary Baptist Church, 1879-1979*, 25; Farris, *Through It All*, 49; Taylor Branch, *Parting the Waters: America in the King Years, 1954-63* (New York: Simon and Schuster, 1988), 77; and Keith D. Miller, *Voice of Deliverance: The Language of Martin Luther King, Jr., and Its Sources* (New York: The Free Press, 1992), 44. Barbour would "raise questions" to King and the other students "about theology and religion and church life much like the ancient philosophers," and the sessions "were more stimulating than the classes at the seminary." See "Remembering Mentor to a Generation of Young Black Preachers," 1-2; Kirk Byron Jones, "Old Chester, PA: Dr. Martin Luther King, Jr.," *Delaware County Daily Times*, "Opinion and Commentary Section" (16 January 1989); and Rufus Burrow, Jr., *Extremist for Love: Martin Luther King, Jr, Man of Ideas and Nonviolent Social Action* (Minneapolis: Fortress Press, 2014), 207.

36. Lewis, *King: A Critical Biography*, 28; Oates, *Let the Trumpet Sound*, 29; and Baldwin, *There is a Balm in Gilead*, 282.

37. Reddick, *Crusader without Violence*, 83. Barbour's parsonage has also been called "King's home away from home," and Barbour "King's father away from father." See Jones, "Old Chester, PA: Dr. Martin Luther King, Jr"; Garrow, *Bearing the Cross*, 39; Baldwin, *There is a Balm in Gilead*, 282; and *The Centennial Yearbook of the Calvary Baptist Church, 1879-1979*, 25.

38. Carson, et al., eds., *King Papers*, I, 161; and *The Centennial Yearbook of the Calvary Baptist Church, 1879-1979*, 25.

the sacred that they brought to Sunday School lessons, Bible study, usher board meetings, and choir rehearsal. These were resourceful women who could take what seemed to be modest scraps of food and prepare large, elaborate meals, and King, Jr. got to know them quite well. "He would go from house to house looking for food and fun," Emma Anderson recounted, "and he loved anything that was 'soul'. He really enjoyed my sweet potato pie."[39] "I would always leave my key under a brick so he could get into my house when I was away," Sara Richardson explained in an interview concerning King, Jr.'s years in Chester, "and he would come here and cook. He really loved soul food. He would eat chitterlings, cornbread, black-eyed peas, rice, spareribs, fried chicken, and especially lemon meringue pie. He would eat with his fingers."[40]

Only on rare occasions did King, Jr. dine at restaurants in and around Chester, mainly because most eateries were owned by whites who routinely discriminated against blacks. As explained in Chapter 1, King, Jr. had experiences during his Crozer years that would have perhaps turned the stomach, destroyed the appetite, or broken the spirit of the average young man of his temperament and social standing. Only months after arriving in Chester, he and Dupree Jordan, one of his white classmates at Crozer, went to Stouffer's Restaurant in downtown Philadelphia where they had to demand service after being ignored for almost thirty minutes. King, Jr. found sand in some of the vegetables he was served, but despite being outraged, took the insult without protesting and he and Jordan soon left the restaurant.[41] In June 1950, at the end of his first year at Crozer, King, Jr. and his black classmate Walter McCall and their dates were denied service and actually forced out of a restaurant in Maple Shade, on the outskirts of Camden, New Jersey.[42] For one who loved food and had so much respect for the

---

39. A Private Interview with Emma Anderson, Chester, Pennsylvania (29 May 1987); and Baldwin, *There is a Balm in Gilead*, 38.
40. A Private Interview with Sara Richardson, Chester, Pennsylvania (29 May 1987); and Baldwin, *There is a Balm in Gilead*, 38.
41. Garrow, *Bearing the Cross*, 40; and Lerone Bennett, Jr., *What Manner of Man: A Biography of Martin Luther King, Jr.* (Chicago: Johnson Publishing Company, 1964), 27.
42. Carson, et. al., eds., *King Papers*, I, 327–29; Garrow, *Bearing the Cross*, 40; Downing, *To See the Promised Land*, 153; Reddick, *Crusader without Violence*, 82–83; and Baldwin, *The Voice of Conscience*, 143.

culinary arts, and who had never known the pain of hunger, the very idea of being denied the right to eat anywhere in America on grounds of race had to be nauseating. After all, King, Jr. had eaten at "one of the finest restaurants" in Hartford while working on the tobacco farm in Simsbury, Connecticut back in 1944, and had actually expressed delight that "a person of my race could eat anywhere" he pleased in that part of the country.[43] But the incidents at the restaurants in Philadelphia and Maple Shade would not have been totally surprising to King, Jr., for his mother had told him about segregated eateries and lunch counters when he was only six, and he had actually been forced to take meals in the rear of segregated dining cars in parts of the South upon his return to Atlanta from Simsbury.[44] In any case, it was in the context of such experiences, however painful, that King, Jr. first thought seriously about access to food and the privilege to eat as being not only practical necessities, but also basic human rights.

Having a more independent existence than he had known with his parents and siblings back in Atlanta, King, Jr. actually learned how to cook for himself for the first time during his Crozer years. Sara Richardson of Calvary Baptist Church remembered those times when the young man either did light cooking or warmed up food to consume at her home.[45] Because of his sensitivity to the racist stereotypes that whites generally accepted about blacks and their eating and drinking habits, King, Jr. was not likely to make a public display of his great love for certain soul foods and drink while on Crozer's campus. This would not have been odd in a campus atmosphere in which an "undercurrent of tension shortened some meals in the cafeteria," despite the emphasis on "racial harmony" as Crozer's "recommended prescription."[46] King, Jr. believed deeply that he and his black classmates had a practical, and perhaps even a moral, responsibility to

43. Carson, et. al., eds., King Papers, I, 112 and 115; King, My Life with Martin Luther King, Jr., 82; and King, Daddy King, 145.
44. Farris, "The Young Martin," 57; King, My Life with Martin Luther King, Jr., 82; and "Face to Face: Dr. Martin Luther King, Jr. and John Freeman," 4.
45. Contrary to what is suggested in some accounts of King, Jr.'s student years, he actually learned to do some cooking before he went to Boston to pursue Ph. D. work. See King, My Life with Martin Luther King, Jr., 86–87; and Reddick, Crusader without Violence, 88.
46. Branch, Parting the Waters, 75.

avoid any actions that reinforced racial stereotypes, which occupied the thinking of whites at virtually every level of the society in the 1940s and '50s.[47]

This explained King, Jr.'s problems with Joseph Kirkland, another black student on campus, who, despite being a minister's son and the product of a highly respectable family in Philadelphia, supposedly became "a numbers runner and bootleg whisky dealer in the ghetto underworld." King, Jr. was deeply concerned about the image Kirkland projected and how his actions reflected upon all of Crozer's black students. One day, he "visited Kirkland's room and objected to the beer kept there in coolers," and he reminded Kirkland that "the burden of the Negro race" was "on their shoulders." Kirkland casually replied, "so what?,"[48] a comment that must have puzzled, and perhaps, upset King, Jr. Having been raised in a family and home environment in which food, fellowship, and fun never included the use of alcoholic beverages, King, Jr. had little patience at that time with those black students, and particularly, those training for ministry, who somehow disregarded or violated this standard.

When King, Jr. graduated from Crozer and left Chester to study for the PhD at Boston University, he looked forward to living in a larger city that afforded virtually unlimited possibilities in terms of the essentials of black life and culture. Boston's black population was significantly larger than Chester's, and so many of its black residents were either migrants from the South or had family ties to that part of the country.[49] This invariably meant more access to homes and restaurants in which the best in soul food and drink could be found. King, Jr. rented an apartment on Massachusetts Avenue, a predominantly black section of Boston, with Philip Lenud, his long-time friend and former Morehouse College classmate, who knew how to prepare a range of southern dishes. The apartment consisted of two bedrooms, a large living room, a kitchen, and a bathroom, and the $60 monthly rent was quite high for that time, but King, Jr. and

---

47. William Peters, "Our Weapon Is Love," *Redbook* (August, 1956), 72.
48. Branch, *Parting the Waters*, 75.
49. Baldwin, *There is a Balm in Gilead*, 39–40 and 283–84.

Lenud managed to keep the apartment for two years "by saving on the food bill and trying their hands at home cooking."[50] This led to some good-natured teasing on the part of some of King, Jr.'s closest friends, who found the idea of him cooking anything at all quite funny. "Your mother said you had taken all of her pots and pans and cut-out for Boston," said H. Edward Whitaker, a former Crozer classmate, in a letter to King, Jr. "You can't wash dishes or can you?," he added. "I certainly would not like to stop by for a meal because I would probably take with acute indigestion and die."[51] Although King, Jr. learned a lot about cooking from Philip Lenud, who was studying for his BD Degree at Tufts College, he mostly assumed the task of washing dishes after meals.[52]

King, Jr.'s exposure to the best sources of cooking and food came in his capacity as the new preaching assistant at the historic Twelfth Baptist Church in the Roxbury area of Boston, where most blacks lived. The pastor of this church was William H. Hester, a dear friend of King, Sr.,[53] and Hester and his wife Beulah, natives of North Carolina, had essentially the same influential role in King, Jr.'s life that J. Pius and Olee Littlejohn Barbour had assumed earlier back in Chester. King, Jr. was called "the adopted son" of Twelfth Baptist Church.[54] Twelfth Baptist was not only his "home away from home," "feeding trough," and "fellowship station," it was also his link to a larger black community in which cooking, food, and eating were not only considered sacred, but critical to the physical, social, spiritual, and

50. Farris, *Through It All*, 74; King, *My Life with Martin Luther King, Jr.*, 55, 64, and 86–87; Reddick, *Crusader without Violence*, 87–88; Baldwin, *There is a Balm in Gilead*, 39–40; and Baldwin Interview with Lenud (7 April 1987).

51. Clayborne Carson, et. al., eds., *The Papers of Martin Luther King, Jr.*, Volume II: Rediscovering Precious Values, July 1951-November 1955 (Berkeley: University of California Press, 1994), 159.

52. Reddick, *Crusader without Violence*, 88; and Baldwin Interview with Lenud (7 April 1987).

53. Michael Haynes, who also served as a preaching assistant at Twelfth Baptist at that time, has reported that "Martin was very special to Reverend Hester. Martin was the most popular among the Reverend Hester's seminary associates, and the one who preached the most regularly." See *One Hundred and Five Years by Faith: A History of the Twelfth Baptist Church, 1840-1945* (Boston: Twelfth Baptist Church,1946), 47–51; *The Souvenir Journal and the Threefold Celebration: The Twelfth Baptist Church* (1985), 19; King, *Daddy King*, 147–49; Carson, et al., eds., *King Papers*, II, 11; and A Private Interview with Michael E. Haynes, Boston, Massachusetts (25 June 1987).

54. *The Souvenir Journal and the Threefold Celebration* (1985), 19; *One Hundred and Five Years of Faith*, 47–51 and 55; and Baldwin Interview with Haynes (25 June 1987).

cultural well-being of the folk. King, Jr. actually dated one of Pastor Hester's nieces who was also pursuing graduate work at Boston University, and the young man frequently visited with the Hesters while taking delight in eating large quantities of soul food prepared by Mrs. Hester. Many of the members at Twelfth Baptist also opened their doors to and invited King, Jr. to lunch or dinner from time to time, and especially after Sunday services, and the youngster was never known to turn down such invitations. King, Jr.'s relationship to the Twelfth Baptist Church family was so similar to what he had known and experienced at Ebenezer Baptist Church in Atlanta and Calvary Baptist Church in Chester. Although the young man was physically removed from the South, he was located there spiritually and culturally—as evidenced by all of the meals, fellowship, and incredibly enjoyable experiences he had with the folk at Twelfth Baptist Church.[55]

It was through the Hesters and others at Twelfth Baptist that King, Jr. got to know about Barbara's Chef, Mother's Lunch, the Western Lunch Box, and other black-owned eating places in and around Roxbury. Mrs. Jackson's Western Lunch Box, owned "by a brown-skinned woman from Kentucky, who specialized in Southern cooking" or "soul food," became "the favorite eating place for Martin and some of his friends, including Mary Powell of Atlanta," who had become well-acquainted with King, Jr. and his family through her own marriage to a nephew of Dr. Benjamin Mays of Morehouse College.[56] Interestingly, it was through the matchmaking efforts of Mary Powell, who was also Reverend William Hester's secretary, that King, Jr. met Coretta Scott, an Alabama native, who would ultimately become his wife.[57] Clearly, food was a critical factor in this web of relationships, for Coretta had grown up on soul food, which was most often "cooked on a big wood-burning iron stove." Her heritage was also "deeply rooted in southern soil," where her parents, Obadiah and Bernice McMurray

55. *The Souvenir Journal and the Threefold Celebration* (1985), 19; Baldwin Interview with Haynes (25 June 1987); and Baldwin, *There is a Balm in Gilead*, 39–40 and 283–85.
56. Baldwin Interview with Haynes (25 June 1987); Baldwin, *There is a Balm in Gilead*, 40 and 284; Reddick, *Crusader without Violence*, 87; and King, *My Life with Martin Luther King, Jr.*, 51.
57. Baldwin Interview with Haynes (25 June 1987); King, *My Life with Martin Luther King, Jr.*, 51; and Farris, *Through It All*, 72.

Scott, "raised corn, peas, potatoes, and garden vegetables," along with "hogs, cows, and chickens."[58]

Food and eating was an important topic of conversation during King, Jr.'s very first date with Coretta in the spring of 1952. King, Jr. drove Coretta to Sharaf's Restaurant on Massachusetts Avenue in Boston, where the couple had lunch cafeteria-style. They soon settled into a serious relationship, agreed to get married, and became engaged to each other—in part, because of their shared sense of place in a southern context, which also entailed a certain perspective on cooking, food, and eating. Their "social life in Boston" was "mostly among other southern blacks who were studying at the various colleges and universities," and was also mostly "conducted at a few 'southern-style restaurants' or at parties in private homes," especially since they "did not feel completely welcome at many white restaurants and nightclubs in the Boston area."[59] King, Jr. and Coretta occasionally went to Mrs. Jackson's Western Lunch Box and other soul food restaurants together, and at other times, Coretta prepared a home-cooked meal. One Sunday evening, Coretta cooked her specialty, banana pudding, "and Martin's favorite cabbage smothered in bacon," and with her sister Edythe's help, also made tossed salad and corn meal bread. King, Jr. and his roommate Philip Lenud ate voraciously and appreciatively, and when they finished, King, Jr. teasingly mentioned that Coretta "had passed the test."[60] He had suggested repeatedly that he wanted to marry a beautiful girl from the South who was also an excellent cook.

The day before King, Jr. and Coretta's wedding, which occurred on June 18, 1953, a feast involving family members and friends from both sides, and also members from Atlanta's Ebenezer Baptist Church, took place at Obadiah and Bernice Scott's home in Marion, Alabama. Those present "had the usual country-style dinner," part of which was cooked by Coretta, "with a variety of southern dishes with their special

---

58. King, *My Life with Martin Luther King, Jr.*, 18 and 23.
59. Ibid., 50, 52, and 90; and Baldwin, *There is a Balm in Gilead*, 41.
60. King, *My Life with Martin Luther King, Jr.*, 50–51 and 64–65; Edythe Scott Bagley, *Desert Rose: The Life and Legacy of Coretta Scott King* (Tuscaloosa: The University of Alabama Press, 2012), 96; and Baldwin, *There is a Balm in Gilead*, 40.

country flavor."[61] Sit-down dinners after wedding rehearsals, and occasionally, after weddings had become, like family reunions, the usual getting together on holidays, and the informal gatherings of friends, a kind of tradition for members of the King family,[62] and King, Jr. was almost never absent. His healthy appetite actually reflected both his zest for and his optimistic view of life and of living.[63]

That first year of marriage afforded opportunities for King, Jr. to display his own cooking skills, and according to Coretta, he "was quite proud of his ability." On Thursday nights, when Coretta was in her six-o'clock class at the New England Conservatory of Music, King, Jr. would smother cabbage and cook pork chops, fried chicken, pigs' feet, pigs' snout, pigs' ears, corn bread, and southern-style turnip greens "with ham hocks and bacon drippings." He and Coretta preferred soul food, or "highly seasoned, overcooked, and delicious southern cooking," partly because it was relatively inexpensive. "I never liked pigs' ears," Coretta recalled, "but Martin liked them because," as he put it, "they're good and they're cheap." The couple added other foods to their menu as time passed, and as they increasingly moved into the public spotlight and expanded their social networking beyond the usual circles of family and friends, but they never surrendered their hearty appetites for southern-style cooking and soul food.[64]

C. Our Daily Bread: Food and the Struggle for Freedom, Justice, and Community

Martin Luther King, Jr.'s experiences as a cook essentially ended when he accepted the position of senior pastor at Montgomery's Dexter Avenue Baptist Church in the spring of 1954. Although the North had yielded so much of what he wished for in terms of culinary practices,

---

61. King, *My Life with Martin Luther King, Jr.*, 70.
62. Farris, *Through It All*, 62.
63. As far back as his Crozer years, King, Jr. had declared that "It is quite easy for me to think of the universe as basically friendly," and "to lean more toward optimism than pessimism about human nature," primarily "because of my uplifting hereditary and environmental circumstances." I submit that this outlook was vividly reflected in his love for food and his eating habits. See Carson, et al., eds., *King Papers*, I, 360.
64. King, *My Life with Martin Luther King, Jr.*, 86–87; and Baldwin, *There is a Balm in Gilead*, 131–32.

elaborate spreads, and delightful and tasty dishes,[65] he had long desired to return to the South where he knew he would be literally surrounded by great cooking and all of the mouth-watering soul food he could possibly have imagined, let alone consumed. "Eating is my great sin," King, Jr. confessed to his friend Lawrence D. Reddick, who had arrived in Montgomery around the time the historic bus boycott began in order to chair the Department of History at Alabama State College.[66] By this time, King, Jr. had become known around Dexter Church as the intelligent and dynamic young pastor whose "favorite expression of enthusiasm" was "Oh Yes!," who routinely greeted his elders with the words "No, Ma'am" and "Yes, Sir," who always expressed a hearty "Thank you!" to those who helped him in any way,[67] and who, perhaps more interestingly, delighted in consuming soft drinks and large helpings of southern foods, especially fried chicken, pork chops, steaks, sauces, gravies, string beans and other vegetables, fruits, cakes, pies, and ice cream.[68] Coretta cooked most of her husband's meals during this early stage in his public life, and she, in "those precious moments" of being alone with him, enjoyed "preparing his favorite dishes, especially home-made vegetable soup."[69] As time passed, an increasingly crowded schedule caused King, Jr. to arrive at the church parsonage on South Jackson Street quite late on some nights, but Coretta adjusted quite well and became accustomed to warming up food for him on such occasions. "Many times Coretta saw her good meals grow dry in the oven when a sudden emergency kept me away,"

65. King, *My Life with Martin Luther King, Jr.*, 50–51; Baldwin Interview with Richardson (29 May 1987); and Lewis, *King: A Critical Biography*, 27–28.
66. Reddick, *Crusader without Violence*, 3; Lewis, *King: A Critical Biography*, 28; and Downing, *To See the Promised Land*, 126. King's point about himself was supported by many who knew him best. For example, see Garrow, *Bearing the Cross*, 122.
67. This kind of behavior was consistent with the values instilled in King as a child. See Reddick, *Crusader without Violence*, 7; Farris, *Through It All*, 18; King, *My Life with Martin Luther King, Jr.*, 59; Telephone Interview with Nelson Malden (15 March 2014); and Telephone Interview with Nelson Malden (23 May 2014).
68. Wally G. Vaughn and Richard W. Wills, eds., *Reflections on Our Pastor: Dr. Martin Luther King, Jr., at Dexter Avenue Baptist Church, 1954-1960* (Dover, MA: The Majority Press, Inc., 1999), 3, 61–62, 82, 128, 153, and 156; Reddick, *Crusader without Violence*, 3, 7, 52–53, 56, and 93; Telephone Interview with Malden (15 March 2014); Telephone Interview with Malden (23 May 2014).
69. Octavia Vivian, *Coretta: The Story of Coretta Scott King*, Commemorative Edition (Minneapolis: Fortress Press, 2006), 47.

King, Jr. recounted. "Yet she never complained, and she was always there when I needed her."[70]

Although King, Jr. disliked the common view of Dexter Avenue Baptist Church as "the 'big folks' church," or as "a sort of silk-stocking church catering to a certain class,"[71] he found that many of the women within its ranks could compete with any ordinary grassroots housewife or unrefined but wise grandmother when it came to cooking soul food. Any questions King, Jr. may have had about the culinary skills of his female parishioners were answered when the Women's Council at Dexter gave him and Coretta "a food shower" soon after their arrival in Montgomery. Mrs. Sallie B. Madison, who also served on the Social Service Committee at Dexter Church, was widely known and appreciated for the quality of her cooking. King and Coretta lived with Mrs. Madison for a brief period on Grove Street in Montgomery until the parsonage was ready for them, and the couple took great pleasure in sitting at her dining table and munching on her southern fried chicken. Mrs. Madison's residence was among King, Jr.'s "favorite homes" in Montgomery, mainly because it allowed for fellowship that was warm and inviting and lively discussions of church affairs in an atmosphere saturated with the aroma of good, tasty food.[72]

When it came to identifying the best places to eat in and around Montgomery, King, Jr. did not limit himself to the homes of the members of Dexter Church. He frequently dined at the home of his best friend Ralph D. Abernathy and his wife Juanita, the pastor and first lady of First Baptist Church in the city.[73] "Because of segregation there were no suitable restaurants we could go to," Abernathy reported, "so we had lively discussions and hearty meals at each others' homes." He sensed that King, Jr. was very fond of Juanita not only "because she was

70. Carson, et. al., eds., *The Autobiography of Martin Luther King, Jr.*, 59 and 72; and King, *Stride toward Freedom*, 123 and 141.
71. King, *Stride toward Freedom*, 25.
72. Evans and Alexander, eds., *The Dexter Avenue Baptist Church, 1877–1977*, 75 and 89; Vaughn and Wills, eds., *Reflections on Our Pastor*, 77 and 128; and Telephone Interview with Malden (15 March 2014).
73. Ralph D. Abernathy, *And the Walls Came Tumbling Down: An Autobiography* (New York: Harper & Row, Publishers, 1989), 125–26 and 470; Baldwin, *There is a Balm in Gilead*, 304; and Baldwin Interview with Abernathy (17 March 1987).

bright and quick-witted," but also, because of the care and skills she brought to her work in the kitchen:

> I remember one night in Montgomery when she had served home-made ice cream and he was about to start on his second bowl. Suddenly he stopped with his spoon in midair. "Juanita," he said, "I believe we can solve this whole boycott problem if we carry a bowl of this ice cream over to George Wallace. I think I'll take it over right now." He started to rise, then sank back in his chair. "No," he said. "He doesn't deserve it. I'm just going to sit here and eat it myself."[74]

Abernathy went on to explain what he and King, Jr. routinely did after dining sufficiently on such occasions: "While the women did the dishes—I guess to a degree we were male chauvinists—we would talk past the midnight hour; often we would go out on the porch. The conversation would be laced with light discussion bordering on gossip, and serious talk on non-violence, Thoreau, the great theologians, Gandhi and Jesus."[75]

The residence of Georgia Gilmore on Dericote Street in Montgomery also registered high on King, Jr.'s list of favorite eating places. King, Jr. and Coretta only lived three blocks from Mrs. Gilmore, and King, Jr. enjoyed her elaborate soul food dishes, and especially, her crispy and juicy fried chicken and her delicious cakes, pies, and pastries. King, Jr. and others in the Montgomery Improvement Association (MIA) actually assisted Mrs. Gilmore in starting her own home-based restaurant after she was fired from her job as a cook at the National Lunch Company due to her civil rights activism. Mrs. Gilmore sold chicken dinners to the boycotters and to those who frequented mass meetings, and donated the proceeds to the bus protest efforts. A very heavy woman whom King, Jr., in his most playful moods, called "Tiny," Mrs. Gilmore contributed substantially to the success of the bus boycott through her vigorous fundraising efforts. She hosted secret MIA meetings in her kitchen, and ran the only restaurant in

74. Ralph David Abernathy, "My Old Friend Martin," *The Tennessean: USA Weekend* (12–14 January 1990), 6; Abernathy, *And the Walls Came Tumbling Down*, 470; Baldwin, *There is a Balm in Gilead*, 304; and Baldwin Interview with Abernathy (17 March 1987).
75. Abernathy, "My Old Friend Martin," 6; Abernathy, *And the Walls Came Tumbling Down*, 125; and Baldwin Interview with Abernathy (17 March 1987).

Montgomery at that time in which blacks and whites "could be served (illegally) at the same table."[76] Undoubtedly, her contributions gave King, Jr. not only a greater appreciation of the sociocultural significance of culinary practices, food, and eating, but also a new and better sense of how these practical necessities related to his people's struggle for freedom, justice, and community.

King, Jr. took a number of VIPs who visited with him in Montgomery to Mrs. Gilmore's restaurant to eat, among whom was Senator Robert Kennedy from Massachusetts. He occasionally took guests to other black restaurants in and around Montgomery as well, while, at the same time, urging blacks in the city not to patronize white-owned eateries that required them to go to the back door before being served.[77] King, Jr. enjoyed the food at Kats Diner, which had a reputation "like no other" when it came to the wonderful taste of its pigs' ears.[78] Although King, Jr. thought a lot during those years about what it meant to live "in true Gandhian simplicity" and abstinence,[79] even when it came to food and eating, he never went as far as the little brown man from India, who occasionally became so weak from fasting until he had to be lifted and literally carried from place to place by his associates and followers. This was most evident to King, Jr.'s old friend and mentor J. Pius Barbour, who remembered something quite interesting about King, Jr.'s appetite when King, Jr. traveled from Montgomery to Chester, Pennsylvania to receive an alumni award from Crozer Seminary in November, 1959, only months after he had

76. Vaughn and Wills, eds., *Reflections on Our Pastor*, 61–62; "Georgia Theresa Gilmore (2014): The Biography." Com website. Retrieved 01:27, 22 May 2014, from http://www.biography.com/people/georgia-gilmore-21392019 (accessed 22 May 2014); Telephone Interview with Malden (15 March 2014); Telephone Interview with Malden (23 May 2014); and David L. Chappell, *Inside Agitators: White Southerners in the Civil Rights Movement* (Baltimore: The Johns Hopkins University Press, 1994), 68 and 245n57. Interestingly enough, King makes only a fleeting reference to Georgia Gilmore in his account of the Montgomery bus boycott, and offers no insight into her importance to the protest. See King, *Stride toward Freedom*, 148.

77. Telephone Interview with Malden (15 March 2014); and Vaughn and Wills, eds., *Reflections on Our Pastor*, 61–62.

78. Vaughn and Wills, eds., *Reflections on Our Pastor*, 61 and 156; Reddick, *Crusader without Violence*, 7; Chappell, *Inside Agitators*, 245n57; Telephone Interview with Malden (15 March 2014); and Telephone Interview with Malden (23 May 2014).

79. King, *My Life with Martin Luther King, Jr.*, 162–65. Also see King's Palm Sunday sermon on Mohandas K. Gandhi in Clayborne Carson, et. al., eds., *The Papers of Martin Luther King, Jr., Volume V: Threshold of a New Decade, January 1959–December 1960* (Berkeley: University of California Press, 2005), 145–56.

spent several weeks touring "the land of Gandhi."[80] Pastor Barbour invited King, Jr. to his home at that time and noticed that he "had not changed his outrageous eating habits." "I gave a steak supper one night, and he gulped down a great big sirloin steak swimming in hot sauce," Barbour later reported. "Where does he put all that food, I wondered?"[81] In the minds of Barbour and his wife, Olee Littlejohn Barbour, the question lingered: Was King, Jr. somehow addicted to food and eating?

King, Jr.'s public persona became fixed in the thinking of many who either heard him on radio, saw him on television, listened to his speeches and sermons at certain major events, or marched with him during civil rights demonstrations in the 1950s and 60s, but that more private side of his life, which included his eating and drinking habits, was known only within a small circle of his family and friends. His great love for food and soft drinks was, of course, no real secret among family members, many of whom prepared food for him or were present at those times when he freely indulged in whatever food items were put before him. King, Jr.'s mother, Alberta and his sister, Christine knew exactly how and what to cook for him. Coretta never complained about her husband's eating, and the opportunity to sit and watch him consume food she had prepared was always one of her greatest delights,[82] especially since an ever increasing busy schedule caused him to miss so many meals at home. "We would often come in off the road at 10 o'clock at night and Coretta would be so glad to see us that she would get up and fix a major meal," according to King, Jr.'s aide Bernard Lee. "Late at night we'd be sitting there eating greens and corn bread."[83] However, Coretta did not like her husband's habit of taking food from the dishes before the family sat down at the table to eat. "He'd pick food from the serving bowl or platter and my mother

80. James M. Washington, ed., *A Testament of Hope: The Essential Writings and Speeches of Martin Luther King, Jr.* (New York: HarperCollins Publishers, 1991), 23–30.
81. Quoted in Garrow, *Bearing the Cross*, 122.
82. Vivian, *Coretta*, 47; and King, *Stride toward Freedom*, 60.
83. A Private interview with Bernard S. Lee, Washington, DC (9 July 1986).

would fuss at him about it all the time, but he did it anyway," King, Jr.'s daughter Yolanda recalled.[84]

When the family moved from Dexter Church in Montgomery back to Ebenezer Baptist Church in Atlanta in January, 1960, King, Jr., in his capacity as both a native son and an associate pastor with his father, reconnected with that larger extended family that also took great pleasure in satisfying his need and desire for home-cooked food. "Sometimes you might drop into the pastor's study at Ebenezer," Coretta recounted, "and there would be my husband gnawing at a pigs' feet while the delighted parishioner who had brought him a jar of her specialty sat proudly watching his enjoyment." King, Jr.'s extended family members at Ebenezer needed "his big appetite for their church dinners" as much as they needed "his visionary leadership,"[85] and their own lives were enriched by the mere opportunity to provide something that he really loved and benefitted from so much.

King, Jr.'s tastes were "wide and varied" and it was never easy for him to fast and watch his diet. While in Montgomery, he had tried to restrict himself on starches and to deny "himself that second helping" at times, but the mere smell of good soul food was always a challenge, and indeed, a threat to any plans he had along these lines. Whenever King, Jr.'s weight or health considerations demanded a change in eating habits, he dropped one meal and ate "a late breakfast and an early dinner" while taking vitamin pills. He occasionally exercised and his "robust health," which was "part of the basis for his energy and poise," was evident to those who observed and spent a considerable amount of time with him.[86] King, Jr. always felt that the "highly seasoned" and "overcooked" soul food he was eating was not sufficiently nutritious, and perhaps, even unhealthy, but it tasted so good. "Dear Martin!," said Coretta as she looked back on those years. "He always complained that our cooking was too fattening, yet it was

84. "'I Remember Martin': People Close to the Late Civil Rights Leader Recall a Down-to-Earth and Humorous Man," *Ebony*, Vol. 39, no. 6 (April, 1984), 38.
85. King, *My Life with Martin Luther King, Jr.*, 87; and Michael G. Long, *Martin Luther King Jr. on Creative Living* (St. Louis, MO: Chalice Press, 2004), 2.
86. Reddick, *Crusader without Violence*, 3; Vaughn and Wills, eds., *Reflections on Our Pastor*, 26, 53, and 60; and Baldwin Interview with Abernathy (17 March 1987).

exactly what he loved, and with a plate of greens before him, he never could remember his diet."[87] King, Jr.'s eating habits, as his son Dexter pointed out, was clearly a product of his cultural heritage:

> Sometimes his mind wandered and he seemed lost in thought, absently eating green onions. My father liked stalks of green onions with sweet, white, bulbous roots. They sat in a plate in water, like celery; before a meal he'd pick and eat them like fruit, especially before meals containing turnip or collard greens. He would say he was laying down a bed of straw before the cows and pigs—the rest of the meal—came home. This was ancestral. His father's family was from rural Georgia, my mother's family from rural Alabama. You can see a plate of green onions in photos of tarpaper shacks in the black belt of Mississippi, Alabama, and Georgia; they were staples of the sharecropper's diet.[88]

Those who worked closely with King, Jr. during his thirteen-year pilgrimage from Montgomery to Memphis, and who knew him best, insisted that his robust appetite merely exposed his profound and recognizable ordinariness, or his basic and genuine "humanness." "And he did enjoy good food," said Dorothy Cotton, who was the education director for King, Jr.'s SCLC. "During one of our trips through the deep South, we stopped in a little country store and bought some pickled pigs' feet and had great fun standing around eating them with only a paper towel in our hands," she recalled. "Now, that's down to earth," Cotton continued. "Dr. King enjoyed good restaurants as well, but he really liked soul food."[89] Cotton also reported that during the trip from Norway back to the United States in December 1964, after King, Jr. had dined with kings and received the Nobel Prize, the civil rights leader was determined to find some soul food:

---

87. King, *My Life with Martin Luther King, Jr.*, 87; and Reddick, *Crusader without Violence*, 3. King was ill at times during his years in the movement, and it is highly possible that some of his sick spells were food-related. See Abernathy, *And the Walls Came Tumbling Down*, 491. In one of his sermons, King talked about the urge to eat too much. "Do you know if you are a slave to food you just eat all the time," he declared. "You can never satisfy your hunger." At first glance, this seems to have been a very personal revelation of stunning proportions. See Martin Luther King, Jr., "The Prodigal Son," unpublished version of a sermon, Ebenezer Baptist Church, Atlanta, Georgia (4 September 1966), King Center Library and Archives, 3.
88. Dexter Scott King, *Growing Up King: An Intimate Memoir*, with Ralph Wiley (New York: Warner Books, Inc., 2003), 21.
89. "'I Remember Martin,'" 34.

Soberly, after the impressive award ceremony, the banquets, the tours and visits with European notables, we headed home, with a stopover in Paris. There Martin insisted we locate an African American woman who now had a very successful restaurant that specialized in African American "soul food." I couldn't help but point out that we could get all that kind of food back home! Why would we order American southern soul food from our culture when we were in Paris? I exclaimed. But the restaurant was contacted, the order was placed, and soul food was soon delivered to our hotel. I'm reminded of a man who called me fairly recently wanting a statement declaring that Dr. King was "totally against eating meat," because of the violence it involves to animals. I know the man was sad to hear me say that "Dr. King was happy when he had a beautiful steak on his plate." Martin loved southern soul food. In any case, we were not as conscious then about the damage this style of cooking could potentially cause. Earlier African American soul food was always cooked with fat and much of it was fried. Fortunately there is now a healthier consciousness about food abroad in the land.[90]

The Reverend Fred Shuttlesworth, who also worked and traveled widely with King, Jr., shared an interesting account of how King, Jr. once continued eating his soul food meal even while conversing by phone with President John F. Kennedy:

Once Dr. King was on the telephone talking to President Kennedy about nonviolence. He'd say: "Yeah, Mr. President, segregation is like a boil. You have to cut down into it and let some sunlight and air get to it before it will heal." Then he'd interrupt his conversation with the President, turn to me and say, "Fred, this is some of the best corn bread," and then start back talking to Kennedy. Then he'd stop again and say, "Ralph, tell them to bring some more of that fried chicken."[91]

The Reverend Willie Barrow, who worked with King, Jr. in her capacity as the Chicago-area SCLC coordinator in the 1960s, remembered that food was always a topic of conversation whenever King, Jr. visited her home, "just to get away from everyone." "We'd send out for ribs, one of his favorite foods, and I'd get out my nice

90. Dorothy F. Cotton, *If Your Back's Not Bent: The Role of the Citizenship Education Program in the Civil Rights Movement* (New York: Atria Books, 2012), 19–20; and "'I Remember Martin,'" 34 and 38. Apparently, King did not fully embrace the Gandhian concept of *ahimsa*, which consisted in non-injury to all creatures or living things. Vegetarianism was never really considered seriously by him, and the very idea of a meal without meat was unthinkable. See John J. Ansbro, *Martin Luther King, Jr.: The Making of a Mind* (Maryknoll, NY: Orbis Books, 1982), 129.
91. "'I Remember Martin,'" 40.

silver, my cloth napkins and my best china," she explained, "and then he'd say, 'Now wait just a minute, Reverend, I have my silver right here,' indicating his fingers. And he'd eat his barbecue and lick his fingers just like we did. He knew how to relax."[92]

Interestingly enough, King, Jr.'s habit of eating with his hands and licking his fingers was quite acceptable in black culture and among southerners generally, and was largely confined to those private moments when he was dining with family and close friends and aides. This habit was also indicative of his earthy humanness. He routinely used a knife, fork, and spoon, or followed dining etiquette and proper and socially acceptable table manners and techniques of eating, when sharing breakfast, lunch, or dinner with dignitaries, particularly in the United States and other parts of the Western world. King, Jr.'s social justice activism took him to many parts of the so-called Third World, where movement business and global problems were discussed around the table at mealtime, and where the rules of table-setting and dining etiquette differed, and he was always flexible and found it easy to adjust to any situation. When traveling in Africa, Asia, or other parts of the dark world,[93] where eating with the hands was not inconsistent with the rules of socially and culturally acceptable behavior, King, Jr. was prone to act accordingly. This also meant expanding his menu significantly beyond the usual southern soul food recipes, and this, he did surprisingly easy at times.[94] In any case, he never wanted to embarrass himself or to make an unfavorable impression on others. In King, Jr.'s own judgment, his eating and table manners were a reflection of both his personal style and values and his fierce desire to enhance the spirit of unity and to find common cause with others.

Food and eating took on special meanings and significance in the context of King, Jr.'s crusade for freedom, justice, human dignity, and peace. Dinner at King, Jr.'s home on Sunset Avenue in Atlanta for the

92. Ibid., 33–34. King, Jr.'s habit of eating with his hands extended at least back to his Crozer years and possibly his early childhood. See Baldwin, *There is a Balm in Gilead*, 38.
93. "Dark world" was a common phrase used at that time in reference to people in the so-called "non-white world" (Africa, Asia, Latin America, Caribbean). King himself used the term or phrase at times, so it seems appropriate here.
94. King, *My Life with Martin Luther King, Jr.*, 87.

entire SCLC staff was common, and on such occasions, King, Jr. was not reluctant to indulge freely.[95] Much of King, Jr.'s fundraising and strategizing for the movement took place in the homes of celebrities where delicious dishes were provided, along with fellowship, entertainment, and fun. He and some of his SCLC aides spent many evenings at the apartment of the entertainer Harry Belafonte in New York, which he considered both his "home away from home" and "the movement's New York headquarters," for food, drink, pleasure, and serious and lively conversation. Whenever King, Jr. stayed at Belafonte's apartment overnight, Belafonte's wife, Julie "would cook a simple kitchen dinner" and, when King, Jr. had dined sufficiently, the two men would "adjourn to the red living room" where they would take off their shoes, put their feet up, drink, and "stay up late into the night talking."[96] Belafonte remembered an occasion when he, King, Jr., and others gathered at the suite of actor Peter O'Toole for "a celebratory dinner" after a benefit concert for the movement, and O'Toole opened his kitchen door "to see Martin with a napkin over his forearm, holding a large tray of fried chicken from Jimmy's and plainly imitating a waiter." "Dinner is served," King, Jr. "said in that baritone voice of his." "As plates were handed out," Belafonte recalled, King, Jr., in a display of "humility" and "abject gratitude," "went from star to star, dispensing chicken and pausing ever so briefly to give each a sense of his personal appreciation for their contribution," noting that "You have no idea what it means for our folks back home."[97] Such moments not only exposed King, Jr.'s appetite for delicious food, but also, revealed his most human side and reinforced his belief that his cause was right and just.

For King, Jr., food and eating were practical needs that reinforced

---

95. Cotton, *If Your Back's Not Bent*, 187; and Baldwin Interview with Lee (9 July 1986).
96. Harry Belafonte, *My Song: A Memoir*, with Michael Shnayerson (New York: Alfred A. Knopf, 2011), 194, 247, 296, 310, and 326–29.
97. King, *My Life with Martin Luther King, Jr.*, 247; and Belafonte, *My Song*, 309–10. King's appearances at the homes and hotel suites of celebrities in New York were sometimes limited mostly to fun and eating, with little attention to the day-to-day struggles he faced. On one occasion, he was invited to a social gathering planned by Sammy Davis, Jr., during which he availed himself to "huge tables of hot hors d'oeuvres." See Sammy Davis, Jr., *Yes I Can: The Story of Sammy Davis, Jr.*, with Jane and Burt Boyar (New York: Pocket Books, 1965), 617.

bonds and obligations not only between himself and other civil rights activists and supporters, but also between black people as a whole. He knew that in so many cases, black women who did not actively participate in the protests, due to old age, disabilities, responsibilities in the home, or fear of economic reprisals, served the cause of black unity and freedom in their kitchens by preparing meals for those involved in the marches, sit-ins, and demonstrations. Black eateries throughout parts of the South were equally important in this regard. Paschal's Restaurant, "that world-famous Atlanta landmark" so "well known for its marvelous chicken dinners," was "the scene of numerous late-night planning meetings and strategy sessions" as King, Jr. and his SCLC "prepared for their battles for justice all across the nation."[98] Beamon's Restaurant, located about one and a half blocks from the SCLC headquarters in Atlanta, was "a favorite lunch spot" for King, Jr. and some of his staffers. Beamon's was "near juke joints, pool halls, and pork sandwich shops," and King, Jr., according to SCLC staffer Dorothy F. Cotton, "would often stop and would appear very much at home talking with the guys who hung out on the street there."[99] It sometimes took King, Jr. "forty-five minutes to an hour to walk" that short distance mainly because he spent so much time talking to people along the way, and the informal conversations undoubtedly continued once he made his way into Beamon's. Meeting, talking, and eating with ordinary people became his habit or disposition, a part of how he lived day to day. "If you wanted to talk to him, he was going to take time to talk to you," said Michael Harrington, an ardent supporter of King, Jr. "That's just the way he was; that was his nature."[100] Dorothy Cotton agreed, noting that King, Jr. "had the special capacity to feel comfortable 'dining with kings' as well as speaking with guys well into their wine."[101] The opportunity to dine in settings such as Beamon's Restaurant,[102] in which movement activists and ordinary people

98. Farris, *Through It All*, 61; and Dora McDonald, *Secretary to a King: My Years with Martin Luther King, Jr., the Civil Rights Movement, and Beyond* (Montgomery, AL: New South Books, 2012), 37–38.
99. Cotton, *If Your Back's Not Bent*, 188; and McDonald, *Secretary to a King*, 38.
100. Garrow, *Bearing the Cross*, 603.
101. Cotton, *If Your Back's Not Bent*, 188.
102. King's secretary, Dora McDonald reported that Beamon's Restaurant, located "on the ground floor

interacted and conversed at least on some levels, could not have been more important for King, Jr., who wanted to connect with as many people at the grassroots as possible, and who was always appreciative of what black cooks were contributing to the struggle through the employment of the culinary arts.

King, Jr. was probably more intentional than any other civil rights leader in his time when it came to associating the pleasures of food and eating with the quest for black unity and freedom. He shared food with fellow protestors along marching routes and in jail cells and modest homes, thus reinforcing, in very practical ways, a spirit of solidarity and a commonality of purpose in the movement. While involved in the crusade against poverty and slum tenements in Chicago in 1966, King, Jr. actually met and shared barbecue in the ghetto with black gang members, one of whom expressed amazement that "this cat who's been up there talking to Presidents" and "eating filet Mignon steaks" is now "sitting here eating barbecue just like me."[103]

In this respect, King, Jr. was quite different from nationalists such as the Black Muslims, who associated soul food with slavery and stereotypical images of black people, and who often alluded to it in distinguishing themselves from the masses who tended to enjoy it tremendously. Malcolm X, one of the leaders of the group, was among the greatest and most consistent critics of soul food in the early 1960s, clearly sharing that distinction with his messenger, Elijah Muhammad, who later wrote a two-volume work entitled, *How to Eat to Live* (1972). Malcolm's comments about blacks who ate chitterlings and other pork products were often scathing, and he was known to teasingly refer to King, Jr. at times as "a Rev. Dr. Chicken wing."[104] Interestingly enough, this was a period during which food was as much in debate as dress

of the Herndon Building on Auburn Avenue," had "excellent food," and King and the members of his "executive staff enjoyed those working lunches in the private dining room." See McDonald, *Secretary to a King*, 38.

103. King, *My Life with Martin Luther King, Jr.*, 262.

104. Elijah Muhammad, *How to Eat to Live* (Chicago: Muhammad's Temple of Islam No. 2, 1972), 7–190; Lewis V. Baldwin, "A Reassessment of the Relationship between Malcolm X and Martin Luther King, Jr.?," *The Western Journal of Black Studies*, Vol. 13, no. 2 (Summer, 1989), 104 and 111n15; and C. Eric Lincoln, *The Black Muslims in America*, Third Edition (Grand Rapids, MI: William B. Eerdmans Publishing Company, 1994; originally published in 1961), 76 and 129.

styles and the proper name for Negroes when it came to the question of the formation of a new and true black identity.

The lunch counter took on both a practical and a symbolic significance in King, Jr.'s thinking as he struggled for that larger communitarian ideal that would involve all Americans, irrespective of race and class, sitting at the table of brotherhood.[105] Having grown up in a society in which blacks and whites were not allowed to sit and eat together in any context, King, Jr. felt that freedom at its best also meant the privilege to eat whenever and wherever he pleased, and he found the very act of kicking people "off of lunch counters" deeply troubling. While acknowledging that the sit-ins at lunch counters were, in some measure, "a demand for food service," King, Jr. held, perhaps more importantly, that these acts of protest also represented "a demand for respect." He spoke of the absurdity of welcoming his people "with open arms at most counters in the store," while denying them "service at a certain counter because it happens to be selling food and drink."[106] He believed that if Americans learned the seemingly simple lesson of sitting and dining at the same table, this would be yet another giant step toward both their own personal maturation and the actualization of what he called the beloved community.[107] King, Jr. knew that food and eating were essential to life and to the social nature of human existence, and it was actually during the sit-ins at lunch counters that he developed a renewed sense of the practical need for food and eating and their connections to the realm of the sacred.

The same might be said of King, Jr.'s involvements in the planning of the Poor People's Campaign in 1967–68, which has been called his "last crusade." The Poor People's Campaign was the only nationwide effort planned from scratch by King, Jr.'s SCLC, and it was projected to be "a symbolic reminder to the nation that the Great Society's declared war

---

105. Washington, ed., *A Testament of Hope*, 219.
106. King, *My Life with Martin Luther King, Jr.*, 22 and 34; Reddick, *Crusader without Violence*, 91; Martin Luther King, Jr., "Address to the National Press Club," unpublished version, Washington, D. C. (19 July 1962), 1 and 14; and Carson, et. al., eds., *King Papers*, V, 449.
107. King understood well the potential of food to bring people together, and he expressed this in even casual and unorthodox ways. See Abernathy, *And the Walls Came Tumbling Down*, 470; Baldwin, *There is a Balm in Gilead*, 79 and 304; and Martin Luther King, Jr., "An Address at a Mass Meeting," Marks, Mississippi (19 March 1968), King Center Library and Archives, 5–6.

on poverty had not produced significant tangible results."[108] Scheduled to occur in Washington, DC in the spring of 1968, it focused to a greater extent than the previous SCLC campaigns on the living conditions of poor people, and food was at the top of its agenda. "And we're talking about bread now," King, Jr. stated emphatically, echoing the words of many of the women in the National Welfare Rights Organization (NWRO) who also supported the effort. "We're talking about the right to eat, the right to live. This is what we're going to Washington about."[109] Much of the organizing, strategizing, and fundraising activities for this proposed Poor People's Campaign occurred under King, Jr.'s leadership, and there was always a sense, on the part of King, Jr. and others in the SCLC, of how it connected with the crusade against poverty worldwide.

Although King, Jr. was assassinated in April 1968, some two months before the Poor People's Campaign actually began, its leaders, among whom were James Bevel, Ralph Abernathy, and Jesse Jackson, were guided by King, Jr.'s conviction that hunger can destroy both the spirit and the bodies of any people, and that the crusade for food was actually a struggle for the very survival and welfare of people, irrespective of race or color. The rallying cry of the most active participants in the Poor People's Campaign, who actually established a 3,000-person temporary tent settlement on the National Mall, called "Resurrection City,"[110] was "Foo-oo-ood," which was heard repeatedly as they marched daily to various federal agencies to demand economic justice

---

108. Gerald D. McKnight, *The Last Crusade: Martin Luther King, Jr., the FBI, and the Poor People's Campaign* (Boulder, CO: Westview Press, 1998), 112 and 127. Another perspective on King's very last campaign is provided, with considerable sophistication, in Michael K. Honey, *Going Down Jericho Road: The Memphis Strike, Martin Luther King's Last Campaign* (New York: W. W. Norton & Company, 2007), 50–75.
109. King, "Why a Movement," 1.
110. Ronald L. Freeman, *The Mule Train: A Journey of Hope Remembered* (Nashville: Rutledge Hill Press, 1998), 108–11; McKnight, *The Last Crusade*, 113–15, 118–20, 130, and 132–33; and Honey, *Going Down Jericho Road*, 500–501. Interestingly enough, as a part of King's funeral the "SCLC staff arranged for his body to be carried from Ebenezer Church to Morehouse College on an old farm wagon drawn by two Georgia mules," symbolizing "the Poor People's Campaign" that he "had been planning." The Poor People's Campaign began about eight weeks after the King assassination with a mule train headed from Mississippi to Washington, D. C., symbolism that King had eagerly supported before his death. See McDonald, *Secretary to a King*, 114; and King, *My life with Martin Luther King, Jr.*, 279.

for the poor. Although the campaign only lasted six weeks and won only minor concessions from the federal government in the form of free surplus food distribution and programs for the poor, King, Jr.'s proclamations about humans' inability to "live without bread" was heard loudly and clearly through the voices and actions of its leaders and their most devout followers. Years later, the story of the Poor People's Campaign would be captured poignantly in the film entitled "The Promised Land, 1968," from the PBS television series *Eyes on the Prize*, which ends with King, Jr. quoting those immortal words of Jesus: "For I was hungry, and you fed me not; I was thirsty and you gave me no drink"(Matthew 25:42). These words stuck with King, Jr. as he called upon the rich in his country to feed the unfed, and as he consistently challenged the federal government to adopt a "war on poverty" that would include education, jobs, food, and other kinds of social welfare intervention.

When King, Jr. spoke in these terms, he had in mind a world in which millions suffered the pains of hunger and thirst, and in which thousands of children died daily from starvation and malnutrition. He insisted that he was concerned "not merely about streets in heaven flowing with milk and honey," but also, "about two-thirds of the people of the world who go to bed hungry at night."[111] Convinced that freedom from hunger and thirst was a fundamental human right, he apparently saw food and eating as practical necessities that embodied potential for uniting humanity. King made this quite clear in "A Christmas Sermon on Peace" in December 1967, in which he evoked the principle of "the interrelated structure of all reality,"[112] and mentioned the ways in which the daily sharing of food, drink, and other basic necessities by humans across national boundaries were already indicative of the workings of what was essentially an interconnected, interrelated, and interdependent world:

111. Martin Luther King, Jr., "Who are We?," unpublished version of a sermon, Ebenezer Baptist Church, Atlanta, Georgia (5 February 1966), King Center Library and Archives, 5; and Martin Luther King, Jr., "What is Man?," unpublished version of a sermon on "Sunday with Martin Luther King, Jr.," WAAF—AM, Chicago, Illinois (17 April 1966), King Center Library and Archives, 3.
112. Martin Luther King, Jr., *The Trumpet of Conscience* (San Francisco: Harper & Row, Publishers, 1987; originally published in 1967), 69–70.

We are made to live together because of the interrelated structure of reality. Did you ever stop to think that you can't leave for your job in the morning without being dependent on most of the world? You get up in the morning and go to the bathroom and reach over for the sponge, and that's handed to you by a Pacific islander. You reach for a bar of soap, and that's given to you at the hands of a Frenchman. And then you go into the kitchen to drink your coffee for the morning, and that's poured into your cup by a South American. And maybe you want tea: that's poured into your cup by a Chinese. Or maybe you're desirous of having cocoa for breakfast, and that's poured into your cup by a West African. And then you reach over for your toast, and that's given to you at the hands of an English-speaking farmer, not to mention the baker. And before you finish eating breakfast in the morning, you've depended on more than half of the world. This is the way our universe is structured; this is its interrelated quality. We aren't going to have peace on earth until we recognize the basic fact of the interrelated structure of all reality.[113]

Food and eating were central to King, Jr.'s vision of "the great world house," in which peoples of different races, nationalities, religions, cultures, ideologies, and interests "who, because we can never again live apart, must learn somehow to live with each other in peace."[114] King, Jr. believed deeply that the possibilities for global community would become greater when the world's leaders chose to share bread and clean, fresh water instead of military technology and weapons of mass destruction. He repeatedly made this point and, on one occasion while viewing a photograph "showing the horrific effects of napalm attacks on Vietnamese children," refused to continue eating his meal. Knowing King, Jr.'s voracious appetite, an aide, clearly surprised, promptly asked: "Doc, doesn't it taste any good?" King, Jr. quickly replied: "Nothing will ever taste any good for me until I do everything I can to end that war."[115] In King, Jr.'s estimation, the very thought of an "arms race" in a world threatened by hunger, malnutrition, and disease defied both simple logic and the standards of basic human decency.[116]

King, Jr. felt similarly about the rich and powerful who lived

113. Ibid.; and Martin Luther King, Jr., *Where Do We Go from Here: Chaos or Community?* (Boston: Beacon Press, 1968; originally published in 1967), 181.
114. King, *Where Do We Go from Here?*, 167.
115. Ibid., 177–91; and Tavis Smiley, *Death of a King: The Real Story of Dr. Martin Luther King Jr.'s Final Year,* with David Ritz (New York: Little, Brown and Company, 2014), 14.

extravagantly while taking food and drink out of the mouths of the poor and the oppressed of the world. He held that the story of Dives and Lazarus in the New Testament, and that of the rich young ruler as well, applied to every individual, group, and nation that could watch "hungry fellowmen smothering in the airtight cage of poverty and not be moved."[117] He strongly criticized the United States, Britain, Canada, Russia, and other wealthy nations in Western Europe for not providing the capital and technical assistance that the underdeveloped nations needed to feed their people, and for using food as part of a surreptitious design to control those nations.[118] Some of King, Jr.'s most celebrated sermons, addresses, and mass meeting speeches were peppered with metaphorical language that highlighted the need for "the haves" to feed "the have-nots" or "the unfed." When he spoke of colonized people worldwide who were in search of "the bread of faith," "the bread of hope," "the bread of freedom," and "the bread of social justice,"[119] he was not oblivious to the food that they needed in order to survive and function physically and spiritually. Whenever he alluded to Jesus' words, "Let this cup pass from me," he was referring to the cup of sorrow, disappointment, and suffering, but he was equally mindful of those who were thirsty and in need of clean, fresh water.[120] For King, Jr., good food and drink necessarily had to be included among a range of life-giving and peace-building resources if humans were to genuinely participate in the world community and an enlightened, globalized rights culture.

King, Jr. also wanted to be an example of how people of goodwill everywhere might respond to the problems of hunger, starvation, and

---

116. King, *Where Do We Go from Here?*, 178 and 181–82; King, *The Trumpet of Conscience*, 68–70; and Baldwin, *The Voice of Conscience*, 99 and 296n250.

117. Martin Luther King, Jr., "Dives and Lazarus," unpublished version of a sermon, Atlanta, Georgia (10 March 1963), King Center Library and Archives, 10–11; King, *The Measure of a Man*, 48–49; and Baldwin, *The Voice of Conscience*, 95.

118. King, *Where Do We Go from Here?*, 178–79.

119. See King's sermon, "A Knock at Midnight," in Clayborne Carson and Peter Holloran, eds., *A Knock at Midnight: Inspiration from the Great Sermons of Reverend Martin Luther King, Jr.* (New York: Warner Books, Inc., 1998), 69–71.

120. Clayborne Carson, et al., eds., *The Papers of Martin Luther King, Jr., Volume VI: Advocate of the Social Gospel, September 1948–March 1963* (Berkeley: University of California Press, 2007), 279–83; and Lewis V. Baldwin, ed., *"Thou, Dear God": Prayers that Open Hearts and Spirits—The Reverend Dr. Martin Luther King, Jr.* (Boston: Beacon Press, 2012), 36–37.

undernourishment among the poor and oppressed of the world. Inspired by Gandhi and the life of Jesus, "he often talked about taking a vow of poverty,"[121] which undoubtedly related to the kind of food he would have eaten. Despite King, Jr.'s great appetite, he sometimes fasted in jail cells as part of his spiritual practice as well as his desire to identify on some levels with those who not only hungered for righteousness sake, but for real food.[122] His greatest dream was not about eating, drinking, and socializing with the rich, powerful, and famous, but about creating a culture in which poor people, and especially, children and the elderly, would be sufficiently fed. Moreover, King, Jr. wanted his own children to see and have some sense of what it was like for people to be hungry and malnourished.[123]

King, Jr. never lost his appetite for good cooking, food, and eating. During those final hours of his life, in Memphis, he thought and talked a lot about good food and drink, and actually shared with his aides a story about a friend who was so "low on money" until he could not afford to feed him.[124] King, Jr. and his friend Ralph Abernathy decided to have lunch together at the Lorraine Motel, and King, Jr., holding "up two fingers," requested "two orders of fried catfish" and "two glasses of iced tea." The waitress mistakenly brought a double order instead of two separate orders, but King, Jr. was not upset. "Don't bother her any more," said he to Abernathy, who sought to remind the waitress of the original order. "She probably doesn't get paid minimum wage," King, Jr. continued, "and you know what the tips must be like here." The two "sat and ate from the same plate," and "it was the last meal" they had together.[125]

121. David J. Garrow, The FBI and Martin Luther King, Jr.: From "Solo" to Memphis (New York: W. W. Norton & Company, 1981), 216–17; King, My Life with Martin Luther King, Jr., 162–63; and Carson, et al., eds., King Papers, V, 152 and 154–55.

122. King decided, at times, during his campaigns that nonviolent direct action should take the form of fasting and prayer vigils. See King, My Life with Martin Luther King, Jr., 189 and 211.

123. Ibid., 189, 211, 258, 260, and 262.

124. "'I Remember Martin,'" 38.

125. Baldwin Interview with Abernathy (17 March 1987); and Abernathy, And the Walls Came Tumbling Down, 436–37. Abernathy later stated that King "worried about hurting the feelings of a tired waitress who had brought the wrong order." This was yet another example of King's amazing capacity for empathy, especially when it came to the poor and under-paid, or what he routinely called "the least of these." See Abernathy, "My Old Friend Martin," 6. For another account of King and Abernathy's last lunch together, see Vivian, Coretta, 79.

Only minutes before the assassin's bullet found its mark, King, Jr. was getting ready to go to the home of his friend, Samuel Billy Kyles, for "a good home-cooked meal." In "a light mood" at that time, King, Jr. teased Kyle and started telling a story about what he had once experienced while at a friend's house for dinner. "We had *cold* potatoes, *cold* ham, *cold* bread and cool aid," he joked. "You see, my friend was low on money because he'd just bought a new house." Knowing that Kyle had only recently settled in a new home, King, Jr. added: "Now Billy, if you've bought this big new house and you can't afford to feed us, I'm going to tell everybody in the country. Your wife can't cook anyway. She's too good-looking."[126] King, Jr. actually started speculating on that occasion about what Mrs. Kyles might be serving." He turned to Ralph Abernathy and said, "Ralph, call her up and ask her what she's having." Ralph made the call, and King, Jr. was literally overjoyed to hear that the menu included "Roast beef, asparagus, and cauliflower," along with "candied yams, pigs' feet, and chitterlings."[127] Sadly, King, Jr. never got the chance to enjoy the meal.

King, Jr.'s ability to indulge himself with delicious dishes placed before him was well-known, and indeed, legendary, and it appears, at first glance, that he was an Epicurean when it came to the pleasures of food and eating.[128] It is better to say that his love for food and eating was reflective of his robust character and his optimistic outlook on and approach to life as a whole, and indeed, his philosophy of life. Life must be lived in its "completeness," or in all of "its dimensions," he so often said,[129] and this, of course, meant the enjoyment of God's bountiful material blessings, including food and drink. Put another way, this entailed, in the words of Harvey Cox, "joy," "living it up," and "saying yes to experience."[130] At dining tables throughout the South, the nation, and the world, King, Jr. affirmed life and experience while

---

126. "'I Remember Martin,'" 38; Baldwin, *There is a Balm in Gilead*, 306–7; and Baldwin Interview with Abernathy (17 March 1987).
127. Vivian, *Coretta*, 79; "'I Remember Martin,'" 38; and Abernathy, *And the Walls Came Tumbling Down*, 438.
128. King actually denounced what he termed "The Epicurean creed—eat, drink, and be merry," because "spiritual values" in a case like this "have given away to temporary bodily satisfaction." See Carson, et al., eds., *King Papers*, VI, 204.
129. King, *The Measure of a Man*, 35–56.

revealing his capacity for festivity and celebration.[131] This was also quite evident in his appreciation for various forms of music, oral and instrumental, which is covered in some detail in the next chapter of this book.

130. Harvey Cox, *The Feast of Fools: A Theological Essay on Festivity and Fantasy* (New York: Harper & Row, Publishers, 1969), 27.
131. McDonald, *Secretary to a King*, 37–38, 77, 81–82, and 105.

4

___

"Let Our Rejoicing Rise": Music as a Central, Living Element in the Life of Martin Luther King, Jr.

Lift ev-'ry voice and sing, till earth and heav-en ring,
Ring with the har-mo-nies of lib-er-ty;
Let our rejoicing rise, high as the lis-t'ning skies,
Let it re-sound loud as the roll-ing sea.
    –Negro National Anthem[1]

Martin had a high baritone voice, and he loved to sing. We and the children used
to sing together whenever we could, but especially at Christmastime.
    –Coretta Scott King[2]

Music was an integral part of the life story of Martin Luther King, Jr.—from the time of his birth to the moment of his tragic and untimely death. He grew up in a society and culture in which the opportunities for exposure to great music were endless, and in which music-making

1. *Songs of Zion: Supplemental Worship Resources 12* (Nashville: Abingdon Press, 1981), 32–33; and *The National Baptist Hymnal* (Nashville: National Baptist Publishing Board, 1983), 477–78.
2. Coretta Scott King, *My Life with Martin Luther King, Jr.*, Revised Edition (New York: Henry Holt and Company, 1993; originally published in 1969), 232.

157

was essentially a communal exercise. As a child, he delighted in "the brassy sounds of marching bands and the sight of the high-stepping majorettes."[3] There were so many occasions for music-making in black Atlanta and in the South, as a whole, in King, Jr.'s youth, and there was always appropriate music for church functions, family reunions, concerts, weddings, funerals, recreational and entertainment purposes, and a variety of other formal and informal social activities that King, Jr. either witnessed or participated in over the course of his life. Music, like words and stories, was part of the rhythm and currency of daily life in the South, and King, Jr. came very early to understand that it was through music that the living heritage of his African forebears was most commonly and vigorously celebrated.[4]

This chapter treats the primacy of music in King, Jr.'s life and experiences. King, Jr.'s lifelong appreciation for music is highlighted, with emphasis on his childhood years in a deeply musical family, his own musical talents and passions, his adjustments to a culture in which both oral and instrumental music was inextricably linked to dance and bodily movement and expression, his attitudes toward the various sacred and secular musical forms, and his sense of the importance of music in his own personal life and in the larger context of both church life and the crusade for freedom, justice, human dignity, peace, and community. Also, much will be revealed about King, Jr. as both a public and private figure, his festive and celebrative approach to life, and his understanding of the roles that artists in the field of music could play in the enduring struggle to enlighten, uplift, and empower humanity. There was a romantic quality about the King, Jr. introduced here—about the human being who grew up around singers and good singing, who sensed and delighted in the true value of music, who appreciated music in various forms, and who consistently urged others to "cultivate a love for great music."[5]

3. Tavis Smiley, *Death of a King: The Real Story of Dr. Martin Luther King Jr.'s Final Year*, with David Ritz (New York: Little, Brown and Company, 2014), 75.

4. Martin Luther King, Sr., *Daddy King: An Autobiography*, with Clayton Riley (New York: William Morrow and Company, Inc., 1980), 14, 27, and 127; and Christine King Farris, *Through It All: Reflections on My Life, My Family, and My Faith* (New York: Atria Books, 2009), 26 and 83.

5. Clayborne Carson, et. al., eds., *The Papers of Martin Luther King, Jr., Volume IV: Symbol of the Movement*,

A. The Sounds of Culture: Music and the Ethos of Family, Church, and Community

Martin Luther King, Jr. was part of a deeply musical family from birth, and his earliest experiences with music occurred in the context of family musical evenings during weekdays and Wednesday night prayer meetings and Sunday morning services at Atlanta's Ebenezer Baptist Church.[6] His early fascination with the sounds of musical instruments and with the singing of Negro spirituals, gospel songs, and the great hymns of the Christian church was nurtured in a culture in which music was a day-to-day, minute-to-minute preoccupation, in which solid musical education was routinely pursued, and in which people were encouraged and expected to exercise the part of their being that involved singing or sounds running through the body. King, Jr. found this art form in abundance in his own family, church, and neighborhood, those influences that were nearest and dearest to him during his childhood. Music, family, religion, and life were so mingled until it was virtually impossible to think of one without the others.[7]

King, Jr.'s family circle was such that he was exposed from birth to the most vital aspects of this culture—particularly music and religion—through his parents. His own father, Martin Luther King, Sr., had grown up in rural Stockbridge, Georgia, where the "human voice was the rural church's organ and piano," and where his own childhood minister had often urged the faithful "to sing with the spirit and understanding." King, Sr. had emerged in his twenties as a "traveling

January 1957-December 1958 (Berkeley: University of California Press, 2000), 504; Martin Luther King, Jr., *Strength to Love* (Philadelphia: Fortress Press, 1981; originally published in 1963), 69; Lawrence D. Reddick, *Crusader without Violence: A Biography of Martin Luther King, Jr.* (New York: Harper & Brothers, Publishers, 1959), 55; Farris, *Through It All*, 26; and Lewis V. Baldwin, *There is a Balm in Gilead: The Cultural Roots of Martin Luther King, Jr.* (Minneapolis: Fortress Press, 1991), 17 and 163–64.

6. Unfortunately, the place of music in the upbringing and life of King has been woefully neglected in even the most celebrated works on this important figure. This explains the difficulty many scholars have encountered in treating King in proper cultural context. See Baldwin, *There is a Balm in Gilead*, 17 and 31–33.

7. King, *Daddy King: An Autobiography*, 26–27 and 127; King, *My Life with Martin Luther King, Jr.*, 59, 77–78, and 82; Reddick, *Crusader without Violence*, 56; Lewis V. Baldwin, *The Voice of Conscience: The Church in the Mind of Martin Luther King, Jr.* (New York: Oxford University Press, 2010), 16–17; Baldwin, *There is a Balm in Gilead*, 17, 31–33, and 163–64; Farris, *Through It All*, 3–54; and King, *My Life with Martin Luther King, Jr.*, 74–84.

preacher" whose "singing," which included what the folk called "the lining out of the old Dr. Watt hymns" with their long and vibrant tradition of call and response, "often brought congregations to a peak of emotional fervor."[8] King, Jr.'s mother, Alberta Williams King, was a highly regarded public school teacher and "an accomplished musician," who "played both the piano and organ," and who served as a leading musician for the Women's Auxiliary of the National Baptist Convention (NBC) for some time. King, Jr. spoke of having accompanied his mother "on two or three occasions" when she played the organ for this group at events held on the campus of the Southern Baptist Theological Seminary in Louisville, Kentucky.[9] Alberta was "Ebenezer's minister of music" from the late 1920s, and by "the 1940s, her annual church choir concerts attracted overflowing crowds."[10] In any case, the influence of King, Sr. and Alberta, more than any others, explained King, Jr.'s "feeling for ceremonies and ritual," and more specifically, his "passionate love of Baptist music" as "a young boy." That influence also accounted for the boy's desire, expressed at the end of his Morehouse college years, to become "a minister of music in church."[11]

These familial and church sources proved all the more fertile and influential in a larger culture in which music was central to the

8. Clayborne Carson, et al., eds., *The Papers of Martin Luther King, Jr., Volume I: Called to Serve, January 1929-June 1951* (Berkeley: University of California Press, 1992), 23; King, *Daddy King*, 23 and 27; Martin Luther King, Sr., "What Part Should Singing Play in Our Church Worship?," *Georgia Baptist* (1 March 1936); and Andrew Young, *An Easy Burden: The Civil Rights Movement and the Transformation of America* (New York: HarperCollins Publishers, 1996), 186–87. E. Franklin Frazier has noted that "the ability to sing" was a "qualification which the slave preacher" had to "possess" in order to establish his "authority" among fellow slaves, and Daddy King was obviously an heir of that long and unbroken tradition. See E. Franklin Frazier, *The Negro Church in America* (New York: Schocken Books, 1964), 18.

9. Ebenezer's choirs actually performed at the premiere of *Gone with the Wind* in Atlanta in 1939. See Christine King Farris, "The Young Martin: From Childhood through College," *Ebony*, Vol. XLI, no. 3 (January, 1986), 56; Carson, et al., eds., *King Papers*, I, 30 and 79; Martin Luther King, Jr., "The Church on the Frontiers of Racial Tension," unpublished version of an address given at the Gay Lectures, Southern Baptist Theological Seminary, Louisville, Kentucky (19 April 1961), Library and Archives of The Martin Luther King, Jr. Center for Nonviolent Social Change, Inc., Atlanta, Georgia, 1; Baldwin, *The Voice of Conscience*, 27 and 267n55; and Peter Ling, *Martin Luther King, Jr.* (New York: Routledge, 2002), 14.

10. When it came to music, and especially instrumental music, Alberta King was apparently the soul and spirit of both the King home and Ebenezer Church. She organized a choir at Ebenezer that would later be named for her famous son. See Farris, "The Young Martin," 56; Carson, et. al., eds., *King Papers*, I, 30, 79, and 143; Ling, *Martin Luther King, Jr.*, 14; and Baldwin, *The Voice of Conscience*, 27 and 267n55.

11. King, *Daddy King*, 127; and Carson, et al., eds., *King Papers*, I, 143.

cultivation of vital spiritual and communal values, and in which the power of music in surviving the unthinkable or unimaginable was well-established. As King, Jr. was growing up in Atlanta in the 1930s and 40s, the Big Bethel African Methodist Episcopal Church (AME), located in close proximity to both the King home and Ebenezer Baptist Church, was widely known for its stress on black sacred music, and especially, for *Heaven Bound*, which was written by some of the members of that congregation. "Utilizing many of the old spirituals in the form of a miracle play," the many performances of *Heaven Bound* attracted large crowds, including members of the King family. Kemper Harreld, the Director of Music at Morehouse College in the early 1940s, did notable work with orchestras and glee clubs in various academic and church settings, usually giving priority to concerts during which Negro spirituals figured prominently.[12] Exposed to an environment in which considerable numbers of ex-slaves and their immediate descendants could be found, King, Jr. heard the spirituals in churches, at home, on the campuses of Atlanta's black colleges, on the streets, and in the everyday processes of living, and there was never any chance of him disrespecting or being ashamed of that music. He sensed early on that that music illuminated the lives of a people struggling to survive against great odds—that it was indeed a balm in the midst of all the suffering and uncertainties of life.

The more secular musical forms were equally important and vital in the Atlanta of King, Jr.'s childhood. In the 1930s and 40s, lively scenes existed with "the thin, fast music of sidewalk phonographs, and always the voices, loud but musical." The city streets were often filled with the sounds and rhythms of work songs coming from the lusty throats of black chain-gang workers, who timed their labor routines to the tempo of music, and at times, grim-faced black men could be seen strumming musical instruments of almost every variety and singing blues that rose to the dizzy heights of emotion.[13] King, Jr. vividly remembered his

---

12. Reddick, *Crusader without Violence*, 69 and 73; Carson, et. al., eds., *King Papers*, I, 25n76; and Baldwin, *There is a Balm in Gilead*, 163–64.
13. *Atlanta: A City of the Modern South*, compiled by workers of The Writer's Program of The Work Projects Administration in the State of Georgia (New York: Smith and Durrell, 1942), 5; Martin

occasional walks down to "Buttermilk Bottom," the chief slum area of Atlanta, to see "a Negro guitarist" sing songs such as "I've Been Down So Long That Down Don't Bother Me."[14] The down-home blues, the music of sorrow and joy, of trials and triumph, typically flowed from the taverns into the streets, as listeners engaged in fluid and lively dance styles. "The neighborhood was always abuzz with activity," King, Jr.'s sister, Christine recalled. "Jazz was a constantly flowing presence coming from the shops and clubs." Some of the leading jazz entertainers and blues artists of that time occasionally performed at nightclubs in Atlanta.[15] While so many of King, Jr.'s elders tended to dismiss work songs, the blues, jazz, and other secular forms as "the devil's music," the youngster nonetheless affirmed all types of black secular music with few, if any, objections on religious grounds.[16] The rising and falling of secular musical forms, with their peculiar cadence and bursts of delightful melody, struck a responsive chord in the very soul of King, Jr., for he sensed something that was genuinely and inherently his own. Indeed, his sense of himself and of place in a southern context owed so much to his exposure to these everyday essentials of black life and culture.

Surrounded by family and church members who were musically inclined, King, Jr. "fell in love with the rousing gospel singing and chants" and was able to develop certain musical skills before he reached school age.[17] "As a four-year old youngster he had already discovered that his singing voice could be exploited," his friend Lawrence Reddick reported. "He began appearing occasionally before churches and church conventions." King, Jr. is said to have "had a

---

Luther King, Jr., *Stride toward Freedom: The Montgomery Story* (New York: Harper & Row, Publishers, 1958), 212; Martin Luther King, Jr., "Address at a Mass Meeting," Yazoo City, Mississippi (21 June 1966), King Center Library and Archives, 2; Clayborne Carson, et. al., eds., *The Papers of Martin Luther King, Jr., Volume V: Threshold of a New Decade, January 1959–December 1960* (Berkeley: University of California Press, 2005), 416; and Baldwin, *There is a Balm in Gilead*, 19 and 32–33.

14. King, *Stride toward Freedom*, 212; Carson, et al., eds., *King Papers*, IV, 433; Carson, et al., eds., *King Papers*, V, 416; and Baldwin, *There is a Balm in Gilead*, 33.

15. King, "Address at a Mass Meeting," Yazoo City, Mississippi (21 June 1966), 2; King, *Stride toward Freedom*, 212; and Farris, *Through It All*, 26.

16. Lewis V. Baldwin and Amiri YaSin Al-Hadid, *Between Cross and Crescent: Christian and Muslim Perspectives on Malcolm and Martin* (Gainesville: University Press of Florida, 2002), 16.

17. David R. Collins, *Not Only Dreamers: The Story of Martin Luther King, Sr. and Martin Luther King, Jr.* (Elgin, IL: Brethren Press, 1986), 6.

performer's voice as well as a performer's ear"[18]—gifts that came naturally due to his familial roots and cultural background. The boy's mother, Alberta, whose activities in the music field figured in some way in the shaping of his own interest in music, often accompanied her son "at the piano" as "he sang out with a rollicking gospel beat or a slow, heart-rending sob."[19] King, Jr.'s "favorite number was 'I Want to be Like Jesus,'" a song that was strangely prophetic in view of who and what he would ultimately become. A "Mr. and Mrs. Roger Anderson booked the little songster for various church programs," and "a special collection" was usually "taken up for him" on such occasions.[20] King, Sr. and Alberta King were present whenever King, Jr. "was going to sing" at some church-related event or in a school choir and the elder King recounted that his son sang "in a fine, clear voice."[21] But King, Jr.'s musical interests and talents never really extended to the playing of musical instruments, and the youngster denounced the "piano lessons" his parents arranged for him and his siblings as "sissy stuff." On one occasion, he and his brother, A. D. actually attacked the family piano with a hammer, and when that did not work, loosened the piano legs so that "it would collapse" when the "music instructor sat on it." The music teacher "was then dumped unceremoniously on the floor," and Daddy King, upon hearing the full story, whipped his children.[22]

King, Jr. did not feel the impact of the Negro spirituals, gospel songs, and the celebrated hymns of the Christian church in any precise way until he was perhaps in his teens. He spent a lot of time with Mattiwilda Dobbs and other high-school classmates who shared his appreciation for music, and was a member of his high-school choir. In a speech entitled "The Negro and the Constitution," the fifteen-year-old King,

18. Reddick, *Crusader without Violence*, 56; Ling, *Martin Luther King, Jr.*, 14; Baldwin, *There is a Balm in Gilead*, 16–17; Carson, et al., eds., *King Papers*, I, 30; and King, *Daddy King*, 127.
19. King, Jr.'s mother Alberta was actually murdered by a crazed gunman named Marcus Chenault "as she played the Lord's Prayer on Ebenezer Baptist Church's organ during the 11:00 A. M. worship service" on June 30, 1974. See Reddick, *Crusader without Violence*, 56; Farris, *Through It All*, 145; and King, *Daddy King* (introduction).
20. Reddick, *Crusader without Violence*, 56; King, *My Life with Martin Luther King, Jr.*, 77–78; and Baldwin, *There is a Balm in Gilead*, 163.
21. King, *My Life with Martin Luther King, Jr.*, 82; and King, *Daddy King*, 127.
22. Farris, "The Young Martin," 56; and Baldwin, *There is a Balm in Gilead*, 164.

Jr. commented on the language of passion and yearning that coursed through the great Marian Anderson's rendition of "Nobody Knows De Trouble I Seen," the popular slave spiritual. By that time, King, Jr. was beginning to understand that music in theoretical terms, and he delighted so much in the artistic genius of Anderson and others, who were known for serious renderings of the spirituals in the tradition of their slave ancestors.[23]

Although King, Jr. deeply appreciated the sacred music that was part of a cherished family and church heritage, he was not as receptive to the frenzy, or holy dancing and shouting, which were inextricably related in performance to the spirituals, the gospel songs, and the hymns typically sung at Ebenezer and other black churches, and which reflected the continuing impact of certain aspects of slave culture.[24] King, Jr. was exposed, time and again, to variants of the shout and the holy dance through his father, King, Sr., who "would start preaching at the front of the church and," as his sermons became songs, would prance "and walk the benches at the back," while all around him stood others who would catch the infection.[25] The image of Luella Allen, "the little Sister" who usually sat "on the left side" at Ebenezer Church, shouting convulsively "against the wall," as others augmented her efforts with singing, chanting, groaning, and expressions of "amen" and "hallelujah," was also indelibly etched in the memories of King, Jr. and others in his family. The seeming excesses of his people while singing, jumping, and vigorously swaying to and fro actually

23. Reddick, *Crusader without Violence*, 55; Carson, et al., eds., *King Papers*, I, 110; and Baldwin, *The Voice of Conscience*, 104.
24. Clayborne Carson, ed., *The Autobiography of Martin Luther King, Jr.* (New York: Warner Books, Inc., 1998), 15; and Zelia S. Evans and J. T. Alexander, eds., *The Dexter Avenue Baptist Church, 1877–1977* (Montgomery, AL: Dexter Avenue Baptist Church, 1978), 69. Andrew P. Watson's clear distinction between "shouting" and the "holy dance" is critical to this discussion, for both figured prominently in the church culture in which King, Jr. was born and raised. Watson describes "shouting" as "a spontaneous act" that "may happen any time the individual feels the spirit." The "holy dance" is a group affair that has "a specified place" in worship, musical instruments are used, and "the dancers move and sway to the music and singing." See Clifton H. Johnson, ed., *God Struck Me Dead: Voices of Ex-Slaves*, with a new introduction by Albert J. Raboteau (Cleveland: The Pilgrim Press, 1993; originally published in 1969), 10–12.
25. A Private Interview with Ralph D. Abernathy, West Hunter Baptist Church, Atlanta, Georgia (7 May 1987); King, *Daddy King*, 27; Carson, ed., *The Autobiography of Martin Luther King, Jr.*, 15; Baldwin, *There is a Balm in Gilead*, 31; Baldwin and Al-Hadid, *Between Cross and Crescent*, 13; and Young, *An Easy Burden*, 186–87.

constituted the primary means of artistic expression in the black worship experience, but King, Jr. found it impossible in his childhood to affirm and legitimate this art on black or any other terms. "I revolted, too, against the emotionalism of Negro religion, the shouting and stamping," he asserted as he looked back on those early years. "I didn't understand it, and it embarrassed me." Evidently, this was not young King, Jr.'s idea of what constituted an "intellectually respectable" religion.[26]

The time-honored tradition of congregational singing, always accompanied by hand-clapping and the patting of the feet, was, aside from preaching, the most widely practiced art during worship in Negro churches in Atlanta and across the southern United States during King, Jr.'s childhood years. Although King, Jr. found much that was emotionally and spiritually satisfying in this style of singing, he had an equally strong preference for choir and quartet singing. He was involved with choirs throughout his years in the public schools in Atlanta, and such involvements reinforced the musical instruction he received at home and at Ebenezer Baptist Church. While working on a tobacco farm in Simsbury, Connecticut in the summer of 1944, King, Jr. sang with a boy's choir that actually appeared on a local radio station.[27] That kind of involvement with music continued when the young man enrolled at Atlanta's Morehouse College, the historically-black, all-male institution. He sang with the Morehouse Glee Club and the Atlanta University-Morehouse-Spelman Chorus, which comprised students from each of the affiliated black colleges in Atlanta, and this experience, along with his participation in the annual J. L. Webb Oratorical Contest at Morehouse, which he won for at least two years,

---

26. But young King did affirm "the noble moral and ethical ideals" of that religion, which for him was intellectually sound. See Clayborne Carson, et al., eds., *The Papers of Martin Luther King, Jr., Volume II: Rediscovering Precious Values, July 1951–November 1955* (Berkeley: University of California Press, 1994), 320; Carson, ed., *The Autobiography of Martin Luther King, Jr.*, 15; Evans and Alexander, eds., *Dexter Avenue Baptist Church*, 69; and Carson, et al., eds., *King Papers*, I, 363.

27. King, Jr.'s mother Alberta reportedly "nurtured his musicality" through his Morehouse College years. Carson, et. al., eds., *King Papers*, I, 36–37, 112, and 116; Farris, *Through It All*, 38; King, *My Life with Martin Luther King, Jr.*, 82–83; Ling, *Martin Luther King, Jr.*, 14; and Baldwin, *There is a Balm in Gilead*, 29.

helped refine the type of skills he needed to excel as both a singer and a speaker.[28]

Morehouse College was essentially an extension of the King family and Ebenezer Church when it came to King, Jr.'s developing love and appreciation for music. The King family was present at "almost all the campus concerts even before" the youngster "entered college, and frequently waited a few moments after the performances were over to congratulate and chat with the singers." King, Jr. developed a close and lasting association with Robert Williams, another Morehouse student, who "had a beautiful tenor voice" and served as "one of the soloists" with both the Morehouse Glee Club and the chorus of the affiliated black colleges. According to King's friend Lawrence Reddick, "These were first class aggregations under the direction of Kemper Harreld and his assistant Willis Laurence James,"[29] who were viewed as two of the most brilliant minds in the music field. Music was all around King, Jr. in those early years, and this explains why the spirituals, gospel songs, hymns, and other musical forms were almost as much a part of his education at Morehouse as his courses in sociology, philosophy, and ethics. When it came to music, the intertwining significance of his family, church, and Morehouse College came together in King, Jr.'s consciousness, and together, they provided the context for a rigorous and generous engagement with the most vital ingredients of black cultural and artistic life.

In this setting of continued racial oppression and segregation, in which art touched virtually every ramification of life, a precocious youngster such as King, Jr. was not likely to reduce music to merely that vital part of his people's expressions of faith which too often swelled and overflowed into joyous shouts. While he understood sacred

---

28. Southern black culture in this period, as had been the case during slavery and countless generations back in Africa, was still largely orality culture. As Lawrence Levine has pointed out, the "spoken arts' were central to that "expressive culture," and "verbal improvisation" was both "encouraged" and "rewarded." Levine's insights are quite useful in locating King, Jr. in that culture, and also for any celebration of his life in song, the verbal arts, or the spoken word. See Reddick, *Crusader without Violence*, 73–74; Baldwin, *There is a Balm in Gilead*, 29; and Lawrence W. Levine, *Black Culture and Black Consciousness: Afro-American Folk Thought from Slavery to Freedom* (New York: Oxford University Press, 1978), 6.

29. Reddick, *Crusader without Violence*, 73–74.

music largely in these terms, he found in black secular music, a rich source of fun, entertainment, and celebration, and was therefore far more receptive to its relationship in performance to dance or bodily movement and expression. In other words, the young man who looked with shame and confusion on his elders' shouting and dancing in church "liked to dance" himself at teen socials, "and was quite a good jitterbug" when attending parties at Atlanta's Booker T. Washington High School, at the homes of friends and neighbors, or at the local community centers.[30] As many as "300 to 400 young people" reportedly showed up for some of the dances King, Jr. attended at the Butler Street YMCA in the city.[31] King, Jr. and his brother A. D. not only danced as teenagers, but began drinking and smoking, repeatedly testing "their father's willingness to impose discipline."[32] This kind of festive and celebrative approach to life continued unabated when King, Jr. enrolled at Morehouse College in 1944 at the tender age of fifteen. Walter R. McCall, one of King, Jr.'s friends and classmates at Morehouse, remembered that King, Jr. did not take "his studies very seriously" and "loved the lighter side of life," even "when it meant disobeying his father's injunctions against sinful behavior."[33]

30. Carson, ed., *The Autobiography of Martin Luther King, Jr.*, 15; Evans and Alexander, eds., *Dexter Avenue Baptist Church*, 69; Reddick, *Crusader without Violence*, 4 and 56; Baldwin, *There is a Balm in Gilead*, 31; Frederick L. Downing, *To See the Promised Land: The Faith Pilgrimage of Martin Luther King, Jr.* (Macon, GA: Mercer University Press, 1986), 126; Farris, "The Young Martin," 57–58; Farris, *Through It All*, 30 and 62; King, *My Life with Martin Luther King, Jr.*, 59; David J. Garrow, *Bearing the Cross: Martin Luther King, Jr., and the Southern Christian Leadership Conference* (New York: William Morrow and Company, Inc., 1986), 34; Carson, et al., eds., *King Papers*, I, 38; and Ling, *Martin Luther King, Jr.*, 20.
31. Warren R. Cochrane, who served as executive director of the Butler Street YMCA in Atlanta at that time, and who recounted "two occasions on which he had substantive conversations with M. L. King, Jr., as a teenager," was actually interviewed in July, 1985. Cochrane reported that King, Sr., a member of both the local ministerial association and the executive committee of the Butler Street YMCA, was "delegated" at one point "to study the dances held there" and to make recommendations "to the group of ministers" about how the situation might be properly and effectively handled. This compelled King, Sr. to make unannounced appearances at dances from time to time. King, Jr. supposedly told Cochrane on one such occasion: "Don't pay any attention to daddy. He just acts that way." See Downing, *To See the Promised Land*, 129n12.
32. Interestingly enough, this is not the image of young King that one gets from a close reading of the autobiographies of his father and sister. There are no suggestions here of a teenager who takes on bad habits while challenging or testing his father. See Keith D. Miller, *Voice of Deliverance: The Language of Martin Luther King, Jr., and Its Sources* (New York: The Free Press, 1992), 39; Farris, "The Young Martin," 57–58; Farris, *Through It All*, 30–31 and 223; King, *Daddy King*, 127 and 130–31; and King, *My Life with Martin Luther King, Jr.*, 77–78 and 83–84.
33. Carson, et al., eds., *King Papers*, I, 38; Miller, *Voice of Deliverance*, 39; Farris, *Through It All*, 223; Downing, *To See the Promised Land*, 129; Garrow, *Bearing the Cross*, 34 and 39; and Baldwin, *There is a Balm in Gilead*, 37–38 and 119.

When it came to the question of how one should view and respond to music and dance in the context of both the sacred and secular realms, the "exceedingly liberal religious views" of King, Jr. clashed with the single-minded moralism that pervaded so much of black church culture in the South generally, and that was embraced wholeheartedly and uncritically by the elder King himself.[34] King, Jr. and A. D. "rebelled" against the hypermoralism of Daddy King and Ebenezer Church, where bodily movement and expression were fine as long as this was done under the power of the Holy Spirit and in the service of the Lord. "Many times his father opposed our dancing and things like that," said McCall of King, Jr., "but he would slip off anyway and go." "Many times he and I as well as his sister and some more girls would congregate at his home while his Daddy was at church and we'd put on a party."[35] One of King's closest teenage friends, Larry Williams, a member at Ebenezer, "never forgot how angrily King, Sr." became "when he once caught Williams" and King, Jr. "dancing with girl friends at a church social." "Shouting furiously, Reverend King told the two young men to leave the YWCA where the social was being held."[36] "I don't approve of dancing and I don't let my children dance," Daddy King declared on one occasion. "But I suppose it is what kids want to do."[37] Even so, King, Sr. did punish his children at times for dancing and partying, often requiring them to do "kitchen duty," especially when they "failed to return" by his curfew. "Part of it, I'm sure, was the generational conflict that every family with teen-aged children goes through," King, Jr.'s sister, Christine recalled. "On the other hand, there were a good number of deacons in the church who frowned upon dancing, and Dad supported them. However, as time went on he grew to tolerate the things the 'young folks' did."[38]

34. One might argue that the differences here brought into focus certain theological and ethical principles over which King, Jr. and his father strongly disagreed. See Miller, *Voice of Deliverance*, 39; Carson, et al., eds., *King Papers*, I, 38; and Farris, "The Young Martin," 57–58.
35. Walter McCall shared these recollections in an interview with Herbert Holmes on 31 March 1970. See Carson, et al., eds., *King Papers*, I, 38. Also see Miller, *Voice of Deliverance*, 39; Farris, *Through It All*, 30–31; and Farris, "The Young Martin," 57–58.
36. Garrow, *Bearing the Cross*, 34.
37. Quoted in Downing, *To See the Promised Land*, 129. Also see Farris, *Through It All*, 223; and Farris, "The Young Martin," 57–58.

As one who was inquisitive from a very young age, and who questioned the Virgin Birth, the physical resurrection of Jesus, and other fundamental church teachings, it is not surprising that King, Jr. categorically rejected the notion that dancing constituted a particularly heinous type of sin.[39] In his formative years, his grounding in the essentials of black art was such that he understood much about the significance of dance in secular forms in the cultures of peoples of African descent worldwide, even if he did not then understand sacred expressions of the dance and the shout in similar terms. During his senior year at Morehouse, King, Jr. wrote an interesting paper on "Ritual," in which he alluded to the Vodun dance in Haiti, in which songs for the deity "are taken up as the drums play the rhythm of the god," as "a symbolic way of becoming possessed of the gods."[40] Exactly why he did not understand the shout and the holy dance in southern Negro churches, which were also linked to forms of spirit possession, in a similar fashion is most difficult to grasp, for no youngster his age in that time had a greater exposure to and knowledge of the spiritual aspects of black culture.

King, Jr.'s experiences at Crozer Seminary in Chester, Pennsylvania and at the Graduate School of Theology at Boston University did not lead to significant or noticeable changes in his attitude toward and approach to the world of music. Surrounded in both cities by blacks who had migrated from different points in the South, and who had recreated a southern sense of place in their new environment, the young man found almost perfect settings in which to avail him self to great artists and to the richest veins of music and dance. King, Jr. discovered at the Calvary Baptist Church in Chester, at which he taught Sunday school and occasionally preached, an emphasis on the spirituals, gospel songs, and the great Christian hymns that reminded

38. Farris, "The Young Martin," 57–58; Farris, Through It All, 30–31; and King, My Life with Martin Luther King, Jr., 12–13.
39. Carson, ed., The Autobiography of Martin Luther King, Jr., 6; Miller, Voice of Deliverance, 39–40; Carson, et al., eds., King Papers, I, 38; Farris, "The Young Martin," 57–58; and Downing, To See the Promised Land, 129.
40. Carson, et al., eds., King Papers, I, 109–11, 121, 131, and 363; Baldwin and Al-Hadid, Between Cross and Crescent, 16–17and 35–36; Baldwin, There is a Balm in Gilead, 30–44; King, Daddy King, 127; and Farris, Through It All, 3–19.

him of Ebenezer Baptist Church back home in Atlanta. There, he delighted in listening to the singing of Olee Littlejohn Barbour, the wife of Pastor J. Pius Barbour, who "was blessed with a memorable voice and inordinate energy," who "devoted many years to the musical training" of Calvary's youth, and who "was the organizer and director" of that congregation's junior choir.[41] Sara Richardson, a devoted member of Calvary Church at that time, recalled that King, Jr. "loved the old-time spirituals, and would sit for hours listening to Mrs. Barbour and Calvary's choirs singing them." Recalling the sheer breadth of King, Jr.'s musical interests, Richardson went on to report that the youngster listened to all types of music on the radio and "loved the blues," and that "Bessie Smith was one of his favorites."[42] Wherever there was music in Chester's black community, there was also dance, and King, Jr., despite becoming more serious about his ministry and academic pursuits, still "carried on a rather busy night life."[43] He occasionally showed up at "parties in Philadelphia and nearby suburbs,"[44] and seemed, at least on the surface, to believe that there was really no bifurcation of the sacred and secular in the music of his people. This perspective was very much in line with the youngster's growing ethical and theological liberalism and also his amazing tendency toward independent thinking.

The social world in Boston was especially fertile for a young man such as King, Jr., who had extraordinary aesthetic sensibilities in music, and who literally enjoyed a variety in vocal and instrumental music. The Roxbury area, where most blacks lived, was known for great art and culture, and King, Jr., who had high cultural standards, looked for

41. "A History of Calvary Baptist Church," in *Program Booklet of the Calvary Baptist Church Centennial Celebration, 1879-1979* (Chester, PA: Linder Printing Company, 1979), 18; A Private Interview with Sara V. Richardson, Chester, Pennsylvania (29 May 1987); A Private Interview with Emma Anderson, Chester, Pennsylvania (29 May 1987); and Baldwin, *There is a Balm in Gilead*, 282.
42. Baldwin Interview with Richardson (29 May 1987); and Baldwin, *There is a Balm in Gilead*, 38 and 282.
43. Garrow, *Bearing the Cross*, 41. King, Jr. "had no time for frivolity" and was apparently "the Faustian student" during the day, but had much fun in his "spare moments" and in the evenings. See David L. Lewis, *King: A Critical Biography* (New York: Praeger Publishers, 1970), 32; and Downing, *To See the Promised Land*, 154.
44. Lerone Bennett, Jr., *What Manner of Man: A Biography of Martin Luther King, Jr.* (Chicago: Johnson Publishing Company, 1964), 26.

and found great music in churches, taverns, nightclubs, poolrooms, and on street corners—music ringing through open windows and heard blocks away. The Twelfth Baptist Church, where considerable numbers of migrants from the South worshipped, and where King, Jr. served as a preaching assistant to Pastor William H. Hester, had been associated with developing trends in black sacred music since antebellum times. King, Jr. was always moved by the rousing renditions of the folksongs and hymns he heard there on Sunday mornings, music that punctuated the doctrinal preaching and fiery exhortation from the pulpit, and the shouts of "yes," "thank God," and "praise the Lord" from the choir stand and pews.[45] When King, Jr. was not in church, relaxing, or studying for classes, he and his friends routinely met for an evening of jazz at the Totem Pole and other night spots in Roxbury, where the rhythmic beating of worn brass drums and the music of violins, guitars, and saxophones created a medley of sounds that set the stage for much wiggling, dancing, and flirting.[46] A more stimulating environment for King, Jr. in those days was almost unimaginable. His experiences in both the sacred space of the church and the more secular world of blacks in Boston contributed substantially to his sense of the spirit of community and cooperation that informed black music and dance, and indeed, black art as a whole.

Boston was also significant because it was the city in which King, Jr. met the one person who, aside from his mother, Alberta, would have the greatest impact on his sense of the beauty and power of

---

45. A Private Interview with Reverend Michael E. Haynes, Twelfth Baptist Church, Boston, Massachusetts (25 June 1987); A Private Interview with Philip Lenud, Vanderbilt Divinity School, Nashville, Tennessee (7 April 1987); and Baldwin, *There is a Balm in Gilead*, 39 and 283. Twelfth Baptist was founded in 1840, and has been referred to over generations as the "abolitionist church" and the "Fugitive Slave Church," because William Lloyd Garrison, Wendell Phillips, Theodore Parker, Charles Sumner, and Frederick Douglass spoke from the pulpit there, and because it emerged "as a primary station in the 'Underground Railroad'." Given the ties of Twelfth Baptist to anti-slavery activities, it is only logical to conclude that slave spirituals were sung or heard there in the Pre-Civil War years. See *One Hundred and Five Years by Faith: A History of the Twelfth Baptist Church, 1840-1945* (Boston, 1846), 9–11 and 18–22; *Three-Fold Celebration Year: Souvenir Journal, Twelfth Baptist Church* (May, 1985), 18–19; and King, *My Life with Martin Luther King, Jr.*, 89–91.
46. Downing, *To See the Promised Land*, 169; Baldwin Interview with Haynes (25 June 1987); Baldwin Interview with Lenud (7 April 1987); Stephen B. Oates, *Let the Trumpet Sound: The Life of Martin Luther King, Jr.* (New York: Harper & Row, Publishers, 1982), 41; Baldwin, *There is a Balm in Gilead*, 40; and King, *My Life with Martin Luther King, Jr.*, 50–51 and 90.

music—namely, Coretta Scott, who, as she herself put it, "was absorbing music" at the highly reputable New England Conservatory of Music at that time.[47] Coretta would become King, Jr.'s wife and partner in the civil and human rights struggles, and she would bring the power of her art to bear on those struggles. When it came to the capacity to cherish and to benefit spiritually from music in all forms, it was difficult to imagine a better-paired couple. Coretta's "world of music" had been "opened" at Lincoln High School in her hometown of Marion, Alabama, where she enrolled in music classes, took voice lessons, played the trumpet, performed vocal solos, and sang solos with choruses, and where she was introduced to classical music, and especially, Handel's *Messiah*. While a student at Antioch College in Ohio in the late 1940s and early 1950s, Coretta studied with a professor who "was at home with Bach as well as bop,"[48] and she actually "had the unusual experience of appearing on a program with the then world-famous baritone Paul Robeson," whose performances were beyond imitation when it came to renditions of the Negro spirituals on the concert stage, and "who commended" Coretta's "voice and encouraged" her "to continue her voice studies." Coretta's voice was as smooth as velvet, and King, Jr. came to view her "as a young lady who was studying music with deep cultural appreciation. . . ."[49]

King, Jr. and Coretta's shared love for music was part of "a heritage deeply rooted in southern soil."[50] Music was the dominant topic of conversation during their very first date at Sharaf's Restaurant in Boston in early 1952, and as the relationship strengthened and became serious, it was clear that the two shared much more than simply being from the deep South. Both had lived in areas saturated with the sounds and rhythms of sacred and secular music from their earliest childhood. Coretta vividly recounted growing up in a black Methodist Church

47. King, *My Life with Martin Luther King, Jr.*, 49; Farris, *Through It All*, 72, 77, and 81; and King, *Daddy King*, 149.
48. Dr. Walter Anderson was "Antioch's lone African American faculty member" at that time, and he was equally and perhaps more important to Coretta as Frances Thomas and Olive J. Williams had been at Lincoln High School in Alabama. See King, *My Life with Martin Luther King, Jr.*, 34–36 and 44–45.
49. Ibid., 35–37, 43, 45, 49, and 58.
50. Ibid., 18; and Baldwin, *There is a Balm in Gilead*, 17, 19, 31–33, and 41.

where her maternal grandfather Martin McMurray would "line the hymns," where "Amazing Grace," "Holy, Holy, Holy," and "all the Methodist hymns" were commonly sung, and where the spirituals and other folksongs—a century-old "mixture of African and American folkways in the context of the Christian religion"—combined with "rousing" sermons and "emotional" shouts of "Amen!," "Yeah!," or "Preach!," producing "a church atmosphere" that constituted both "the cultural haven" and the birth of "the concept called 'soul'." Coretta also remembered a home environment in which "such treasures as Clara and Bessie Smith recordings, sermons, and jazz recordings, as well as popular songs and hymns"[51] could be found and heard. In these contexts of church, home, and family, it is not surprising that Coretta, like King, Jr., was encouraged very early to pursue training in vocal and instrumental music. Both were song leaders and soloists as children, and as they reached adulthood, wondered why so many black "performers in Jazz and popular music," with "extraordinary talent," either "were not able to get professional training at first-rate institutions or, if they had training," were "not able to find jobs" with the "many symphonies."[52] Both were cultured and well-traveled by the time they became engaged to each other, and their romantic side was quite evident not only in their love for music, but also literature and the broader sphere of art. In short, King, Jr. and Coretta's encounter with the power of different kinds of music and art, in general, united them in mind, heart, and body, and was part of the magic that produced the romance. Indeed, this is largely what anchored their relationship for life.

The music scene in Boston was broad and diverse enough in the 1950s to meet the spiritual, social, and recreational needs of any young black couple anticipating marriage, and King, Jr. and Coretta availed themselves to as much of it as their schedules permitted. They were

---

51. In view of the richness and vitality of that culture, it is difficult to understand Coretta's claim that she was from "such a culturally deprived background." See King, *My Life with Martin Luther King, Jr.*, 18, 28–29, 36, 52–53, and 58–59.
52. Ibid., 31, 35–36, 44–50, and 85; Farris, "The Young Martin," 56; and Reddick, *Crusader without Violence*, 56.

convinced that great music and dancing feet did, in fact, go together, even in worship, as long as it was not excessive and did not degenerate into what King, Jr. regarded as sheer entertainment, unrestrained exhibitionism, or an "ecclesiastical circus."[53] Exposure to the church experience on Sunday mornings—the chanted sermon, the spontaneous humming, the improvisatory singing, the stirring piano or organ pieces, the vigorous handclapping and foot-stomping that added a kind of percussive quality—remained central to the spiritual life of the couple, but this constituted only a small segment of their social world, especially when it came to the enjoyment of music. King, Jr. also introduced Coretta to a side of the city's night life, filled with secular musical forms, that she had not come to know well because of her rather sheltered existence and her devotion to her jobs and studies. "I remember the first concert he took me to at Symphony Hall in Boston," Coretta recalled. "I was touched that Martin, who knew how much music meant to me, would think of that kind of date. The great Polish artist Artur Rubenstein was the pianist, and this was the first time I had heard him play."[54]

Convinced that music and dance were central facts of life, King, Jr. and Coretta frequented "parties in private homes," mainly because they "did not feel completely welcome" at white "nightclubs in the Boston area." "He loved to dance and was a good dancer," said Coretta of King, Jr. "He loved people and enjoyed parties and, especially, good conversation. He loved music too."[55] The partying was mostly among other southern Negroes who were also studying at one of the academic

---

53. During this period in Boston, King, Jr. was still a bit uneasy about what he considered excessive emotionalism during worship exercises, and especially, dancing and the shout, despite their inseparability from music in Negro church culture. Preachers who shouted or engaged in a sacred dance while singing their sermons were, in his estimation, too often "showmen giving the people what they want rather than what they need," and he criticized "songs in our worship periods which appeal to the feet and hands rather than to the heart and mind." See Clayborne Carson, et al., eds., *The Papers of Martin Luther King, Jr., Volume VI: Advocate of the Social Gospel, September 1948–March 1963* (Berkeley: University of California Press, 2007), 223–25 and 295.

54. King, *My Life with Martin Luther King, Jr.,* 59–60. The reader may recall that it was Coretta's enjoyment of concerts and plans to perform on the concert stage that actually accounted for King, Jr.'s father's initial opposition to the couple's relationship and plans for marriage. See, King, *Daddy King*, 149.

55. King, *My life with Martin Luther King, Jr.,* 50 and 59–60; and Edythe Scott Bagley, *Desert Rose: The Life and Legacy of Coretta Scott King* (Tuscaloosa: The University of Alabama Press, 2012), 98.

institutions in and around Boston.[56] King, Jr. made the best of such experiences, for they not only satisfied his desire for entertainment, but also reinforced his southern sense of place and his desire to ultimately return to the South. Daddy King wondered at times if his son was "partying too hard,"[57] but he never interfered in any serious fashion. The conflict between King, Jr.'s position and that of his father over music and dance and their proper place in life would ultimately end, particularly as Daddy King became increasingly tolerant of secular music and dance.[58]

Secular music and dance figured as prominently in King, Jr.'s growing sense of the extended family and of the larger ideal of human community as music and dance in sacred forms. He delighted in various types of music whenever there were weddings, gatherings with friends, and other activities of a social nature, and he and Coretta often "danced publicly" up to the time he became the pastor at Montgomery's Dexter Avenue Baptist Church in 1954.[59] When that time came, King, Jr. told Coretta that as pastor and first lady of a southern black Baptist Church, they were not "able to dance anymore in public because it would be distasteful to the older members of the congregation."[60] While King, Jr. always saw differences between secular musical and dance forms and sacred musical and dance forms, he ultimately came to appreciate both and considered both when speaking of the role that art could play in enlightening, empowering, and bringing people together.[61]

56. King, My Life with Martin Luther King, Jr., 90.
57. King, Daddy King, 148.
58. Daddy King actually approached the membership at Ebenezer Baptist Church about providing space for young people to dance. Pounding the pulpit on one occasion, he told his rather conservative folk at Ebenezer: "I know how you feel about this, but you're going to have to accept it. It is better to provide for them to dance here than for them to go somewhere else." See King, My Life with Martin Luther King, Jr., 12–13; and Farris, "The Young Martin," 58.
59. Reddick, Crusader without Violence, 56; Bagley, Desert Rose, 102; and King, My Life with Martin Luther King, Jr., 12.
60. King, My Life with Martin Luther King, Jr., 12–13; and Reddick, Crusader without Violence, 4.
61. Bagley, Desert Rose, 102; King, My Life with Martin Luther King, Jr., 12; Carson, et al., eds., King Papers, IV, 392–93 and 402; and Baldwin and Al-Hadid, Between Cross and Crescent, 35–42.

B. The Language of Faith: Sacred Music in the Context
of Congregational Life

Martin Luther King, Jr. saw vocal and instrumental music as *de rigueur* in congregational life and as an essential component of Christian ministry, and this perspective largely defined his approach to the pastoral role at Dexter Church. Arriving in Montgomery after almost six years of seminary and graduate studies in the northeast, King reclaimed southern black Baptist life in its most original context and in all of its ritualism, ceremonialism, and traditionalism, which included music in its most sacred and vital expressions. Although Dexter had a highly educated membership, was known for its classism, and was quite unlike the typical Negro congregation in the South,[62] liturgically speaking, King became a participant in that larger black church culture in which faith was largely expressed and celebrated through music and the frenzy—characteristics that W. E. B. DuBois had associated with the slave church.[63] Powerful singers moving and swaying and holy rollers shouting almost to the point of pure exhaustion were very much a part of the very fabric of Negro congregational life, and King acknowledged and became more respectful of this kind of spiritual and emotional release as a pastor.[64] His effort to change the image of Dexter from a "big folks' church" to a "whosoever will, let him come" church with a lively and appealing worship experience had much to do with a revitalization of its music ministry. Some of King's earliest recommendations at Dexter, expressed orally and in writing,

---

62. King, *Stride toward Freedom*, 25; Baldwin, *There is a Balm in Gilead*, 174–206; Baldwin, *The Voice of Conscience*, 114–40; and Lewis V. Baldwin, *Never to Leave Us Alone: The Prayer Life of Martin Luther King Jr.* (Minneapolis: Fortress Press, 2010), 72.

63. "Frenzy" for DuBois meant "Shouting," which occurred, as he put it, "when the Spirit of the Lord passed by, and seizing the devotee, made him mad with supernatural joy." This, DuBois added, was an "essential of Negro religion and the one more devoutly believed in than all the rest." See W. E. B. DuBois, *The Souls of Black Folk in Three Negro Classics* (New York: Avon Books, 1965), 339.

64. King himself explained how he, while praying at a mass meeting in a Negro Church in Montgomery during the bus boycott, was "caught in the grip of an emotion I could not control," a stunning admission from one who, as a boy, had been ashamed of "the emotionalism of much Negro religion." King actually broke down on this occasion and, at one point, simply stood "unable to move" with the arms of fellow ministers around him. See King, *Stride toward Freedom*, 178; Carson, ed., *The Autobiography of Martin Luther King, Jr.*, 15; Baldwin, *There is a Balm in Gilead*, 187–92; and Baldwin, *The Voice of Conscience*, 117.

called for the hiring of a new organist, the organization of "musical units" to take charge of church music and to "give encouragement to promising artists," and the formation of a "Department of Music" to "coordinate the efforts and aims of the musical units of the church." King, Jr. further recommended that "members of this department shall meet with the pastor once quarterly to discuss ways to implement the technical, artistic, and worship aims of the master."[65] King's efforts to reorganize and revitalize the music ministry were greeted with enthusiasm at Dexter, a congregation that claimed a rich musical history and that included not only a number of musicians, but also many who were musically inclined. Dexter's music program had already achieved much success and wide popularity in the late 1940s and early 50s under accomplished musicians such as Altona Trent Johns, the wife of King's predecessor, Vernon Johns. Largely because of the ground prepared by Mrs. Johns, "a professor of music" at Montgomery's Alabama State University, "a concert pianist of the first magnitude," and "the author of books on the subject of play songs and other helps for children,"[66] the people at Dexter were receptive to King, Jr.'s idea of music ministry as a high calling, and also, his conviction that music was as essential to the witness and mission of the church as preaching.

Having either observed or worked with choirs and music departments in black Baptist Churches virtually all of his life, King, Jr. fully understood the place and power of music in southern black

65. King declared that all of these recommendations were part of a larger effort to "lift the general cultural appreciation of our church and community." See King, *Stride toward Freedom*, 25; Carson, et al., eds., *King Papers*, II, 289–90; and Wally G. Vaughn and Richard W. Wills, eds., *Reflections on Our Pastor: Dr. Martin Luther King, Jr., at Dexter Avenue Baptist Church, 1954-1960* (Dover, MA: The Majority Press, Inc., 1999), 63. King must have had Dexter Church in mind whenever he spoke of the kind of Negro church that "freezes with classism"—that "boasts of its dignity, its membership of professional people, and its exclusiveness," and in which "the worship service is cold and meaningless, the music dull and uninspiring, and the sermon little more than a homily on current events." See King, *Strength to Love*, 63.
66. Some of the members at Dexter recalled Mrs. Johns's "skillful attainment in her chosen field" and noted that "On television she is portrayed as a woman who took music around the corner for twenty-five cents." See Evans and Alexander, eds., *Dexter Avenue Baptist Church*, 64; Vaughn and Wills, eds., *Reflections on Our Pastor*, 63; Charles Emerson Boddie, *God's "Bad Boys": Eight Outstanding Black Preachers* (Valley Forge, PA: Judson Press, 1980), 62; and King, *My Life with Martin Luther King, Jr.*, 121.

Baptist life and he freely drew on the musical resources of Dexter's membership, friends, and family to accomplish his goals. In the spring of 1955, King, Jr. hired Althea Thompson Thomas, a young but promising musician whom he baptized at Dexter, to fill the position of organist at the church, and he chose another Dexter member and longtime friend, Dr. J. T. Brooks, a "self-taught organist" who "mastered the technique of legato playing" and "hymn playing," to chair the church's "Department of Music."[67] Both Thomas and Brooks also had connections to the Music Department at Alabama State University, and this provided yet another resource that King, Jr. exploited to strengthen Dexter's music ministry. King, Jr. discussed music for hours with Robert Williams, one of his friends and former classmates at Atlanta's Morehouse College, who "had a beautiful tenor voice" and who also taught music at Alabama State. Both had been a part of the Morehouse Glee Club and the Atlanta University-Morehouse-Spelman Chorus years earlier, and their "mutual interest in music" largely explained their lasting association.[68]

King highly respected Thomas, Brooks, Williams, and other musical minds and talents in Montgomery, but he frequently turned to family first when making plans for great musical events at Dexter Church. Church music was almost always mentioned whenever King spoke by telephone or exchanged letters with his parents and siblings, and especially, in his many conversations with his sister, Christine and his mother, Alberta. Christine remembered her brother's installation ceremony as senior pastor at Dexter, in October, 1954, as "a King family affair" because their parents were present along with the Ebenezer Baptist Church choir from Atlanta. According to Christine, "Daddy preached" and "I led the singing of the anthem, 'I Will Give Thanks,' accompanied by Mother on the organ."[69] Knowing that his church

---

67. Vaughn and Wills, eds., *Reflections on Our Pastor*, 63–64; and Carson, et al., eds., *King Papers*, II, 289–90.
68. Williams was very close to both King and his wife Coretta, and "was often around as a guard and protector" of the King home when white mob violence surfaced in response to the Montgomery bus boycott. See Reddick, *Crusader without Violence*, 73, 130, 177, and 230; and King, *My Life with Martin Luther King, Jr.*, 114 and 122.
69. Farris, *Through It All*, 83.

members enjoyed concert music, King, Jr. later approached both his mother and his wife Coretta about providing this type of music periodically for the congregation. He invited Alberta to direct Ebenezer's choir in a number of Sunday afternoon concerts that would be "tailored for Dexter," but the only concert with Alberta as choir director actually occurred in April 1955, at which time the song, "I Fall on My Knees, and Cry Holy," was labeled "the best selection rendered."[70]

Coretta was in a much better position as Dexter's pastor's wife to meet many of the musical needs of that congregation. She had graduated from the New England Conservatory of Music in Boston in June 1954, with a degree in music education and a major in voice, and with some expertise in piano and violin, in choir directing, in orchestral arrangement and directing, and in the instrumental classes of percussion, strings, woodwinds, and brass, and that kind of knowledge and experience, in addition to the years of singing and playing musical instruments in black churches, equipped her to assume a special role in both the music ministry at Dexter and the freedom movement that would unfold in Montgomery after the arrest of Rosa Parks. King urged Coretta to either teach music or give concerts, and he experienced great joy when she sang solos or gave voice recitals at Dexter and at other Negro churches in Montgomery and other parts of the South. Coretta was "a soprano" and her Freedom Concerts, in which she told the story of the Montgomery bus boycott in song, or wove it into the spirituals and the freedom songs, undoubtedly became her most significant contribution to Dexter Church, to the civil rights struggle, and to the world of music.[71] Needless to say, King Jr.'s broad knowledge of church music as a work of art, as a necessary force in creating the atmosphere and mood for worship, and as a positive

---

70. Vaughn and Wills, eds., *Reflections on Our Pastor*, 67; Carson, et al., eds., *King Papers*, II, 43 and 45; and Evans and Alexander, eds., *Dexter Avenue Baptist Church*, 71.
71. King, *My Life with Martin Luther King, Jr.*, 36, 41, 43, 85, 88, 101, 133, 230–32, and 243; Carson, et al., eds., *King Papers*, II, 44; Reddick, *Crusader without Violence*, 6 and 217; Clayborne Carson, et al., eds., *The Papers of Martin Luther King, Jr., Volume III: Birth of a New Age, December 1955–December 1956* (Berkeley: University of California Press, 1997), 407; and Dorothy F. Cotton, *If Your Back's Not Bent: The Role of the Citizenship Education Program in the Civil Rights Movement* (New York: Atria Books, 2012), 233 and 271.

factor in faith formation, owed much to the influence of Coretta. When it came to the role of music in the congregational life of Dexter Church, she was to King, Jr. what Altona Johns had been to Vernon Johns.[72]

King himself displayed musical gifts at Dexter on Sundays that delighted, and at times, amazed its membership and its visitors. People were visibly moved whenever he lifted his voice in song, and his artistic ability and/or genius were as evident when he sang the spirituals and the great hymns of the church as when he delivered dynamic sermons, addresses, and mass meeting speeches. King had that wonderful ability to spontaneously break out in sermon and song at the same time, and this was not particularly surprising since great preachers in the culture were almost always great singers as well. Simply put, King's sermons were, in effect, songs or speech music, with much of the sound, phrasing, and rhythms of Negro folksongs. Those who knew him best and listened to him at Dexter and in other church settings recalled how he epitomized the beauty and vitality of the human voice whenever he spoke or sang.[73] "King's voice is possibly his most magnetic power," wrote the historian Lawrence Reddick, who was often present for Sunday services at Dexter Avenue Church. Reddick also noted how King used "his voice as an instrument, fitting its inflections to the tempo of his sentences and to the mood and thought that they are meant to convey."[74] King's own brother A. D. stated that King could "sing bass in a chorus and then double with a second tenor solo." Art Carter, an editor and commentator for the *Afro-American* newspaper, declared that King had "a soft musical voice

---

72. Charles Emerson Boddie, a Baptist minister who knew the Johns very well, reported that Mrs. Johns "abilities and graces made her husband what he could not have been without her." King often made similar comments about Coretta. See Boddie, *God's "Bad Boys,"* 62.

73. Vaughn and Wills, eds., *Reflections on Our Pastor*, 25, 32, 40, 47, 69, 75, 91, and 94; and Baldwin, *There is a Balm in Gilead*, 296.

74. Reddick's reference to King here clearly calls to mind James Weldon Johnson's statement regarding the slave preacher, or "old-time Negro preacher," who "knew the secret of oratory," who "was a master of all the modes of eloquence," and who "possessed a voice that was a marvelous instrument." See Reddick, *Crusader without Violence*, 8 and 12; and James Weldon Johnson, *God's Trombones: Seven Negro Sermons in Verse* (New York: The Viking Press, 1977; originally published in 1927), 5. Ralph Abernathy also located King in that tradition of the old-time Negro preacher, concluding that "he could lift that robust, beautiful, and musical voice just like his daddy." See A Personal Interview Ralph D. Abernathy, West Hunter Baptist Church, Atlanta, Georgia (17 March 1987); and Baldwin, *There is a Balm in Gilead*, 299.

which he uses without oratorical tricks." Almena Lomax of the *Los Angeles Tribune* essentially agreed, asserting that King's "voice has great power, passion, great depths of tenderness and an overlay of gentleness to charm your heart out of your body." Mrs. Lomax went on to explain that "the impact of Martin Luther King is in his delivery, which is all of a piece, like a narrative poem," and that his "elocution has the beauty and polish of Roland Hayes singing a spiritual. . . ."[75]

King sang as much as he preached during his years as pastor of Dexter Church, and he was always in search of a more fertile ground for that congregation's exposure to new and different forms of sacred music. More specifically, he sought to expand Dexter's repertoire of music beyond classical organ and piano pieces and the singing of traditional hymns such as "Just as I Am, Without One Plea," "Holy, Holy, Holy," and "Amazing Grace," to include more selections from black folk music, and especially, the spirituals, gospel songs, and anthems of the movement.[76] Time and context were quite relevant to these efforts on King's part, for King, due to a burgeoning civil rights crusade in the late 1950s, was rapidly becoming the preeminent voice of blacks in the South. Knowing the importance of music in sustaining his people's spirit of community and sense of cultural identity, he encouraged a liturgical atmosphere at Dexter that highlighted those types of vocal and instrumental music that triggered thoughts of their long history of suffering and struggle. This alone had tremendous spiritual and therapeutic value for church folk who functioned in a society in which there was so much that challenged their faith and sense of a fundamentally ordered world. While Dexter Church did not become known for the chanting, stomping, shouting, bring-down-the-house style of worship characteristic of the typical Negro Baptist church in and around Montgomery, it did inject more black sacred songs into its services and rituals, and was as active as any other black congregation in reclaiming the songs sung by slaves in antebellum times for the modern civil rights cause.[77]

---

75. Reddick, *Crusader without Violence*, 8 and 12.
76. Vaughn and Wills, eds., *Reflections on Our Pastor*, 36; King, *Stride toward Freedom*, 86–87 and 149; and King, *My Life with Martin Luther King, Jr.*, 133–35.

The rich and melodious voices of King, Jr. and his wife, Coretta blended well into the participatory singing at Dexter Church. Congregational singing there took on a special life of its own as events connected to the bus protest unfolded and gradually reached fever pitch, but there were also choir singing, concerts, solos, and other types of musical performances. Coretta "became a regular member of the choir" at Dexter, worked with its music units, served as co-chairman of its Department of Music, and occasionally, sang solos, even as she began to "consider the options for a broader musical career."[78] She added significantly to the flavor of the worship experience at Dexter with her renderings of spirituals such as "Go Down Moses," "Walk Together, Chillun," "Lord I Can't Turn Back, Just Because I've Been Born Again," "Keep Your Hands on the Plow," and "Honor, Honor," which was one of her husband's "favorite songs." Coretta's singing was apparently well-received by the congregation, and also, her style of telling the story of the movement in Montgomery through the prism of the old spirituals, which was taken beyond Dexter and other black churches in the South to the concert stage in places as far away as the Manhattan Center in New York City.[79] Consequently, Coretta and her husband developed a stronger sense of the impact that music and song, and especially, the singing of the spirituals, might have not only in the context of the congregational worship experience, but also, in larger and more inclusive efforts to frame and spread the message of human freedom.

The couple's interest in and involvements with church music never really waned, even as King, Jr. himself took on a greater and more demanding role in his people's struggle against bigotry and discrimination. In January 1960, after resigning as senior pastor of Dexter, King, Jr. became a co-pastor with his father, King, Sr. and

77. King, *Stride toward Freedom*, 86–87 and 149; King, *My Life with Martin Luther King, Jr.*, 133–35; and Baldwin Interview with Abernathy (17 March 1987).
78. Bagley, *Desert Rose*, 108–9; Carson, et al., eds., *King Papers*, II, 289; and Evans and Alexander, eds., *Dexter Avenue Baptist Church*, 74.
79. King, *My Life with Martin Luther King, Jr.*, 133–34; Bagley, *Desert Rose*, 108–9; Octavia Vivian, *Coretta: The Story of Coretta Scott King*, Commemorative Edition (Minneapolis: Fortress Press, 2006), 25–26; and Baldwin Interview with Abernathy (17 March 1987).

brother, A. D. at the Ebenezer Baptist Church in Atlanta, the congregation that first introduced him to much of the world of sacred music. At Ebenezer, he and Coretta re-entered a community in which the spirituals and other black sacred songs were routinely sung with virtually no barriers of technique and feeling. It was a community of spiritually-minded folks who responded with cries of joy, raised hands, the nodding of heads, handclapping, and the movement of bodies in accordance with the meter of hymns sung. Members of the King family once again came together in a familiar environment in which their musical talents essentially defined the artistic and liturgical life of the congregation. From that point, perhaps the most striking images of Ebenezer Church on Sunday mornings were revealed in the rhythmic eloquence of the sermons preached by King, Jr., his father, and his brother, in the captivating performances of King, Jr.'s mother, Alberta on piano and organ, and in the solos of Coretta and King, Jr.'s sister, Christine—both of whom were members of the church choir as well.[80]

On some Sundays, when King, Jr. was scheduled to preach at Ebenezer, he asked Coretta to sing a solo. Sometimes, at Christmastime and Easter, he called on her to do the Meditation Hymn, and especially, "Sweet Little Jesus Boy," which "was one of his favorites."[81] At other times, King, Jr. would lead in the singing of some Negro spiritual, gospel song, or hymn himself, and would follow with a dynamic and moving sermon. Coretta has shared more than anyone else about King, Jr.'s singing ability during his years as Ebenezer's co-pastor, noting that he also occasionally served as a song leader at other gatherings that included church people as well. She recalled one particular occasion when her husband's "willingness to sing in public caused" him "a very embarrassing time":

> He was speaking at a large meeting, and when he finished, he had wanted the audience to join him in singing "His Eye Is on the Sparrow." But the

---

80. King, *My Life with Martin Luther King, Jr.*, 232–33; Vivian, *Coretta*, 26; Baldwin Interview with Abernathy (17 March 1987); and Baldwin Interview with Abernathy (7 May 1987).
81. After her husband's death, Coretta found "a new meaning and interpretation of the words of this song," for it seemed "so reminiscent of Martin's own life experiences." See King, *My Life with Martin Luther King, Jr.*, 232. Also see Baldwin Interview with Abernathy (17 March 1987); and Baldwin, *There is a Balm in Gilead*, 299.

people had not understood what he meant, and Martin was left standing there, only *his* voice sounding in the large auditorium. He told me how emotionally the people responded when he came to the part that said:

I sing because I'm happy,
I sing because I'm free. . . .

It was as if the emotional pull on the audience had lifted them from their seats. Martin continued singing:

His eye is on the sparrow,
And I know He's watching me.

He told me that he had real stage fright, but had no choice but to sing through to the end. The audience responded with great emotion, shouting and applauding. When Martin got home, he told me proudly, "I really did well. You think I can't sing, but the people say I can."[82]

Singing, for King, Jr., was always a necessity in the life of the person of faith, and he freely exercised this part of his being in various settings. "And yes, Dr. King would be up and energetically singing along with his mom and the rest of us," reported Dorothy Cotton, one of King's aides in the SCLC. "He loved to sing and always had fun doing so."[83] King, Jr. found new life in the joyous and transformative power of church music. Aside from preaching, prayer and meditation,[84] and testimony, this was the one medium through which he most often expressed his own deep personal spirituality.[85] Knowing that his people's response to oppression was not only political, but liturgical as well, he really cherished the many worship experiences during which he united his voice in song with the members of Ebenezer and countless other churches in black communities. The same might be

---

82. King, *My Life with Martin Luther King, Jr.*, 232–33.
83. According to Cotton, "Dr. King loved poetry; he loved beautiful language and the songs of our people," and "was indeed a poet" as well as a good singer himself. See Cotton, *If Your Back's Not Bent*, 13, 89, 98, and 220.
84. Baldwin, *Never to Leave Us Alone*, 9–90; Baldwin, *There is a Balm in Gilead*, 287–321; King, *My Life with Martin Luther King, Jr.*, 134 and 232–33; Cotton, *If Your Back's Not Bent*, 13; and King, *Daddy King*, 147.
85. Although King's "life's thrust was made through the medium of preaching," more attention needs to be devoted to his involvement with music and song if his artistic ability is to be properly and fully understood. See Boddie, *God's "Bad Boys"*, 77; Baldwin, *There is a Balm in Gilead*, 86–87; and King, *My life with Martin Luther King, Jr.*, 8–9, 59, and 232–33.

said of those rare but special moments when King, Jr. sat around the piano at home with his wife and children and other family members, singing the great hymns of the church. Faced with a crowded schedule and increasing demands on his time and energy, Christmas was the occasion during which he was most often available to participate in such displays of artistic talent and ability, and he freely lifted his "high baritone voice" in singing a variety of Christmas carols.[86] Although King, Jr. had virtually no training, in a formal sense, as a singer, the image of him bringing the full force of his vocal power to bear on the great body of Christian music actually reinforces the claim that he was, at heart, an artist of considerable ability and skill.

C. Lift Every Voice: Songs Rolling Down Like a Mighty Stream

It was through his involvements with and studies of vocal music, in particular, that Martin Luther King, Jr. came to a theoretical understanding of certain essentials of black culture and American culture in general.[87] He repeatedly referred to a range of sacred and secular songs in his sermons, speeches, and writings, and his comments about these songs were rooted in a more general concern for what they revealed about the human spirit, higher human values, and the struggle to enlarge the reach of the human endeavor, especially as it related to freedom, justice, equality of opportunity, and self-determination. What made King, Jr.'s statements concerning the Negro spirituals, gospel songs, hymns, the blues, and other vocal musical forms so keen and penetrating had to do with much more than just the formal scholarly training he received at Morehouse College, Crozer Theological Seminary, and Boston University. Significantly more important was what he observed, experienced, and felt as he availed

---

86. King, *My Life with Martin Luther King, Jr.*, 232; Baldwin Interview with Abernathy (17 March 1987); Baldwin Interview with Abernathy (7 May 1987); Baldwin and Al-Hadid, *Between Cross and Crescent*, 15–17 and 35; and Reddick, *Crusader without Violence*, 8.
87. For an earlier attempt to explore King's understanding of certain aspects of black culture in theoretical terms, see Baldwin, *There is a Balm in Gilead*, 30–339; and Baldwin and Al-Hadid, *Between Cross and Crescent*, 22–30.

himself to different kinds of songs and singing in black churches, historically black colleges, and various other settings over time.[88]

King, Jr. probably said more about the Negro spirituals than he said about any other type of vocal music, and this was to be expected since this type of music had been part of the very air he breathed from his childhood years. Quoting W. E. B. DuBois, King, Jr. called the spirituals "that most original and beautiful of all American music," and he spoke, with telling insight, of the artistic genius of his "slave foreparents," who created this music out of their suffering and sorrow and pioneered in making it an American folk classic.[89] King, Jr. was equally perceptive when recognizing those scholars whose insights into the cultural significance of the spirituals were so creative and searching, and also, those artists who had been so instrumental in capturing and preserving the beauty and power of this music in their own performances in churches, on the concert stage, and in other settings. Although King, Jr. apparently knew about DuBois's important references to the spirituals and the frenzy in *The Souls of Black Folk* (1903) and other works, and also about James Weldon Johnson's *American Negro Spirituals* (1925), in which the shout is discussed as "semi-barbaric music," he never commented in any serious way on the importance of these sources for understanding the history of black music, and he virtually ignored DuBois's and Johnson's claim that the counterparts of the Negro spiritual and shouting could be found in Africa.[90] While King, Jr. also made no mention of DuBois's references

---

88. Baldwin, *There is a Balm in Gilead*, 17, 31–33, 35, 38, 40, 42, 86, 168–70, 173, 196–97, 201, and 205; Lewis V. Baldwin, *To Make the Wounded Whole: The Cultural Legacy of Martin Luther King, Jr.* (Minneapolis: Fortress Press, 1992), 64–66; and King, *My Life with Martin Luther King, Jr.*, 8–9, 134, and 232–33.

89. See DuBois, *The Souls of Black Folk in Three Negro Classics*, 220 and 338; Martin Luther King, Jr., "Pre-Washington Campaign," unpublished version of a Speech to the Mississippi Leaders on the Washington Campaign, St. Thomas AME Church, Birmingham, Alabama (15 February 1968), King Center Library and Archives, 12; Martin Luther King, Jr., "The Meaning of Hope," unpublished version of a sermon, Dexter Avenue Baptist Church, Montgomery, Alabama (10 December 1967), King Center Library and Archives, 16; King, "Address at a Mass Meeting," Clarksdale, Mississippi (19 March 1968), King Center Library and Archives, 7; and Baldwin, *There is a Balm in Gilead*, 57.

90. King read Dubois, Johnson, and also Melville Herskovits, and there is reason to believe that he knew that slave music reflected the unity of African cultures through syncopation, antiphony, group singing, improvisation, instrumental qualities, and the organic connection to dance, but he never committed his thoughts on the subject to paper. See DuBois, *The Souls of Black Folk in Three Negro Classics*, 220 and 338–39; and James Weldon Johnson and J. Rosamond Johnson, *The Books of*

to the spirituals as a vital part of "the gifts of black folk" to the world, he must have had this and other considerations in mind when he, in "Honoring Dr. DuBois," a centennial address delivered at Carnegie Hall in New York in February 1968, alluded to DuBois's "genius and pride" and referred to him as "a historian of Negro life" who "rescued for all of us a heritage whose loss would have profoundly impoverished us."[91] King, Jr. had a similar regard for Johnson's genius in recreating for the singer that strange amalgam of heartache and hope in the black experience in "Lift Ev-ry Voice and Sing," or the Negro National Anthem,[92] which he also felt embodied the rhythmic beauty and poetic sublimity so characteristic of Negro spirituals.

Marian Anderson, Roland Hayes, and Paul Robeson were the names most often mentioned when King, Jr. discussed great artists who brought their own techniques to the singing of the spirituals professionally.[93] Always moved by Anderson's skill in capturing for audiences the great sorrow of the African slave in "Nobody Knows de Trouble I Seen," King, Jr. called her "probably the greatest singer of the twentieth century," and noted further that she embodied "all of the beauty of blackness and black culture."[94] King, Jr. saw in Hayes the

American Negro Spirituals (New York: The Viking Press, 1953; originally published in 1925), 33. For a brilliant treatment of DuBois and Johnson around the question of African influences on slave art, and especially the spirituals and dance, see Sterling Stuckey, *Slave Culture: Nationalist Theory and the Foundations of Black America* (New York: Oxford University Press, 1987), 254–55 and 319.

91. This address was given on the centennial of DuBois's birth. See Martin Luther King, Jr., "Honoring Dr. DuBois," *Freedomways*, Vol. 8, no. 2 (Spring, 1968), 104–11. The spirituals actually figured into both DuBois and King's sense of the potential messianic role of the American Negro. When DuBois declared "that Negro blood has a message for the world," and when King so often alluded to "The spiritual power that the Negro can radiate to the world," both had in mind, among other things, the values conveyed through the Negro spiritual. See DuBois, *The Souls of Black Folk in Three Negro Classics*, 215; King, *Stride toward Freedom*, 224; Baldwin, *There is a Balm in Gilead*, 229–43; and Vincent Harding, "W. E. B. DuBois and the Black Messianic Vision," *Freedomways*, Vol. 9, no. 1 (Winter, 1969), 49–57. For other indications of Dubois's relationship to King, see Carson, et al., eds., *King Papers*, III, 180; and Carson, et al., eds., *King Papers*, VI, 365–66.

92. King was known to include verses from the Negro National Anthem in some of his addresses. See Carson, et al., eds., *King Papers*, IV, 208n3; and Reddick, *Crusader without Violence*, 4. King called Johnson "a star in the poetic sky." See Martin Luther King, Jr., *Where Do We Go from Here: Chaos or Community?* (Boston: Beacon Press, 1968; originally published in 1967), 127.

93. King once noted that whenever Anderson, Hayes, and Roberson sang, "the very fibers of the souls are shaken. . . ." See Carson, et al., eds., *King Papers*, VI, 89 and 365.

94. Martin Luther King, Jr., "Training Your Child in Love," unpublished version of a sermon, Ebenezer Baptist Church, Atlanta, Georgia (8 May 1966), King Center Library and Archives, 5; Clayborne Carson and Peter Holloran, eds., *A Knock at Midnight: Inspiration from the Great Sermons of Reverend Martin Luther King, Jr.* (New York: Warner Books, 1998), 152–54; Carson, et. al., eds., *King Papers*, V, 285 and 340; Carson, et al., eds., *King Papers*, VI, 89; Carson, et al., eds., *King Papers*, I, 110; and Martin

preeminent example of the great artist, for he had risen from humble beginnings in "the red hills of Gordon County, Georgia" to become "one of the world's great singers," and had "carried his melodious voice to the palace of King George the fifth and the mansion of Queen Mother of Spain."[95] King, Jr. spoke of Robeson with the same respect and admiration, despite the latter's leftist ties, for Robeson had achieved greatness as a singer and actor, and had done more to recreate the voice of the slave in the singing of the spirituals than any other artist before him. King, Jr.'s opinion of Robeson probably had much to do with his wife, Coretta, who had performed with Robeson while an undergraduate at Antioch College and still thought highly of him.[96] Although King, Jr. sensed enduring value in what Robeson and Hayes, and also, Anderson, had done to advance the spirituals on concert stages and in other contexts, he never really addressed Robeson's and Hayes's sophistication as theoreticians of that music.[97]

King felt well-placed to interpret the spirituals for himself, especially since they had been a crucial part of his upbringing and also stood as the basis of his cultural bond with his slave forebears. Having grown up in the South, where "racial segregation" was "a new form of slavery covered up with the niceties of complexity,"[98] King, Jr. understood the exile's lot, or the experience of the resident alien, singing the Lord's song in a strange land, and this is why he was so deeply moved when listening to Negro spirituals. "On the Statue of Liberty we read that America is the mother of exiles but it does not take us long to realize that America has been the mother of its white exiles from Europe," King, Jr. declared. "America has never demonstrated

Luther King, Jr., "Speech in Savannah," unpublished version (1 January 1961), King Center Library and Archives, 11.

95. Carson, et al., eds., *King Papers*, V, 285 and 339–40; and Carson, et al., eds., *King Papers*, VI, 89.

96. King, *My Life with Martin Luther King, Jr.*, 43. Coretta and Robeson appeared together at the Majestic Hotel in Cleveland on March 10, 1950, on a program sponsored by the Progressive Party of Ohio. "Accompanied by Larry Brown, Robeson's pianist, Coretta sang 'Vedrai Carino' from *Don Giovanni*, 'Bird Courtships,' *and* 'Let Us Break Bread Together.'" After the performance, Robeson congratulated Coretta, commented favorably on her voice, and encouraged her to continue her voice studies. See Bagley, *Desert Rose*, 80–81; and King, *My Life with Martin Luther King, Jr.*, 43.

97. Robeson and Hayes are treated as both singers and theoreticians of the spirituals in Stuckey, *Slave Culture*, 314–15, 318–19, and 406n37.

98. Martin Luther King, Jr., "Remarks on Interfaith Conference on Civil Rights," unpublished version, Chicago, Illinois (15 January 1963), King Center Library and Archives, 1.

the same kind of maternal care for her black exiles who were brought here in chains from Africa," he added, "and it is no wonder that in one of our sorrow songs, our forebears could sing out, 'sometimes I feel like a motherless child'." The metaphorical language and lyrical quality of this song, and especially, "sometimes I feel like a motherless child, a long ways from home," reminded King, Jr. of the great "sense of estrangement, rejection, and hurt" endured by the slaves.[99] Interestingly enough, his interpretation of the song probably benefitted from the influence of Paul Robeson, who had, since the late 1920s, made it one of his signature pieces as he shared the spirituals with people worldwide.[100]

King, Jr. repeatedly quoted lines from spirituals which extolled the joys of heaven while also excoriating, openly or by implication, the earthly hardships of slaves in an alien world. Among these were "Bye and Bye, I'm Gonna Lay Down My Heavy Load," "Over My Head, I See Freedom in the Air," "I Heard of a City Called Heaven," "All God's Chillun Got Wings," "Swing Low, Sweet Chariot," "Free at Last," and "Oh Freedom!"—songs which penetrated the deeper fibers of the soul while giving vital expression to the human spirit.[101] In King, Jr.'s

99. Martin Luther King, Jr., "The Crisis of Civil Rights," unpublished version of an address at an Operation Breadbasket Meeting, Chicago, Illinois (10 July 1967), King Center Library and Archives, 10; Martin Luther King, Jr., "Transforming a Neighborhood," unpublished version of a speech, the NATRA Convention, RCA Dinner, Atlanta, Georgia (10 August 1967), King Center Library and Archives, 7–8; Martin Luther King, Jr., "Address at a Mass Meeting," unpublished version, Maggie Street Baptist Church, Montgomery, Alabama (16 February 1968), King Center Library and Archives, 4; Baldwin, The Voice of Conscience, 105–6; and Baldwin, There is a Balm in Gilead, 42.
100. Robeson was known to "re-create for an audience the great sadness of the Negro slave" in his rendering of this song. King's comments on the song at different places in his writings and speeches are amazingly similar to points made by Robeson. The idea that King's sense of the meaning of the song drew on Robeson is not beyond the realm of the possibility, especially since King and his wife Coretta were quite familiar with Robeson's music and his contributions to his people's struggle through song and his larger artistic achievements. See Paul Robeson, Songs of My People, RCA Victor (recorded on 7 January 1926). LM–3292; Stuckey, Slave Culture, 315–16; King, My Life with Martin Luther King, Jr., 43; and Bagley, Desert Rose, 80–81 and 293n6.
101. Carson, et al., eds., King Papers, VI, 365; King, Strength to Love, 95; King, "The Meaning of Hope," 16–17; Martin Luther King, Jr., "Sleeping through a Revolution," unpublished version of a speech, Sheraton Hotel, Chicago, Illinois (10 December 1967), King Center Library and Archives, 5; Martin Luther King, Jr., "A Knock at Midnight," unpublished version of a sermon, All Saints Community Church, Los Angeles, California (25 June 1967), King Center Library and Archives, 16; Martin Luther King, Jr., "Interruptions," unpublished version of a sermon, Ebenezer Baptist Church, Atlanta, Georgia (21 January 1968), 9; Martin Luther King, Jr., "A Knock at Midnight," unpublished version of a sermon, Canaan Baptist Church, New York, New York (24 March 1968), 14–16; Martin Luther King, Jr., The Trumpet of Conscience (New York: Harper & Row, Publishers, 1987; originally

estimation, these songs were living proof of how tragedy is so often the catalyst for great art. In a larger sense, they were, for him, enduring testimonies to the agony and ecstasy of the black experience in America. King skillfully employed the images of "midnight" and "morning" to illustrate how paradoxical notions of suffering and celebration, of sorrow and joy, course through the spirituals, thus providing grounds for hope for generations that descended from a people in bondage:

> Don't give up. Midnight is not here to stay. You know, our old slave parents used to see this—our foreparents—and they thought about midnight, and they worked out a little song to deal with midnight: "Nobody knows the trouble I see. Nobody knows but Jesus." And that described midnight for them. But something reminded them that morning would come, and they started singing, "I'm so glad that trouble don't last always." Morning will come.[102]

"Nobody knows the trouble I see" and "I'm so glad trouble don't last always" appear as much or perhaps more in King, Jr.'s sermons and speeches than any other lines from the spirituals, probably because of the profound coupling of heartache and hope that finds expression. King, Jr. detected here a glaring and striking example of how pain and affirmation existed side by side in slave art. Also, his sense of the relationship between art and labor, and indeed, art and life, for the slave was significantly enhanced. Ultimately, his knowledge of the history of slavery and of slave culture was such that he understood the place of work routines in his ancestors' creation and singing of the spirituals.[103]

published in 1967), 3–4; Carson, et al., eds., King Papers, V, 248–49; Baldwin, There is a Balm in Gilead, 168–70; and Baldwin, To Make the Wounded Whole, 64–66.
102. King, "A Knock at Midnight" (24 March 1968), 13; Martin Luther King, Jr., "Why a Movement," unpublished version of a speech (28 November 1967), King Center Library and Archives, 11; King, "A Knock at Midnight" (25 June 1967), 15; King, "Training Your Child in Love," 5; Martin Luther King, Jr., "Ingratitude," unpublished version of a sermon (18 June 1967), King Center Library and Archives, 6; Carson, et al., eds., King Papers, I, 110; Carson, et al., eds., King Papers, VI, 365 and 502; Carson, et al., eds., King Papers, IV, 330; Carson and Holloran, eds., A Knock at Midnight, 75–76; King, Strength to Love, 64–65; Michael Thurman, ed., Voices from the Dexter Pulpit (Montgomery, AL: New South Books, 2001), 60–61; Baldwin, To Make the Wounded Whole, 64–65; and Alex Ayres, ed., The Wisdom of Martin Luther King, Jr.: An A-to-Z Guide to the Ideas and Ideals of the Great Civil Rights Leader (New York: Penguin Books USA, Inc., 1993), 110.
103. These reflections are essential for locating King in black culture and also for understanding him

The depth of insight King, Jr. brought to his assessment of the meaning and artistic value of spirituals such as "All God's Chillun Got Wings" and "There is a Balm in Gilead," in which the rhythms of lament and hope also rise and fall, apparently owed much to his reading of certain works by the black theologian Howard Thurman. King concluded that the promise of shoes and robes in "All God's Chillun Got Wings" spelled relief for a people who had to work in the cotton and tobacco fields "in their bare feet" and in ragged cast-off clothes, and who also knew that the God of the Bible "was not a God that would subject some of his children and exalt others." Thus, "they could sing in their broken language":

> I got shoes, you got shoes,
> All of God's chillun got shoes.
> When I get to heaven gonna put on my shoes
> And just walk all over God's heaven.
> I got a robe, you got a robe,
> All of God's chillum got a robe.
> When I get to heaven gonna put on my robe
> And just gonna shout all over God's heaven.[104]

The visions of freedom in this song, highlighted by the security of shoes and robes and the walking and shouting "all over God's heaven," were particularly meaningful and inspiring for King, Jr. as he led his people in continuing efforts to win freedom from poverty, economic injustice, and political disenfranchisement. Drawing on Thurman, King, Jr. noted that another line in this spiritual—"Everybody talkin' 'bout heaven ain't goin' there!"—was sung as slaves cast a steady eye on the big house where the slave owner lived.[105] The interrelationship

---

as a cultural figure. See King, "The Meaning of Hope," 15–17; King, "A Knock at Midnight" (25 June 1967), 15–16; Carson, et al., eds., *King Papers*, VI, 365 and 502; and Lewis V. Baldwin, "'A Home in Dat Rock': Afro-American Folk Sources and Slave Visions of Heaven and Hell," *The Journal of Religious Thought*, Vol. 41, no. 1 (Spring–Summer, 1984), 43–44.

104. This spiritual also speaks of the slaves' plan to "put on my wings" and "take up my harp." See Carson, et al., eds., *King Papers*, VI, 316; King, "Interruptions," 9; King, "The Meaning of Hope," 16–17; and Johnson and Johnson, *The Books of American Negro Spirituals*, 71–73.

105. It is abundantly clear that King was borrowing from Howard Thurman, *Jesus and the Disinherited* (Nashville: Abingdon Press, 1949), 61. Also see Howard Thurman, *Deep River and the Negro Spiritual Speaks of Life and Death* (Richmond, IN: Friends United Press, 1975), 48; and King, "The Meaning of Hope," 16.

between earthly and otherworldly concerns in "All God's Chillun Got Wings" squared well with King, Jr.'s own outlook, and he was particularly intrigued by what this and other spirituals conveyed about his forebears' undeniably unique capacity to look critically and prophetically at life and at the conventions of power and authority.

The rare passion of insight that King, Jr. brought to his reading of the spiritual, "There is a Balm in Gilead," is most evident in certain versions of his popular sermon, "A Knock at Midnight." Here again, King, Jr. detected what Thurman called "the peculiar genius of the Negro slave," and, quoting Thurman directly at points, he spoke compellingly about how this song, which was based on scripture, gave expression to his ancestors' unconquerable spirit and audacity to hope:

> Centuries ago Jeremiah, the great prophet, raised a very profound question. He looked at the inequities around and he noticed a lot of things. He noticed the good people so often suffering, and the evil people so often prospering. Jeremiah raised the question: "Is there no balm in Gilead? Is there no physician there?" Centuries later our slave forefathers came along, and they too were confronted with the problems of life. They had nothing to look forward to morning after morning but the sizzling heat, the rawhide whip of the overseer, long rows of cotton. But they did an amazing thing. They looked back across the centuries, and they took Jeremiah's question mark and straightened it into an exclamation point. And they could sing:
>
> > There is a balm in Gilead,
> > To make the wounded whole.
> > There is a balm in Gilead,
> > To heal the sin-sick soul.
>
> Then they came with another verse:
>
> > Sometimes I feel discouraged,
> > And feel my work's in vain.
> > But then the Holy Spirit,
> > Revives my soul again

King, Jr. frequently ended these reflections with explanations of how the faith, hope, and vision expressed here informed his own perspective on and approach to life.[106] "There is a Balm in Gilead," in his own thinking, affirmed his people's ability to "hope against hope."[107]

The great body of Negro spirituals was a great comfort to King, Jr. personally, and he discovered there core ideas and values that he sought to translate into practical action and reality in the context of the civil rights movement. He recalled that many of these songs to which he was exposed, from the time of his sojourn in Montgomery, were nonviolent in quality and effect—that they, much like his preaching, conveyed rich and empowering lessons about peace, forgiveness, and reconciliation.[108] "Honor, Honor," which expressed reverence for the "dyin' lamb," embodied what he considered to be the true spirit of sacrificial love and redemptive suffering.[109] Spirituals such as "Walk Together, Children" and "Let Us Break Bread Together" captured his sense of the communitarian ideal.[110] "Lord, I Can't Turn Back," "Keep Your Hands on the Plow," "Go Down, Moses," and "Joshua Fit the Battle of Jericho"[111] were infused, in King, Jr.'s judgment, with the spirit of perseverance and no surrender. Having a keen sense of that long history involving the messianic expectation of his people, or that longing for a deliverer, King, Jr. found much inspiration in spirituals that focused on biblical figures such as Moses, Joshua, and Jesus, who were vehicles for the fulfillment of God's plan for the weak,

---

106. Carson, et al. eds., *King Papers*, VI, 229; King, "A Knock at Midnight" (25 June 1967), 16; Martin Luther King, Jr., "A Christian Movement in a Revolutionary Age," unpublished version of a sermon (Fall, 1966), King Center Library and Archives, 1; Carson and Holloran, eds., *A Knock at Midnight*, 164; Baldwin, *To Make the Wounded Whole*, 65; and King, *My Life with Martin Luther King, Jr.*, 9.
107. King, "A Knock at Midnight" (25 June 1967), 16; King, "The Meaning of Hope," 17; King, *Where Do We Go from Here?*, 113; Baldwin, *To Make the Wounded Whole*, 65; and King, *My Life with Martin Luther King, Jr.*, 9.
108. King, *Stride toward Freedom*, 88.
109. King, *My Life with Martin Luther King, Jr.*, 134.
110. Carson, et al., eds., *King Papers*, III, 199; Carson, et, al., eds., *King Papers*, V, 579n24; King, *My Life with Martin Luther King, Jr.*, 134; and Baldwin, *There is a Balm in Gilead*, 173.
111. King, *My Life with Martin Luther King, Jr.*, 134; King, "A Christian Movement in a Revolutionary Age," 1; and Carson, et al., eds., *King Papers*, IV, 155. King occasionally quoted from "Joshua Fit the Battle of Jericho," despite its martial imagery and seemingly violent tone, to illustrate that "Freedom is never voluntarily granted" but "must be demanded by the oppressed." For King, "the Biblical march of Joshua around the walls of Jericho" carried essentially the same significance as Moses walking "into the courts of Pharaoh" and thundering "forth with the call to 'Let my people go'." See Martin Luther King, Jr., "Address at the Chicago Freedom Movement Rally," Soldier Field, Chicago, Illinois (10 July 1966), King Center Library and Archives, 3.

downtrodden, and outcast. Such spirituals had a deep personal and immediate meaning for King, Jr., much as they did for his ancestors in bondage.[112]

The fact that a large number of the spirituals were both religious and political in content never really escaped King, Jr. He made significant references at times to double-meaning spirituals, which carried religious messages as well as hidden meanings, hints, and signals for slaves plotting to escape:

> Our spirituals, now so widely admired around the world, were often codes. We sang of "heaven" that awaited us, and the slave masters listened in innocence, not realizing that we were not speaking of the hereafter. Heaven was the word for Canada, and the Negro sang of the hope that his escape on the Underground Railroad would carry him there. One of our spirituals, "Follow the Drinking Gourd," in its lyrics contained disguised directions for escape. The gourd was the Big Dipper, and the North Star to which its handle pointed gave the celestial map that directed the flight to the Canadian border.[113]

King, Jr. spoke similarly of the disguised political-temporal messages in other spirituals. He explained that "Steal Away to Jesus," for slaves who "couldn't worship" freely, "meant that we got to get together tonight," a veiled reference to secret plantation gatherings called "Hush Harbor" meetings or "the invisible institution," at which the participants worshipped while also occasionally planning escape or revolt. When slaves sang "I Heard of a City Called Heaven," "the white folks thought they were talking about heaven up yonder," King, Jr. maintained, "but they were talking about Canada, the other end of the Underground Railroad."[114] It is highly likely that these observations grew out of a

---

112. King, "A Christian Movement in a Revolutionary Age," 1; King, "Address at the Chicago Freedom Movement Rally," 3; Carson, et al., eds., *King Papers*, IV, 155–66; King, *Strength to Love*, 76–85; Martin Luther King, Jr., "Why We Must Go to Washington," unpublished speech, SCLC Staff Retreat, Ebenezer Baptist Church, Atlanta, Georgia (15 January 1968), King Center Library and Archives, 14; Clayborne Carson and Kris Shepard, eds., *A Call to Conscience: The Landmark Speeches of Dr. Martin Luther King, Jr.* (New York: Warner Books, Inc., 2001), 17–18; James M. Washington, ed., *A Testament of Hope: The Essential Writings and Speeches of Martin Luther King, Jr.* (New York: HarperCollins Publishers, 1991), 281 and 495; Baldwin, *The Voice of Conscience*, 105; and Harold Courlander, *Negro Folk Music, USA* (New York: Columbia University Press, 1963), 42 and 45.

113. King, Jr., *The Trumpet of Conscience*, 3–4; King, "The Meaning of Hope," 16; and Baldwin, *There is a Balm in Gilead*, 226–27.

114. King, "The Meaning of Hope," 16.

reading of the ex-slaves Harriet Tubman and Frederick Douglass, King, Jr.'s boyhood hero, both of whom reported that heaven was identified in the minds of many slaves with the North and Canada.[115] There is also reason to believe that King, Jr. was aware of some of the scholarship on the spirituals completed in the early 1960s, and particularly, the work of Harold Courlander, which afforded an insightful look into the slave spirituals as "conscious disguises for political, temporal meanings."[116] This would not have been at all surprising in view of the continuing involvements of King, Jr. and his wife, Coretta with folk music in churches and in academic settings as well. King, Jr. would have been mindful of how Courlander's interpretive work on the spirituals essentially built on contributions made earlier by the likes of DuBois, James Weldon Johnson, and Howard Thurman.

Some of King, Jr.'s favorite spirituals were created and popularized in the immediate aftermath of the Emancipation Proclamation and the Civil War, the period during which newly freed slaves resolved never to forget nor repeat the experiences they had known in bondage. These included "Free at Last" and "Oh Freedom," which contained the lines, "before I'll be a slave, I'll be buried in my grave and go home to my Lord and be free."[117] For King, Jr., both testified to his forebears' indomitable spirit and audacity to hope. King, Jr. ended many of his sermons and addresses, and most notably, his celebrated "I Have a Dream" speech, quoting the lines, "Free at last, free at last, thank God almighty, we're free at last."[118] This was not simply a declaration and an

---

115. Reddick, *Crusader without Violence*, 14; Frederick Douglass, *Life and Times of Frederick Douglass*, revised edition (New York: The Crowell-Collier Publishing Company, 1962; reprint, 1892), 159–60; Sarah Bradford, *Harriet Tubman: The Moses of Her People*, 2nd edition (New York: Corinth Books, 1961; reprint, 1886), 27–28; and Baldwin, "'A Home in Dat Rock,'" 55.
116. Courlander, *Negro Folk Music, USA*, 41–43. King actually exchanged letters with Courlander around the comparability of Jim Crow in the American South and apartheid in South Africa in the 1960s, and his comments on disguised meanings and messages in the spirituals echo Courlander's. See King, "The Meaning of Hope," 16; King, *The Trumpet of Conscience*, 3–4; and Lewis V. Baldwin, *Toward the Beloved Community: Martin Luther King, Jr. and South Africa* (Cleveland: Pilgrim Press, 1995), 27 and 201n12.
117. King, "Pre-Washington Campaign,"13; Carson, et al., eds., *King Papers*, IV, 179; and Carson, et al., eds., *King Papers*, V, 248–49, 269, 288, and 339. Lawrence Levine brilliantly discusses these and other spirituals as post-Emancipation Proclamation creations. It was the time during which ex-slaves thought of the South's defeat as the fulfillment of a prophecy that they had long sung about. See Levine, *Black Culture and Black Consciousness*, 136–55.
118. Carson, et al., eds., *King Papers*, IV, 179; King, "Pre-Washington Campaign," 13; and Washington,

---

expression of thanksgiving, but also, by implication, a firm albeit un-vocalized determination to experience the fullness of freedom while also struggling against all that threaten freedom. King, Jr. noted that the choice of the grave over slavery, or "physical death" over "a permanent death of the spirit," as expressed in "Oh Freedom," conveyed essentially the same message, but that there is also, in this spiritual, the sense that freedom "is not a struggle to attain some ephemeral desire," but "to maintain one's very selfhood."[119]

King, Jr. spoke of the spirituals in terms that he hoped would inspire pride rather than shame in the masses of his people, so many of whom struggled with deeply entrenched feelings of inferiority and inadequacy, which prevented them from accepting the power and richness of black culture as a whole. He had little patience with black intellectuals who, driven to become as nearly like the white elite as possible, considered the singing of the spirituals to be an affront to their dignity and class status.[120] King, Jr. was equally disturbed by ordinary black church folk who seemingly reduced the spirituals to merely a source of entertainment without adequate appreciation for their artistic, cultural, and sociopolitical value. Although rural black southern churches, in which the folk sang the spirituals with all the strength of their voices, and in which bodies moved in perfect time to the songs, were always fertile ground when King, Jr. needed an experience of renewal and reaffirmation through an existential appropriation of black faith, he felt that the spirituals were too often associated with worship reduced to outright showmanship or exhibitionism.[121] This was not his idea of expressing and celebrating faith with genuine joy and meaning.

The spirituals revealed what King, Jr. regarded as the "profound

---

ed., *A Testament of Hope*, 220. So many people worldwide became familiar with certain Negro spirituals because of King's habit of quoting repeatedly from them in his sermons, addresses, and speeches.

119. Carson, et al., eds., *King Papers*, V, 248–49, 269, 288, and 339; and King, *Where Do We Go from Here?*, 123.

120. Carson and Holloran, eds., *A Knock at Midnight*, 74; Thurman, ed., *Voices from the Dexter Pulpit*, 59; and King, *Strength to Love*, 63.

121. Carson, et al., eds., *King Papers*, VI, 223 and 295; King, *Strength to Love*, 63; and Baldwin, *The Voice of Conscience*, 72–73.

psychological vision" of his slave forebears and their descendants.[122] In other words, in the spirituals, he heard the voices of generations who had learned to cope not only spiritually, but psychologically and emotionally, with victimization and suffering. Although King understood and respected the deep links of common songs between southern blacks and whites, the Negro spirituals were distinctive and infinitely more important as he defined himself and what linked him, in matters of spirit, to the mass of his people.[123] The Negro spirituals were, for him, melodic statements that bore witness to the power and uniqueness of black history, life, and culture. King, Jr. saw in them the poetic character, the rhythmic qualities of language, and the kind of beautiful, imaginative, elevated thoughts that were also present in black sermons and in the works of Langston Hughes and other poets.[124]

The same might be said of King, Jr.'s perspective on black gospel songs, for which he also displayed a decided preference. Like the spirituals, gospel songs spoke of "the troubles, sorrows, and burdens of everyday existence," of "hope and affirmation," and of a "God who was an immediate, intimate, living presence"[125] in human experience, and this largely accounted for King, Jr.'s love of that music. Although King, Jr. grew up in an age when gospel music was considered anathema

122. Carson, et al., eds., *King Papers*, IV, 330.
123. King knew that there was a history of both black and white spirituals stretching back to the slave South, but he said little or nothing about white spirituals, undoubtedly because they merely afforded additional proof of the ambivalent soul of white America. See Baldwin, *There is a Balm in Gilead*, 82. For a brilliant treatment of the similarities and differences between black and white spirituals during slavery, which is useful for putting much of what King said about southern history and culture in proper context, see Levine, *Black Culture and Black Consciousness*, 22–23.
124. For studies that make significant references to King in relation to the folk sermon and poetry as works of art, see Gerald L. Davis, *I Got the Word in Me and I Can Sing It, You Know* (Philadelphia: University of Pennsylvania Press, 1985), 11–12 and 77; Jon Michael Spencer, *Sacred Symphony: The Chanted Sermon of the Black Preacher* (Westport, CT: Greenwood Press, 1987), 4–5; and W. Jason Miller, *Origins of the Dream: Hughes's Poetry and King's Rhetoric*, unpublished manuscript (14 April 2014), Author's files.
125. Lawrence Levine provides one of the best comparative treatments of the Negro spirituals and gospel songs, though some of his claims and conclusions are open to question and debatable. In pointing out differences between the two black sacred musical forms, he notes that gospel songs were more otherworldly in their "overriding thrust," were dominated by Jesus and the New Testament rather than the Hebrew Children, Joshua, Daniel, and other Old Testament figures, and were defined by an emphasis on a concept of heaven that remained firmly in the future. Levine's claim that "from the 1930s on" gospel songs "displaced the spirituals as the most important single body of black religious music" is not borne out by this study of King. See Levine, *Black Culture and Black Consciousness*, 174–76.

in some black church circles, mainly because many of its pioneering artists, and most notably, Thomas A. Dorsey, had been blues musicians,[126] King, Jr. nevertheless sang rollicking gospel songs such as "I Want to Be More and More Like Jesus" from the time he was a child.[127] This music was as much a part of his family and church heritage as the Negro spirituals, the chanted sermon, and the old Watts lining hymns.

Among the gospel songs King, Jr. appreciated most were "Thank You, Lord," "Walk with Me, Lord," "Some Day," "Because He Lives," "How I Got Over," "I've Been 'Buked and I've Been Scorned," "Never Grow Old," and "Precious Lord, Take My Hand," which was his favorite. Some of his sermons, speeches, and addresses were punctuated with references to or lyrics from these songs, mainly because they, much like the spirituals, spoke to his sense of the black experience, embodied his enduring cry for what he called "divine companionship," captured his idea of a loving, merciful, rational, and personal God who is ever close to and delivers divine creation, affirmed his belief in an afterlife in which joys denied in this life would be fulfilled, and gave him meaning and hope.[128] The song "Precious Lord, Take My Hand," which contains the lines—"lead me on, let me stand, I am tired, I am weak, I am worn"—had a very personal meaning for King, Jr., especially in the last days of his life, when he himself conceded that he was exhausted and discouraged, and that he had entrusted himself to God, and therefore, had no nagging regrets or fears. Only seconds before the assassin's bullet found its mark on that fateful night in Memphis in April 1968, King, Jr. asked Ben Branch, known for brilliant displays of

126. Michael W. Harris, *The Rise of the Gospel Blues: The Music of Thomas A. Dorsey in the Urban Church* (New York: Oxford University Press, 1992), 182–83; and Levine, *Black Culture and Black Consciousness,* 179 and 182–83.

127. Reddick, *Crusader without Violence,* 56; and King, *My Life with Martin Luther King, Jr.,* 78.

128. King, "Ingratitude," 8; Martin Luther King, Jr., "Answer to a Perplexing Question," unpublished version of a sermon (3 March 1963), King Center Library and Archives, 1; Ralph D. Abernathy, *And the Walls Came Tumbling Down: An Autobiography* (New York: Harper & Row, Publishers, 1989), 440; Reddick, *Crusader without Violence,* 195; Jesse Jackson, *Make a Joyful Noise Unto the Lord!: The Life of Mahalia Jackson, Queen of Gospel Singers* (New York: Dell Publishing Company, Inc., 1974), 72; Tony Heilbut, *The Gospel Sound: Good News and Bad Times* (New York: Anchor Books/Anchor Press/Doubleday, 1975), 31; King, *My Life with Martin Luther King, Jr.,* 221; King, "A Christian Movement in a Revolutionary Age," 8; and Juliann DeKorte, *Ethel Waters: Finally Home* (Old Tappan, NJ: Fleming H. Revell Company, 1978), 127–28.

musical talent on trumpet, to play the song "real pretty for me" at the next mass meeting.[129]

Gospel music was heard and promoted in many contexts in the 1950s and 60s, and King, Jr. seldom, if ever, passed on an opportunity to avail himself to the religiously animating power of these songs. He was exposed to gospel songs in churches, where they were participatory in performance and so often accompanied by the pulsing rhythms of the shout,[130] through quartets, during street demonstrations, in jail cells, and even at the great march on Washington in 1963, where Mahalia Jackson stirred the crowd with a rousing rendition of "How I Got Over."[131] Much like the spirituals, gospel songs reflected the spirituality and artistic genius of the folk, and King, Jr. was fully convinced that they had a special significance not only in congregational life and on the concert stage, but also in the movement, and this, too, offered a glimpse into his spiritual heart.

King, Jr. held the many creators and artists in the field of gospel music, from Charles A. Tindley and Thomas A. Dorsey to Julius Cheeks, J. Robert Bradley, Rosetta Tharpe, Edna Gallman Cooke, Clara Ward, Mahalia Jackson, James Cleveland, and Aretha Franklin, in the highest esteem, and he had a close personal relationship with some of them. He was a friend to Aretha Franklin and her father, C. L. Franklin, who was a Baptist pastor and civil rights activist in Detroit, and Aretha was actually honored by King and his SCLC on at least one occasion. Her singing of "Never Grow Old" when she was still very young always touched King, Jr.'s soul. But King, Jr.'s favorite gospel singer, by far, was recording artist Mahalia Jackson,[132] who, perhaps more than any other gospel musician, devoted her talent to the service of the civil rights cause. King, Jr. and his wife, Coretta occasionally stayed at Mahalia's

129. Abernathy, And the Walls Came Tumbling Down, 440–41; Heilbut, The Gospel Sound, 31; King, My Life with Martin Luther King, Jr., 292–93; Baldwin Interview with Abernathy (17 March 1987); and Oates, Let the Trumpet Sound, 490.
130. It has been noted that "some middle-class blacks derided" this music "as 'cotton-picking songs,' calling gospel singers 'nappy-headed shouters'." See Jackson, Make a Joyful Noise Unto the Lord!, 72.
131. Baldwin and Al-Hadid, Between Cross and Crescent, 189; and Martin Luther King, Jr. to Mahalia Jackson (10 January 1964), King Center Library and Archives, 1–2.
132. Phyl Garland, The Sound of Soul (Chicago: Henry Regnery Company, 1969), 196; Private Interview with Abernathy (17 March 1987); and King, "Answer to a Perplexing Question," 1.

home in Chicago, and Mahalia sometimes sang to large crowds before or after King, Jr. spoke. The two appeared at the annual National Baptist Convention in Denver in 1956, at the Prayer Pilgrimage in Washington, DC in 1957, at the march on Washington in 1963, and at a mass rally in support of open housing and fair real estate practices at Soldier Field in Chicago in 1966,[133] and images of King, Jr. speaking and Mahalia singing were always a powerful and effective combination, artistically and from a cultural and sociopolitical standpoint. King, Jr. sensed the magic of Mahalia's art. Concerning her performance at the great march in Washington, he declared: "You have sung before kings and potentates, but never have you sung the Lord's song like you did that day. When I got up to speak, I was already happy."[134] When Mahalia appeared in Atlanta in November 1963, three months later, King, Jr., who placed such huge expectations on musicians and artists in general, was equally charitable in showering her with words of praise and gratitude, noting that "This world-famous gospel singer has willingly lifted her great voice over and over again in an inspiring appeal for moral, spiritual, and financial support of this great thrust of today's freedom champions."[135]

King, Jr. obviously drew spiritual strength from the songs of Mahalia and other gospel artists, but equally important was the impact that he and his freedom crusade had on gospel music as it took shape in the 1950s and 60s. King, Jr.'s aide, Wyatt Tee Walker, has concluded

133. Mahalia Jackson sang "Precious Lord, Take My Hand" at King's funeral in Atlanta on 9 April 1968. See King, *My Life with Martin Luther King, Jr.*, 221, 263–67, and 306; Farris, *Through It All*, 136; Jackson, *Make a Joyful Noise Unto the Lord!*, 99–100, 104, and 117–18; King to Jackson (10 January 1964), 1–2; "Festival of Faith and Freedom 1962: Special Citation to Miss Mahalia Jackson," Bushnell Auditorium, Hartford, Connecticut (28 October 1962), King Center Library and Archives, 1; "MLK Rally with Mahalia Jackson," Chicago, Illinois (4 August 1966), King Center Library and Archives, 1–4; Martin Luther King, Jr., "Statement Regarding Mahalia Jackson's Appearance in Atlanta," Atlanta, Georgia (26 November 1963), King Center Library and Archives, 1; Heilbut, *The Gospel Sound*, 58, 70, and 72; and Lewis, *King*, 91.

134. King to Jackson (10 January 1964), 1. King said of Mahalia what he had long said of Marian Anderson, whose rendering of slave spirituals impacted him so much, noting that "a voice like this comes only once in a millennium." He told Mahalia personally that "It really has become difficult to say to you how much you mean and have meant to the Negro revolution and especially SCLC." See "MLK Rally with Mahalia Jackson," 1; King to Jackson (10 January 1964), 1; and Baldwin and Al-Hadid, *Between Cross and Crescent*, 189–90.

135. King, "Statement Regarding Mahalia Jackson's Appearance in Atlanta," 1; and Baldwin and Al-Hadid, *Between Cross and Crescent*, 189–90.

that modern gospel came to reflect "the influences of both the quartet era and the period symbolized by Martin Luther King's leadership," for both "ushered in a period of broad acceptability of the Gospel idiom, which had not been altogether welcome in all-Black church circles prior to that time."[136] Tony Heilbut, known for his scholarly interpretation of that music, has advanced essentially the same conclusion, while suggesting that the "assassination of King may well have hastened the demise of the faith that sustained gospel music."[137]

While immersing himself in the sacred songs of the black folk heritage, King, Jr. also freely assimilated many of the great hymns and musical styles of that broader Christian tradition. Both came together quite naturally in his consciousness whenever he considered any music setting of church liturgy. He cherished opportunities to sing classic hymns and contemporary church hymns, and always enjoyed them when they were rendered instrumentally or sung as either solos or in unison or congregational style. As a product of black church traditions, King, Jr. always had exposure to musically inclined congregations in which treasured hymns were sung both *a cappella* and with the accompaniment of piano and organ, and at times, with drums, tambourines, and other instruments. The hymns he preferred most and so often quoted from were testimonies to his sense of the power of faith and the meaning of life and ultimate reality. His sermons, which, in effect, were songs themselves, were literally peppered with lyrics from hymns written by Isaac Watts, John Newton, John Oxenham, Edward Perronet, Civilla D. Martin, Frank E. Graeff, Fanny Crosby, Charlotte Elliot, John Oatman, John Bowring, Charles W. Fry, Joseph H. Gilmore, Edward Mote, Charles H. Gabriel, James C. Moore, Eldon Burkwall, Robert MacGimsey, Julia Ward Howe, Alma Bazel Androzzo, and others, thus affording solid proof that he was never limited to black musicians and the songs of his own people.[138]

136. Wyatt Tee Walker, *"Somebody's Calling My Name": Black Sacred Music and Social Change* (Valley Forge, PA: Judson Press, 1979), 130, 136, and 175–76.
137. Heilbut, *The Gospel Sound*, 31.
138. For references to the many hymns and hymn writers King quoted, see Carson, et al., eds., *King Papers*, VI, 99n5, 132n6, 133n12, 142, 163, 170n15, 181, 185n3, 192, 270n21, 283, 289n17, 292, 300–301, 342n21, 353n7, 390–91, 405, 410n15, 429, 444–45, 450, 454, 486, 494, 519–20, 526–27, and

King, Jr.'s involvements with both the church and the movement were determinative for how he interpreted and made use of his favorite hymns. He often urged congregations to join him in singing hymns such as "Just As I Am," "Amazing Grace," "Thank You, Lord," "Where He Leads Me," "I Surrender All," and "Jesus is Tenderly Calling You Home" when he was extending the invitation to Christian discipleship after he preached on Sunday mornings, most often at Atlanta's Ebenezer Baptist Church.[139] For meditation hymns such as "Lift Him Up," "All Hail the Power of Jesus Name," "I Trust in God," and "Sweet Little Jesus Boy," also a Christmas hymn, King, Jr. routinely turned to either his wife, Coretta or Mrs. Mary Gurley, an Ebenezer church member who was also his "favorite meditation singer."[140] The messages imparted in the hymns of meditation King, Jr. cherished were amplified many times over in the "Hallelujah Chorus" of George Frideric Handel's 1741 oratorio, "Messiah," especially the lines, "He's King of King and Lord of Lords, hallelujah! Hallelujah!," and "He shall reign forever and ever, hallelujah! Hallelujah!," which King, Jr. so often quoted.[141] Lenten hymns such as "In the Cross of Christ I Glory," "When I Survey the Wondrous Cross," "The Old Rugged Cross," and "Were You there When They Crucified My Lord," which affirm the power of unmerited, sacrificial love and redemptive suffering, were personal in

---

702–3; Carson, et al., eds., *King Papers*, IV, 249, 258, and 506; Carson, et al., eds., *King Papers*, III, 199; Carson, et al., eds., *King Papers*, V, 145, 250, 289–90, 343, and 375; King, *My Life with Martin Luther King, Jr.*, 107, 231–33, and 304–5; Carson and Holloran, eds., *A Knock at Midnight*, 31, 58–59, 186, and 209; King, *Strength to Love*, 55, 89, and 97; Carson, ed., *The Autobiography of Martin Luther King, Jr.*, 59; Martin Luther King, Jr., "The Agenda for the Meeting of the SCLC," unpublished version, Richmond, Virginia (31 October 1958), King Center Library and Archives, 1; King, "Ingratitude," 8; Martin Luther King, Jr., "Lost Sheep or the God of the Lost," unpublished version of a sermon (18 September 1966), King Center Library and Archives, 8; and King, "Answer to a Perplexing Question," 1 and 21–22.

139. This was the point at which the so-called "lost" or "unsaved" were invited to join the church. See King, "Answer to a Perplexing Question," 21–22; Martin Luther King, Jr., "The Prodigal Son," unpublished version of a sermon, Ebenezer Baptist Church, Atlanta, Georgia (4 September 1966), King Center Library and Archives, 9; King, "Lost Sheep or the God of the Lost," 8; King, "Ingratitude," 8–9; and Carson, et. al., eds., *King Papers*, VI, 283, 390–91, 445, and 454.

140. King, *My Life with Martin Luther King, Jr.*, 232 and 304–5.

141. Carson, et al., eds., *King Papers*, V, 285 and 339; Carson, et al., eds., *King Papers*, VI, 170n16, 248, 292n30, 328n19, 355n6, 454n22, and 600; King, "Interruptions," 8; Martin Luther King, Jr., "Making the Best of a Bad Mess," unpublished version of a sermon, Ebenezer Baptist Church, Atlanta, Georgia (24 April 1966), King Center Library and Archives, 5; and King, "Pre-Washington Campaign," 11–12.

the most private sense to King, Jr., especially since he thought of the trials and persecution he faced as an advocate for freedom, justice, and peace in terms of bearing a cross. Lenten hymns gave expression to King, Jr.'s conviction that a cross had to be borne before a crown could be worn.[142]

There were other Christian hymns that also evoked strong feelings in King, Jr. and gave him a sense of inner peace because they carried profound messages about the mercy and power of God, human frailty and limitations, the interrelated structure of all reality, and the moral responsibility of believers in the face of sin and evil. When he felt lonely, discouraged, and devoid of a clear sense of direction, he evidently found hope, inspiration, and reasons to keep moving forward in hymns such as "God Will Take Care of You," "Oh God Our Help in Ages Past," "His Eye is on the Sparrow," "Leaning on the Everlasting Arms," "The Lily of the Valley," "What a Friend We Have in Jesus," "Never to Leave Us Alone," "Mine Eyes Have Seen the Glory," "My God and Father, While I Stray," "He Leadeth Me," and "God Moves in a Mysterious Way."[143] In "In Christ there is No East or West" and "Dear Lord and Father of All Mankind," King, Jr. discovered echoes of his own widely expressed convictions that all barriers that separate humans from each other and the creator are artificial, and ultimately, meaningless.[144] Hymns such as "Onward, Christian Soldiers" and "If I Can Help Some Body" were, for him, clarion calls to action in a world haunted by bigotry, intolerance, injustice, and human need.[145] It was

---

142. King once said of the hymn, "When I Survey the Wondrous Cross": "I think if there is any hymn of the Christian church that I would call a favorite hymn, it is this one." The hymn, "Were You there When They Crucified My Lord," also viewed as a spiritual and likely composed by slaves, must have caught King's attention, imagination, and sympathy in a particularly striking way. In this song, the slaves identified with the suffering of Jesus on a very personal level. This explained their tendency to combine belief and experience when singing spirituals like "Were You there When They Crucified My Lord," a tendency that King also had as he pondered his own crucifixion at the hands of white mobs. See Carson, et. al., eds., King Papers, V, 145–46; Carson, et al., eds., King Papers, VI, 181, 444, 486, and 494; King, My Life with Martin Luther King, Jr., 304; and Sterling Brown, "Negro Folk Expression: Spirituals, Seculars, Ballads and Work Songs," in August Meier and Elliot Rudwick, eds., The Making of Black America: Essays in Negro Life & History, 2 vols. (New York: Atheneum, 1974), I, 212–13. For a rich discussion of how King's sense of mission unfolded over time, see Garrow, Bearing the Cross, 18–624; and Washington, ed., A Testament of Hope, 41–42.
143. Carson, et al., eds., King Papers, VI, 132n6, 163, 193, 249, 270n21, 300–301, 353, 405, 410n15, 506, 519–520, and 526–27.
144. Ibid., 133n12, 170n15, 292, 342n21, and 450n15; and King, Strength to Love, 55.

essentially the imaginative power King, Jr. brought to these hymns, and not simply his interpretive skills, that made them so meaningful and relevant for humanity and the whole of life.

King, Jr.'s love for popular and well-known hymns such as "My Country 'Tis of Thee," also known as "America," and "Mine Eyes Have Seen the Glory," commonly called "The Battle Hymn of the Republic," were equally telling, for this, too, was indicative of his thinking about God, humanity, and life, and also, of his pride in country despite his basic quarrel with it. These hymns fused religious and patriotic themes, and reflected, in King, Jr.'s reasoning, much of the spirit and founding principles upon which the nation stood. King, Jr. joined others in singing both songs on many occasions and in various settings, and he commonly used lyrics from both in advancing his vision of a more democratic and inclusive America. The line, "let freedom ring," from "My Country 'Tis of Thee," reverberated throughout parts of his "I Have a Dream" speech in August 1963, and verses from "Mine Eyes Have Seen the Glory" were included in his very last speech in Memphis the day before his death in April 1968.[146] In King, Jr.'s mind, these patriotic hymns were in the very best tradition of both the nation and the Christian church.

King, Jr.'s appreciation for the great hymns as artistic treasures was actually in phase with what had long been his deepening interest in classical music as a whole. He had been, by some standards, a student of the classics in seminary and graduate school, familiarizing himself with certain trends in the development of the world's literature and art, including music. Having a sensitive ear and a feeling for great music, and a wife who was prepared and willing to perform classical music in any form and in any setting, King, Jr. was not likely to value the great Christian hymns while simultaneously devaluing other types of classical music. Thus, he and Coretta occasionally attended classical music performances in concert halls and ballrooms in parts of this

---

145. Carson and Holloran, eds., *A Knock at Midnight*, 186; King, *My Life with Martin Luther King, Jr.*, 305; and Carson, et al., eds., *King Papers*, III, 71.
146. King, "Speech in Savannah," 24; Washington, ed., *A Testament of Hope*, 220 and 286; and Carson and Shepard, eds., *A Call to Conscience*, 86–87.

country and abroad. Also, King, Jr. spoke highly of the musical genius of the German composers Bach and Beethoven, who represented the golden age of classical music, noting on one occasion that "we marvel when we hear" Beethoven's "fifth symphony or his moonlight sonata. . . ."[147] For King, Jr., the great musical compositions of Bach and Beethoven, like the Norwegian violinist Olee Bull's creative ability to play the violin polyphonically, were examples of the heights to which humans in any field of endeavor could climb if they dared to dream, to work hard, and to strive for excellence.[148]

But talented musicians and the great music of the world, vocal and instrumental, had a much more personal and practical significance for King, Jr. that had to do, among other considerations, with entertainment and enjoyment. He understood music as a social activity, and was entertained and gratified by all kinds of music, including classical Western music, sacred music, rhythm and blues, and jazz, even as he cautioned against any tendency to reduce music to mere entertainment.[149] Apparently, his aesthetic sensibilities were such that he could spend an evening thoroughly enjoying the symphonic and orchestral music of a Leonard Bernstein while also lavishly praising the artistic genius that resulted in folk classics such as "Ave Maria" and "Goodnight Irene."[150] King, Jr. sensed the artistic and cultural importance and impact of these works of art, and also of the pioneering blues compositions of W. C. Handy and Huddie "Lead Belly" Ledbetter, the "calypso" music of the Caribbean-American Harry Belafonte, the beat and romantic ballads of Sammy Davis, Jr., the Jazz

---

147. Carson, et al., eds., *King Papers*, VI, 89, 154n15, 189, 297, 308, 333, 355n6, 482n13, and 600; Carson, et al., eds., *King Papers*, IV, 79; Martin Luther King, Jr., *The Measure of a Man* (Philadelphia: Fortress Press, 1988; originally published in 1959), 41; King, "Making the Best of a Bad Mess," 5; and King, "Address at a Mass Meeting," Clarksdale, Mississippi (19 March 1968), 7.
148. Carson, et al., eds., *King Papers*, VI, 89; King, "Address at a Mass Meeting," Clarksdale, Mississippi (19 March 1968), 7; and King, "Why a Movement," 8–9.
149. King, *My Life with Martin Luther King, Jr.*, 59–60; Carson, et al., eds., *King Papers*, IV, 504; and Cotton, *If Your Back's Not Bent*, 13.
150. Bernstein actually contributed to the fundraising side of King's civil rights campaign. "Ave Maria," a song based on Walter Scott's popular epic poem, "Lady of the Lake," was composed by the Austrian composer Franz Schubert in 1825, and "Goodnight Irene" is a 20th century American folk standard originally recorded by the folk and blues artist Huddie "Lead Belly" Ledbetter in 1933. See King, *My Life with Martin Luther King, Jr.*, 247; King, "Pre-Washington Campaign," 11; and King, "Interruptions," 8.

orchestras of Duke Ellington, the jazz genres of Nat King Cole, the "bebop" music of Billy Eckstine, and Nina Simone's contributions to a range of musical styles, including classical, jazz, blues, folk, R&B, gospel, and pop, and he counted all of these artists among the supporters of the civil rights cause.[151] King's wife, Coretta was actually "the featured performer" at a concert that also included Belafonte and Ellington in 1956.[152]

King, Jr. undoubtedly had this and much more in mind whenever he considered seriously what his own people had contributed to "the great folk music of the ages, the great jazz, the great blues," which, in his estimation, had "made America beautiful." Toward the end of his life, King, Jr. recommended, as part of the Poor People's Campaign planned for the nation's capital, "bringing in folk musicians from everywhere" to participate in the kind of "music festivals" or "song festivals" that would highlight the richness and power of the black cultural heritage as it related to both secular and sacred musical forms. King, Jr. felt that these festivals would not only educate his people and instill black pride, but would also demonstrate "that Bach and Beethoven were not the only great musicians."[153] His thinking along these lines was amazingly perceptive, for music had long been one of the fields in which his people had the freedom to be creative and to fully exercise their gifts and talents without threatening white people, and especially, the power elite.

Having grown to manhood in a culture in which all too many of his people distinguished church music from the music of the night club and concert hall,[154] it was not always easy for King, Jr., especially in

---

151. King, *My Life with Martin Luther King, Jr.*, 133 and 247; Carson, et al., eds., *King Papers*, IV, 208, 373n1, and 514; Carson, et al., eds., *King Papers*, VI, 603 and 607–8; Carson, et al., eds., *King Papers*, V, 15, 16n78, 25, 41, 47, 54, 160–61, 381, 476, 519–20, 582n1, and 583; Carson, et al., eds., *King Papers*, III, 317; King, "Pre-Washington Campaign," 11; Martin Luther King, Jr. to Sammy Davis, Jr. (28 March 1961), King Center Library and Archives, 1; Nat King Cole to Martin Luther King, Jr. (25 June 1963), King Center Library and Archives, 1; and Martin Luther King, Jr. to Nat King Cole (18 July 1963), King Center Library and Archives, 1.

152. King, *My Life with Martin Luther King, Jr.*, 133; and Carson, et al., eds., *King Papers*, III, 407–8.

153. King, "Address at a Mass Meeting," Clarksdale, Mississippi (19 March 1968), 7; and Martin Luther King, Jr., "Rally Speech on the Georgia Tour," unpublished version, Albany, Georgia (22 March 1968), 5.

154. Lawrence Levine has written about "this context of a sharpening dichotomy between sacred

his capacity as a Christian pastor, to assess the legitimacy and power of certain secular musical forms on their own or any other terms. In response to a question raised by a seventeen-year-old musician in April 1958, King, Jr., who was in the earliest stages of his work as a pastor and civil rights leader, essentially denied that one could "be consistent in playing gospel music and rock and roll music" simultaneously:

> It seems to me that one must decide to either play gospel music or rock and roll. The two are totally incompatible. The profound sacred and spiritual meaning of the great music of the church must never be mixed with the transitory quality of rock and roll music. The former serves to lift men's souls to higher levels of reality, and therefore to God; the latter so often plunges men's minds into degrading and immoral depths. Therefore, I would say that you would be giving your life to a more noble purpose if you concentrated on the music of the church rather than rock and roll. Never seek to mix the two.[155]

At that time, King, Jr. would have drawn the same contrast between the spirituals and the blues. But the distinctions between these two genres of music were never so clear-cut or complete for King, Jr., especially since he had been exposed in his youth to a culture in which blues artists such as Blind Willie McTell, Charley Patton, Barbecue Bob, Blind Lemon Jefferson, and Thomas A. Dorsey recorded "religious songs as well as blues."[156] As King, Jr. increasingly became friends and comrades in the struggle with musicians such as Harry Belafonte and entertainers like Sammy Davis, Jr., and as he and young activists in the movement routinely sang freedom songs and anthems together that embodied sacred and secular elements, and that had much of the same rocking, driving beat as the blues and jazz, he became more respectful of secular music and more prone to see that it, like sacred music, reflected the mind, soul, and spirit of a people who affirmed and celebrated freedom and life despite oppression.[157] In other words,

---

and secular music" in the 1930s, King's childhood years. See Levine, *Black Culture and Black Consciousness*, 179–83.

155. Carson, et al., eds., *King Papers*, IV, 392–93; and Martin Luther King, Jr., "Advice for Living," *Ebony*, 13 (April, 1958), 104.

156. This idea was framed on the basis of my reading of Lawrence Levine. See Levine, *Black Culture and Black Consciousness*, 179–84.

157. Harry Belafonte, *My Song: A Memoir*, with Michael Shnayerson (New York: Alfred A. Knopf, 2011),

King, Jr. ultimately came to appreciate secular musical forms with few, if any, objections on religious terms, and there was no longer that glaring dichotomy between the sacred and secular when it came to his understanding of music as a whole. Thus, he could appreciate the artistic, cultural, and spiritual significance of the American popular music of Johnny Mathis and the soul and R&B of Sam and Dave, and he included these forms among his favorite music.[158] This is why King, Jr. experienced great sadness one night after attending an event called "Great American Music Night" at his daughter Yolanda's elementary school, "where different kinds of 'American' music were celebrated" with the exception of the blues, gospel, the spirituals, R&B, and jazz, and where the program ended with the playing of "Dixie."[159]

An appreciation for secular music on King, Jr.'s part translated quite naturally into an appreciation of dance as well, for the two had always been inseparable in his mind. He was never uncomfortable with the fact that secular music was closely tied to bodily movement, and even during his most active years in the church and the movement, he and his wife, Coretta occasionally took time to dance.[160] During a visit to Stockholm, Sweden in December 1964, while en route to Norway to receive the Nobel Peace Prize, King and Coretta actually danced "the opening selection together" at a ball given by African students who were celebrating the independence of Kenya.[161] On their trip back to the United States, they had a stopover in Paris, during which they

10, 33, 134, 172, 174, 190–91, and 326; and Baldwin, *There is a Balm in Gilead*, 61 and 86. Rufus Burrow, Jr. also attributes King's evolving views on music to personalism, which holds that "the facts of experience are never all in, but are always forthcoming (since we humans always know only in part)." Burrow goes on to say that King "knew he had to be open to the possibility that some fact could emerge that would necessitate him altering his views on some things." See Rufus Burrow, Jr., "Behind the Public Veil—Comments," unpublished (7 February 2015), 8. In light of such growth on King's part, Michael Eric Dyson's references to similarities between King and Tupac Shakur and Biggie Smalls are not blasphemous or far-fetched in any respect, especially since Dyson also acknowledges "huge differences between King and many hip-hop artists." See Michael E. Dyson, *I May Not Get there with You: The True Martin Luther King, Jr.* (New York: Simon & Schuster, 2000), 177–96.

158. King, *My Life with Martin Luther King, Jr.*, 59; and Dexter Scott King, *Growing Up King: An Intimate Memoir*, with Ralph Wiley (New York: Warner Books, Inc., 2003), 100.

159. King, *Growing Up King*, 100.

160. Coretta reported that they developed the habit of not dancing "publicly" because such behavior was widely considered sinful in black church circles, and especially among the elderly in the South. See King, *My Life with Martin Luther King, Jr.*, 12–13.

161. Referring to this occasion, Coretta reported that this was the very first time that she and her

joined Dorothy Cotton, Andrew Young, and other SCLC staffers in enjoying "an evening at a nightclub that" they "had been told had an array of dancers and singers and other first-class entertainers." "It was a very pleasant interlude," Cotton recounted, and "We thoroughly enjoyed the show."[162]

On rare occasions, King, Jr. attended private parties during which singing and dancing occurred, and he was not particularly disturbed if drinking took place, as long as those who drank acted sensibly, courteously, and responsibly. Although he appreciated certain types of wine and beer, Harvey's Bristol Cream was his drink of choice, and those who knew him best have reported that he sang and danced and was, at times, "the life of the party."[163] The SCLC staffer Dorothy Cotton recounted that on some nights after taking care of movement business, "we'd move the chairs and tables and put on some recorded dance music and have almost a dance competition." "Having this close-up time with Dr. King, when he was able to attend," and "feeling his pleasure in being with all of us," Cotton declared, "contributed to the joy of coming together in a CEP workshop week." Cotton went on to note that Andy Young would "regale us with the music of Louis Armstrong, Ella Fitzgerald, and others," and "We would dance the night away."[164]

Caught up in the daily stresses and strains of the movement, King, Jr. needed this kind of social outlet and release, but he, at the same time, offered a word of caution to those who took partying too far, insisting that life should have "meaning beyond a bottle of whisky" and "a beautiful night club."[165] He was concerned that excessive celebration was too often resulting in precious lives being maimed and even lost

husband "danced publicly since our college days in Boston." See King, My Life with Martin Luther King, Jr., 12–13.

162. Cotton, If Your Back's Not Bent, 20.

163. Belafonte, My Song, 247 and 326–28; Stewart Burns, To the Mountaintop: Martin Luther King, Jr.'s Sacred Mission to Save America, 1955-1968 (New York: HarperCollins Publishers, Inc., 2004), 217; King, My Life with Martin Luther King, Jr., 12–13, 59, and 232–33; "'I Remember Martin,'" 34; Abernathy, And the Walls Came Tumbling Down, 468; Ralph David Abernathy, "My Old Friend Martin," The Tennessean: USA Today Weekend (12–14 January 1990), 6; and Taylor Branch, Parting the Waters: America in the King Years, 1954-63 (New York: Simon & Schuster, 1988), 706.

164. Cotton, If Your Back's Not Bent, 142 and 198.

165. Carson, et al., eds., King Papers, VI, 204; and Carson, et al., eds., King Papers, IV, 268, 444, and 503.

in bar fights or Saturday night brawls.[166] Even so, King, Jr.'s sacred mentality was not such that he persisted in reducing the experience of the secular to something sinister, and thus, meaningless. He remained open to an appreciation and enjoyment of the secular side of life, while also maintaining that it should be properly balanced with an affirmation and celebration of that which is sacred as well. This is the key to understanding how he approached the rich and diverse world of music. The discussion that follows will afford additional information and yield deeper insights into how the lines between what might be regarded as purely religious songs and purely secular songs became increasingly blurred in King, Jr.'s consciousness.[167]

D. Rhythms of Discontent and Hope: The Freedom Songs and Anthems of the Movement

In a statement entitled, "Message for My People," prepared for release on New Year's Day in 1966, Martin Luther King, Jr. perceptively referred to the relationship between art and his people's historic struggle for freedom. "There is a great body of material—prose, poetry, and novels—which concerns itself with the trouble Negro Americans have seen during 200 years of physical slavery and 100 years of segregation," he wrote. "Songs, ranging from the spirituals of the slaves through the folk music of the freedom riders, have dramatized those traumatic years." King, Jr. went on to point out that "The fervor of countless orators, the genius of many playwrights, the sensitivity of artists, great and small, have made the world well aware of the crippling crises through which the black American has moved." Such a contribution, he felt, could not have been more commendable, and it was, for him, a model for what was to be expected of blacks in various fields of endeavor in his own time.[168] While King, Jr. appreciated art

---

166. King, *Where Do We Go from Here?*, 125; Carson, et al., eds., *King Papers*, IV, 268, 306, 444, 503, and 520–21; and Carson, et al., eds., *King Papers*, VI, 204.
167. This is yet another indication of King's cultural and spiritual links with his African and slave ancestors who, according to Lawrence Levine, never "drew modernity's clear line between the sacred and the secular." See Levine, *Black Culture and Black Consciousness*, 30–33 and 177. Also see Stuckey, *Slave Culture*, 24 and 330.
168. Martin Luther King, Jr., "Message for My People," unpublished version prepared for release to the

for art's sake, he was far more interested in the potentially creative ways in which art could be put to the service of his people's continuing efforts to make real the promises of democracy in his own time.[169]

King, Jr. knew as far back as the Montgomery years that a great part of the movement was about singing, or expressing the values of the movement through song. This is why he was among the earliest and strongest supporters of his wife, Coretta's Freedom Concert, which was originally entitled "Portrait of the Montgomery Bus Boycott," and which "told the story of Montgomery in words and songs." This concert developed as part of a fundraising effort for the boycott in 1956.[170] As the movement progressed, the concert was slightly revised and renamed "The Story of the Struggle from 1955 to 1965," and Coretta, as she herself reported, "wove the spirituals and the freedom songs into the narration which I had written." For Coretta, and undoubtedly, for her husband as well, the Freedom Concert "was an inspired concept seeking to combine, in dramatic form, art and experience in a practical, relevant, and meaningful way."[171] In other words, Coretta set out to achieve in churches and on the concert stage what many blacks at the grassroots level were accomplishing, in their own unique ways, in the streets, in jail cells, and in other more informal settings.

King, Jr. revealed much about how the freedom songs and anthems of the movement developed and took shape over time, and as events unfolded from Montgomery to Memphis. He reported that singing occurred in various settings during the Montgomery bus protest. The meetings of the Montgomery Improvement Association (MIA), the

Associated Negro Press, New York City (1 January 1966), King Center Library and Archives, 1; King, *Where Do We Go from Here?*, 126–27; Baldwin, *There is a Balm in Gilead*, 61; and Carson, et al., eds., *King Papers*, VI, 402.

169. For King, the uplift and empowerment of his people remained "a challenge for Negro artists and entertainers as well as writers." See Carson, et al., eds., *King Papers*, IV, 402; and Martin Luther King, Jr., "Advice for Living," *Ebony*, 13 (May, 1958), 112.

170. King, *My Life withy Martin Luther King, Jr.*, 133, 230–31, and 243. Dorothy Cotton, who headed SCLC's Citizenship Education Program, cherished the "public role" Coretta played in the movement, insisting that she "had special skills that helped it as well." See Cotton, *If Your Back's Not Bent*, 233 and 271.

171. There were eight parts to Coretta's Freedom Concert, in which she "alternated between narrating and singing." See King, *My Life with Martin Luther King, Jr.*, 230; and Carson, et al., eds., *King Papers*, IV, 464.

organization that King, Jr. headed and that spearheaded the boycott, always began with scripture readings and prayer, followed by the singing of songs such as "When the Saints Go Marching In," "What a Friend We Have in Jesus," "Onward Christian Soldiers," and "My Country 'Tis of Thee."[172] As the boycotters walked to and from work, they sang "Walk Together Chillum, Don't You Get Weary," "Walk With Me, Lord," "Lord I Can't Turn Back, just because I've been born again," "Keep Your Hand on the Plow," and "We ain't gonna ride the buses no more"—all of which evoked deep thoughts and emotions in King, Jr.[173] King, Jr. noted that the mass meetings in his Dexter Avenue Baptist Church and other neighboring black churches, which "cut across class lines," were the primary context for "group singing," which included mostly "hymns," "traditional songs," or "unaccompanied lined tunes of low pitch and long meter."[174] The singing of the old spirituals, which some in Dexter Church had previously frowned upon, often swelled into an overpowering mass of voice, thus reinforcing that musical thread that extended back generations in slavery. For King, Jr., who always responded to this music on a very human level, the songs triggered thoughts of the long history of black suffering, and were, perhaps more importantly, imbued with the spirit of love and nonviolence.[175]

When King, Jr. moved into Albany, Georgia in 1961 to launch his second major attempt at organized social protest, he was both proud and deeply moved to see and struggle with ordinary black citizens and youngsters, some members of the Student Nonviolent Coordinating Committee (SNCC), who created songs spontaneously during mass meetings, public demonstrations, and while incarcerated, thus suggesting, once again, a close connection between art and struggle. Traditional songs such as "Sometimes I feel Like My Time Ain't Long," "This Little Light of Mine," "Swing Low, Sweet Chariot," "Ain't Gonna

172. Carson, et al., eds., King Papers, III, 70, 150–51, and 369–70.
173. King, My Life with Martin Luther King, Jr., 134; Baldwin Interview with Abernathy (17 March 1987); and King, Stride toward Freedom, 149.
174. King, Stride toward Freedom, 86; and Carson, ed., The Autobiography of Martin Luther King, Jr., 59.
175. King, Stride toward Freedom, 86 and 88; Washington, ed., A Testament of Hope, 448; and King, My Life with Martin Luther King, Jr., 134.

Let Nobody Turn Me Round," and "Oh, Freedom!" were often sung, but so were newly created songs such as "Wallace, Betcha Can't Jail Us All" and "Oh Pritchett, Oh Kelly," composed to the tune of "Oh Mary, Oh Martha," and used as powerful statements against the oppressive actions of Albany's Police Chief Laurie Pritchett and Mayor Asa D. Kelly.[176] A "song parody" which King, Jr. "enjoyed very much" in Albany went as follows: "I'm coming,' I'm comin'/And my head *ain't* bendin' low/I'm walkin'/I'm walkin' tall, I'm talking strong/I'm America's *New* Black Joe."[177]

Although King, Jr. characterized the freedom crusade as "a spiritual movement," he was obviously becoming more favorably disposed to the fact that so many of the songs of the movement, such as "The Movement is a-Movin' All Over this Land" and "Pick 'em Up and Lay 'em Down," were not particularly religious in language, melody, and performance, and that some, such as "Everybody Sing Freedom," "I'm Gonna Do What the Spirit Say Do," "Ain't Gonna Let Nobody Turn Me 'Round," and "I'm on My Way to Freedom Land," actually embodied elements of two disparate genres, one sacred and the other secular.[178] In other words, it was clear to King, Jr. that the freedom songs drew heavily on not only the spirituals and gospel, but on rhythmic chants, rhythm and blues, and calypso forms as well. It was equally evident to him that there was no real distinction between sacred songs and secular songs when it came to the question of their significance in mobilizing and inspiring the folk, and in giving voice to black cultural

176. "Why Our Prayer Vigil," unpublished version of a group statement of the Negotiating Committee of the Albany Movement and its Chief Consultants, Dr. Martin Luther King, Jr. and Dr. Ralph Abernathy, Albany, Georgia (1962), 1–2; Guy and Candie Carawan, *Sing for Freedom: The Story of the Civil Rights Movement through Its Songs* (Bethlehem, PA: Sing Out Corporation, 1990), 62; and Baldwin, *There is a Balm in Gilead*, 196–97. Apparently, what Lawrence Levine calls "spontaneity" and "elasticity of forms" were critical ingredients in the creation and performance of these songs, much as was the case with the slaves in antebellum times, and King understood this. See Levine, *Black Culture and Black Consciousness*, 25–55.

177. This song is a perfect example of how protesters not only in Albany, but across the South, displayed levels of creative genius as they struggled for freedom and justice. See Washington, ed., *A Testament of Hope*, 348.

178. Martin Luther King, Jr., "An Ambitious Dream Confronts Reality," unpublished version of an essay written for *Amsterdam News*, New York, New York (23 June 1965), King Center Library and Archives, 1; Washington, ed., *A Testament of Hope*, 84; Carawan and Carawan, eds., *Sing for Freedom*, 24 and 62–63; Cotton, *If Your Back's Not Bent*, 232, 239, 302, and 312; and King, *My Life with Martin Luther King, Jr.*, 214.

values. With movement songs as a whole in mind, King, Jr. declared: "The freedom songs are playing a strong and vital role in our struggle. They give the people new courage and a sense of unity. I think they keep alive a faith, a radiant hope in the future, particularly in our most trying hours."[179]

King, Jr. called the freedom songs "the soul of the movement," and not "just incantations of clever phrases designed to invigorate a campaign." He also said repeatedly, as in 1963, that these songs were "as old as the history of the Negro in America," and that they testified to his cultural bond with his ancestry, linking him, in matters of spirit, to the mass of his people over many generations in America, despite his own formal training, amazing achievements, and standing on both the national and global scenes:

> They are adaptations of the songs the slaves sang—the sorrow songs, the shouts for joy, the battle hymns, and the anthems of our movement. I have heard people talk of their beat and rhythm, but we in the movement are as inspired by their words. "Woke Up This Morning with My Mind Stayed on Freedom" is a sentence that needs no music to make its point. We sing the freedom songs today for the same reason the slaves sang them, because we too are in bondage and the songs add hope to our determination that "We shall overcome, Black and white together, we shall overcome someday."[180]

In another statement, King, Jr. commented further on the history and

179. Robert Shelton, "Songs a Weapon in Rights Battle," *New York Times* (20 August 1962); Washington, ed., *A Testament of Hope*, 348; and Martin Luther King, Jr., *Why We Can't Wait* (New York: The New American Library, Inc., 1963), 61. SCLC's Dorothy Cotton essentially agreed with King, insisting that the songs "energized us when we were tired," "made us feel better and stronger," and "advanced the movement." In this sense, Cotton concluded, the songs were "cathartic." Cotton said that she, King, and others rediscovered "the wonder-working power of music." See Cotton, *If Your Back's Not Bent*, 150, 158, and 292.

180. King, *Why We Can't Wait*, 61; and Washington, ed., *A Testament of Hope*, 348. King's point that the freedom songs were passed down from slavery and slightly revised to meet the challenges of a more contemporary context is widely supported by the testimonies of other activists and by the most recent scholarship on the subject. King's former aide Wyatt Walker has noted that "The nonviolent movement in the South, at its inception, 'updated' many of the historic Negro spirituals and transformed them through slight word changes into Freedom Songs." In a similar vein, Sterling Stuckey writes: "What a splendid affirmation of the hopes and dreams of their slave ancestors that some of the songs being sung in antebellum days are the ones Afro-Americans are singing in the freedom movement today: 'Michael, row the boat ashore'; 'Just like a tree planted by the water, I shall not be moved'." See Walker, *"Somebody's Calling My Name"*, 176; and Sterling Stuckey, "Through the Prism of Folklore: The Black Ethos in Slavery," in Eric Foner, ed., *America's Black Past: A Reader in Afro-American History* (New York: Harper & Row, Publishers, 1970), 111.

multiform character of the freedom songs, while drawing an analogy between them and songs that spoke to America's mission in the world:

> Consider, in World War II, *Praise the Lord and Pass the Ammunition*, and in World War I, *Over There* and *Tipperary*, and during the Civil War, *Battle Hymn of the Republic* and *John Brown's Body*. A Negro song anthology would include sorrow songs, shouts for joy, battle hymns, anthems. Since slavery, the Negro has sung throughout his struggle in America. *Steal Away* and *Go Down, Moses* were the songs of faith and inspiration which were sung on the plantations.[181]

For King, Jr., nothing was more heart-warming, thought-provoking, and encouraging than the experience of actually singing the songs of the movement with groups of his people, especially youngsters, who too often seemed unmindful and even unappreciative of the rich heritage passed down by the generations before them. Referring specifically to the campaign in Birmingham in 1963, King, Jr. captured the power of those moments in graphic terms:

> I have stood in a meeting with hundreds of youngsters and joined in while they sang "Ain't Gonna Let Nobody Turn Me 'Round." It is not just a song; it is a resolve. A few minutes later, I have seen those same youngsters refuse to turn around from the onrush of a police dog, refuse to turn around before a pugnacious Bull Connor in command of men armed with power hoses. These songs bind us together, give us courage together, help us to march together.[182]

The impact of such experiences on King, Jr. personally is rather easy to imagine, for he literally adored children and youth and also had a remarkable ability to empathize with others. The very sound of young protesters locking arms with adults and singing "We Shall Overcome," after the homes of black leaders had been bombed and four black girls killed in the bombing of the Sixteenth Street Baptist Church in Birmingham, shook King, Jr. to the core and actually overwhelmed him, for he was never stoic in the face of tragedy. "Tears came into my eyes that at such a tragic moment, my race could sing its hope

---

181. Washington, ed., *A Testament of Hope*, 348.
182. King, *Why We Can't Wait*, 61; Washington, ed., *A Testament of Hope*, 348 and 535–36; and Baldwin, *There is a Balm in Gilead*, 200–201.

and faith,"[183] he declared, as he reflected on the spiritual texture of the movement, and on how musicality, spirituality, and physicality were intimately intertwined in its ranks. He became more convinced that even the most abject brutality was no match for the spirit of people who sang about hope and faith even in the face of death, for they had, in his judgment, a freedom within that nothing in their external world could vanquish. "We all are free in the sense that freedom is that inner power that drives us to achieve freedom,"[184] King, Jr. occasionally remarked, as he considered the energizing spirit and sustaining power of the movement's songs and anthems. In words that further clarified his point, he held that "The within is that realm of spiritual ends expressed" not only in "literature, morals and religion," but "in art" as well.[185]

"We Shall Overcome" became not only "the anthem, or symbol, of the Movement," particularly during and after Birmingham, it also became the chief expression of King, Jr.'s hopes for the movement and the future of humankind.[186] "I've joined hands so often with students and others behind jail bars singing 'We shall overcome,'" he said in an interview. "Sometimes we've had tears in our eyes when we joined together to sing it, but we still decided to sing it."[187] King, Jr. felt uplifted whenever the churched and non-churched among his people

183. Washington, ed., *A Testament of Hope*, 347–48.
184. Martin Luther King, Jr., "See You in Washington," unpublished version of a speech at the SCLC Staff Retreat, Ebenezer Baptist Church, Atlanta, Georgia (17 January 1968), King Center Library and Archives, 11.
185. Martin Luther King, Jr., "Moving to Another Mountain," edited version from the transcript of a baccalaureate sermon delivered at Wesleyan University, Middletown, Connecticut (7 June 1964), King Center Library and Archives, 3.
186. For an account of how the song became the anthem of the movement, beginning with the student demonstrations, see King, *My Life with Martin Luther King, Jr.*, 173. Eileen Southern claims that the text of "We Shall Overcome" "apparently derived from Charles Tindley's gospel song *I'll Overcome Some Day*" (1900). Southern also discusses King's view of the song as "a spiritual." See Eileen Southern, *The Music of Black Americans: A History*, second Edition (New York: W. W. Norton & Company, Inc., 1983), 546–47; and Cotton, *If Your Back's Not Bent*, 211. For yet another perspective on the development of the song, see Carawan and Carawan, eds., *Sing for Freedom*, 15. Also see Martin Luther King, Jr., "The Ballot," unpublished version of an interview (17 July 1962), King Center Library and Archives, 2–4; "Remarks of Dr. Martin Luther King, Jr.: '*EN GRÄNSLOS KVÄL PÅ OPERAN*'," unpublished version, Stockholm, Sweden (31 March 1966), 4; King, "Address at a Mass Meeting," Clarksdale, Mississippi (19 March 1968), 7; and Baldwin, *There is a Balm in Gilead*, 77 and 202.
187. King, "The Ballot," 4. King's testimony is supported by the SCLC staffer Dorothy Cotton. See Cotton, *If Your Back's Not Bent*, 211.

united and sung this song with all of the power of their souls. He heard it in Negro churches in St. Augustine in 1964, in the streets during the campaign for voting rights in Selma in 1965, at Soldier Field in Chicago at the height of the Chicago Freedom Movement in 1966-67, and in Memphis while marching with sanitation workers in 1968. Oftentimes, the singing of "We Shall Overcome" was followed by stirring renditions of "This Little Light of Mine," a song of both personal and collective empowerment, as was the case at Selma's Brown Chapel African Methodist Episcopal Church (AME), where "the worn brown benches were packed with people clapping and swaying to the music, which grew louder and more enthusiastic as the crowd grew steadily larger."[188] King, Jr. always looked forward to participating in the circle formation in which prayers were recited and the freedom songs and anthems of the movement were sung, and he was captured on film in Memphis, shortly before his death, singing with folded arms in a circle of ministers, with his eyes fixed upward toward the heavens.[189]

Not so well-known are those precious moments King, Jr. spent accompanying his closest SCLC aides in singing movement songs. Coretta King reported that her husband and Andrew Young, Ralph Abernathy, Wyatt Walker, and Bernard Lee often sang these songs "to break up the seriousness" of their "staff conferences and retreats." While in Oslo, Norway to receive the Nobel Peace Prize in December, 1964, King, Jr. and the group actually formed a quintet "and sang freedom songs in beautiful harmony."[190] After they had created the

---

188. Charles E. Fager, *Selma, 1965: The March that Changed the South* (Boston: Beacon Press, 1985), 8, 40, and 116; Robert M. Mikell, *Selma* (Huntsville, AL: Publishers Enterprise, Inc., 1965), 23; Sheyann Webb and Rachel West Nelson, *Selma, Lord, Selma: Childhood Memories of the Civil Rights Days*, as told to Frank Sikora (Tuscaloosa: The University of Alabama Press, 1997), xiv (foreword); and Baldwin, *There is a Balm in Gilead*, 205.

189. The circle was apparently as significant in the singing of movement songs as it was in prayer, and this too owed much to traditions stretching back to the slave forebears. Sterling Stuckey has argued convincingly that "The ring in which Africans danced and sang is the key to understanding the means by which they achieved oneness in America." See Baldwin, *Never to Leave Us Alone*, 16–17 and 83; and Stuckey, *Slave Culture*, 12–13. The importance of the "circle" or "ring" is also underscored in Lewis V. Baldwin, *"Invisible" Strands in African Methodism: A History of the African Union Methodist Protestant and Union American Methodist Episcopal Churches, 1805-1980* (Metuchen, NJ: The American Theological Library Association and The Scarecrow Press, Inc., 1983), 137–41.

190. King, *My Life with Martin Luther King, Jr.*, 8–9. Dorothy Cotton pointed out that this was "a popular form of singing among Black men in the South at the time," and King loved it. See Cotton, *If You Back's Not Bent*, 13.

proper atmosphere, Coretta, her in-laws, King, Sr. and Alberta King, her sister-in-law, Christine, and the other family members and friends in the traveling party joined in and collectively they all "sang freedom songs and hymns together," with words ringing "louder than ever before." According to Coretta, "We sang 'Oh Freedom,' 'Ain't Gonna Let Nobody Turn Me Round,' 'Were You There When They Crucified My Lord?,' and 'Balm in Gilead,' which my husband often quoted when he needed a lift."[191] King, Jr.'s associate Dora McDonald, who was present on that occasion, remembered that the group "sang freedom songs" in the hotel lobby there in Norway, sparking a kind of "impromptu freedom rally" and attracting the attention of curious hotel employees and other onlookers.[192] These songs took on new life, and indeed, a life of their own, in the context of King, Jr.-led civil rights campaigns. Thus, they were never outdated remains of a slave past.

The marches, demonstrations, and experiences in and outside jail cells were the contexts in which King, Jr. most often united his voice in song with both famous artists and ordinary freedom singers. According to King, Jr.'s secretary Dora McDonald, King "would rally our troops with the eloquence of his speeches and the singing of spirituals such as 'Ain't Gonna Let No Injunction. . . .' or 'Ain't Gonna Let No Police Dogs. . . .' or 'Ain't Gonna Let No Water Hose Turn Me 'Round.'"[193] During the mammoth march from Selma to Montgomery in 1965, King, Jr. walked, chanted, and sang with Harry Belafonte, whose song, "Day O!" (1956), a Jamaican folk song about a worker being fairly compensated for a long night on the graveyard shift, impacted the civil rights movement substantively and symbolically. King, Jr. marched and sang with the gospel artists Mahalia Jackson and Dorothy Coates, the freedom singers

191. King's voice often radiated outward whenever he quoted the vitally expressive lyrics of "Balm in Gilead," and especially, "Sometimes I feel discouraged, And think my work's in vain, But then the Holy Spirit, Revives my soul again." See King, *My Life with Martin Luther King, Jr.*, 9; Carson and Holloran, eds., *A Knock at Midnight*, 164; King, "The Meaning of Hope," 16–17; Martin Luther King, Jr., "Early Days," Excerpts from "Thou Fool," unpublished version of a sermon, Mt. Pisgah Missionary Baptist Church, Chicago, Illinois (27 August 1967); Baldwin, *There is a Balm in Gilead*, 77 and 196; and Baldwin, *To Make the Wounded Whole*, 65.

192. Dora McDonald, *Secretary to a King: My Years with Martin Luther King, Jr. the Civil Rights Movement, and Beyond* (Montgomery, AL: New South Books, 2012), 81; and King, *My Life with Martin Luther King, Jr.*, 9.

193. McDonald, *Secretary to a King*, 49 and 97.

Fannie Lou Hamer and Bernice Johnson Reagon, and the American folk singer and activist Joan Baez during the Vietnam protests. These experiences, along with those King, Jr. shared with his wife, mother, and sister, who also sang in the cause of freedom,[194] must have reminded him that women, and especially black women, were not only great nurturers, but also worthy contributors to the protest, and also, the artistic and spiritual sides of the movement. King, Jr. knew that women outnumbered men among the freedom singers and in the choirs of the most progressive Negro churches, which were the primary sources for the music of the movement.

Although King, Jr. viewed the freedom songs and anthems as integral to his people's struggle to expand the reach of democracy in the United States, he also had a sense of their world value and felt that they were meaningful and magnetic enough to appeal to poor and oppressed people everywhere. While visiting India in 1959, King, Jr. discovered that "The Indian people love to listen to the Negro spirituals," and his wife, Coretta actually "ended up singing as much" as he lectured.[195] Exposed to a range of musical forms, sounds, and genres over time, and sensitive to the power and appeal of music as a universal language, King, Jr. felt that musicians everywhere had a role to play in support of human liberation efforts. He actually joined Miriam Makeba, the famous South African folk singer who introduced the Western world to Xhosa and Zulu songs, as an international sponsor of the *Appeal for Action Against Apartheid* in 1962, and the two participated, along with the American folk singer Pete Seeger, in a fundraising event on behalf of South African liberation at Hunter College in New York in December, 1965.[196] King, Jr. was convinced that music gave vital expression to the

194. Carson, et al., eds., *King* Papers, IV, 373; Heilbut, *The Gospel Sound*, 165; Garland, *The Sound of Soul*, 40; Carson, et al., eds., *King Papers*, V, 353; King, *My Life with Martin Luther King, Jr.*, 36, 133, 230–32, and 243; Cotton, *If You Back's Not Bent*, 302; Smiley, *Death of a King*, 116; Marcus "Goodie" Goodloe, "Coalition of Conscience: An Assessment of Martin Luther King Jr.'s Leadership with Athletes and Entertainers During the Civil Rights Movement," unpublished PhD dissertation, Dallas Baptist University, Dallas, Texas (May, 2011), 190; and McDonald, *Secretary to a King*, 49, 74, 81, and 95–97.
195. Carson, ed., *The Autobiography of Martin Luther King, Jr.*, 123; King, *My Life with Martin Luther King, Jr.*, 164; and Carson, et al., eds., *King Papers*, V, 233.
196. Baldwin, *Toward the Beloved Community*, 48, 169, and 173; and "Observe Human Rights Day December 10 by Answering this Appeal for Action Against Apartheid: International Sponsors," a pamphlet, The American Committee on Africa (July, 1962), King Center Library and Archives.

reciprocity, the deep kinship, and the shared sense of higher human values that joined the cultures and the freedom movements of oppressed peoples everywhere, and he delighted in the ways in which different kinds of music challenged and inspired peoples of all racial and ethnic backgrounds to work for positive and much-needed social change.

King, Jr.'s sense of the importance of music in the shaping of a new humanity and a new world became evident on so many levels. As he elevated his cry against Vietnam and the haunting threat of war to what he called "the great world house" in the late 1960s, he occasionally requested the senior choir at his Ebenezer Baptist Church to sing "Down By the Riverside," also known as "Ain't Gonna Study War No More," and he used this line in sermons and speeches as well. "I believe there is a need for all people of goodwill to come with a massive act of conscience and say in the words of the old Negro spiritual, 'We ain't gonna study war no more,'" said King, Jr. in a sermon toward the end of his life. It was his conviction that "peace represents a sweeter music, a cosmic melody that is far superior to the discords of war."[197]

King, Jr. was prone to use similar analogies and metaphors when considering music in relationship to the disturbing cycles of grinding poverty, and he made this known amidst the setbacks and sheer frustration that attended his proposed Poor People's Campaign. For him, food and other basic necessities for the poor constituted "a sweeter music" than the surreptitious means the rich and powerful employed to control the poor.[198] He thought a lot about this in his final days, and it appeared, at times, that he was restless. Unable to sleep in hotel room after hotel room, he, according to sources analyzing him, found "himself singing those same words he sang in Acapulco," words from "the ancient hymn whose meaning penetrates the heart":

Nothing in my hand I bring,
Simply to Thy cross I cling.
Naked, come to Thee for dress,

197. Carson and Holloran, eds., *A Knock at Midnight*, xix (introduction); and King, *Where Do We Go from Here?*, 185.
198. King, *Where Do We Go from Here?*, 178–79.

Helpless, look to Thee for grace
Foul, I to the fountain fly
Wash me, Saviour, or I die.

While I draw this fleeting breath,
When mine eyes shall close in death.
When I soar to worlds unknown,
See Thee on Thy judgment throne.
Rock of ages, cleft for me,
Let me hide myself in Thee.[199]

There were other musical analogies and metaphors King, Jr. employed in articulating his vision of a society and world free of the barriers imposed by the race-caste system. "We've come to the point of knowing that every man from a bass black to a treble white is significant on God's keyboard," he maintained. He stated on another occasion that "Life's piano can only produce the melodies of brotherhood when it is recognized that the black keys are as basic, necessary and beautiful as the white keys." Noting that the "hopes of our childhood and the promises of our mature years are unfinished symphonies," King, Jr. longed to see a world in which the "jangling discords" of humankind would be transformed "into a beautiful symphony of brotherhood."[200]

King, Jr. has been memorialized and celebrated in song. "Supplication," Nina Simone's "The King of Love is Dead," and Stevie Wonder's "Happy Birthday"[201] are fitting tributes to a man who found, in music, a means of offering praise and thanks to his creator, of

199. Smiley, Death of a King, 186–87.
200. King, "Pre-Washington Campaign," 7; King, *Where Do We Go from Here?*, 123; and Washington, ed., *A Testament of Hope*, 219. Also see the beautiful analogy King drew between the challenges confronting him and his people and the sense of urgency the Norwegian violinist Olee Bull faced when he "transposed the composition and finished it on three strings" after his "A string snapped" during "a concert in Paris." King noted: "This is life, to have your A string snap, and yet finishing on three strings. Most of us have to do it that way. Our A string often snap and we have to go on in on three strings. But this is life, injecting meaning into difficult, sometimes messy situations. And going on in on broken pieces." See King, "Making the Best of a Bad Mess," 5; King, "Why a Movement," 8–9; and Ayres, ed., *The Wisdom of Martin Luther King, Jr.*, 110.
201. "Supplication" was actually written by the father of Althea Thompson Thomas, the woman who served as King's organist at Dexter Avenue Baptist Church in Montgomery. Thomas's father put the words to the song after hearing of King's assassination. In Althea Thomas's references to the song, she did not mention her father's full name. See Vaughn and Wills, eds., *Reflections on Our Pastor*, 68; Garland, *The Sound of Soul*, 179 and 184; and Daryl Miller, "King's Dream Endures Mixture of Music and Drama," *Los Angeles Times* (6 February 2000).

enjoying and celebrating life, of relaxing in the midst of tension-packed situations, of relieving his high stress levels, of stimulating his mind, and of giving expression to his own "humanness" as well as his shared humanity with others. Music was a part of the whole of King, Jr.'s life, making it virtually impossible at times to neatly distinguish between King, Jr. the public figure and King, Jr. the private person. By affirming, appreciating, and getting involved with music, King, Jr. was actually displaying his capacity for what has been called "celebrative affirmation," which means "saying yes to life" despite its demands, hardships, and disappointments.[202] The next chapter will advance this claim in greater depth, with major attention to King, Jr.'s attitude toward and approach to play and games and how this translated into a sense of the value of sports and sports heroes to life and the human struggle.

---

202. Harvey Cox, *The Feast of Fools: A Theological Essay on Festivity and Fantasy* (New York: Harper & Row, Publishers, 1969), 25–26.

5

"His Child's Heart": Martin Luther King, Jr.'s World of Play and Sports

The great man is he who does not lose his child's heart.
–Mencius[1]

Daddy was such a fun-loving person. He was as much a kid at heart as we were.
–Yolanda D. King[2]

A genuine and abiding love for fun remained one of the greatest and most attractive qualities of Martin Luther King, Jr. He affirmed, enjoyed, and celebrated life not only through food, eating, sex, and music, but also through the phenomenon of play. Play is most often associated with children and childlike activities, but King, Jr. evidently understood that play could be a positive, meaningful, and enlightening experience for adults as well, especially in cases where they were burdened with the stresses and strains of a deeply committed and

1. Quoted in Katie J. Dubaj, "My Translucent Father," *Human Architecture: Journal of the Sociology of Self-Knowledge*, Vol. I, Issue 2 (2002), article 8. For similar quotes by Heraclitus, Johann Friedrich von Schiller, Friedrich Nietzsche, Pablo Neruda, and other great thinkers, see James H. Evans, Jr., *Playing: Christian Explorations of Daily Living* (Minneapolis: Fortress Press, 2010), 7, 20, 29, and 45.
2. "'I Remember Martin': People Close to the Late Civil Rights Leader Recall a Down-to-Earth and Humorous Man," *Ebony*, 39, no. 6 (April, 1984), 38.

unusually busy and hurried life. King, Jr. developed a play ethic, and he played, at times, with the joyful abandon of a child, even into his adult years.

This chapter is about the development of King, Jr.'s attitude toward and approach to play and sports over the course of his life. Much of the discussion covers King, Jr.'s involvements with basketball, baseball, football, pool, billiards, golf, and other pastime recreational activities and pleasures, which tended to be somewhat structured, focused toward some specific goal or objective, and designed to advance physical, mental, and intellectual growth, social skills, and moral and spiritual development as well. Some attention is also given to King, Jr.'s favorite sports heroes, to his work with famous sports figures in the interest of civil and human rights, and to his use of sports metaphors to convey certain ideas and values that were dear to him personally and that related well to that larger cause for which he struggled so gallantly. The more general concern here is about the ways in which King, Jr. injected play into his relationships and interactions with family, friends, and co-workers.

A. Learning to Play: Moving Freely in Specified Spaces

The black community along Auburn Avenue in the northeast section of Atlanta, Georgia constituted the world in which Martin Luther King, Jr. learned to play as a child in the 1930s and 40s. King, Jr. described that world as "quite ordinary in terms of social status" and "characterized with a sort of unsophisticated simplicity."[3] It was a segregated world with a life of its own. Here, a vibrant atmosphere existed, imbued with animation and an ever recurring symphony of gay noises—the crack of balls in poolrooms, the loud roar of vehicles slowly passing by, the barking of stray dogs on street corners, and always, the sounds of children playing and laughing, loud and occurring with measured regularity. Having the usual growing boy's love for the outdoors, King, Jr. found the warm and balmy weather in the South ideal for satisfying

3. Clayborne Carson, et al., eds., *The Papers of Martin Luther King, Jr., Volume I: Called to Serve, January 1929–June 1951* (Berkeley: University of California Press, 1992), 360.

his habits of play and love of sports.[4] Described by relatives as the "typical, active, outgoing," and "fun-loving" child, who was also "small, but very strong and quick, good at sports," King, Jr. poured his very heart and soul into basketball, baseball, football, stickball, dodge ball, tennis, and other sports or games.[5] He was also "a strong swimmer" and literally enjoyed "playing sand-lot and street baseball," riding his bikes, making and flying "kites and model planes," throwing rocks "for distance" and as "a test of accuracy," and "bouncing rubber balls off the side of the house, a wall or a fence."[6] His very first playmates were his siblings, Christine and A. D., and most of his earliest experiences playing occurred on "a basketball court" in the backyard of the King family home or on "a baseball diamond" in the "open field behind the King property."[7] Although King, Jr. and A. D. had moments during which they disagreed, hit each other, and antagonized each other and their sister, the time the trio spent together playing ball and staging pranks or mischievous tricks[8] not only delighted them, but also strengthened their sense of kinship and reinforced bonds of mutual love, respect, obligations, and cooperation between them that extended into their adulthood.

Aside from family, church, and the lessons received in nursery school, David T. Howard Elementary School, Atlanta University's Laboratory High School, and Booker T. Washington High School, play constituted the most important means of learning for King, Jr. during

---

4. Christine King Farris, *Through It All: Reflections on My Life, My Family, and My Faith* (New York: Aria Books, 2009), 16–31; and Lewis V. Baldwin, *There is a Balm in Gilead: The Cultural Roots of Martin Luther King, Jr.* (Minneapolis: Fortress Press, 1991), 19 and 23.

5. Farris, *Through It All*, 21–25 and 223; Christine King Farris, "The Young Martin: From Childhood through College," *Ebony*, Vol. LXI, no. 3 (January, 1986), 56–57; Coretta Scott King, *My Life with Martin Luther King, Jr.* (New York: Henry Holt and Company, 1993; originally published in 1969), 78; Lawrence D. Reddick, *Crusader without Violence: A Biography of Martin Luther King, Jr.* (New York: Harper & Brothers, Publishers, 1959), 53; Alberta King, "Dr. Martin Luther King, Jr.: Birth to Twelve Years Old by His Mother," a recording, Ebenezer Baptist Church (18 January 1973), Library and Archives of the Martin Luther King, Jr. Center for Nonviolent Social Change, Inc., Atlanta, Georgia; and Frederick L. Downing, *To See the Promised Land: The Faith Pilgrimage of Martin Luther King, Jr.* (Macon, GA: Mercer University Press, 1986), 43–44.

6. King, "Dr. Martin Luther King, Jr.: Birth to Twelve Years Old"; King, *My Life with Martin Luther King, Jr.*, 78; and Reddick, *Crusader without Violence*, 53.

7. King, "Dr. Martin Luther King, Jr.: Birth to Twelve Years Old"; Downing, *To See the Promised Land*, 43; and Reddick, *Crusader without Violence*, 53.

8. Farris, *Through It All*, 21–25; and Martin Luther King, Sr., *Daddy King: An Autobiography*, with Clayton Riley (New York: William Morrow & Company, Inc., 1980), 126–27.

those early years. He and his siblings played ball and other sports and games with children of different classes in the backyard of the King family home, on the property of neighbors, and on the playgrounds of segregated schools and other public places, facilities, and accommodations.[9] Apparently, King, Jr. eagerly and enthusiastically devoted everything at his disposal to play, especially his body and mind, and the goal was, as with every child, always fun and pleasure. But the associative and cooperative nature of play taught him crucial lessons about how to relate in positive ways to people, and thus, fueled his healthy development, physically, intellectually, emotionally, and otherwise. This is why the youngster "was strong and sturdy" and, as he himself put it, "precocious, both physically and mentally," with an "I. Q." that "stands somewhat above average."[10] As King, Jr. talked and interacted with other children, and repeatedly participated in the same activities with them, he naturally learned words and concepts, how to express himself, how to make choices and reach goals, how to be resourceful and creative, and how to live and function well in the strange world in which he found himself.

Perhaps King, Jr.'s most eye-opening, memorable, and enduring lesson in the context of child's play occurred when he, at about age six, lost two white playmates due to racism. As discussed to some extent in Chapter 1, King, Jr. and the white boys played together freely until they entered racially separate schools, at which time, the white boys' father abruptly demanded an end to the friendship. This was the beginning of King, Jr.'s struggle with Christian love (*agape*) at the level of his thinking, and also, his emotional and spiritual crisis around the ethics of love and community.[11] Beset by bitterness and feelings

---

9. Farris, *Through It All*, 24–25; Carson, et. al., eds., *King Papers*, I, 360; King, "Dr. Martin Luther King, Jr.: Birth to Twelve Years Old"; and Downing, *To See the Promised Land*, 43–44.
10. Reddick, *Crusader without Violence*, 53; and Carson, et al., eds., *King Papers*, I, 359.
11. John Ansbro mistakenly suggests that this crisis began with King, Jr.'s reading of the works of the nineteenth century German philosopher Friedrich Nietzsche, especially *On the Genealogy of Morals* (1887) and *The Will to Power* (1910). This was clearly not the case. See John J. Ansbro, *Martin Luther King, Jr.: The Making of a Mind* (Maryknoll, NY: Orbis Books, 1982), 1–2; Carson, et al., eds., *King Papers*, I, 362–63; and "Face to Face: Dr. Martin Luther King, Jr. and John Freeman," London, recorded from transmission and aired (29 October 1961), King Center Library and Archives, 2–3. Interestingly enough, King, Jr.'s sister Christine concludes that her brother's response to

of vindictiveness, the boy would have developed a deep and lasting hatred for all whites had it not been for the Christian teachings of his parents, King, Sr. and Alberta King.[12] The youngster was made to understand why he experienced community among his own people and non-community in his dealings with whites, and also, why it was necessary for him to struggle for a higher and more inclusive communitarian ideal. The lesson he learned from his mother on that occasion about the origins of slavery and segregation as social conditions rather than the products of "a natural order," and about the need to be proud of himself as a Negro in spite of his encounters with racism and hatred on the playground and elsewhere, helped make it possible for King, Jr. to speak and write in rather sophisticated terms about race and black history and culture while still in his teens.[13]

The world of play presented challenges that inspired and shaped young King, Jr.'s intolerance for injustice of any kind, and especially, racial injustice. Barred from access to swimming pools, public parks, the YMCA, and other arenas in which white children in Atlanta freely played,[14] he resolved early on that he would not bow to segregation because it defied basic standards of Christian morality and human decency. His mind was always on integrated swimming pools, parks, baseball diamonds, football fields, and basketball and tennis courts, and he vowed to one day put his body where his mind was.[15] The spirited nature of King, Jr.'s play as a child, and his courage and

this crisis "would ultimately be the foundation of his successful leadership in the civil rights movement." See Farris, *Through It All*, 25.

12. Carson, et. al., *King Papers*, I, 362; Farris, *Through It All*, 25; Farris, "The Young Martin," 57; King, *Daddy King*, 130; King, "Face to Face: Dr. Martin Luther King, Jr. and John Freeman," 2–3; and King, "Dr. Martin Luther King, Jr.: Birth to Twelve Years Old."

13. Martin Luther King, Jr., *Stride toward Freedom: The Montgomery Story* (New York: Harper & Row, Publishers, 1958), 18–19; Farris, *Through It All*, 25; Farris, "The Young Martin," 57; King, *Daddy King*, 130; Carson, et al., eds., *King Papers*, I, 109–11, 121, and 362–63; "Rev. M. L. King, Jr. Guest Speaker for Cultural League," *Atlanta Daily World*, Atlanta, Georgia (11 July 1948), 3; and "Face to Face: Dr. Martin Luther King, Jr. and John Freeman," 2–3.

14. King, *Stride toward Freedom*, 18–21; "Face to Face: Dr. Martin Luther King, Jr. and John Freeman," 3–5; and Clayborne Carson, ed., *The Autobiography of Martin Luther King, Jr.* (New York: Warner Books, Inc., 1998), 8–11.

15. Martin Luther King, Jr., "A Speech," unpublished version, Grenada, Mississippi (15 June 1966), King Center Library and Archives, 3; King, *Stride toward Freedom*, 20–21; "Face to Face: Dr. Martin Luther King, Jr. and John Freeman," 3–5; Farris, *Through It All*, 17; and Baldwin, *There is a Balm in Gilead*, 21 and 24.

tendency to take risks while playing sports and other games, became oddly symbolic of the values and virtues he would later bring to the freedom struggle. The youngster risked limb, and even life, each time he and his playmates innocently engaged in "the rough sport of throwing rocks at each other," and whenever he went "into the streets after a ball." On at least two occasions, King, Jr. "was knocked from his bike by automobiles" and "landed on his head," and he is reported to have jumped from the upstairs window of the King family home a number of times as well. On yet another occasion, when King, Jr. was a catcher in a baseball game, the bat got away from his brother, A. D. and struck him "on the right side of the head," knocking him to the ground, but King, Jr. "bounced right up" and reminded A. D. that "he was 'out' since he missed that third strike when the bat flew out of his hands." "Well, I guess God was looking out for me even then," said King, Jr. to a friend in Montgomery many years later. He went on to say that "the Lord must have been preserving him for something by giving him a hard head."[16]

Being the son, grandson, and great grandson of Baptist preachers and God-fearing, church-going women, it is not surprising that King, Jr. brought certain moral and spiritual values into his field of play. As his childhood letters to his parents indicate, the boy had a keen sense of what constituted right and wrong behavior, and he knew that the world of child's play had clear boundaries in terms of what was acceptable and unacceptable.[17] Play was to be a positive and building experience and fighting, racial epithets, offensive acts or name-calling, or anything else that undermined this goal were categorically prohibited. King, Jr. and his parents never drew class and race lines, "but there was parental concern about the behavior pattern of playmates. Badly behaved children were to be avoided,"[18] and King,

---

16. Reddick, *Crusader without Violence*, 53; King, "Dr. Martin Luther King, Jr.: From Birth to Twelve Years Old"; Downing, *To See the Promised Land*, 43–44; Clayborne Carson, et al., eds., *The Papers of Martin Luther King, Jr., Volume IV: Symbol of the Movement, January 1957–December 1958* (Berkeley: University of California Press, 2000), 227; Ted Poston, "Fighting Pastor: Martin Luther King, Jr.," in *New York Post*, New York, New York (8 April 1957); and Stephen B. Oates, *Let the Trumpet Sound: The Life of Martin Luther King, Jr.* (New York: Harper & Row, Publishers, 1982), 4.

17. Carson, et al., eds., *King Papers*, I, 102–7 and 111–17; and "Face to Face: Dr. Martin Luther King, Jr. and John Freeman," 2.

Jr. acted accordingly. "I can well remember that all of my childhood playmates were regular Sunday School goers," he reported years later. He went on to recount that "it was very difficult to find playmates in my community who did not attend Sunday School," and that "it was the Sunday School that helped me to build the capacity for getting along with people."[19] Evidently, images of Ebenezer church, the King family, and the schools King, Jr. attended came together in his consciousness with memories of his experiences on the playground, and the values of each reinforced those of the others in his young life. The youngster also had all of these various contexts in mind when he wrote: "It is quite easy for me to think of the universe as basically friendly mainly because of my uplifting hereditary and environmental circumstances. It is quite easy for me to lean more toward optimism than pessimism about human nature mainly because of my childhood experiences."[20] A more intriguing comment from a youngster who confronted daily "the usual stresses and strains" of being raised in a segregated society is difficult to imagine.[21]

Always sociable and eager to meet friends, King, Jr. continued to play with abandon during his time at both Atlanta University's Laboratory High School and Booker T. Washington High School, and it appeared, at times, that he was obsessed with the pleasure principle. Much has been said about King, Jr.'s tendency to be rebellious during those years, but the teenager never really clashed in any serious manner with his parents over his habit of delighting in the worldly pleasures of sports. Although King, Sr., or Daddy King, objected to his son's partying and to some of his very liberal religious ideas and views on the Bible, the elder King never thought that King, Jr.'s involvement with sports were somehow sinful, immoral, or even repugnant, for that matter.[22] King,

18. Farris, *Through It All*, 23–24; "Face to Face: Dr. Martin Luther King, Jr. and John Freeman," 1–3; King, "Dr. Martin Luther King, Jr.: Birth to Twelve Years Old"; Reddick, *Crusader without Violence*, 53; and Downing, *To See the Promised Land*, 42–46.
19. Carson, et al., eds., *King Papers*, I, 360; and Carson, ed., *The Autobiography of Martin Luther King, Jr.*, 6.
20. Carson, et al., eds., *King Papers*, I, 360; and Carson, ed., *The Autobiography of Martin Luther King, Jr.*, 2–3.
21. Lerone Bennett, Jr., *What Manner of Man: A Biography of Martin Luther King, Jr.* (Chicago: Johnson Publishing Company, 1964), 26.
22. Keith Miller seems to suggest that King, Sr. was as opposed to King, Jr. playing pool as he was to

Jr. played pool quite often and apparently channeled an amazing store of energy into swimming, baseball, basketball, football, and track, but his parents were always there to remind him that athletics should never be allowed to interfere in any way with his academic performance and pursuits.

King, Jr.'s enrollment at Atlanta's Morehouse College in the fall of 1944 afforded a range of opportunities in the sports area, despite the fact that he was only fifteen. He was a member of the basketball and track teams,[23] and is reported to have played quarterback for the Morehouse football squad "because in spite of his light weight, his compact body and tremendous spirit made him very hard to stop." Whenever King, Jr. was on the football field, "Mamma and Daddy King were sure to be in the audience rooting for him."[24] Although the young man was not known for raw, God-given talent, he apparently brought to college sports not only vibrancy, excellent health, abundant energy and sturdiness, and a determination to win, but also a willingness to understand how the phenomenon of play and the world of sports related to life, culture, and the prospects for a better and more just society for his people. For King, thinking along these lines would have come naturally, for he was already "deeply interested in political matters and social ills," and was also considering how he might contribute to "breaking down the legal barriers to Negro rights."[25] Furthermore, it was the period during which Jackie Robinson, one of King, Jr.'s favorite sports heroes, was breaking the color barrier in professional baseball. At that particular point, involvement in play and a number of sports, for King, Jr., no longer connoted merely fun and pleasure. In other words, he came to see that excelling in these fields, like achievements in the classroom, was part of his people's struggle.

While King, Jr. had become more serious about life when he became

the youngster's habit of dancing and also his growing biblical and theological liberalism, which is quite open to debate. Although some blacks at that time, clergy and laity, tended to associate sports with personal sins, there is no evidence that Daddy King felt similarly. See Keith D. Miller, *Voice of Deliverance: The Language of Martin Luther King, Jr., and Its Sources* (New York: The Free Press, 1992), 39.

23. Carson, et al., eds., *King Papers*, I, 144.
24. King, *My Life with Martin Luther King, Jr.*, 78 and 82.
25. Downing, *To See the Promised Land*, 134.

a seminary student in the fall of 1948, he never lost that tendency to occupy himself in amusement, sports, or other recreational activities. At Crozer Theological Seminary, he ran with students who "relieved the day-by-day tension" by going bowling or playing billiards or card games, and often, "with pranks and hijinks," such as room raids.[26] Although cultural and recreational attractions in Chester, Pennsylvania did not compare with what he had come to know in Atlanta, King, Jr. found much in Chester's black community that brought gratification. His tendency to alternate between being serious and behaving playfully became widely known, especially among his seminary classmates and the members of Calvary Baptist Church, where he served as a student minister. He was known to wrestle, play games, and speak in a playful tone of voice with Walter McCall and other black seminary classmates and friends his age, and at other times, he delighted in exposing himself to sports events on radio and television. He enjoyed listening to prizefights at the home of J. Pius Barbour, the pastor of Calvary Church. "Having a love for sports, he would come to my house on Wednesday nights to watch boxing matches and to eat with his friends," said Sara Richardson, a member of that same congregation.[27] Such experiences for young men King, Jr.'s age seemed commonplace or not particularly unusual or special, but they benefitted King, Jr. emotionally and spiritually, and they had much to do with the kind of person he ultimately became.

This was equally true of King, Jr.'s experiences in Boston in the early 1950s, the period during which he balanced serious attention to his graduate studies and ministry at Twelfth Baptist Church with an enjoyment of the fun things of life. Occasionally, he shot pool and played basketball with the youngsters at the social service center across the street from Twelfth Baptist, and according to Michael Haynes, who associated with King, Jr. as a young preacher at the

26. Bennett, *What Manner of Man*, 26; David J. Garrow, *Bearing the Cross: Martin Luther King, Jr., and the Southern Christian Leadership Conference* (New York: William Morrow and Company, Inc., 1986), 39; and Reddick, *Crusader without Violence*, 81–82.
27. Garrow, *Bearing the Cross*, 39; Reddick, *Crusader without Violence*, 81–83; A Private Interview with Sara Richardson, Chester, Pennsylvania (29 May 1987); and Baldwin, *There is a Balm in Gilead*, 38.

church, these moments at play actually strengthened King, Jr.'s belief that perhaps his special calling involved ministry to youth. "That was an area that Martin really wanted to look at—working with young black people," Haynes recalled. On further reflection, Haynes added: "And had he not been thrust into the movement, I think he would have spent some time with a special focus on young black people. He was carried so fast into the broader arena that this very genuine interest never really had time to reach its fullest potential."[28]

King, Jr.'s playful spirit was one of the personality traits that drew so many children, youth, and adults to him during those Boston years. He had a rare capacity to make those around him feel so much at ease. Apparently, this was the case at Twelfth Baptist Church and in other circles in which he frequently moved. This was most certainly the case with Coretta Scott, who was studying at the New England Conservatory of Music in Boston at the time, and who would eventually become King, Jr.'s wife. Coretta found that King, Jr.'s playfulness was one of the reasons he radiated so much charm the first time they met, and after the couple married, she came to enjoy seeing him in a playful mood and fondly recalled the many times he teased and toyed with her.[29] Coretta remembered that her husband and Philip Lenud, his closest friend and once his roommate in Boston, often joked around and engaged in horseplay, and sometimes carried on like children. She vividly recalled one experience that fully revealed King, Jr.'s playful tendencies:

> I remember that in the early summer of 1954 my mother came to visit with me in Boston for my graduation. We went out to an amusement park at the beach where they had all the hair-raising rides, roller coasters, a Ferris wheel, and a roller-skating rink. Martin rode all the rides, and he and Philip roller-skated until they were ready to drop, laughing and roughhousing and doing fancy turns and gyrations. . . . My husband had preached that Sunday morning, and Mother had been tremendously impressed with his sermon. Now he was having so much

---

28. King, *My Life with Martin Luther King, Jr.*, 85–91; A Private Interview with Reverend Michael E. Haynes, Twelfth Baptist Church, Boston, Massachusetts (25 June 1987); and Baldwin, *There is a Balm in Gilead*, 40 and 283–84.

29. King, *My Life with Martin Luther King, Jr.*, 24, 52–55, 59, and 72; Edythe Scott Bagley, *Desert Rose: The Life and Legacy of Coretta Scott King* (Tuscaloosa: The University of Alabama Press, 2012), 97–99; and Baldwin, *There is a Balm in Gilead*, 129.

fun that she could hardly believe that it was the same serious-minded young man who had spoken so wisely and well a few hours before. "You know," she said to him, "you act like you are about four years old."[30]

Clearly, King, Jr. did not equate this kind of innocent, free-spirited, and good-natured play with immaturity, silliness, or behavior unbecoming for adults. Even before he became the nation's leading voice for civil rights, he had some understanding of the necessity and deeper meaning of childish play, especially in the context of life's challenges, stresses, and strains, and was open to it to the degree that it arose out of and gave expression to positive emotions, and as long as it occurred within reasonable and acceptable boundaries.

B. Staying, in Part, a Child: An Enduring Freedom of Play and Love of Sports

"If you want to be creative, stay in part a child, with the creativity and invention that characterizes children before they are deformed by adult society," wrote the Swiss philosopher Jean Piaget.[31] It is as if Martin Luther King, Jr. took these words to heart, for the child continued to live in him throughout his adult life. This explained, in part, his creative mind and willingness to test new ideas, and also, why he, from the time he was catapulted to leadership in the Montgomery bus boycott in 1955, brought such a distinctive, dynamic, and refreshing approach to his efforts to improve the human condition.

It is difficult, in hindsight, to think of King, Jr. as being both playful and highly interested in sports in his adult life, for he seemed so serious-minded and committed to uplifting and empowering humanity, and also, because the challenges he faced daily as both a pastor and a civil rights leader consumed so much of his time, energy, and resources. But King, Jr. always had that playful nature that found expression in so many ways, and that, more specifically, translated into, and was inseparable from, his lasting involvement on some levels

30. King, *My Life with Martin Luther King, Jr.*, 89; and A Private Interview with Philip Lenud, Vanderbilt University Divinity School, Nashville, Tennessee (7 April 1987).
31. Quoted in Evans, *Playing*, 82.

in the world of sports. While in Montgomery in the mid-to-late 1950s, he enjoyed "weekend visits with a small party of friends in the mountains, on the seashore or at some suburban home," where he could "let his hair down," so to speak, or act playfully, without being judged or misunderstood. At times, the group played golf, billiards, ping pong, basketball, touch football, or baseball. King, Jr. also loved to fish, and occasionally, spoke of a desire "to go yachting in pursuit of the prizes of the deep sea," but his "favorite exercises" were "walking, tennis, and swimming," as had been the case during his seminary and graduate school years.[32] Making every effort "to identify with 'the boys,'" he was said to be "extremely good" at pool tables, and "could beat most of the fellows" who hung out with him "around High and Jackson Streets" in Montgomery. "Only a few pool players around here could beat King," said Nelson Malden, who was King, Jr.'s barber and also a member at Dexter Avenue Baptist Church, where King, Jr. was pastor.[33] Apparently, King, Jr. savored the feelings of comaraderie, the fun, and the competition that pool and other games and sports provided.

Sports created opportunities for King, Jr. to mingle with ordinary people in ordinary situations without the glare of media coverage, and this is what he wanted and needed for his own personal satisfaction as well as the quality of his own spirit. Knowing how he loved "to be around students and ordinary people," friends and church members occasionally invited him to attend sports events at high schools and colleges in and around Montgomery. One night, King, Jr. accompanied Deacon John Fulgham from Dexter Church and another male member from First Baptist Church to a basketball game at Dunn Arena on the campus of Montgomery's Alabama State College, and King, Jr. "enjoyed himself to the fullest," especially since Alabama State was playing against his alma mater, Atlanta's Morehouse College. According to

---

32. King, *My Life with Martin Luther King, Jr.*, 78 and 82; Reddick, *Crusader without Violence*, 3–4; and Dora McDonald, *Secretary to a King: My Years with Martin Luther King, Jr., the Civil Rights Movement, and Beyond* (Montgomery, AL: New South Books, 2012), 29, 40, and 75–76.
33. Wally G. Vaughn and Richard W. Wills, eds., *Reflections on Our Pastor: Dr. Martin Luther King, Jr., at Dexter Avenue Baptist Church, 1954-1960* (Dover, MA: The Majority Press, Inc., 1999), 60 and 70; and "'I Remember Martin,'" 33 and 38.

Deacon Fulgham, "The game was exciting," and "Dr. King was cheering, smiling, and supporting his favorite team like everyone else." "Without question, he was relieved being among the crowd," the deacon added. "Much of the stress that had been mounting found an avenue of escape."[34]

When an increasingly demanding schedule made it virtually impossible for King, Jr. to be present for such activities, he found other ways of satisfying his love for sports. "As a sports spectator," wrote King, Jr.'s friend Lawrence Reddick in 1959, "King keeps up fairly well with big-time football, baseball and boxing, although most of the games and bouts that he sees now are by way of television." King, Jr.'s "long-time ring heroes were Joe Louis and Sugar Ray Robinson," and he sometimes took time to watch their bouts on television or to listen to blow-by-blow accounts on radio. The same applied in the cases of other boxers King, Jr. admired and respected, such as Gene Tunney, Henry Armstrong, and Tiger Flowers, the great middleweight from Atlanta, King, Jr.'s hometown. When King, Jr. was not up to watching sports events or movies on TV, he turned to game shows or "quiz programs," during which he delighted in trying to "beat the contestants to the answers."[35] As insignificant as this tendency may appear at first glance, it was, in some measure, reflective of the kind of free, engaging, and competitive spirit with which King, Jr. approached the life of play.

King, Jr.'s playfulness or habits of play endeared him to blacks of all age groups as he moved through certain cities and small towns across the South. He was habitually playful with children and youth he encountered in places such as Albany, Birmingham, St. Augustine, Selma, and Memphis, and he delighted in recalling touching but amusing incidents involving children during civil rights campaigns.[36] In the course of the campaign for voting rights in Selma in 1965, he actually befriended eight-year-old Sheyann Webb and her nine-year-old playmate, Rachel West, with whom he was often conversationally

---

34. Vaughn and Wills, eds., *Reflections on Our Pastor*, 40–41.
35. Reddick, *Crusader without Violence*, 3–4.
36. "'I Remember Martin,'" 38; and Martin Luther King, Jr., *Why We Can't Wait* (New York: The New American Library, Inc., 1963), 97–98.

playful. Once when King, Jr. had to be away from Selma for a few hours, he, with a playful expression on his face, told the girls to "watch over things until I get back," and he repeatedly reminded them, "Just keep your marching shoes on because I'll be calling on you." Once they reached adulthood, Sheyann and Rachel collaborated on a book in which Rachel recounted their experiences of playfulness with King, Jr.:

> I remember he said something about our singing, shook hands with us and then asked our names. Then he leaned down closer and said to us, "What do you want?" And we said, "Freedom." "What's that?" he says. "I couldn't hear you." So we say, louder this time, "Freedom." And he shakes his head and kind of smiles a little. "I still don't believe I heard what you said." So we laugh, and then real loud we yelled, "We want freedom!" "I heard you that time," he says. "You want freedom? Well, so do I." We got to be friends from then on. Every time he'd see us he'd play that little game with us, asking what we wanted, pretending he couldn't hear what we'd say until we were shouting at the top of our lungs, "Freedom." Sometimes during the rallies at Brown Chapel, when Shey and I would sing, he would call us over where he would be sitting at the altar and lift us up on his lap and we'd sit there with him until it was time for him to speak. I'm sure many of the other people envied us. We'd be sitting up there so proud![37]

King, Jr.'s relationship with Sheyann and Rachel clearly revealed his amazing capacity for child's play even as he constantly reminded the girls, in both subtle and more intentional ways, of the seriousness of a cause in which they were all involved. King, Jr. had similar experiences while playing pool with youngsters in Chicago, Memphis, and other cities. These meaningful encounters not only brought pleasure, but also provided opportunities for him to enlighten youngsters about the movement and how it related to their own well-being and futures.[38] They also gave King, Jr. a more expansive view of what it meant to live and function in relation to other human beings.

King, Jr.'s capacity for and willingness to play was the one quality that actually made his relationships with family, friends, and comrades, or the people with whom he interacted and worked on

37. Sheyann Webb and Rachel West Nelson, *Selma, Lord, Selma: Girlhood Memories of the Civil Rights Days,* as told to Frank Sikora (Tuscaloosa: The University of Alabama Press, 1979), 31–32 and 41–42.
38. "'I Remember Martin,'" 38.

a day-to-day basis, most gratifying, empowering, and fulfilling. The little, amusing mind games he played in privacy with his wife, Coretta around her country upbringing, her place as his wife, and other matters have already been discussed in connection with his role as husband in chapter 2 of this book. King, Jr. was also known to act in playful ways with other members of his family, but almost never in public. He occasionally spoke in fun to Daddy King about his "thoroughgoing capitalism" and habit of going to such great lengths just to save a penny. Knowing that he "had been a heavy child to carry," and thus, "a burden" to his mother, Alberta in the period before he was born, he teased her at times, suggesting that he was perhaps not worth the pain. He loved to shoot pool and tussle with his brother, A. D. after a stressful day of protest activities. At other times, King, Jr. and his brother, A. D. "would both be on the phone with their mother, laughing and riding each other about their huge appetites and what they were doing to their respective waistlines."[39] In such instances, King, Jr. released negative energy and his playfulness also reinforced the already strong familial bonds.

The time King, Jr. spent playing with his own children also deserves further mention, despite the fact that this subject, too, was given some attention in Chapter 2 in reference to King, Jr.'s image as a father. Occasionally, when King, Jr. was home, his boyish zeal for fun took over and he found much joy in riding bicycles and playing baseball and basketball with his sons, Marty and Dexter, in twirling hula hoops around Marty's and his oldest daughter, Yolanda's waist, and in throwing his youngest daughter, Bernice up in the air and catching her as you came. Even when dressed in shirt and tie, King, Jr. never hesitated to get on the floor and crawl and rock and roll around with his children, and his wife, Coretta sometimes found the children sitting on his stomach or riding on his back and the house in disarray. The "refrigerator game," during which each child jumped off the top of the refrigerator into King's arms, always brought a lot of pleasure and

39. Reddick, *Crusader without Violence*, 50; King, *Daddy King*, 188; and King, *My Life with Martin Luther King, Jr.*, 56, 76, and 292.

laughter, and so did the "kissing game," which involved the children identifying their mother's and their own "sugar spot" on their daddy's face.[40] It was playfulness that seemingly came naturally and effortlessly for King, Jr., and it revealed so much about the passion, enthusiasm, and fun-loving spirit with which he approached life generally. "He was such a kid," said Yoki of her father, and she further noted that "the play and the fun" always came to mind whenever she recalled her father's spirit. King, Jr.'s son Dexter also remembered those times when his father exuded the spirit of a child at play:

> Every time I was in his presence, I felt deep compassion from him. Many times he felt like a playmate, like somebody who was Dad in terms of compassion and sensitivity, but was not so removed, because he enjoyed playing too, and could relate to a child's problems. We had fun playing softball. He'd pitch. If I swung and missed he'd be disappointed. "Aw Dexter," he'd say, lobbing in another underhand toss. When he'd come back from a trip, we'd hide from him, trembling with excitement; he'd find us, have us jump off the refrigerator top into his arms.[41]

The quality of this kind of interaction between King, Jr. and his children is not difficult to assess in view of King, Jr.'s time and context. Obviously, the benefits were never exclusively physical in nature, but were spiritual, emotional, and cognitive as well. Those experiences with child's play were a vital source of amusement and relaxation for King, Jr., and they also calmed him, made it possible for him to temporarily forget his activities and commitments, relieved tension and stress, stimulated his mind, sparked his imagination, helped him to become more focused, and put him in touch with his true self. Knowing not what to expect from day-to-day as he traveled in decidedly hostile environments, and constantly confronted by people who were uncaring and capable of the most vicious attacks against his people, King, Jr. discovered, in the unconditional love and innocence of his

40. King, *My Life with Martin Luther King, Jr.*, 78, 198, and 200–201; *Martin Luther King, Jr., 1929–1968: An Ebony Picture Biography* (Chicago: Johnson Publishing Company, Inc., 1968), 30; "'I Remember Martin,'" 38; and Dexter Scott King, *Growing Up King: An Intimate Memoir*, with Ralph Wiley (New York: Warner Books, Inc., 2003), 22, 44–45, and 59.

41. Roger Simon, "To Her, Rev. King was Simply Dad," *Los Angeles Times* (14 January 1985) and *Chicago Tribune* (14 January 1985); and King, *Growing Up King*, 22.

children during play, reasons for hope and for looking out on the world in a more optimistic light. Had it not been for those rare but precious moments, the pressures King, Jr. faced on a daily basis would have taken a much greater toll on him emotionally.[42]

The benefit to Yolanda, Marty, Dexter, and Bernice, who spent days, and sometimes, weeks without the comforting and reassuring presence of their father, was equally significant. Play was pivotal in building a strong relationship between them and their father. While playing baseball, basketball, the "refrigerator game," "the kissing game," and other sports and games with his children, King, Jr. taught them how to share, how to choose love over violence and conflict, the priority of familial ties, the meaning of courage, ways of being creative in word and deed, the positive effects of learning and memory, and other values essential to human growth and empowerment. Also, the children learned, as had King, Jr. in his own childhood, that play was not unrelated to moral and spiritual values, and that there were times to play and times to approach life and its demands in more of an attitude of seriousness.[43] King, Jr.'s son Dexter explained:

> The one thing Daddy didn't like was to be disturbed when he was in his study, writing down his thoughts, scheduling, composing sermons, reading and making notes in the margins of his books. There was a contemplative thought process at work in him. He compartmentalized it. If he was working, then he worked. If he was playing, then he played. He didn't mix the two. "Now, Dexter, when Daddy's working, don't disturb him. Daddy will play with you soon." Most people might think, because of the way he was projected as such a serious person, that he was always so, but sometimes he was the opposite of that, or the balance of that;

---

42. These assertions are supported by a careful reading of King, *My Life with Martin Luther King, Jr.*, 78, 99, 195–201, 263–64; "'I Remember Martin,'" 38; and Baldwin, *There is a Balm in Gilead*, 136–41.

43. King, *My Life with Martin Luther King, Jr.*, 78 and 198–201. King clearly understood the significance of these and other values for children. See Martin Luther King, Jr. to Mr. Robert Pobuda, Crowell School, Albion, Michigan (1 December 1960), King Center Library and Archives, 1; Martin Luther King, Jr. to the Student Body of Jesse Crowell School, Albion, Michigan (1 December 1960), King Center Library and Archives, 1–2; James R. Wood, Martin Luther King, Jr.'s Administrative Assistant, to Mr. L. F. Palmer, Jr. (23 February 1961), King Center Library and Archives, 1–2; Martin Luther King, Jr., "What a Mother Should Tell Her Child," unpublished version of a sermon, Ebenezer Baptist Church, Atlanta, Georgia (12 May 1963), King Center Library and Archives, 1–13; and Martin Luther King, Jr., "Training Your Child in Love," unpublished version of a sermon, Ebenezer Baptist Church, Atlanta, Georgia (8 May 1966), King Center Library and Archives, 1–11.

he needed an outlet, a way to break the tension. He sought refuge in his children, his family. He became us.[44]

As noted previously, King, Jr.'s friends and closest associates in the movement felt that his ability to approach life in more playful and less structured and stressful ways figured among his most coveted character traits.[45] At times, King, Jr. was almost effortlessly carefree and playful with his male aides in the SCLC., and the experiences of play ranged from spontaneous, relaxed, and free-spirited teasing to horseplay to carefully planned and organized recreational pleasure and enjoyment. King, Jr. and his dearest friend, Ralph Abernathy, frequently teased each other, and sometimes, wrestled in a playful manner when the fellows gathered in hotel rooms. "He was the strongest little man I've ever seen in my life," said Abernathy of King, Jr. "He could out-box you, out-wrestle you, and out-run you."[46] Bernard Lee, another prominent SCLC member, remembered that King, Jr. was the quintessential teaser, and that there were so many times when King, Jr. enriched and revitalized himself by engaging his closest aides playfully. Interestingly enough, on his very last birthday, January 15, 1968, the thirty-nine-year-old King spent much of the day teasing staff members who met to discuss movement business with him in the basement of his Ebenezer Baptist Church, thus softening the impact of the heated debates that swirled around SCLC's proposed Poor People's Campaign. As Fred Bennett and Bernard Lee entered the church for the meeting, King, Jr. commented: "Come on in Brother Bennett; take off your coat. And I see Bernard has on his coat. They act like its cold in my church." Lee later dropped something behind King, Jr. as he was speaking to the group, causing a crashing sound, and King, Jr., interrupting his own remarks, promptly asked: "What you been drinking, Bernard?" "He could really tease you or, as the fellows said,

44. King, *Growing Up King*, 22–23.
45. "'I Remember Martin,'" 33–34, 36, 38, and 40; and Ralph David Abernathy, "My Old Friend Martin," *The Tennessean: USA Weekend*, Nashville, Tennessee (12–14 January 1990), 6–7.
46. Private Interview with Reverend Ralph D. Abernathy, West Hunter Baptist Church, Atlanta, Georgia (17 March 1987); Baldwin, *There is a Balm in Gilead*, 303–4; "'I Remember Martin,'" 33–34, 36, 38, and 40; and Abernathy, "My Old Friend Martin," 6–7.

'crack on you,'" Lee recounted. "And then he could be very serious," Lee continued. "We'd sit and talk about the issues very seriously."[47]

On those occasions when King, Jr. was able to carve out some playtime, he never hesitated to challenge his staff to one of his favorite games or sports. Fancying "himself something of a pool shark," and feeling "a close bond with the man in the streets," he "loved to go into pool halls in the different cities and show the fellows he had a good touch," reported Samuel Billy Kyles,[48] and he never hesitated to brag mildly whenever he won. Dorothy Cotton, who directed SCLC's Citizenship Education Program (CEP), and who always valued "this close-up time with Dr. King," remembered those rare but "fun and festive" occasions when King, Jr. played ping-pong and threw balls over the volleyball net, and she saw in him "a jolly good fellow who loved to relax and play."[49] Basketball, baseball, and swimming were other pleasurable activities in which King, Jr. and his staff comfortably immersed themselves together when they felt lighthearted and playful.[50] This type of interaction was always both gratifying and fulfilling, and it naturally fostered intimacy and enhanced the quality of their relationship to each other in other ways. It had a human and spiritual effect, especially since the SCLC staff members involved were most often male and clergy as well. For King, Jr., more specifically, the opportunity to inject his own unique playful attitude into these activities could not have been more important since threats against his life came in increasingly, with time. Play was essential to the wholeness of the man.

Those moments of free, relaxed, and unstructured activity on the part of King, Jr. and his staff, perhaps to a greater extent than the

47. Martin Luther King, Jr., "Why We Must Go to Washington," unpublished version of a speech, SCLC Staff Retreat, Ebenezer Baptist Church, Atlanta, Georgia (15 January 1968), King Center Library and Archives, 1 and 5; Private Interview with Bernard S. Lee, Washington, DC (9 July 1986); "'I Remember Martin,'" 34; Dorothy F. Cotton, *If Your Back's Not Bent: The Role of the Citizenship Education Program in the Civil Rights Movement* (New York: Atria Books, 2012), 186–87 and 211; and Baldwin, *There is a Balm in Gilead*, 305.
48. "'I Remember Martin,'" 38.
49. According to Cotton, SCLC.'s staff members thought of themselves as "the King team." See Cotton, *If Your Back's Not Bent*, 142–43, 186–87, 191, 199, 205, 274, and 311.
50. King, *My Life with Martin Luther King, Jr.*, 78; and Baldwin Interview with Abernathy (17 March 1987).

"bull" or "brainstorming sessions" in closed-door meetings, as some of the men in the SCLC called them, took on the character of brotherly associations. When the pastor's study or hotel rooms in which King, Jr. and his staff routinely met seemed eerily silent after heated arguments in staff meetings, or after some disappointing civil rights campaign, King, Jr. was always able to bring some life to the group with his cheerfulness and playful manner. This happened in a most memorable fashion on the last day of King, Jr.'s life, April 4, 1968, in Memphis, as the SCLC staff still brooded over a march that had been marred by violence in that city a week earlier—the first of this kind led by King, Jr. King, Jr. was in a playful mood that whole day, and his playfulness bordered on silliness, but was nevertheless genuine and infectious. That afternoon, he and his brother A. D. "kidded each other and wrestled together boisterously like boys," after which they phoned and tried to fool their mother, Alberta "for a while, disguising their voices, each pretending to be the other."[51] Andrew Young arrived at the Lorraine Motel and found King, A. D., "and other SCLC folk gathered in A. D.'s room on the first floor," "just sitting around clowning in an extremely playful, happy-go-lucky way, in complete contrast to the tension of the last few days." "When I came in," Young recalled, "Martin yelled, in mock anger, 'Lil' nigger, just where you been?'" Young vividly recalled how the rest of his playful encounter with both King, Jr. and Abernathy unfolded:

> Of course, he knew where I had been, but he was enjoying the pretense of being angry with me, and Ralph joined in. "You ought to stay in touch with me," Martin said, keeping it up. "You're always running off doing something without me knowing about it." Then he sprang up from the bed, grabbed a pillow, and swung at me. The next thing I knew, both Martin and Ralph were beating on me with pillows. After all the tension we had been through, this kind of childlike play was exhilarating. It was a big room with two double beds, so I dodged and ducked my way over to the other bed, grabbed a pillow, and fought them off. Pretty soon our nervous energy was expended and I explained what had transpired in court.[52]

51. King, *My Life with Martin Luther King, Jr.*, 292; King, *Daddy King*, 188; and Baldwin, *There is a Balm in Gilead*, 151.

King, Jr.'s playfulness on that fateful day did not end with Andy Young. He teased Samuel Kyles, at whose home he was getting ready to have dinner, about his wife's cooking and good looks and about whether Kyles was actually able to meet the demands of his appetite. In those final moments, King, Jr., appearing very happy and content, looked down from the balcony of the Lorraine Motel and pestered Jesse Jackson about not being properly dressed for dinner. "You aren't going to Billy's house looking like that are you?," King, Jr. asked. Also in a playful spirit, Jesse, who had on a leather coat, fired back: "Well, Doc, I didn't think a shirt and tie were prerequisites for an appetite."[53] Then, the bullet struck. Andy Young later put the events of those final moments into some perspective, capturing the spirit of a man who was both playful and serious until the very end:

> He had been laughing and joking a few minutes earlier as though he didn't have a care in the world. . . . We were on the way out to dinner when I heard the sound. *Some jerk is playing with firecrackers*, I thought. Then I looked to the balcony and saw no Martin. My first thought was, *He's clowning again. He probably went back into the room with Ralph*. Then I saw his shoe sticking through the iron railing. His foot was no longer in it. I rushed up the stairs and there he was. At peace, maybe for the first time in his young thirty-nine years.[54]

The physical presence King, Jr. brought to his world of play and sports was amazing. He frequently described himself as "extraordinarily healthy" and had long been known among friends as "the athletic type." He combined this with a tremendous depth of emotional and spiritual security, and this is why he was able to be

---

52. Andrew Young, *An Easy Burden: The Civil Rights Movement and the Transformation of America* (New York: HarperCollins Publishers, Inc., 1996), 463–64; and Andrew Young, *A Way Out of No Way: The Spiritual Memoirs of Andrew Young* (Nashville: Thomas Nelson Publishers, 1994), 101. King used the "N word" and even cursed occasionally but only within very small circles of his family and SCLC staff. He would never have done these things in the presence of whites, including whites like the Jewish lawyer Stanley Levison, who was very close and dear to King. See Michael Eric Dyson, *I May Not Get There with You: The True Martin Luther King, Jr.* (New York: The Free Press, 2000), 177.

53. "'I Remember Martin,'" 38; Young, *A Way Out of No Way*, 101; Young, *An Easy Burden*, 463–65; King, *My Life with Martin Luther King, Jr.*, 89 and 292; and Octavia Vivian, *Coretta: The Story of Coretta Scott King*, Commemorative Edition (Minneapolis: Fortress Press, 2006), 79–81.

54. Young, *A Way Out of No Way*, 101.

playful and to have fun doing so without feeling foolish, inauthentic, guilty, and ashamed.[55]

C. The Will to Win: King, Sports Heroes, and the Movement

The historical Martin Luther King, Jr. is virtually impossible to recognize and hold in perspective without serious attention to how he viewed sports heroes, both on a personal level and in the context of the movement.[56] King, Jr.'s knowledge of the history of various sports in the United States, and especially, baseball and boxing, was quite extensive, and he brought that knowledge, coupled with his deep love for sports, to his relationships with certain sports heroes, and also, to his sense of the contributions he thought sports figures might make to the black freedom movement, in particular, and the human struggle, in general.

King, Jr. often said that a critical part of "the Negro struggle" involved breaking through "the shackles of circumstance" and achieving excellence in various fields of endeavor. Black sports figures, in his estimation, were among those who had, despite a "lack of full freedom," risen "to the heights of genius." King, Jr. pointed specifically to great boxers such as Jack Johnson, Joe Louis, and Muhammad Ali; celebrated baseball figures such as Jackie Robinson, Roy Campanella, Don Newcombe, Willie Mays, Hank Aaron, and Frank Robinson; basketball stars Bill Russell and Wilt Chamberlin; the track and field gold medalist Jesse Owens; the football hero Buddy Young; the professional tennis player and golfer Althea Gibson; the tennis star Arthur Ashe; and others who "rose to the heights of the athletic world."[57] In numerous speeches and writings in the late 1950s and 60s,

---

55. Carson, et al., eds., *King Papers*, I, 359; King, *My Life with Martin Luther King, Jr.*, 78; Vivian, *Coretta*, 59; Baldwin Interview with Abernathy (17 March 1987); Reddick, *Crusader without Violence*, 2–4; and Baldwin, *There is a Balm in Gilead*, 303–4.
56. This topic is treated in what might be considered, on some levels at least, a groundbreaking work. See Marcus "Goodie" Goodloe, "Coalition of Conscience: An Assessment of Martin Luther King Jr.'s Leadership with Athletes and Entertainers During the Civil Rights Movement," unpublished Ph. D. dissertation, Dallas Baptist University, Dallas, Texas (May, 2011). 1–254.
57. Martin Luther King, Jr., *Where Do We Go from Here: Chaos or Community?* (Boston: Beacon Press, 1968; originally published in 1967), 127; King, *Why We Can't Wait*, 65; Oates, *Let the Trumpet Sound*, 426; Baldwin, *There is a Balm in Gilead*, 61; Clayborne Carson, et al., eds., *The Papers of Martin Luther*

King, Jr. mentioned stars "in the athletic star," referring mostly to "Joe Louis with his educated fist, Jesse Owens with his fleet and dashing feet, and Jackie Robinson with his calm spirit and powerful bat."[58] For King, Jr., the many great Negro sports heroes throughout American history had epitomized the creative spirit and competitive nature of play while simultaneously striking a blow for freedom.

The lives of great sports heroes carried timeless lessons that King, Jr. felt were meaningful and relevant for people of all ages who wished to free, uplift, and empower themselves. "We say that Joe Louis was a great boxer and...we marveled as we heard him end a colorful career as probably the greatest boxer in history," King said in a sermon, "but Joe Louis realized early that he could not stay up all night drinking...if he was to be the champion of the world."[59] On April 24, 1966, King, Jr. shared a personal conversation he had with an unidentified person concerning Willie Mays that further illustrated his point that "freedom demands sacrifice," and that one should accept oneself as one is and become the very best that one can be with what one has if life is to be truly meaningful:

I was talking to somebody yesterday and I said, "You know, I'm not in Atlanta too much, but I'm gonna make it clear, and I'm gonna make it my business to be here when the San Francisco Giants come because I just like to see that fellow Willie Mays." I said, "He can really hit that ball," and the person with whom I was talking said, "He just can't talk too well." I said, "Well, a brother that can hit a ball like that doesn't need to talk." Maybe he doesn't have much education; he didn't have the opportunity. But somehow he educated his hands and his feet. And his personal response said "even though I was born in the Crete of Alabama, I'm going to be somebody anyway. I may not be able to articulate my words but I will be able to articulate a ball and a bat. And I will rise up and be somebody in history."[60]

King, Jr., Volume VI: Advocate of the Social Gospel, September, 1948–March 1963 (Berkeley: University of California Press, 2007), 89; Ansbro, *Martin Luther King, Jr.*, 226; and James M. Washington, ed., *A Testament of Hope: The Essential Writings and Speeches of Martin Luther King, Jr.* (New York: HarperCollins Publishers, 1991), 212.

58. Clayborne Carson, et al., eds., *The Papers of Martin Luther King, Jr., Volume V: Threshold of a New Decade, January 1959–December 1960* (Berkeley: University of California Press, 2005), 285 and 340.

59. Carson, et al., eds., *King Papers*, VI, 89.

60. King's sermon was actually based on the book of Titus in the New Testament, in which Paul wrote his disciple Titus "on the great island known as Crete," around "the eastern Mediterranean,"

In King, Jr.'s thinking, Willie Mays and other sports figures who moved from lowly beginnings to greatness demonstrated that people in search of some experiential or existential ideal should never become "inflicted with 'give-up-itis' "—that "we must have that something that the existential philosophers call 'the courage to be,' that 'in spite of quality'."[61] In a speech in November 1967, King referred to an experience he had at another sports event years earlier, which also reflected this "refusal to be stopped," or this will to go "on *anyhow*." In terms that merit extensive quotation, King, Jr. declared:

> I remember back in the fifties going to a game in Brooklyn between the Brooklyn Dodgers and the New York Giants. The Giants were leading 1–0. The last inning came, and then came that last part of the last inning. The score was still 1–0. The pitcher for the Giants went to the mound; he pitched his first ball to the first batter—strike one, strike two, strike three—he was out. Next batter came up, hit a single. And then the next batter came up; he struck out. The game was about to close now; the score was 1–0 in favor of the New York Giants. The next batter came up, and the pitcher started pitching and he threw the ball and it was ball one. He threw another one, strike one; another one, ball two; another one, strike two; another one, ball three. And now the last moment had appeared—the last part of the last inning, two outs, one man on base, the last batter facing the fact of two strikes and three balls. And then the pitcher pitched the ball, getting ready to close out the game. But there is a law of physics which says when two objects meet, the object with the greatest power moves the other object. That ball met that bat, but at that moment that bat had the greatest power. And that bat hit that ball, and it went up in the air and moved out and out and out over the fence of right field. The game was over, 2–1 in favor of the Brooklyn Dodgers. This is what the Book of Revelation means when it says making it in on what you have left, even if it is near nothing.[62]

which "was not at all a desirable place for a Christian to be left." "The Cretans," said King, quoting Paul, were always not only "liars" but "evil beasts and idle gluttons." This must be considered in putting the long quote from King's sermon in proper context. See Martin Luther King, Jr., "Making the Best of a Bad Mess," unpublished version of a sermon, Ebenezer Baptist Church, Atlanta, Georgia (24 April 1966), King Center Library and Archives, 6–7.
61. Martin Luther King, Jr., "Why a Movement," unpublished version of a speech (28 November 1967), King Center Library and Archives, 6.
62. Martin Luther King, Jr., "A Knock at Midnight," unpublished version of a sermon, Canaan Baptist Church, New York, New York (24 March 1968), King Center Library and Archives, 15; King, "Why a Movement," 6–8; and Martin Luther King, Jr., "See You in Washington," unpublished version of a speech, SCLC Staff Retreat, Ebenezer Baptist Church, Atlanta, Georgia (17 January 1968), King Center Library and Archives, 12–13.

King, Jr. was convinced that talented, highly accomplished, and celebrated athletes, like entertainers and artists in other fields, had a special role to play in expanding the parameters of the human struggle and endeavor. Their contributions, he felt, could never be legitimately limited to what they achieved in their different sports, especially since they were most often in a position to have a far greater impact socially, politically, culturally, and otherwise.[63] Thus, King, Jr. sought from the time of his pilgrimage in Montgomery to collaborate with certain sports celebrities in addressing a range of civil and human rights issues and concerns. Of particular importance was his view of and work with Jackie Robinson, who broke baseball's color barrier in 1947, becoming the first black man in the major leagues. King, Jr. thought that Robinson's role in integrating professional baseball helped prepare the ground for the organized protests against Jim Crow that would occur later, and Robinson saw King, Jr. as the man most equipped to lead in the struggle for a freer and more just and inclusive society.[64]

The lives of King, Jr. and Robinson became intertwined on so many levels. The two men appeared at a number of educational events and freedom rallies together in the late 1950s, and signed a number of petitions, declarations, and appeals covering issues from segregated schools and economic equality in the United States to apartheid practices in South Africa. They took part in the commencement exercises at Howard University in Washington, D. C. in June, 1957, and, in October 1958, served as honorary chairmen of Youth March for Integrated Schools in that city.[65] In October 1959, King, Jr. represented

---

63. Carson, et al., eds., *King Papers*, IV, 402; Lewis V. Baldwin and Amiri Yasin Al-Hadid, *Between Cross and Crescent: Christian and Muslim Perspectives on Malcolm and Martin* (Gainesville: University Press of Florida, 2002), 33–42.

64. Robinson, who was one of King's heroes and friends, left baseball in 1957 and became one of the most recognized voices for the freedom of his people. See Carson, et al., eds., *King Papers*, V, 184n1 and 475–78; Jackie Robinson to Martin Luther King, Jr. (9 October 1962), unpublished version of a letter, Martin Luther King, Jr. Papers, Special Collections, Mugar Memorial Library, Boston University, Boston, Massachusetts, 1; Martin Luther King, Jr., "Hall of Famer," *New York Amsterdam News*, New York, New York (4 August 1962), 11; Jackie Robinson, "What I Think of Dr. Martin Luther King," *Chicago Defender*, Chicago, Illinois (1 July 1967); and Goodloe, "Coalition of Conscience," 77n128.

65. Carson, et al., eds., *King Papers*, IV, 484 and 514–15; Washington, ed., *A Testament of Hope*, 21–22; David L. Lewis, *King: A Critical Biography* (New York: Praeger Publishers, 1970), 91; and Goodloe, "Coalition of Conscience," 141.

his SCLC and Robinson the NAACP in staging a voting rights rally in New York City.[66] In February 1960, Robinson became part of the much-needed Committee to Defend Martin Luther King and the Struggle for Freedom in the South, and Robinson and King, Jr. denounced the emerging tensions between the SCLC and the NAACP over "divisive fundraising efforts" and "derogatory comments" in June of that same year.[67] In July 1962, Robinson donated the proceeds from his Baseball Hall of Fame dinner to SCLC's voter registration drive, and two months later, he and King, Jr. united in establishing a fund to rebuild Negro churches that had been damaged or destroyed due to their involvements in the civil rights struggle in Albany, Georgia and other parts of the South.[68] Robinson showed up in support of King, Jr. and SCLC's campaign in Birmingham in the spring of 1963, and was also among the platform guests when King, Jr. delivered his famous "I Have a Dream" speech in Washington, DC in August 1963.[69] The two men were ideologically aligned, and King, Jr., in an article on Robinson, once noted that "back in the days when integration wasn't fashionable, he underwent the trauma and the humiliation and the loneliness which comes with being a pilgrim walking the lonesome byways toward the high road of freedom." King, Jr. went on to say that Robinson "was a sit-inner before the sit-ins, a freedom rider before the Freedom Rides."[70]

It was evident to King, Jr. that Jackie Robinson was more the exception than the rule when it came to professional athletes actively contributing to the civil rights program. Robinson provided not only financial and moral support, but physical support as well, and in this

---

66. Roy Wilkins and Daisy Bates were also representatives of the NAACP at this event. All of the civil rights groups involved organized under the umbrella of The Federation of Negro Civil Service Organizations, Inc. See Carson, et al., eds., *King Papers*, V, 316–17.

67. Carson, et al., eds., *King Papers*, V, 25, 380–81n1, 403n2, 454–55, 475–78, and 570n1; Oates, *Let the Trumpet Sound*, 157; Lewis, *King*, 118.

68. Martin Luther King, Jr. to Leroy Freeman (8 October 1962), unpublished version of a letter, King Center Library and Archives, 1; and "Dr. King and Jackie Robinson Head Rebuilding for Burned Churches," unpublished version of a SCLC Press Release (12 September 1962), King Center Library and Archives, 1–2.

69. Lewis, *King*, 225; Goodloe, "Coalition of Conscience," 134 and 205; Taylor Branch, *Parting the Waters: America in the King Years, 1954-63* (New York: Simon and Schuster, 1988), 647 and 726; and Ralph David Abernathy, *And the Walls Came Tumbling Down: An Autobiography* (New York: Harper & Row, Publishers, Inc., 1989), 278.

70. King, "Hall of Famer," 11.

regard, King thought, he made sacrifices that few sports figures of his statue were prepared to make in that explosive and tension-packed period. In terms of support for civil rights activism, King, Jr. saw that most of these figures fell into three general categories. First, there were those such as baseball greats Willie Mays and Willie McCovey who, perhaps out of a fear of negative publicity or economic and political reprisals, refused to get physically involved. Second, most professional athletes who recognized the need for King, Jr.'s leadership and the movement openly expressed their support physically, morally, and financially. Third, there were those such as the Olympians Tommie Smith and John Carlos who, inspired by black power cry in the late 1960s, declined to actively support the movement because they found King, Jr.'s approach seriously lacking in terms of militancy and a strong black programmatic thrust.[71] These varying responses, which extended into King, Jr.'s struggle for economic justice, actually mirrored what King, Jr. detected at all levels of society when it came to civil rights, including among clergymen.

Sports heroes were equally divided, though in more complicated ways, over the question of the logic and acceptability of King, Jr.'s tendency to link the American civil rights movement to liberation movements abroad, and to insist that he had a special responsibility, as a prophet and Nobel laureate, to address world problems involving not only racism and poverty, but war as well. King, Jr. believed this unequivocally and had long felt that famous athletes, whose performances on the field earned them much respect and admiration among people worldwide, had rare opportunities to become voices for the oppressed everywhere. In 1957, King, Jr. served with Jackie Robinson on the National Committee of the American Committee on Africa (ACOA), a New York-based organization of Christian pacifists, which actually started in 1951 as the Americans for South African Resistance (AFSAR). Robinson gave his support when King, Jr. became the US vice chairman, along with the international chairman Eleanor

---

71. This conclusion is seemingly borne out by a reading of Goodloe, "Coalition of Conscience," 91, 112, 134, 166, and 176–77.

Roosevelt and US Chairman Bishop James A. Pike, of the ACOA's universal *Declaration of Conscience*, a document proclaiming "December 10, 1957, Human Rights Day, as a Day of Protest against the organized inhumanity of the South African Government and its *apartheid* policies." This *Declaration of Conscience* bore the signatures of some 123 world leaders.[72]

But King, Jr. knew that promoting declarations targeting world problems was not nearly enough; that such a move was merely symbolic at best. The real challenge would come as he sought the support of sports celebrities for more substantive and radical approaches to ending global problems, such as South African apartheid and America's ill-conceived military mission in South Vietnam. As early as November 1962, King, Jr., in what was a clear message to professional athletes everywhere, joined Roy Wilkins, Whitney Young, Dorothy Height, and others in the newly-formed American Negro Leadership Conference on Africa (ANLCA) in urging "the American Olympic Committee to fight for the exclusion of South Africa from the Olympic games unless that nation permits all South African athletes to compete for places on its team without regard to race or color."[73] Jackie Robinson worked with King, Jr. and other civil rights leaders on this initiative, and the support received from athletes worldwide actually accounted for the barring of South Africa from participation in the Olympic Games in Tokyo in 1964.

Three years later, in April 1967, King, Jr. joined Jackie Robinson, George Houser, T. Wendell Foster, and other ACOA representatives in pushing for the exclusion of South Africa from the 1968 Olympic Games in Mexico City. Robinson, the main force behind this effort, sought to accomplish this goal by working through the channels of the US Olympic Committee (USOC) and the International Olympic Committee

---

72. George M. Houser, *No One Can Stop the Rain: Glimpses of Africa's Liberation Struggle* (New York: The Pilgrim Press, 1989), 12–20; George M. Houser to Lewis V. Baldwin (9 October 1987), unpublished version of a letter, author's files; A Private Interview with George M. Houser, Pomona, New York (26 May 1993); and Lewis V. Baldwin, *Toward the Beloved Community: Martin Luther King, Jr. and South Africa* (Cleveland: The Pilgrim Press, 1995), 13–23.

73. *The American Negro Leadership Conference on Africa: Resolution*, presented at Arden House, Columbia University, Harriman, New York (23–25 November 1962), King Center Library and Archives, 1; and Baldwin, *Toward the Beloved Community*, 40.

(IOC), by actively seeking the support of civil rights leaders and other world-class athletes, and by drawing on the insights and influence of social activists, heads of state, and people in other fields across the globe. Robinson appealed to King, Jr. as "one deeply interested in sports and as a firm believer in interracialism," declaring, in a letter to the civil rights leader, that "I hope you will agree with me that it is essential for American representatives, particularly those involved in the Civil Rights struggle and concerned athletes, to speak with a clear voice on such a crucial issue."[74] King, Jr. actually met with Olympic athletes to discuss the merits of a possible boycott in November 1967. He urged the athletes to draft a formal letter to both the USOC and the IOC stating their demands, which included expelling South Africa from the Olympic Games. King, Jr. also recommended that informational pamphlets concerning the proposed boycott be distributed to athletes throughout the United States.[75] Taking on such initiatives were obviously not in the tradition of American and world athletics, for the common tendency on the part of athletes worldwide was to see a dichotomy between sports and politics.

Responses to the appeal were mixed. The Olympic great Jesse Owens, of whom King, Jr. spoke very highly because of his amazing achievements in track and field, spoke for the IOC and against a boycott. The idea was fully embraced by the Olympic sprinter and professional football star Bob Hayes, and also by Rafer Johnson, the winner of the Olympic decathlon in Rome in 1960, and Ralph Boston, who was known for his accomplishments in the long jump in Rome.[76] Many athletes vowed not to participate in the Olympics if South Africa was invited. Once again, support from athletes and civil rights activists such as King, Jr., while not unanimous, would figure into the IOC's decision to exclude South Africa from the Olympic Games. In his typically unselfish manner, King, Jr. gave the credit for this unfolding

74. T. Wendell Foster to Martin Luther King, Jr. (10 April 1967), unpublished version of a letter (10 April 1967), King Center Library and Archives, 1; Jackie Robinson to Martin Luther King, Jr. (10 April 1967), unpublished version of a letter, King Center Library and Archives, 1; and Baldwin, *Toward the Beloved Community*, 52.
75. Goodloe, "Coalition of Conscience," 176–77.
76. Ibid., 177.

effort primarily to the athletes. "I would like to commend the outstanding athletes who have the courage and the kind of determination not to participate in the 1968 Olympics in Mexico City unless something is done about these terrible problems, these terrible evils, and injustices," said he in a press conference in New York City.[77] For King, Jr., the mere opportunity to unite in thought, spirit, and activism with professional sports figures around concerns essential to world peace and community was historically significant, and it obviously set a new precedent that future athletes could follow in addressing glaring social evils on a global scale.

The support professional athletes gave to the anti-apartheid cause in South Africa was not there when King, Jr. needed it to make his case against the US involvement in Vietnam in the late 1960s. Interestingly enough, both Jackie Robinson and Jesse Owens were openly critical of King, Jr.'s stance on Vietnam, and especially, his suggestion that the United States end all bombing in North and South Vietnam, declare a unilateral cease-fire, and remove all troops from Vietnam in conformity with the 1954 Geneva Agreement. Robinson and Owens felt that King, Jr. was not sophisticated enough militarily to criticize the nation's war effort, and that his criticisms opened him to the charge of being a traitor to his country. The two also declared that King, Jr.'s civil rights campaigns and Vietnam were completely separate issues, and that he was endangering the civil rights movement by exposing it to the charge of communist infiltration and control.[78] Although Robinson later tried to save face and to smooth things over by calling King, Jr. "the finest leader the Negro people have and one of the most magnificent leaders the world has today,"[79] King, Jr. was

77. King's support for this initiative was largely moral in nature, because so much of his time, energy, and resources were being devoted to the planning of the Poor People's Campaign and to the crusade against the war in Vietnam. See "Martin Luther King Press Conference," unpublished version of an interview, ABC, New York, New York (14 December 1967), Stock Library # 29376, King Center Library and Archives, 1; Baldwin, *Toward the Beloved Community*, 52; and Lewis V. Baldwin, ed., *"In a Single Garment of Destiny": A Global Vision of Justice—Martin Luther King, Jr.* (Boston: Beacon Press, 2012), 195.
78. Eugene Patterson, "Martin Luther King, Jr.: Where the Action Is?," *The Atlanta Constitution* (9 April 1967), editorial section; Oates, *Let the Trumpet Sound*, 438; Washington, ed., *A Testament of Hope*, 239; Jackie Robinson, "An Open Letter to Martin Luther King, Jr.," *Chicago Defender*, Chicago, Illinois (13 May 1967); and Goodloe, "Coalition of Conscience," 166, 171, and 188.

understandably hurt, for it was always quite difficult for him to deal with public ridicule from those whom he considered friends. He must have been deeply troubled that great men such as Robinson and Owens could not see that both the civil rights struggle and the problem of war were manifestations of the same structure of social evil.[80]

Strangely, King, Jr. found a strong ally among the unlikeliest of persons; namely, Muhammad Ali, the heavyweight boxing champion who had become a member of Elijah Muhammad's Nation of Islam, a group committed to a strict racial separatism and an unwavering self-defense ethic. Ali had previously rejected King, Jr.'s invitation to join the civil rights movement, but the two men, based on a shared opposition to the nation's adventure in Vietnam, met in March, 1967 to discuss Ali's refusal to register for the draft and his plan to file as a conscientious objector. The possible consequences of Ali's actions, including the loss of his heavyweight title, widespread criticism and rejection, and incarceration, were discussed at some length. Although well-known sports figures such as the Cleveland Browns's Jim Brown, the Boston Celtics's Bill Russell, and the legendary UCLA coach John Wooden advised Ali not to risk his career, reputation, and livelihood by taking sides with King, Jr. against Lyndon B. Johnson's war strategy, King, Jr. and Ali obviously had a meeting of the mind and heart, and they would never falter in their attacks on the Vietnam war.[81] After their March meeting, both spoke in a joint interview about the forces that brought them together despite their differences at the levels of religion, philosophy, and methods. Ali likened their coming together to a meeting between Khrushchev and Kennedy, noting that "Although

79. Robinson, "What I Think of Dr. Martin Luther King"; and Robinson, "An Open Letter to Martin Luther King, Jr."
80. Herbert Richardson rightly argues that King saw all of the connections here, and that this "showed the profundity of his theological insight into the nature of evil today." See Herbert Warren Richardson, "Martin Luther King—Unsung Theologian," in Martin E. Marty and Dean G. Pearman, eds., *New Theology No. 6: On Revolution and Non-Revolution, Violence and Non-Violence, Peace and Power* (New York: The Macmillan Company, 1972), 181; and Baldwin, ed., *"In a Single Garment of Destiny"*, 1–21, 23–132, 134–49, and 189–209.
81. Goodloe, "Coalition of Conscience," 165–67; "Cassius Clay (Muhammad Ali) and Martin Luther King Being Interviewed," unpublished version of a transcribed document, Louisville, Kentucky (29 March 1967), King Center Library and Archives, 1; and Muhammad Ali to Martin Luther King, Jr., unpublished version of a letter (2 November 1967), King Center Library and Archives, 1.

they believe differently, think differently, whites can come together and discuss the common cause." King, Jr. quickly agreed, and, in a common expression of his enthusiasm, asserted:

> Oh, yes, yes, we had a very good discussion uh on matters and of course these are not things that we would discuss here, but we do have common problems and common concerns, and above all, as Muhammad Ali has just said, uh, we are all victims of the same system, of oppression, and even though we may have different religious beliefs, uh this is not at all a thing about a difference in terms of our concern.[82]

King, Jr. would later mention Ali in a number of his interviews, speeches, and sermons on Vietnam, as was the case when he preached at his Ebenezer Baptist Church in Atlanta in April 1967, a week or so after his historic address, "A Time to Break Silence," at the Riverside Church in New York City. "No matter what you think about Mr. Muhammad Ali's religion," said King, Jr. to the audience on that Sunday morning, "you certainly have to admire his courage." "For here is a young man," King, Jr. continued, "who is willing to give up fame and fortune if necessary, willing to give up millions of dollars, to do what conscience tells him is right." And, with the challenges facing Ali uppermost in mind, King, Jr. went on to paraphrase verse 11 from Matthew Chapter 5: "Blessed are ye when men revile you and persecute you and utter all kinds of evil against you. Rejoice and be exceedingly glad, for great is your reward."[83] Apparently, Ali became the model for what King, Jr. hoped to find increasingly in the athletic world, and indeed, across the entire human landscape as he expanded his own commitments in the interest of a new world and a new humanity. He discovered in Ali what he never saw in any other professional athlete in his time; namely, an uncompromising spirit, a willingness to sacrifice all for a higher human ideal, and the will and determination to win in life as he had won in the boxing ring.

King, Jr. never hesitated to use game and sports analogies and

---

82. "Cassius Clay (Muhammad Ali) and Martin Luther King Being Interviewed," 1; and Reddick, *Crusader without Violence*, 7.
83. "Martin Luther King: An Amazing Grace," a 60 Minutes Videotape, 831V (Huntsville Texas: Educational Video Network, Inc., n.d.); and Washington, ed., *A Testament of Hope*, 231–44.

metaphors to explain what it meant to lose and to win in life. He equated capitalism, which he included among the three great evils of the world, with a "losing football team in the last quarter trying all types of tactics to survive," contending that "We are losing because we failed to check our weaknesses in the beginning of the game."[84] In an equally compelling statement, made even before the beginning of the Montgomery bus protest, King, Jr. used football to drive home the point that the struggle for civil rights will not be easily won:

> To use an analogy at this point, since the turn of the century we have brought the football of civil rights to about the fifty yard-line. And now we are advancing in the enemy's territory. The problem for the next few years will be to get the ball over the goal line. Let's not fool ourselves, this job will be difficult. The opposition will use all the power and force possible to prevent our advance. He will strengthen his line on every hand. But if we place good leaders in the back field to call the signals and good fellows on the line to make the way clear; we will be able to make moves that will stagger the imagination of the opposition. Some mistakes will be made, yes, the ball might be fumbled, but for God's sake, recover it! Teamwork and unity are necessities for the winning of any game.[85]

In King, Jr.'s estimation, what mattered most was the spirit of hope and perseverance which, for him, was ultimately grounded in faith, that seemingly invincible force that had always sustained his people's strides toward freedom.[86] Always apt to use very "personal" and "human" experiences when offering an insight into the movement and life generally, King, Jr., reminiscing about fishing and a fishing boat in a sermon in April 1966, elaborated the point in a lengthy comment that registers best when quoted in its fullness:

> I never will forget, Mrs. King and I were down in Mexico; we

84. Carson, et al., eds., *King Papers*, VI, 105. For King, capitalism loomed large within what he variously termed "the giant triplets," "the triple evils," or "the evil triumvirate," meaning racism, poverty, and war. See King, *Where Do We Go from Here?*, 186; and Lewis V. Baldwin, *To Make the Wounded Whole: The Cultural Legacy of Martin Luther King, Jr.* (Minneapolis: Fortress Press, 1992), 258.
85. Carson, et al., eds., *King Papers*, VI, 215; Goodloe, "Coalition of Conscience," 184; and Taylor Branch, *At Canaan's Edge: America in the King Years, 1965-68* (New York: Simon & Schuster, 2006), 556.
86. Martin Luther King, Jr., "Discerning the Signs of History," unpublished version of a sermon, Ebenezer Baptist Church, Atlanta, Georgia (15 November 1964), King Center Library and Archives, 4–5; and Baldwin, *There is a Balm in Gilead*, 226.

had journeyed from Mexico City down to Acapulco, and one afternoon I decided that I wanted to do some deep sea fishing. We had been there several days and the money was now very low, so we had to rent a rather cheap and poorly equipped boat. And we moved out on our fishing trip. And we got out some ten miles from shore. I never will forget it. When we got way out I looked at the captain, and I started talking with him, and I said, "Do you have a phone on this plane..., on this boat?" And he said, "No." Said, "You know this is uh one of our cheaper boats, and it's not equipped like the others." And as we moved around fishing I heard the motor begin to sputter a bit, and the thing kind of conked out right there ten miles from shore. And while he was working on it, I looked up and saw the clouds, and they had begun to hover mighty low. And the wind started blowing; it seemed that a storm was getting ready to rage. And I was looking and turning and fretting and in deep fear. Finally, he got it started up again, but still I was afraid. And you know what I was afraid for, the reason I was afraid? Because strong winds were blowing and we had a weak boat. Oh this morning if I can leave anything with you, let me urge you to be sure you have a strong boat of faith. The winds are going to blow, the storms of disappointment are coming, the agonies and anguishes of life are coming. And be sure that your boat is strong, and also be very sure that you have an anchor. In times like these you need an anchor. And be very sure that your anchor holds.[87]

King, Jr. was anchored by a vital faith, and so much more, in the realm of values that made him feel free and secure within, despite the many demands and challenges before him, and this feeling of inner freedom and security helps explain why he approached the world of play and sports, and indeed, life as a whole, in a celebratory manner. His goal was to celebrate life and his shared humanity with others in some fashion every day, and he accomplished this not only through worship, his own personal devotional experiences of prayer and meditation, and his participation in the movement, but also through his appreciation of and involvements with sports and sports heroes, and by finding the will, time, and energy to play.[88] Convinced that

---

87. King, "Making the Best of a Bad Mess," 8–9. Dora McDonald's claim that King "was not a fisherman" is not supported by King's own testimony. See McDonald, *Secretary to a King*, 76.
88. King, *My Life with Martin Luther King, Jr.*, 89; and Abernathy, "My Old Friend Martin," 6. For a sense of how King celebrated the beauty and blessings of life through worship and acts of personal devotion, see Lewis V. Baldwin, *The Voice of Conscience: The Church in the Mind of Martin Luther King, Jr.* (New York: Oxford University Press, 2010), 13–216; Lewis V. Baldwin, *Never to Leave Us Alone: The Prayer Life of Martin Luther King Jr.* (Minneapolis: Fortress Press, 2010), 9–89; Lewis V. Baldwin, ed., *"Thou, Dear God": Prayers that Open Hearts and Spirits—The Reverend Dr. Martin Luther King, Jr.* (Boston:

playing and sports were not necessarily antithetical to higher spiritual and moral values, King, Jr., as noted earlier, rejuvenated play in ways reminiscent of his childhood, but his playfulness never resulted in a lack of seriousness or a failure to meet responsibility.[89]

King, Jr. knew that playing, like sports, was very much an essential of culture, and, interestingly enough, this is how he expressed himself not only culturally, socially, and recreationally, but also spiritually. This conclusion takes seriously James H. Evans, Jr.'s thesis that playing is not merely about "frivolity"; that it, like cooking, eating, singing, parenting, and other "ordinary routines," is a response "to the life God gives to the world," and it also "lies at the heart of the Christian faith in the triune God."[90] There was a spiritual side to King, Jr.'s playfulness that must be kept in view if he is to be properly understood and appreciated as a human being.

The next chapter, the last in this volume, advances this discussion of King, Jr. at play to another level, with special attention to folk wit, humor, and laughter. It affords additional evidence of the quality of King, Jr.'s life as a person who shared the interests, needs, habits, and tendencies of ordinary human beings.

Beacon Press, 2012), 3–238; Baldwin, *There is a Balm in Gilead*, 187–89; and Tavis Smiley, *Death of a King: The Real Story of Dr. Martin Luther King Jr.'s Final Year* (New York: Little, Brown and Company, 2014), 44.

89. King, *My Life with Martin Luther King, Jr.*, 89; "'I Remember Martin,'" 38; and Baldwin Interview with Lee (9 July 1986).

90. Evans argues that "play has to be taken seriously as a theological subject matter," which would yield even more insight into King's personal and spiritual life, especially since he was both a minister and a theologian by training. Evans, *Playing*, vii, x (foreword), and 86–87.

6

"To Joy and Mirth": Martin Luther King, Jr. and the Gift of Folk Wit, Humor, and Laughter

And yet they are the outcasts of the earth,
A race oppressed and scorned by ruling man;
How can they thus consent to joy and mirth,
Who live beneath a world-eternal ban?
  –Claude McKay[1]

"Let me ask you very directly," I said. "Do you take my son seriously, Coretta?"
She thought I was joking with her, because M. L. had been displaying his dry
sense of humor most of the afternoon.
  –Martin Luther King, Sr.[2]

It has often been said that "Religious people tend to be hypercritical and lack a sense of humor."[3] This was not the case with Martin Luther

1. Claude McKay, "Negro Dancers," in Alain Locke, ed., The New Negro: An Interpretation (New York: Albert and Charles Boni, 1925), 215.
2. Martin Luther King, Sr., *Daddy King: An Autobiography*, with Clayton Riley (New York: William Morrow and Company, Inc., 1980), 150.
3. Risto Saarinen, "Luther the Urban Legend," in Christine Helmer, ed., *The Global Luther: A Theologian for Modern Times* (Minneapolis: Fortress Press, 2009), 19.

King, Jr., who had a boyish zeal for fun and laughter, who personified playfulness as a sense of humor, and who found folk wit and humor in the day-to-day processes of living, especially as he observed and interacted with his people.[4] Humor for King, Jr. was never an inappropriate subject for religious people, and nor was it incompatible with his sense of the proper deportment and spirit of a Christian minister. He absolutely refused to box himself into that typical image of the overly serious, excessively pietistic figure who paraded as if he had an angelic halo hovering over his head. On the contrary, King, Jr. came to see wit, humor, and laughter as natural tendencies in the human spirit, and he had a disposition to tell jokes, to tease others, and to find causes and reasons for amusement and pleasure from one of the most exalted positions in the world.[5]

This chapter casts light on the comical side of King, Jr.'s life and personality. Its focus is threefold. First, it explores King, Jr.'s gift of wit, humor, and laughter through the lens of his familial and cultural traditions.[6] Second, the good-natured and jovial attitude he displayed when using humor in the pulpit and joking about religious figures, including him self, will be discussed in some detail. Finally, attention is given to the ingeniously humorous attitude King, Jr. injected into the movement, particularly as he sought to not only entertain and relax himself and those closest to him in the Southern Christian Leadership Conference (SCLC), but also to ease the fears, relieve tension and stress, and invigorate the minds and spirits of every foot soldier who marched and went to jail with him. The point is to explain, at greater length and

4. Coretta Scott King, *My Life with Martin Luther King, Jr.* (New York: Henry Holt and Company, 1993; originally published in 1969), 59 and 89; "'I Remember Martin': People Close to the Late Civil Rights Leader Recall a Down-to-Earth and Humorous Man," *Ebony*, 39, no. 6 (April, 1984), 33–34, 36, 38, and 40; Ralph David Abernathy, "My Old Friend Martin," *The Tennessean: USA Weekend*, Nashville, Tennessee (12–14 January 1990), 6; and Ralph David Abernathy, *And the Walls Came Tumbling Down: An Autobiography* (New York: Harper & Row, Publishers, 1989), 468–70.
5. Abernathy, *And the Walls Came Tumbling Down*, 468; and King, *My Life with Martin Luther King, Jr.*, 78.
6. My interest in this subject goes back more than thirty years, when I first thought seriously about King's roots in African American cultural traditions. At that time, even the most reputable King scholars were either ignoring or giving only fleeting attention to those formative influences that figured most prominently in King's life. See Lewis V. Baldwin, *There is a Balm in Gilead: The Cultural Roots of Martin Luther King, Jr.* (Minneapolis: Fortress Press, 1991), 33–34, 37, and 303–10.

in more precise terms, how a man who captured the imaginations of millions found privacy, relaxation, joy, and inner peace.

A. A Jokester in the Family: King, Jr.'s Playful Sense of Humor

Martin Luther King, Jr., was shaped and nurtured in a culture marked by a fascinating mix of people, stories, and traditions, and there was always folklore, humor, and laughter. Black life in Georgia in the 1920s, 30s, and 40s had so many sides, and this could not have been more evident to a sensitive and perceptive boy such as King, Jr., who was growing up in Atlanta in that period. People greeted each other with a smile, laughter, and a hearty, "how are you doing?," and they took pride in the ingenious ways in which they maneuvered and survived in a society in which they were too often abused, maimed, and even killed simply because they were black.[7] Having descended from a people who brought "the gift of laughter" to America aboard slave ships, they were a resilient people who told tales, celebrated special moments, and exuded a general aura of merriment that too often played into the common narrative that blacks were "happy-go-lucky."[8] James Weldon Johnson had observed as much and more while teaching the parents and grandparents of these people in Georgia as far back as the 1890s, and he wrote:

> The situation in which they were might have seemed hopeless, but they themselves were not without hope. The patent proof of this was their ability to sing and to laugh. I know something about the philosophy of song; I wish I knew as much about the philosophy of laughter. Their deep, genuine laughter often puzzled and irritated me. Why *did* they laugh so? How *could* they laugh so? Was this rolling, pealing laughter merely echoes from a mental vacuity or did it spring from an innate power to rise above the ironies of life? Or were they, in the language of a line from one of

---

7. King, *Daddy King*, 15–16 and 71–72; Baldwin, *There is a Balm in Gilead*, 30 and 33–34; Christine King Farris, *Through It All: Reflections on My Life, My Family, and My Faith* (New York: Atria Books, 2009), 3–16; and Robert E. Johnson, "Daddy King's Own Book about His Tragedies," *Jet*, Vol. 59, no. 2 (25 September 1980), 16.
8. Lawrence W. Levine, *Black Culture and Black Consciousness: Afro-American Folk Thought from Slavery to Freedom* (New York: Oxford University Press, 1978), 299–300. Martin Luther King, Sr., or Daddy King, grew up in this period and among these people in Georgia, and he recalled those times when his vehicle "was rocking with laughter." See King, *Daddy King*, 15.

the blues, "Laughing to keep from crying"? Were they laughing because they were only thoughtless? Were they laughing at themselves? Were they laughing at the white man? I found no complete answer to these questions.[9]

While summing "up his experience in the form of a conundrum," Johnson nonetheless hinted at qualities passed on from one generation of ex-slaves and their descendants eventually to inhere in King, Jr., who also possessed the ability to laugh in the face of adversity, disappointment, and uncertainty.[10] Born nine months before the stock market crashed in October 1929, King, Jr., commonly called M.L., grew up at a time when both the tragic effects of the Great Depression and the violence of Jim Crow left little or nothing for his people to laugh about, and yet, the boy was viewed in familial circles as funny and clever. Alberta King reported that her son "M. L.'s proclivity as a joke teller went back to childhood, and longtime intimates knew him as a relentless teaser and 'a perfect mimic.'"[11] The youngster grinned a lot, often teased playmates and schoolmates, pulled pranks, feigned illness, and made other excuses to avoid household chores, and routinely made funny comments. His competition with his sister, Christine and his occasional conflict and experiences at play with his brother, A. D. also carried hints of humor. These tendencies owed much to King, Jr.'s childhood home environment.[12] There was always a lot of storytelling,

9. Johnson would later admit that "I have since learned that this ability to laugh heartily is, in part, the salvation of the American Negro; it does much to keep him from going the way of the Indian." Black thinkers such as Claude McKay and W. E. B. DuBois offered similar insights while acknowledging that the ability to laugh in the face of oppression was perhaps their people's greatest gift from God. See Levine, *Black Culture and Black Consciousness*, 298–99; and James Weldon Johnson, *Along This Way: The Autobiography of James Weldon Johnson* (New York: The Viking Press, 1969; originally published in 1933), 120.

10. Levine, *Black Culture and Black Consciousness*, 298–99; James Weldon Johnson, *The Autobiography of an Ex-Colored Man* (New York: Alfred Knopf, 1927), 56; and King, *My Life with Martin Luther King, Jr.*, 78 and 89.

11. David J. Garrow, *Bearing the Cross: Martin Luther King, Jr., and the Southern Christian Leadership Conference* (New York: William Morrow and Company, Inc., 1986), 550; Alberta King, "Dr. Martin Luther King, Jr.: Birth to Twelve Years Old by His Mother," a recording, Ebenezer Baptist Church (18 January 1973), Library and Archives of the Martin Luther King, Jr. Center for Nonviolent Social Change, Inc., Atlanta, Georgia; Clayborne Carson, et al., eds., *The Papers of Martin Luther King, Jr., Volume I: Called to Serve, January 1929–June 1951* (Berkeley: University of California Press, 1992), 359–60; and Farris, *Through It All*, 22–23, 30–31, and 223.

12. Christine King, Farris, "The Young Martin: From Childhood through College," *Ebony*, Vol. XLI, no. 3 (January, 1986), 57–58; Garrow, *Bearing the Cross*, 550; Farris, *Through It All*, 22–23, 27, 30–31, and

joking, laughter, and joy around the dining room table in the King home, and the quiet atmosphere was broken on other occasions by the "cheerfulness" of Grandma Jennie and King, Sr. and Alberta's wonderful sense of humor. In this setting, in which discipline was also encouraged and demanded, King, Jr. and his siblings, Christine and A. D., found an outlet to express their own wittiness or hearty, joyous humor, and they routinely resorted to all kinds of tricks in order to date, to attend parties, to dance, and to take part in other activities that youngsters enjoyed, but that King, Sr., or Daddy King, found unacceptable.[13]

It is said that King, Jr. inherited his "keen sense of humor" from his mother, Alberta, who had gotten her "constant good spirits" from her own mother, Jennie C. Parks Williams, and her "quiet humor" from her father, Adam Daniel Williams, who had pastored Atlanta's Ebenezer Baptist Church, the King's home congregation, from 1894 until his death in 1931. Interestingly enough, King, Jr.'s ability to "tease with a dry, erupting humor" actually reminded "his mother of her father."[14] In any case, Alberta "had many wonderful stories to tell," and she passed them down to her children, especially King, Jr., who had an incredibly accurate and retentive memory, and who seemed to delight most in merry-making and the fun-filled life.[15]

But the impact of that larger black culture in Georgia and throughout the South, in which King, Jr.'s parents and grandparents were rooted, and in which folk wit, humor, and laughter were so pervasive, must also be seriously considered. King, Jr. spent so much of his childhood around elders who were masters of what Lawrence Levine calls "the humor of absurdity," which "worked through a

223; and Frederick L. Downing, *To See the Promised Land: The Faith Pilgrimage of Martin Luther King, Jr.* (Macon, GA: Mercer University Press, 1986), 43–44, 126, and 154.

13. Lawrence D. Reddick, *Crusader without Violence: A Biography of Martin Luther King, Jr.* (New York: Harper & Brothers, Publishers, 1959), 49–51; and King, *Daddy King*, 190–91. King, Jr.'s sister Christine acknowledged having "a good sense of humor," and she made essentially the same point about her bothers. See Farris, *Through It All*, 14, 16, 22–24, 123–24, and 142; Farris, "The Young Martin," 56–58; and Carson, et al., eds., *King Papers*, I, 359.

14. Reddick, *Crusader without Violence*, 7.

15. King, *My Life with Martin Luther King, Jr.*, 76–77; Reddick, *Crusader without Violence*, 49–50; and Baldwin, *There is a Balm in Gilead*, 107–8.

straight-faced assumption of the rationality of the system" of Jim Crow "and the belief structure upon which it rested." "No institution or custom, South or North," wrote Levine, "lent itself better to this humor than segregation, and the amount of wit devoted to it is difficult to assimilate no less summarize."[16] Black southerners often played the fool, grinned, scratched their heads, pretended to believe in the legitimacy and morality of racial apartheid when in the presence of whites, laughed in the faces of whites, mimicked and made fun of whites in their absence, and used various other deceptive means as a survival strategy, without surrendering their dignity as individuals and as a community.[17] Such amazing displays of folk wit, humor, and laughter during King, Jr.'s childhood years, which almost always escaped detection from whites, did much to ease the hardship of racial injustice and the Great Depression, and this, perhaps more than anything else, spoke to his people's ingenuity in dealing with difficult and seemingly insurmountable circumstances. King, Jr. was very much a part of a people who brought the gift of wit, humor, and laughter to so much of what they did, said, and experienced, and in so doing, epitomized the power of the human spirit and the harmony of the human heart.[18] He would later write about this with telling insight.[19]

What King, Jr. witnessed and experienced growing up in Georgia helped keep him from losing a sense of the needs and uses of black humor, even as he moved through the ranks of academia. While studying at Atlanta's Morehouse College from 1944 to 1948, he was literally surrounded by joke-cracking funny guys who routinely gathered in each other's rooms to clown, tell jokes, and tease each

16. Levine, *Black Culture and Black Consciousness*, 310. Also see the chapter on "Deception" in Howard Thurman, *Jesus and the Disinherited* (Nashville: Abingdon Press, 1949), 58–73.

17. This explained the widespread and enduring popularity of the Brer Rabbit tales among blacks, especially in the South, in this period. Like Brer Rabbit, blacks learned to maneuver as best they could from their point of disadvantage, freely employing wit, humor, and laughter. See Ibid., 81–135 and 298–366; Reddick, *Crusader without Violence*, 49–50; and King, *My Life with Martin Luther King, Jr.*, 76–77.

18. These claims are supported by a careful reading of Lawrence Levine's treatment of black wit, humor, and laughter, which covers the period from slavery up through the 1940s, when King was growing up in Georgia. See Levine, *Black Culture and Black Consciousness*, 298–366; and Baldwin, *There is a Balm in Gilead*, 33–37 and 303–10.

19. See Martin Luther King, Jr., "True Dignity," unpublished version of a speech (n.d.), King Center Library and Archives, 1–7.

other. Although King, Jr. seemed rather quiet and reserved to most of his classmates,[20] it would have been virtually impossible for him to escape the influence of this kind of campus culture, especially since he already had a habit of making family members and friends laugh through jokes and amusing situations. During his years at the predominantly white Crozer Theological Seminary in Chester, Pennsylvania in the late 1940s and early 50s, he was something of a jokester while also being careful not to project the image of the thoughtless, happy-go-lucky Sambo.[21] "He loved to smile, laugh, joke, and have a good time," said Sara V. Richardson, who knew King, Jr. quite well while he was a student minister at the Calvary Baptist Church in Chester. She went on to note that King, Jr. "could tell jokes so dry and then burst out laughing himself, and then you had to laugh."[22]

King, Jr. met blacks from the South in Chester who enjoyed his sense of humor and shared his thirst for fun and pleasure. This was also the case in Boston, where King, Jr.'s pursued his graduate studies from 1951 to 1954. In Boston, most of King, Jr.'s social life was among other southern blacks studying at colleges and universities in and around the city, and the young man was often the entertainer when they all got together for pleasant chat or parties. His playful comments, hilarious facial expressions, and the rollicking humor and laughter must have brought some measure of stress relief, especially since all involved dealt daily with the challenges that came with being black students on predominantly white campuses.[23]

20. Some of the jokes that had become widely known and shared at Morehouse by the 1950s focused on the excessive self-interest of "Morehouse men," and also on their "reputed aggressiveness" toward beautiful girls, their self-confidence and egoism, and the rumor that they "ate peas with their knives." King undoubtedly knew many of these jokes and undoubtedly shared them with his friend and first biographer, Lawrence D. Reddick. See Reddick, *Crusader without Violence*, 65–66; A Private Interview with Philip Lenud, Vanderbilt University Divinity School, Nashville, Tennessee (7 April 1987); and Garrow, *Bearing the Cross*, 37.
21. Lerone Bennett, Jr., *What Manner of Man: A Biography of Martin Luther King, Jr.* (Chicago: Johnson Publishing Company, 1964), 26; William Peters, "Our Weapon Is Love," *Redbook* (August, 1956), 72; David L. Lewis, *King: A Critical Biography* (New York: Praeger Publishers, 1970), 28; and Clayborne Carson, "Martin Luther King, Jr.: The Crozer Years," *The Journal of Blacks in Higher Education* (Summer, 1997), 123–24.
22. A Private Interview with Sara V. Richardson, Chester, Pennsylvania (29 May 1987); and Baldwin, *There is a Balm in Gilead*, 37.
23. King, *My Life with Martin Luther King, Jr.*, 90; A Private Interview with Michael E. Haynes, Twelfth Baptist Church, Boston, Massachusetts (25 June 1987); and Baldwin, *There is a Balm in Gilead*, 36–39.

These gatherings, which were very much like the coming together of an extended family, actually set the stage for King, Jr. to meet Coretta Scott, a native of rural, black belt Alabama. Coretta had grown up in an atmosphere in which the telling of tales and raw wit and humor marked the spirit of everything, from church meetings to parties to informal family reunions to dealings with whites, and she really appreciated King, Jr.'s fun side from the moment she met him in early 1952. She immediately sensed that he fitted none of the stereotypes she had always associated with ministers; namely, rigidly fundamentalist in their reading of Scripture, narrow in their thinking, and typically having the "look of sanctity that they seemed to put on like their suits." Struck by King, Jr.'s humility, teasing, and playful sense of humor, Coretta recalled that he "was so alive and funny, and so much fun to be with." King, Jr. often teased her throughout their courtship, and the joking and laughter continued into their marriage,[24] as discussed earlier at points in chapters 2 and 5, which examine King's role as a husband and father. According to Coretta, her husband would "just tell jokes for hours," and "he'd say to me, 'You don't laugh enough'." She went on to characterize King as "a big teaser," and noted that "This was part of his technique for really sort of getting back at me when I would say something that he didn't like."[25] King, Sr. was probably the only one in the family who thought his son was not very funny during those Boston years, referring, on one occasion, to his "dry sense of humor."[26] There were times when King, Jr. was the only one laughing at his jokes.

Poking fun at and laughing with family members literally became a pastime for King, Jr. during his adult years. A man whose affectionate tendencies seemed inexhaustible, he loved to tease and play practical

24. King, *My Life with Martin Luther King, Jr.*, 19, 24, 30, 50, 52, 54–55, 58–59, 65, 67, 72, 88, 90, and 124; Farris, *Through It All*, 72–73; Reddick, *Crusader without Violence*, 105 and 182; and Baldwin, *There is a Balm in Gilead*, 129 and 131. Harry Belafonte's sense of how Coretta responded to teasing and humor seems to contrast sharply with what Coretta herself stated repeatedly. Belafonte reports that Coretta's "manner was stately and stern," and that one "could never tell an off-color joke around Coretta, or even make a teasing remark if it had some salacious spin." "I know Martin Chafed at that, and so did I," Belafonte added. See Harry Belafonte, *My Song: A Memoir*, with Michael Shnayerson (New York: Alfred A. Knopf, 2011), 298.
25. Quoted in Garrow, *Bearing the Cross*, 550–51.
26. King, *Daddy King*, 150.

jokes on his mother, sister, and brother.[27] Although King, Sr. was not the kind who tolerated a lot of playfulness, he was occasionally the target of his son's joking and laughter as well. King, Jr. had a great time riding his father about his "thoroughgoing" capitalism and his spending habits, as his wife, Coretta recounted:

> Daddy King had always been a great penny-saver. Even after Martin and I were married his father carried thrift to an extreme we would often joke about. If chickens were on sale somewhere in town, he would drive across the city to save ten cents, ignoring the cost of the gasoline he used, for the pleasure of a bargain. He would complain about our paying to have our car washed, saying "You should wash it yourself. . . ." Martin, the sociologist, would answer, "Daddy, I have a theory about that. You know society is based on the division of labor, and if I wash my own car it means somebody else doesn't have a job." His father would smile and say, "You go ahead, son. Spend your money! If you go broke, I guess I'll always have a dime in my pocket for you." He meant it too. He may have been thrifty, but, particularly where his family was concerned, he was very generous.[28]

In "an amusing chat" between King, Jr. and one of his friends, in which the name of the calypso singer Harry Belafonte also came up, King, Jr. related another funny story concerning a conversation he had had with his father about the burden of maintaining and compensating good and dependable housekeepers. Daddy King "complained that" his housekeeper "cost him twenty-five dollars a week." "Highway robbery," the elder King exclaimed. King, Jr. quickly responded by telling Daddy King that he paid his housekeeper "a hundred dollars a week," which "really shamed him." "But," King added, "I didn't tell him that Harry was paying for it."[29]

---

27. Ibid., 188; King, *My Life with Martin Luther King, Jr.*, 292; and Baldwin, *There is a Balm in Gilead*, 151. King's image as a jokester was such that it even left an impression on his oldest child Yolanda. "Daddy used to love to tell jokes—a whole lot of them," she reminisced. "He could tell jokes with such a straight, poker face that it only added to the humor." See "'I Remember Martin,'" 38.

28. King called his father "a thoroughgoing capitalist," which he insisted he could never be since that kind of self-identification encouraged one, consciously or unconsciously, to make "all the money you can" while "ignoring people's needs." At the same time, King highly respected his father's handling and/or wise use of money despite all the teasing. See King, *My Life with Martin Luther King, Jr.*, 56 and 76; and Carson, et al., eds., *King Papers*, I, 359–60.

29. As indicated previously in this book, Belafonte used his talent to raise money for King's SCLC. See Belafonte, *My Song*, 258; and Martin Luther King, Jr., *Why We Can't Wait* (New York: The New American Library, Inc., 1963), 57–58 and 75.

Not surprisingly, many of King, Jr.'s humorous comments and stories about his father King, Sr. had to do with morality and religion—matters over which they did not always agree. "My old man has always been a moralist," he jokingly said at times. "He doesn't drink liquor, and he doesn't chase women."[30] King, Jr. remembered one amusing incident that happened in Norway just after he had received the Nobel Peace Prize in a special ceremony. Someone in the group of celebrants "produced champagne and gave a toast to Martin." Daddy King, apparently unmindful of what this really meant, quickly "said with a smile, 'Now I want to give a toast to the person who really is responsible. I want to give a toast to God'." The incident "was so sweet and funny" that everyone present "burst out laughing."[31] King, Sr.'s methods of asserting his authority as Ebenezer's senior pastor and his pulpit manner were also subjects of King, Jr.'s humor on certain occasions. "Well, he makes it clear, sometimes consciously and sometimes unconsciously, that he is the pastor and I'm the co-pastor," said King, Jr. with a wide grin on his face. King, Jr. also had much fun describing how his father "would often get up and ramble for ten minutes after he had preached" at Ebenezer Church on Sunday mornings, "saying nothing." His humor about King, Sr.'s ways or habits was always in good taste, so to speak, and it usually evoked spontaneous laughter.[32]

King, Jr. knew a number of droll stories about his father and mother's experiences as they visited Negro churches in parts of rural Georgia. One of his favorite, which his mother so often told as well, was about a certain Sunday morning, when his parents "were driving

---

30. Coretta Scott King, "Address at the National Conference on Civil Rights," Fisk University, Nashville, Tennessee (5 April 1986); and Baldwin, *There is a Balm in Gilead*, 119.
31. King, *My Life with Martin Luther King, Jr.*, 12; Dorothy F. Cotton, *If Your Back's Not Bent: The Role of the Citizenship Education Program in the Civil Rights Movement* (New York: Atria Books, 2012), 14–15; and Dora McDonald, *Secretary to a King: My Years with Martin Luther King, Jr., the Civil Rights Movement, and Beyond* (Montgomery, AL: New South Books, 2012), 80.
32. Martin Luther King, Jr., "Transcript of an Interview on the Merv Griffith Show," NBC sitcom, New York, New York (6 July 1967), King Center Library and Archives, 2; and Baldwin, *There is a Balm in Gilead*, 317. King's SCLC associate Bernard Lee, who was exposed to this humor, insists that King understood that his father "was one of those preachers from the old school," and he was thus able to tolerate his ways. See A Private Interview with Bernard Lee, Washington, DC (9 July 1986).

through the country trying to find a small church at which" Daddy King had "been invited to preach." The story unfolded in these terms:

> They stopped an old black man walking down the road and asked him for directions. He said, "Let's see, now. To get to that church, you go down this road about two miles, then turn right . . . No, that's not right. What you do is, you turn around and go up to the crossroads, then turn left and . . . No, that's not right, either. Let's see..." He scratched his head and said, "You know, I reckon I don't know *where* that church is." The Kings thanked him for his trouble and pulled away. Suddenly they heard someone calling, and looking back, they saw the old man huffing and puffing down the road to catch up with them. They stopped, backed up the car, and waited while he tried to catch his breath and then listened expectantly. He panted out, "I just wanted to say . . . I just wanted to tell you . . . I just saw my brother, and I asked him . . . and he don't know where that church is either."[33]

King, Jr.'s humor did a lot in terms of reinforcing and solidifying family ties. It drew him closer to his parents, his siblings, his wife, and his children, and helped make it possible for them all to have fun and to enjoy life while also feeling alive and secure in their culture and in their basic humanity.

B. Wholly Laughter: King's Comedy and the Soundscape of Religious Life

Although Martin Luther King, Jr. brought a lot of sincerity and dedication to his roles as preacher and religious leader, he never ceased to laugh and to cherish humor as a gift from God and as a vital and necessary expression of the human spirit. From the very beginning of his tenure as pastor of the Dexter Avenue Baptist Church in Montgomery in 1954, he was known as the fun-loving preacher who relaxed easily, often teased and cracked jokes, and tended to delight in his own funny puns, quips, and stories. Thelma Austin Rice, one of Dexter's most devoted members, described him as "Jovial," "full of life," and blessed with "a grand sense of humor." "In spite of his

---

33. King, *My Life with Martin Luther King, Jr.*, 76–77; Baldwin Interview with Lee (9 July 1986); and Baldwin, *There is a Balm in Gilead*, 305.

humor," she continued, "there was always an immovable dignity." Althea Thompson Thomas, who also attended Dexter, remembered that King, Jr. "was not a stone face," and that "His words were strong, but when appropriate he laced them with humor." "Every time you were around him or engaged in a conversation," said Maggie Shannon, another Dexter member, "you found something to laugh about." "I can see him laughing now," remarked Verdie Davis, one of the church mothers.[34] According to Nelson Malden, a Dexter member and also King, Jr.'s barber, King, Jr.'s down-to-earth jocularity and off-the-cuff quips often sparked sudden laughter, even from people who did not know him well. Apparently, this was one of many qualities that endeared him to people from various walks of life.[35] He never hesitated to share his affection for people through humor and laughter.

King, Jr. joked a lot about what he observed and experienced during those years. During a trip to Chester, Pennsylvania to receive an alumni award from Crozer Theological Seminary, where he had studied years earlier, King, Jr. and his old friend J. Pius Barbour ran into and shook hands with one of King, Jr.'s "old flames." "Great God, Barbour," King, Jr. commented, "she looks like she fell into a concrete mixer."[36] King, Jr. was seldom so harsh and insensitive in his remarks about women or anyone else, and was careful not to push this kind of humor beyond the borders of reason. His friend Lawrence D. Reddick, who taught at Montgomery's Alabama State College, recounted that King, Jr.'s humor was most often clean and wholesome, and that he was also a mimic and quite good at putting on a show:

> Never given to clowning in public, King will regale his friends at private parties with his imitations of religious entertainers and fellow preachers. At a birthday celebration that his wife gave for him and about a dozen guests, King and his close friend, the Rev. Ralph Abernathy, "carried on."

34. Reddick, *Crusader without Violence*, 2. Member after member at Dexter Church vividly recalled King's gift of humor and laughter. See Wally G. Vaughn and Richard W. Wills, eds., *Reflections on Our Pastor: Dr. Martin Luther King, Jr., at Dexter Avenue Baptist Church, 1954-1960* (Dover, MA: The Majority Press, Inc., 1999), 26, 34–35, 53–54, 65, and 87.
35. A Telephone Interview with Nelson Malden (15 March 2014). Mr. Malden's impression of King's very human qualities are offered at greater length in Vaughn and Wills, eds., *Reflections on Our Pastor*, 57–62.
36. Garrow, *Bearing the Cross*, 122.

Pretending to be two semiliterate singers doing a TV program, they began by "dericating" the number to Miss Coretta King, "a dear sister over there in Montgomery, Alabama." Then followed off-key, off-beat singing, slurring, grimacing, and prancing that kept the party howling for half an hour.[37]

During King, Jr.'s years as a pastor at Dexter and a co-pastor with his father and brother at Atlanta's Ebenezer Baptist Church, so much of his humor was church-related humor, and understandably so. While he was always serious-minded and focused when he ascended the pulpit, he never lost that genuine, deep sense of humor for which he was so well-known, and he used it to elevate the power of preaching as the spoken word and the performed art. Having that rare ability to simultaneously entertain, enlighten, and move people to tears, King, Jr. always began his sermons and speeches with jovial informality, and he routinely warmed up his audiences by turning to measured humor, joking with them, sharing humorous anecdotes, and making them laugh, thus putting them at ease with him and preparing them for his message. His intention was to not only induce laughter, but to create a climate conducive to participatory preaching, which typically involved both the proclaimer of the word and the lively, responsive congregation. For example, whenever he was introduced in glowing terms as the guest preacher at various churches throughout the country, he typically began his message with the comical anecdote about "the old maid," as was the case at the Canaan Baptist Church in New York in March, 1968, when Dr. Richard Dixon introduced him:

> As he introduced me, I felt something like the old maid who had never been married. One day when she went to work, the lady for whom she worked said, "Mary, I hear you're getting married." And she said, "No, I'm not getting married, but thank God for the rumor." Well, I know all of these marvelous things that Richard Dixon said about me can't be true, but thank God for the rumor.[38]

37. Reddick, *Crusader without Violence*, 7–8. Mrs. Thelma Austin Rice says King's playful sense of humor was similar at "church or club meetings" and also "our tea gatherings." See Vaughn and Wills, eds., *Reflections on Our Pastor*, 26.
38. Martin Luther King, Jr., "A Knock at Midnight," unpublished version of a sermon, Canaan Baptist Church, New York, New York (24 March 1968), King Center Library and Archives, 1; Martin Luther King, Jr., "Transforming a Neighborhood," unpublished version of a speech, NATRA Convention

Many in the congregation chuckled and some laughed heartily. In his celebrated sermon, "The Drum Major Instinct," preached at his Ebenezer Baptist Church around the same time, King, Jr. used a different humorous incident to make a point about that basic human desire for attention and recognition, thus evoking spontaneous laughter on that occasion as well. He said to his listeners:

> I got a letter the other day. It was a new magazine coming out. And it opened up, "Dear Dr. King, as you are on many mailing lists, and you are categorized as highly intelligent, progressive, a lover of the arts, and the sciences, and I know you will want to read what I have to say." Of course I did. After you said all of that and explained me so exactly, of course I wanted to read it.[39]

Oftentimes, King, Jr. would warm up his audience in this manner. He would announce his intention to be brief and to the point in his sermon, noting, in a joking fashion, "you know, brevity for a Baptist preacher is a magnificent accomplishment. A Baptist preacher is always tempted to preach, and preach a long time, when he's before a very enthusiastic crowd."[40] Known for showing up late at meetings, and sometimes, speaking engagements, King, Jr. at times amused his

RCA Dinner, Atlanta, Georgia (11 August 1967), King Center Library and Archives, 1–2; and Baldwin, *There is a Balm in Gilead*, 294. King's use of humor in the pulpit is yet another indication of how he drank from the wellsprings of a preaching tradition that extended back to the slave preacher. One significant aspect of the black folk sermon, according to Andrew P. Watson, was "the warming-up period," during which the preacher sought to get his hearers involved in the sermon, thus creating the atmosphere for participatory preaching, or the kind of sermonizing that involves the entire congregation. If the congregation is not responsive, with shouts of "Amen," "God, help him," and "make it plain," then the sermon is not in the best tradition of black preaching. See "Negro Primitive Religious Services," in Clifton H. Johnson, ed., *God Struck Me Dead: Voices of Ex-Slaves* (Cleveland: The Pilgrim Press, 1993; originally published in 1969), 5; and Baldwin, *There is a Balm in Gilead*, 293. At times King warmed the people up through prayer or a song. See Lewis V. Baldwin, *The Voice of Conscience: The Church in the Mind of Martin Luther King, Jr.* (New York: Oxford University Press, 2010), 117; and King, *My Life with Martin Luther King, Jr.*, 232–33.

39. Martin Luther King, Jr., "The Drum Major Instinct," unpublished version of a sermon, Ebenezer Baptist Church, Atlanta, Georgia (4 February 1968), 2–3; and Clayborne Carson and Peter Holloran, eds., *A Knock at Midnight: Inspiration from the Great Sermons of Reverend Martin Luther King, Jr.* (New York: Warner Books, Inc., 1998), 172–73.

40. Martin Luther King, Jr., "An Address at the Freedom Fund Report Dinner," unpublished version, 53rd Annual Convention of the NAACP, Atlanta, Georgia (5 July 1962); King Center Library and Archives, 1; Johnson, ed., *God Struck Me Dead*, 5; Martin Luther King, Jr., "Speech at a Mass Meeting," unpublished version, Grenada, Mississippi (19 March 1968), King Center Library and Archives, 1; Martin Luther King, Jr., "Speech at a Mass Meeting," unpublished version, Augusta, Georgia (22 March 1968), King Center Library and Archives, 3; Baldwin, *There is a Balm in Gilead*, 293; and Lewis V. Baldwin, *Never to Leave Us Alone: The Prayer Life of Martin Luther King Jr.* (Minneapolis: Fortress Press, 2010), 46–47.

audience with references to the problems and uneasiness he and his aides experienced while flying to their destination, highlighting feelings and tendencies that were fundamentally human and with which everyone present could identify:

> We did have those moments when our pilots had to make sure that the engine was working, and that held us up some; and I was agreeing that we certainly should take all care and be as scrutinizing as possible in attempting to deal with that problem, because when you get in the air, you want everything right. Now I don't want to give any of you the impression that I don't have faith in God in the air, its simply that I have had more experience with him on the ground.[41]

King, Jr. usually ended his account of this rather humorous, and yet, serious situation with the expression, "I would rather be Martin Luther King late than the late Martin Luther King"[42]—a point that always generated smiles and outright laughter. Having deep roots in the black church and its preaching tradition, and apt to use everything in his communicative power to get his points across, King, Jr. instinctively knew what it took to move people in this way, and to insure their responses to and participation in his sermons.[43] He was like countless other black preachers throughout the country in his time, who integrated humorous anecdotes in their sermons to warm up

41. King, "Speech at a Mass Meeting," Augusta, Georgia (22 March 1968), 1; Martin Luther King, Jr., "Address at a Mass Meeting," unpublished version, St. James Baptist Church, Birmingham, Alabama (31 January 1966), King Center Library and Archives, 3; Martin Luther King, Jr., "Rally Speech on the Georgia Tour 'Pre-Washington Campaign,'" unpublished version, Albany, Georgia (22 March 1968), King Center Library and Archives, 1; Baldwin, There is a Balm in Gilead, 293–94; and Baldwin, Never to Leave Us Alone, 46–47.
42. King made essentially the same statement to a young cab driver who was trying to get him from New York's LaGuardia Airport one night for an appearance with Harry Belafonte on The Tonight Show, declaring that "I'd rather be known as Dr. King late than the late Dr. King." King shared this also with Belafonte and The Tonight Show audience, and Belafonte and the "crowd laughed." See Martin Luther King, Jr., "Speech at a Mass Meeting," unpublished version, Macon, Georgia (22 March 1968), King Center Library and Archives, 1; Baldwin, There is a Balm in Gilead, 294n69; and Belafonte, My Song, 324–25.
43. This point brings to mind John Dollard's experience during the early part of the twentieth century while listening to a southern Negro revivalist. "The revivalist had done his best to arouse the congregation, but no one shouted and no one came forward to confess religion," wrote Dollard. "In this emergency the preacher had to beat a retreat and he did it by lightening the tone of the meeting." Dollard went on to point out that the revivalist "told several humorous anecdotes, joked with the congregation, and actually made them laugh. It was, of course, an atypical performance." See John Dollard, Caste and Class in a Southern Town (New York: Doubleday & Company, Inc., 1949), 234.

congregations. This habit stretched back generations to slave preachers, and it showed how raw but measured humor could be a great asset in the preaching of the gospel.[44]

Considering the religious, intellectual, political, social, and larger cultural milieu in which King, Jr. functioned, it is small wonder that he made black preachers and their attitudes, habits, activities, and shortcomings a central butt of his humor. Jokes and anecdotes targeting preachers had always pervaded Negro lore, focusing primarily on ignorance, greed, hypocrisy, and gluttony,[45] and King, Jr. knew this and did not deviate in any serious way from that tradition. His secretary, Dora McDonald reported that sometimes his mother, Alberta would call "to tell him jokes—usually 'preacher jokes'—and the two of them would have a great mother-son laugh together."[46] In any case, the preachers coursing through King, Jr.'s humor were often stereotypical figures. He "particularly enjoyed jokes or stories that poked fun at overly pompous clergymen,"[47] many of whom had little or nothing to show for their arrogance. He personally knew untrained black preachers who appeared to celebrate ignorance while dwelling on their "calling," and he had much "fun joking about their call." He mentioned one such preacher who claimed to see "GP" "written in the clouds" one day while "he was plowing." "I know God was telling me to 'go preach,'" the preacher explained. After hearing "one of this man's sermons," King, Jr., "in the midst of raucous laughter," said "I think God was telling him to go on and plow!"[48]

Not surprisingly, King, Jr. had much fun with the excessively pious Negro preachers, who, as his wife, Coretta put it, wore "a look of sanctity that they seemed to put on like their black suits." While King, Jr. appreciated genuine piety and found it renewing and empowering, he was turned off by what he considered false piety, and was known

44. Baldwin, *There is a Balm in Gilead*, 293–95; Baldwin, *Never to Leave Us Alone*, 46–47; and Levine, *Black Culture and Black Consciousness*, 317 and 328–29.
45. Lawrence Levine's treatment of humor in this form is among the best on record. See Levine, *Black Culture and Black Consciousness*, 317 and 326–29.
46. McDonald, *Secretary to a King*, 119.
47. Garrow, *Bearing the Cross*, 550.
48. Cotton, *If You Back's Not Bent*, 118.

to laugh at preachers who always walked around with a "holier than thou" disposition. According to Dora Mcdonald, a number of preachers with such an attitude and demeanor "stood around" King, Jr.'s hospital bed after he was stabbed by Izola Curry in Harlem in September 1958, and he sometimes "joked about" them. "He would describe a kind of out-of-body experience with the preachers praying over his body in bed," Mcdonald explained, "but he was in the upper corner of the room." Most of these preachers "wanted me to go on to glory," King joked, "but I kept saying from my corner, 'Don't worry, I'm not going yet'."[49]

The Negro preacher who "preached a great whooping, loud, emotional sermon," or who "depended on the volume of his voice rather than the content of his message," was repeatedly targeted in King, Jr.'s humor. He was both amused and disturbed on one occasion while listening to a young preacher who "was just jumping all over the pulpit and jumping out and spitting all over everything and screaming with his tune, and moaning and groaning."[50] During a meeting of the Montgomery Improvement Association (MIA), King, Jr. listened to a "whooping" or "singing prayer" by a clergyman in attendance, and had to muster "all of his resources to prevent his smiles from leading to open laughter." Witnessing King, Jr.'s reaction, the note taker at the meeting reported that "It was comical to see him 'fighting' with himself and to note his definite relief once the prayer had ended."[51]

49. King obviously shared his wife, Coretta's attitude toward overly pious preachers, but he really had no problem with preachers praying over his hospital bed. While in St. Joseph Hospital in Atlanta, in November, 1964, suffering from a respiratory ailment, King warmly and sincerely accepted the offer of a Bishop Hallinan of the Catholic Diocese of Atlanta to give him his blessing. The bishop knelt beside King's bed and prayed. Then, the bishop asked King: "'May I receive yours?'" King "then blessed the bishop with a brief prayer." Dora McDonald recounted that "It was a tremendously moving moment for all of us." See King, My Life with Martin Luther King, Jr., 50; and McDonald, Secretary to a King, 29 and 75.
50. Martin Luther King, Jr., "New Wine in Old Bottles," unpublished version of a sermon, Ebenezer Baptist Church, Atlanta, Georgia (2 January 1966), King Center Library and Archives, 8; Clayborne Carson, et al., eds., The Papers of Martin Luther King, Jr., Volume VI: Advocate of the Social Gospel, September 1948–March 1963 (Berkeley: University of California Press, 2007), 223 and 295; and Martin Luther King, Jr., "Transformed Nonconformist," unpublished version of a sermon, Ebenezer Baptist Church, Atlanta, Georgia (16 January 1966), King Center Library and Archives, 9. Apparently, King had felt this way as far back as his childhood years. See Clayborne Carson, ed., The Autobiography of Martin Luther King, Jr. (New York: Warner Books, Inc., 1998), 15.
51. Clayborne Carson, et al., eds., The Papers of Martin Luther King, Jr., Volume III: Birth of a New Age, December 1955–December 1956 (Berkeley: University of California Press, 1997), 150–51.

King, Jr. obviously had problems with what he regarded as excessive displays of emotionalism on the part of Negro preachers, noting at one point that "Monkeys are to entertain not preachers."[52] But he himself was known to whoop at times, and his own humor in the pulpit was, in effect, a form of entertainment.[53] Perhaps the "whooping or "tuning up" style of preaching was acceptable to King, Jr. as long as it did not relegate "the gospel to showmanship," and to the degree that it did not turn the church into "an entertainment center."[54] The other problem King, Jr. had with this preaching style is that too many otherwise perceptive, dedicated, and spirit-filled church folk got caught up in "the volume" of the preachers' "voices and how they can twist their moan," while essentially missing what they were actually saying in their sermons. King, Jr. once humorously described how this so often happened with the person of faith who "confused overt emotionalism with the true holy spirit." "Such a person," he declared, is prone to say that "the preacher sure did preach this morning!" "Well, what did he say?" "I don't know, but he sure did preach this morning!"[55] This kind of emotional and unenlightened approach to religious expression, when carried to extremes, was always problematic for King, Jr., and he consistently made this clear in his humor and in his more serious

---

52. Martin Luther King, Jr., "Guidelines for a Constructive Church," unpublished version of a sermon, Ebenezer Baptist Church, Atlanta, Georgia (5 June 1966), King Center Library and Archives, 2.

53. A Private Interview with Ralph D. Abernathy, West Hunter Baptist Church, Atlanta, Georgia (17 March 1987); King, *My Life with Martin Luther King, Jr.*, 5 and 95–96; Carson and Holloran, eds., *A Knock at Midnight*, 106; and Baldwin, *There is a Balm in Gilead*, 285–86 and 299. During an address in Montgomery in December 1957, King made an interesting comment that was greeted with spirited laughter from the audience: "Preachers? We going to get ready for integration, and we can't spend all our time trying to learn how to whoop and holler. We've got to study some." He went on to say, "Now I'm going to holler tonight, because I want to get it over to you. I'm going to be a Negro tonight." On yet another occasion, King declared: "I am a Baptist preacher. And of course, I can get fired up just like Baptist preachers generally get fired up," a comment that drew laughter and a chorus of "Amens" from the congregation. See Clayborne Carson, et al., eds., *The Papers of Martin Luther King, Jr., Volume IV: Symbol of the Movement, January 1957–December 1958* (Berkeley: University of California Press, 2000), 338; and Clayborne Carson, et al., eds., *The Papers of Martin Luther King, Jr., Volume VII: To Save the Soul of America, January 1961–August 1962* (Berkeley: University of California Press, 2014), 592.

54. King, "Transformed Nonconformist," 9; King, "Guidelines for a Constructive Church," 2; and Carson, et. al., eds., *King Papers*, VI, 223 and 295; King, "New Wine in Old Bottles," 8; Carson and Holloran, eds., *A Knock at Midnight*, 106; and Baldwin, *The Voice of Conscience*, 72–73.

55. King often injected this point into versions of his sermon, "A Knock at Midnight." See Baldwin, *Never to Leave Us Alone*, 127n21; Carson, et al., eds., *King Papers*, VI, 223 and 295; and Carson, et al., eds., *King Papers*, IV, 338.

proclamations, during which he often spoke about the dangers of playing with God.

Negro preachers who refused to join the struggle and who put their own needs and desires above the welfare of their people were portrayed in King, Jr.'s humor as selfish and guilty of acts of woeful neglect and shameful ingratitude. He joked at times about "scared Negro preachers" who lacked the courage to stand up against the structures of social injustice, and "Cadillac preachers" who were "more concerned about the size of the wheel base on their automobiles than about the quality of their service to the Negro community."[56] Even as such jokes brought vigorous laughter from those who heard them, the seriousness of the point King, Jr. was trying to make about the need for commitment and sacrifice was never really lost. Bernard Lee, also a Baptist clergyman who served on King, Jr.'s staff, put it best when he, referring to King, Jr., explained that "a lot of times when he was teasing, he was also making a point. . . . This was his manner of saying in a jocular fashion what he wanted to say. . . . He did it teasingly."[57]

Although King, Jr. admired and respected preachers who lived by the strength of their convictions, and who joined the crusade for civil rights, they did not escape the force of his humor. Such preachers who paraded through his humorous stories and anecdotes possessed "ingenuity in dealing with difficult situations." One of his favorite stories involved a preacher he asked "to give prayer during a street demonstration." A white mob surrounded the demonstrators, and the "situation was so hostile and tense," King, Jr. recalled, "that the brother prayed with his eyes open." Another story King, Jr. loved to tell was about a Baptist preacher who was not seminary or college-trained, but who was blessed with great wit and raw natural talents.[58] At the

---

56. Martin Luther King, Jr., *Where Do We Go from Here: Chaos or Community?* (Boston: Beacon Press, 1968; originally published in 1967), 36, 124, and 132; Baldwin Interview with Abernathy (17 March 1987); Baldwin Interview with Lee (9 July 1986); Taylor Branch, *Parting the Waters: America in the King Years, 1954–63* (New York: Simon and Schuster, 1988), 701–2; and Taylor Branch, *Pillar of Fire: America in the King Years, 1963–65* (New York: Simon and Schuster, 1998), 207.
57. Quoted in Garrow, *Bearing the Cross*, 551.
58. Interestingly enough, King may well have been talking about himself during a demonstration for voting rights near the Edmund Pettus Bridge in Selma, Alabama in 1965. There is a scene in the film, "Selma, 1965," from "The Eyes on the Prize" series, during which King is on his knees with

beginning of the movement "when tensions were high," the mayor of Atlanta brought "the top ministers in the city together," including this particular minister, to discuss the racial climate. "Let's see how many people in the black community we have represented here today," said the mayor. One minister claimed 3,000 members, another 2,000, another 2, 500, and so on. When the mayor got to the Baptist preacher, "who had a small church and was hesitant" to share numbers "when the others had such large congregations," the preacher commented, "Sir, I have a church full."[59]

Most of King, Jr.'s funny stories about Negro preachers focused on Vernon N. Johns and Hilly Thomas, who were quite different from each other in educational achievement, attitude, temperament, style, and behavior, but equally accessible as targets of humor and laughter. The two men are discussed separately here to further illumine King, Jr.'s humor and skills as a comedian. Johns was King, Jr.'s immediate predecessor as pastor of Montgomery's Dexter Avenue Baptist Church, serving from 1947 to 1952, and he literally turned the congregation into almost five years "of awe, laughter, inspiration, fear, and annoyance."[60] King, Jr. saw Johns as "a brilliant preacher" who could "quote from the classics of literature and philosophy for hours without ever referring to a manuscript," and also as a "fearless man" who "never allowed an injustice to come to his attention without speaking out against it."[61] "Martin was just fascinated with Vernon Johns," Philip Lenud reported, viewing him as not only "heavy," but also, "complex and funny."[62] While impressed with Johns's "creative mind," his "theological genius," and his "incredibly retentive memory," King, Jr.

his eyes wide open while his associate and friend, Ralph Abernathy, offers a stirring prayer. See "'I Remember Martin,'" 40; and Baldwin, There is a Balm in Gilead, 307.
59. "'I Remember Martin,'" 40; Baldwin Interview with Abernathy (17 March 1987); and Baldwin, There is a Balm in Gilead, 307.
60. Zelia S. Evans and J. T. Alexander, eds., The Dexter Avenue Baptist Church, 1877-1977 (Montgomery: Dexter Avenue Baptist Church, 1978), 64-65; Branch, Parting the Waters, 7; Vaughn and Wills, eds., Reflections on Our Pastor, 46-47 and 57; and Troy Jackson, Becoming King: Martin Luther King Jr. and the Making of a National Leader (Lexington: The University Press of Kentucky, 2008), 25-27 and 31-33.
61. Martin Luther King, Jr., Stride toward Freedom: The Montgomery Story (New York: Harper & Row, Publishers, 1958), 38.
62. Baldwin Interview with Lenud (7 April 1987); and Baldwin, There is a Balm in Gilead, 299. Lawrence D. Reddick recalled that King's use of the word "heavy" meant so much when he was describing a person. Reddick noted that "King characterizes statements that have little intellectual content

was perhaps most fascinated and amused by his tendency to ignore distinctions between those statements and actions that were appropriate in public settings and those that were not.[63] "My husband and his friends could sit for hours swapping stories about this outspoken minister who always gave his middle class congregation a very hard time," remarked Coretta King. "According to Martin," she added, "Dr. John's main purpose was to rock the complacency of the refined members of the Dexter Avenue Baptist Church—in whatever way he could."[64]

King, Jr. and his friend, Ralph Abernathy, had tons of fun joking and laughing about Johns's careless attitude about his personal appearance, his shocking and controversial statements and behavior in public, and his challenge to both complacent and elitist blacks and vicious, diehard white racists. When it came to matters of personal appearance and "trappings of protocol or formal dress," Johns, in King, Jr.'s mind, could not have been funnier. Johns "thought nothing of walking into distinguished assemblies wearing mis-matched socks, with farm mud on his shoes," and he was known to appear in pulpits in various parts of the country with no socks on at all, without laces in his shoes, in wrinkled suits, or with the sleeves of pajama tops showing under the arms of his long sleeve shirts.[65] He routinely carried his suits, underwear, and shirts in a paper bag with his books and other personal belongings. At times, Johns actually preached in his work clothes, or the clothes he had worn while plowing in his field. After giving a commencement address at Virginia Seminary in the mid-1950s, Johns, without a trace of shame, stated to Henry Powell: "I'll bet you that in

as 'pretty light' and a person who makes them as 'a light sister' or 'a light brother'." See Reddick, *Crusader without Violence*, 7–8.

63. This was the case with King's closest aides in the movement as well. See Cotton, *If Your Back's Not Bent*, 62–63.

64. King, *My Life with Martin Luther King, Jr.*, 91 and 94. For similar observations, see Farris, *Through It All*, 83; Taylor Branch, *At Canaan's Edge: America in the King Years, 1965–68* (New York: Simon & Schuster, 2006), 265; King, *Stride toward Freedom*, 38 and 41; Branch, *Parting the Waters*, 12 and 16–17; Garrow, *Bearing the Cross*, 48; and Clayborne Carson, et al., eds., *The Papers of Martin Luther King, Jr., Volume II: Rediscovering Precious Values, July 1951–November 1955* (Berkeley: University of California Press, 1994), 29–30.

65. Branch, *Parting the Waters*, 10 and 18; Vaughn and Wills, eds., *Reflections on Our Pastor*, 39, 57, 70, and 94; Cotton, *If Your Back's Not Bent*, 63; Branch, *At Canaan's Edge*, 265; and King, *My Life with Martin Luther King, Jr.*, 60.

the history of American education, this was the first graduating class that was ever addressed by a speaker who didn't have any underwear on." Powell, who knew Johns rather well and occasionally drove him to his destinations, said that Johns's "kids were always after him about his clothes." Johns's son Billie told Powell once "that his father was going somewhere and looked so bad that Billie took off his shoes or his pants to give to his father. He absolutely didn't care."[66] It is not at all difficult to imagine the great time King, Jr. had talking about and laughing at Johns, especially since King, Jr. himself was always very fastidious about how he appeared in public. When it came to personal appearance, it was clear to King, Jr. that Johns was quite unlike the typical black preacher.[67]

Johns had other habits that must have come up whenever King, Jr. and Abernathy were joking and sharing funny stories about preachers. Johns often hitchhiked wherever he went to save money, and when he bought a car, he often forgot where he parked and was unable to locate it for days. One day, Abernathy dropped by Dexter Church to invite Pastor Johns to his home for lunch. The two agreed to go in Johns's car. As they walked from the church, Johns "suddenly stopped and snapped his fingers." "Ralph," he said, "I just remembered where my car is." "And where is that?," Abernathy asked. Johns replied: "I parked it on Auburn Avenue in Atlanta, Georgia."[68] Johns had other habits that were tailored more toward shocking and annoying the middle-class, elitist members at Dexter Church. He "cultivated a garden in the yard behind" the church "parsonage on South Jackson Street and set many worshippers' teeth on edge with a running description of the cultivation process." At one point, he stored collard greens, cabbage,

---

66. Branch, *Parting the Waters*, 11. Johns often said that "There is nothing in clothes. Some people think you got to wear it in the clothes. A man's mind is what you got to develop. It's not in the clothes." At other times, he scolded those among his people who delighted in dressing well, insisting that "You pride yourself on your expensive wardrobe and your brothers are naked." See Patrick L. Cooney and Henry W. Powell, *The Life and Times of Prophet Vernon Johns: Father of the Civil Rights Movement*, sponsored by the Vernon Johns Society, *http://www.vernonjohns.org/teal1001/vjtofe.html* (8 October 2004), chapter 16, page 6 and chapter 26, page 3.
67. Baldwin Interview with Abernathy (17 March 1987); and Baldwin Interview with Lenud (7 April 1987).
68. Abernathy, *And the Walls Came Tumbling Down*, 117–18 and 124.

and other vegetables in Dexter's basement and never hesitated to bring vegetables into the pulpit. One Sunday, Johns "pulled a huge cabbage and a plump onion from behind the pulpit and held them up for the congregation to inspect," insisting that he simply wanted to show his parishioners "what can be done on a tiny patch of land."[69] After preaching, he frequently sold greens, potatoes, onions, watermelons, hams, and sausage on the street in front of the church, and was known to eat watermelon in public and to sell them on the campus of Alabama State College.[70] It is reported that one Sunday, Johns "had a load of fish iced down on the back of a truck, and the odor, together with the traditionally low estate of the fishmonger, created a rebellion within the church."[71] King, Jr. got "a big kick" out of the lengths to which Johns was willing to go to outrage the folk at Dexter and to bring them down to earth.[72]

Although King, Jr. admired and appreciated the many gifts and talents Johns brought to the pulpit, he was both intrigued and amused by Johns's boldness and audacity in speaking his mind, often insulting and angering people. At times, Johns cursed in the pulpit, walked out if he disliked the music, or abruptly resigned if he could not have his way or felt that his authority as pastor was being undermined.[73] One Sunday, Dr. H. Councill Trenholm, a member of Dexter and the president of Alabama State College, took a seat in church and drew much attention when Johns called him out, so to speak. "I want to pause here in the service," Johns remarked, "until Dr. Trenholm can

69. Branch, *Parting the Waters*, 18 and 24; and Vaughn and Wills, eds., *Reflections on Our Pastor*, 105.
70. Vaughn and Wills, eds., *Reflections on Our Pastor*, 46; Cotton, *If Your Back's Not Bent*, 62; Branch, *Parting the Waters*, 17–18, 21, and 24; Branch, *At Canaan's Edge*, 265.
71. Branch, *Parting the Waters*, 18 and 24.
72. King, *My Life with Martin Luther King, Jr.*, 91; Baldwin Interview with Abernathy (17 March 1987); and Baldwin Interview with Lenud (7 April 1987).
73. Branch, *Parting the Waters*, 18–19 and 24; Vaughn and Wills, eds., *Reflections on Our Pastor*, 106; Abernathy, *And the Walls Came Tumbling Down*, 122; and Rufus Burrow, Jr., *Extremist for Love: Martin Luther King Jr., Man of Ideas and Nonviolent Social Action.* (Minneapolis: Fortress Press, 2014), 149, 164, and 166. Johns resigned at least five times before he was replaced by King at Dexter Church. Johns told his people "that there were greater men than he, but they could not get them," words he was forced to eat, so to speak, when King was selected as his replacement. See Branch, *Parting the Waters*, 15, 19 and 24; and Clayborne Carson, et al., eds., *The Papers of Martin Luther King, Jr., Volume V: Threshold of a New Decade, January 1959–December 1960* (Berkeley: University of California Press, 2005), 245.

get himself seated here on his semi-annual visit to the church." Utterly embarrassed and angered, Trenholm never returned to Dexter while Johns was pastor. Johns's outburst concerning another Dexter member, the prominent physician Dr. R. T. Adair, who was exonerated after killing his wife on suspicion of adultery, was even more shocking. "There is a murderer in the house," Johns cried on that particular Sunday. "God said, 'Thou shalt not kill.'" Johns was especially harsh in scolding and embarrassing those members known for poor church attendance, especially if they were otherwise "big shots" in the community. One day, Johns encountered Rufus Lewis, a Dexter member, funeral director, football coach, and "pioneer in voter registration," on the streets in Montgomery, and "drew a crowd" as he questioned Lewis about his activities and ended with this comment: "Lewis, this is fine, but you don't come to church. You better hope you don't die while I'm here, because if you do you'll have a hell of a funeral."[74]

After King, Jr. moved to Montgomery in 1954, he heard one amusing account after another about Johns's off-the-cuff and offensive comments and behavior from Dexter's members and from Ralph Abernathy, who had accepted a pastorate at the First Baptist Church in Montgomery a few years earlier. There were so many amusing stories about Johns that were known among blacks and some whites in Montgomery. King, Jr. made many of the stories and anecdotes a vital part of that body of humorous incidents that he routinely shared with preacher friends as he traveled around the country.[75]

The same was true of the many funny stories about Johns's actions while officiating at weddings and funerals. Coretta King recalled one such story that she heard from her husband, a story "that must have been as hilarious as it was disconcerting to those in attendance at a certain wedding":

One time Dr. Johns was performing a very staid and elegant wedding

---

74. Branch, *Parting the Waters*, 15.
75. Baldwin Interview with Abernathy (17 March 1987); Baldwin, *There is a Balm in Gilead*, 304; and Abernathy, *And the Walls Came Tumbling Down*, 116–28.

ceremony for one of the most outstanding Negro families in Montgomery. The church wedding had been proceeding, but just before the marriage was final, the minister stopped. He peered up and said, "I would like to announce that right after the wedding there will be a watermelon cutting in the church basement. It will be twenty-five cents a slice, and for all of you economical-minded people who order a half melon, the price will be a dollar fifty." Then, without stopping for a minute, Dr. Johns continued, "I now pronounce you man and wife." (Martin was a wonderful mimic, and when he would tell this story, you could just hear Dr. Johns' thick Virginia drawl.)[76]

Needless to say, the bride was reduced to tears, and she never forgot the casual and insensitive way in which Johns ruined her wedding.[77] While not unmindful of the pain that the couple must have felt, King, Jr., who had that rare ability to see humor in some of the most tragic experiences, found this story to be incredibly funny, for it exposed in graphic detail the quintessential Johns.

So it was also with Johns's performance at funerals. Johns was notorious for being abrasive in his language at funerals, especially if he felt the deceased had failed to live a morally and spiritually respectable life. Speaking over "the remains of an unfortunate Charlestonian who died in a brawl," Johns declared that "Anyone who stops by a grog shop with his paycheck instead of going straight home to his wife and family ought to be struck over the head with a ball bat and killed." Johns then said to those present, "The benediction will take place at the cemetery."[78] At another funeral, during which the family screamed and carried on, Johns instructed the undertaker to open up the casket so he could "see this man." "I ain't never seen this man, this niggra in church before," Johns asserted. "I just wanted to see what these folks are hollering about."[79] On yet another occasion, Johns literally hit the ceiling when he was approached about having the funeral of "a

76. This account is not included in the 1993 edition of Coretta King's book, which is the revised edition. See Coretta Scott King, *My Life with Martin Luther King, Jr.* (New York: Holt, Rinehart & Winston, 1969), 95–96; Burrow, *Extremist for Love*, 157; and Branch, *At Canaan's Edge*, 265.

77. Branch, *Parting the Waters*, 1001n902; and Burrow, *Extremist for Love*, 158.

78. Charles E. Boddie, *God's "Bad Boys": Eight Outstanding Black Preachers* (Valley Forge, PA: Judson Press, 1972), 72; and Burrow, *Extremist for love*, 164.

79. Lamont H. Yeakey, "The Montgomery, Alabama Bus Boycott, 1955–56," unpublished PhD dissertation, Columbia University, New York, New York (1979), 107; and Burrow, *Extremist for Love*, 164.

somewhat disreputable member of a very prominent family" at Dexter Church in the church sanctuary. "He didn't come to church when he was alive," said Johns to the church deacons, "why you want to drag him in here now?" The congregation voted at a church meeting to have the funeral over Johns's objections, and Johns, who "appeared to concede to the decision," "presided over the funeral." "Amos Jefferson lived a trifling, meaningless, worthless life," Johns declared to a stunned audience. Johns went on to say of the deceased: "He went around trying to be a bully and daring someone to cut his throat. The other night at the bar in the Bed Moore Hotel somebody obliged him. He lived like a dog. He died like a dog." Johns then waved his hand and added, "Undertaker, take the body."[80]

Apparently, King, Jr.'s "mock eulogies" of Ralph Abernathy, Wyatt Tee Walker, Andrew Young, and other close associates, occasionally delivered in closed-door meetings to ease any tension they felt before facing white mobs in street demonstrations, were inspired in large measure by these stories about Johns. Young would write about this some years later. "Some of us are going to lose our lives in Birmingham," King, Jr. would say, according to Young, "actually joking about the danger ahead." King, Jr. would "tease us," Young continued, "by telling us how he was going to preach at our funerals. . . . He would then go around the room, taking some embarrassing aspect of each of our lives that he threatened to use in our eulogies." "Martin loved to preach our eulogies in that manner, saying openly and frankly the most humiliating things about us," Young further explained, "preaching our eulogies like Vernon Johns would preach if we had made him mad." Young went on to report that "when Martin started to sound like Vernon Johns, I knew we were in for a rough time."[81] Abernathy must have had a similar feeling about King, Jr. on such occasions, for he, much like Young, saw King, Jr. as "a mimic, with an ear for peculiarities of speech and an eye for facial mannerisms and gestures."[82]

80. Andrew Young, An Easy Burden: The Civil Rights Movement and the Transformation of America (New York: HarperCollins Publishers, Inc., 1996), 195.
81. Ibid.; and Baldwin, There is a Balm in Gilead, 299–300.

There was yet another side to Johns's personality that King, Jr. found not only amusing, but most instructive, and that had to do with Johns's assault on both the Negroes' failure to sufficiently challenge racial and economic inequality and the whites' refusal to honestly confront and address their racism. Johns kept his people laughing at themselves and their seeming inability to resist segregation and to overcome their almost total dependence on white people.[83] On one occasion prior to the Montgomery bus boycott, he boarded the city bus, paid his fare, and refused to move to the back, thus infuriating the white bus driver, who threatened to put him off the bus. "Obviously this driver doesn't want us on the bus, so let's all get off," said Johns to the rest of the black passengers. No one moved. With biting humor, Johns later noted:

> I saw the ugliest woman that day on the bus. I could not forget that face. I saw her a few days later, and asked, "What did they say about me after I got off the bus?" She laughed, "he-he-he-he-he." I said to her, "I did not ask you about 'he-he-he-he'." I asked "what did they say after I got off the bus." She told me, "They said you ought to knowed better."[84]

On the many occasions Johns shared this account, he always ended on a sad note that almost always brought laughter as well. "Even God can't free people who behave like that," he declared, sometimes shaking his head.[85] Johns complained that "everywhere I go in the South the Negro is forced to choose between his hide and his soul." "Mostly he chooses his hide," Johns concluded. "I'm going to tell him that his hide is not worth it."[86]

Johns put forth countless quips about his people's sad economic

82. Abernathy, *And the Walls Came Tumbling Down*, 468–69; and Baldwin Interview with Abernathy (17 March 1987).
83. King saw Johns as standing in the tradition of Booker T. Washington, particularly in terms of "the pull yourselves up by your own bootstraps" philosophy. But Johns also stood in the tradition of W. E. B. DuBois, especially in terms of his advocacy for both civil rights and economic advancement. In a practical sense, Johns came down on the side of both Washington and DuBois. See King, *Stride toward Freedom*, 38–40.
84. Abernathy, *And the Walls Came Tumbling Down*, 117; and Vaughn and Wills, eds., *Reflections on Our Pastor*, 45–45.
85. Abernathy, *And the Walls Came Tumbling Down*, 117; Vaughn and Wills, eds., *Reflections on Our Pastor*, 45–46; and Baldwin Interview with Abernathy (17 March 1987).
86. Branch, *Parting the Waters*, 23. Johns said on another occasion that "The Negro will send his soul to hell to save his hide, and his hide is not worth it." See Vaughn and Wills, eds., *Reflections on Our Pastor*, 47.

state. "If every Negro in the USA dropped dead today," he exclaimed, "it would not affect any important business activity." "You said you want a definition of perpetual motion?," he asked in his usual challenge to black people. "Give the Negro a Cadillac and tell him to park it on some land he owns." One Sunday, Johns flatly stated to those in his congregation, many of whom were staring at him because he had no shoelaces, that "I'll wear shoestrings when Negroes start making them." "In a most bold and totally unashamed way," he said to students, staff, and faculty at Virginia State College, "You sit rather arrogantly up here on this hill, and you walk through the town acting as though you are oblivious to the fact that you can't even urinate under your own auspices."[87] Johns's numerous quips about the sad economic state of his people obviously carried shades of humor, and King, Jr. would have been among the first to acknowledge this, but he, in the midst of all the fun and roaring laughter, sensed that Johns was making profound points about the need for black people to assume primary responsibility for their own liberation, uplift, and empowerment. King, Jr., Ralph Abernathy, and others in his SCLC were helped immensely, spiritually, intellectually, emotionally, and otherwise, by both the humor and the wisdom that Johns brought to his diagnosis of the black condition.[88]

Equally important were the great pleasure and insight King, Jr. must have derived from the humorous stories about Johns's fearless encounters with whites and Jim Crow in Montgomery. Johns's rather amusing account of the circumstances surrounding his experience while boarding a city bus, during which "he responded with defiance rather than fear," has already been mentioned.[89] Segregation was ideally suited for his brand of wit and humor. During one week in 1949, Johns posted his upcoming sermon topic, "Segregation after Death,"

87. Branch, *Parting the Waters*, 16 and 18; Cotton, *If Your Back's Not Bent*, 63; and Burrow, *Extremist for Love*, 159.
88. King, *Stride toward Freedom*, 38–40; Cotton, *If Your Back's Not Bent*, 63; Young, *An Easy Burden*, 194–96; Baldwin Interview with Abernathy (17 March 1987); and Baldwin Interview with Lenud (7 April 1987).
89. Abernathy, *And the Walls Came Tumbling Down*, 117; Branch, *Parting the Waters*, 14; and Vaughn and Wills, eds., *Reflections on Our Pastor*, 45–46.

in bold letters on the large bulletin board at Dexter Church, causing a mixture of amusement and uneasiness among blacks and curiosity, suspicion, and discomfort on the part of whites in the city. He preached the sermon despite attempts by the police chief and his men to intimidate and instill fear in him.[90] Johns posted other controversial sermon titles and messages on his church's bulletin board from time to time, such as "It's Safe to Murder Negroes in Montgomery" and "When the Rapist is White," thus highlighting the cruelty and absurdity of the racist system. On one occasion, he actually walked into and requested service at a white restaurant, much to the shock and anger of the white patrons. When told by the attendant that "We don't serve niggers here," the outspoken minister declared, "That's fine because I don't eat them," and he proceeded to order a chicken sandwich and a drink. The attendant made the sandwich, but slowly poured the drink on the counter in front of Johns. "There is something in me that doesn't like being pushed around," Johns uttered, "and it's starting to work." That remark compelled several customers to run to their cars for guns, and Johns was chased out of the restaurant. He later told his people at Dexter: "I pronounced the shortest blessing of my life over that sandwich. I said 'Goddam it.'"[91]

So much of Johns's wit and humor revealed, unmistakably, a real contempt for white people and their attitudes, values, and practices, and this would not have escaped King, Jr., for he had detected this same spirit in his father and in countless other Negroes who recklessly and singlehandedly struck blows against a system that only the force of the many could topple. Culturally speaking, Johns epitomized the image of "the bad nigger," who fearlessly challenged the racial convention of his time, and also of Brer Rabbit, who, though smaller and less powerful than his foes, used his good sense and quick wit to humiliate them, or to make them feel awkward and foolish.[92] Johns was a master of

90. For a more detailed account of this story, see Branch, *Parting the Waters*, 12; and Burrow, *Extremist for Love*, 153–54.
91. Branch, *Parting the Waters*, 12, 14–15, and 22–24; Abernathy, *And the Walls Came Tumbling Down*, 120; and Baldwin Interview with Abernathy (17 March 1987).
92. Since slavery, blacks in the South had lived vicariously through both "the bad nigger" and Brer Rabbit, and it is not difficult to imagine blacks in Montgomery living vicariously through

"the humor of absurdity," and he gave his people reasons to laugh at themselves, at white people, and the whole system of racial apartheid in the South, and this helps explain why so many stories about him became a part of the repertory of King, Jr.[93] King, Jr. discovered in Johns what he had detected in generations of black preachers, and that was, among other things, the capacity to inject humor into even the most painful circumstances.

The funny stories King, Jr. shared about the Negro preacher Hilly Thomas of Atlanta were not particularly significant in this regard, but they, too, yielded certain insights into the nature of the black experience in the South as King, Jr. understood it. Unlike Johns, Thomas lacked formal education and was not known for inattentiveness to dress and appearance, for constant rants about his people's cowardice, complacency, and irresponsibility, for directing harsh pronouncements to whites, and for personal attacks on and challenges to Jim Crow policies and practices. Thomas "had a stutter that became increasingly pronounced as he became more and more excited," and he "would mess up verbs, nouns, and sentences," and King, Jr., according to his long-time friend Philip Lenud, "really got a big charge out of that." Lenud added: "Martin talked about how this preacher would announce, while extending the call to Christian discipleship to the unsaved after his Sunday sermons, that there *is* two seats up here at the front—'*are* there one?'"[94] Ralph Abernathy recalled

Johns, despite the sense among some that his actions could possibly bring the wrath of the white community down upon them. For the best treatments of the adventures of both "the bad nigger" and Brer Rabbit types, See Levine, *Black Culture and Black Consciousness*, 85, 106, 131, 301, 310–12, 361 and 413–15; Sterling A. Brown, "Negro Folk Expression," *Phylon*, Vol. 11, no. 4 (4th Quarter, 1950), 322–23; and Sterling Stuckey, "Through the Prism of Folklore: The Black Ethos in Slavery," in Eric Foner, *America's Black Past: Reader in Afro-American History* (New York: Harper & Row, Publishers, 1970), 109.

93. In his treatment of folk wit and humor from slavery up to the 1940s, Lawrence Levine stresses the psychic needs of blacks, which included the need to laugh at themselves, whites, and their condition. This is much of what Levine has in mind when he discusses "the humor of absurdity." See Levine, *Black Culture and Black Consciousness*, 300–301, 314, and 317. Also see Baldwin Interview with Abernathy (17 March 1987); Baldwin Interview with Lenud (7 April 1987); and King, *My Life with Martin Luther King, Jr.*, 91 and 94.

94. Abernathy, *And the Walls Came Tumbling Down*, 468; Baldwin Interview with Lenud (7 April 1987); and Baldwin, *There is a Balm in Gilead*, 307–8.

a very interesting and humorous story King, Jr. loved to tell about an experience he had with Thomas in a classroom setting:

> As a service to the black religious community, Martin used to teach a course in grammar to seminarians. Some of the older preachers would also sit in, just to give them a little extra polish; and Hilly Thomas was among them. One day Martin was dealing with pronoun case endings, and more particularly with the question of when to use "I" and when to use "me." Having finished his explanation he put a hypothetical question to the class: "Let's say you've been out too late at night, you come home at 2:00 A. M., and you find your wife has locked the door. You knock and in a minute you hear her voice saying, 'Who is it?' Which do you say? 'It is I,' or 'It is me'?" Hilly waved his arms and begged to be allowed to answer. "If I stayed out to t-t-two in the m-m-morning and knocked on the d-door and m-m-my wife asked m-me, 'Who is it?' I'd answer," he said in his most seductive voice, "*B-b-baby*, this is m-m-me."[95]

King, Jr. remembered yet another occasion when Hilly Thomas was driving his Cadillac in downtown Atlanta and mistakenly rear ended a white man's car. Angered by the incident, the white man quickly exited the vehicle and started yelling, "Nigger, why did you hit my car? I have my mother in this car." Thomas responded, "*Are* your m-m-mama hurt?" "No Nigger," said the white man, "but you hit my car and almost knocked my mama out." "I s-s-said, are your m-m-mama hurt?," repeated Thomas. "Nigger, if you had hurt my mother, I would beat your brains out," the white man added. At this point, the old preacher lost his temper, pointed his finger at the white man, and spoke in a loud voice: "Wait, let m-m-me tell y'all w-w-white folks something r-r-right now. If y'all don't get the hell away from h-h-here, m-m-mama's son are gonna be hurt."[96] "Martin was just rolling with these jokes," Philip Lenud recounted. "He knew so many humorous stories about this preacher." Ralph Abernathy agreed, noting that "Martin had a repertoire of Hilly stories that could keep people laughing for hours."[97]

95. Abernathy, *And the Walls Came Tumbling Down*, 469; Baldwin Interview with Abernathy (17 March 1987); and Baldwin, *There is a Balm in Gilead*, 308.

96. Baldwin Interview with Abernathy (17 March 1987); and Baldwin, *There is a Balm in Gilead*, 308–9.

97. Baldwin Interview with Lenud (7 April 1987); Abernathy, *And the Walls Came Tumbling Down*, 468–69; Baldwin Interview with Abernathy (17 March 1987); and Baldwin, *There is a Balm in Gilead*, 309. Interestingly enough, Coretta King mentioned her husband's body of humor relative to

When surrounded by his close, inner circle of ministers in the SCLC, King, Jr. sometimes delighted in doing imitations of Thomas's pulpit mannerisms and preaching style. Abernathy related this account:

> Martin used to recite an entire sermon he once heard Hilly Thomas preach at Chapel Hill Baptist Church on Northside Drive. "Hilly began," Martin said, "by announcing, 'I'm going to preach this m-morning on the t-text, 'God is Love.' And m-my subject is: 'is.' Now 'is' is not a noun; 'is' is not a verb. 'Is' is just 'is.' Like 'is you got your ticket?' 'Is you going?' 'Is' is just 'is'. . . ." At that point Martin would be screaming, whooping, and waving his arms and the rest of us would be on the floor, holding our sides. He could continue the sermon until we gasped for breath and begged him to stop. When I finally met Hilly Thomas one day at Operation Breadbasket headquarters, I broke into a big grin the moment he opened his mouth. Martin had him down so perfectly I almost had to leave the room.[98]

Nothing was more hilarious and pleasurable for King, Jr. than imitating preachers, but he usually did this only in the presence of his closest aides, almost all of whom were preachers themselves. "He had a perfect sense of timing and he instinctively knew what was funny," said Abernathy of King, Jr. Abernathy went on to acknowledge that "Some people have that gift and some people don't. He had it. I'm convinced that if he had wanted to be a stand-up comic he could have been almost as famous in that role." Speaking specifically to King, Jr.'s skills as a mimic, Abernathy further asserted that "When he imitated somebody the resemblance was always uncanny and usually extremely funny. I have seen a room of staff members helpless with laughter as he launched into one of his routines."[99]

Three points should be explained in greater detail here if King, Jr.'s

Vernon Johns but not Hilly Thomas, an omission that should not be trivialized in view of her stress on King's robust sense of humor. See King, *My Life with Martin Luther King, Jr.*, 59, 89, and 91.

98. Abernathy, *And the Walls Came Tumbling Down*, 469; and Abernathy, "My Old Friend Martin," 6. Abernathy shared a similar version of what was perhaps another sermon King heard Hilly Thomas deliver. See Baldwin Interview with Abernathy (17 March 1987); and Baldwin, *There is a Balm in Gilead*, 308. King's ghostwriter Al Duckett also recalled "King's 'fantastically funny impersonations of other people.'" This capacity on King's part actually supports Lawrence Levine's contention that mimicking and role-playing remained "chief mechanisms of black laughter long after slavery, not only in the trickster tales which continued to be popular but in the entire body of jokes which the freedmen and their descendants told one another." See Garrow, *Bearing the Cross*, 550; and Levine, *Black Culture and Black Consciousness*, 301.

99. Abernathy, *And the Walls Came Tumbling Down*, 468; and Abernathy, "My Old Friend Martin," 6.

tendency to make fun of preachers—and especially, Hilly Thomas—is to be properly digested and understood. First, King, Jr.'s imitations of and funny stories about preachers, as noted briefly earlier, might be called a form of "intragroup humor" or "inner circle humor," and not "on-stage humor."[100] In other words, it was humor that found its fullest expression when King, Jr. was sitting around with preacher friends in hotel rooms and other more private settings, engaging in "preacher talk." In such settings, King, Jr. could freely exercise his skills as a preacher-entertainer without opening himself to the opinions and judgments of the average lay persons, and especially, those in Negro churches, many of whom were not likely to understand that kind of playfulness on the part of one whom they viewed as a no-nonsense man of God.[101]

The second point is that King, Jr. was not the kind of arrogant, snobbish, self-centered PhD who looked down upon preachers who were not as well-trained, respected, and celebrated as he was, and he had no appreciation for humor that was insensitive, cruel, and demeaning to them or anyone else.[102] Although Hilly Thomas fit the mold of the typical old-time, unlearned southern Negro preacher, King had a high regard for his common sense and mother wit. He respected the wit and practical wisdom of the slave preacher who, as he put it, "didn't know anything about Plato or Aristotle," but "knew that the God he had heard about" was "not a God who would subject some of His children, and exalt the others."[103] King, Jr. never intended to

100. The term "intragroup humor" comes from Lawrence Levine, who uses it in reference to the kind of humor that circulates and is understood only or primarily among black people. See Levine, *Black Culture and Black Consciousness*, 322. Ralph Abernathy supports the view that King joked and teased when he was not on the stage or platform. See Abernathy, *And the Walls Came Tumbling Down*, 468.
101. "'I Remember Martin,'" 38; Abernathy, "My Old Friend Martin," 6; Young, *An Easy Burden*, 194–96 and 463–64; and Andrew Young, *A Way Out of No Way: The Spiritual Memoirs of Andrew Young* (Nashville: Thomas Nelson Publishers, 1994), 75.
102. Humor of this nature would have been inconsistent with King's personal idealism, which categorically affirmed the dignity and worth, and indeed the sacredness, of all human personality. See "'I Remember Martin,'" 33–34, 36, 38, and 40; and Carson et al., eds., *King Papers*, IV, 541.
103. Martin Luther King, Jr., "Is the Universe Friendly?," unpublished version of a sermon, Ebenezer Baptist Church, Atlanta, Georgia (12 December 1965), King Center Library and Archives, 6; Carson, et al., eds., *King Papers*, I, 281; King, *Stride toward Freedom*, 63; Baldwin, *The Voice of Conscience*, 108; and Baldwin, *There is a Balm in Gilead*, 308n115.

reduce Hilly Thomas, who stood squarely in this tradition, to the kind of ignorant and unenlightened Negro religious figure so prominent in much of America's folklore.[104] When focusing on Thomas, King, Jr.'s humor was never couched in terms that were disrespectful of the man, though it is doubtful that it would have been understood and acceptable to most in the Negro church. His humor was simply that of a man who enjoyed teasing, joking, and laughing. As Ralph Abernathy put it, "Martin was fun-loving, and when he was offstage you could usually find him telling a joke or teasing somebody."[105]

It should also be noted that King, Jr. never really disassociated himself from Hilly Thomas, Vernon Johns, and other preachers who were both subjects and objects of his humor. When he laughed at them, he was also, in some strange way, laughing at himself because he, like them, was a preacher of the gospel committed to what he considered the highest spiritual and ethical ideal. This point must be taken into account in any serious and credible study of King, Jr.'s preacher-related and church-related humor. His spiritual and emotional security was such that he was never reluctant to take a long, humorous look at himself. He was known to joke about and laugh at the way he looked at times. According to his long-time friend Philip Lenud, "Martin had this idea that he was too short and not very good looking, but he was really a handsome guy."[106] King, Jr.'s wife, Coretta remembered times when King, Jr. poked fun at the very thought of having to dress in formal wear, as was the case when he had to wear "striped trousers and a gray tailcoat," which he laughingly referred to as "a morning suit" with "funny-looking pants," to receive the Nobel Peace Prize in December 1964. "Martin kept fussing and making funny comments about having to wear such a ridiculous thing," she reminisced. "Finally,

---

104. The old-time Negro preacher has been widely portrayed as one who virtually celebrated ignorance, and King knew this well. For a discussion of this kind of mischaracterization, see H. Beecher Hicks, Jr., *Images of the Black Preacher: The Man Nobody Knows* (Valley Forge, PA: Judson Press, 1977), 31–33.

105. Abernathy, *And the Walls Came Tumbling Down*, 468.

106. King had a habit of standing on his tiptoes when he really got into his sermons and speeches, as was the case with the "I Have a Dream" oration, and one wonders if this had anything at all to do, from a psychological point of view, with his uneasiness about his height. See Baldwin Interview with Lenud (7 April 1987); and Baldwin, *There is a Balm in Gilead*, 309.

he said, 'I vow never to wear one of these things again.' He never did."[107] Dorothy Cotton recalled the hearty laughter that followed a wardrobe malfunction King had had while addressing an enthusiastic crowd:

> He was making one of his speeches and, as was his style, as he approached the end there was the crescendo and the words we heard so often. "Free at last, free at last!! Thank God Almighty, I'm free at last." As he raised his arms, we noticed that the seam of his sleeve had ripped apart. We laughed about that for a long time, but he laughed about it more than we did. Actually, he was a careful dresser and very well-groomed. That's why it was so funny.[108]

There were concerns even more personal that evoked King, Jr.'s humor. Dorothy Cotton reported that "Sometimes Martin would joke about the fact that many people couldn't seem to pronounce his name: something like 'Maphin' or 'Marfin Luther' would come out." "He would laugh heartily as he reflected with us, 'I never realized my name was such a tongue twister for so many people!'" Cotton added.[109] After a private audience with Pope Paul VI in Rome in 1964, King, Jr. jokingly referred to the irony surrounding the meeting, asserting that "things have really changed a lot when a pope will agree to see a fellow by the name of Martin Luther."[110] King was frequently called so many bad names by his enemies, such as "Martin Lucifer Coon" and "that Nigger preacher," and the fact that he made his name the butt of occasional humor spoke volumes about his being comfortable with who and what he was.

King, Jr. was surprisingly free-spirited and playful when reflecting on his experiences in jail or on unwise decisions he made concerning the movement. When fellow activist Charles Jones approached King about going to jail in Albany in 1962 to highlight the injustice of a

---

107. King, *My Life with Martin Luther King, Jr.*, 10; and McDonald, *Secretary to a King*, 76. King's friend Lawrence Reddick recalled comments about King's "conservative good taste in dress." "He favors gray or brown suits," Reddick wrote. "He does not care for formal attire, has no tails, but does have a tuxedo and a light summer tux jacket." See Reddick, *Crusader without Violence*, 3–4.
108. "'I Remember Martin,'" 34.
109. Cotton, *If Your Back's Not Bent*, 260–61.
110. King, "An Address at the National Conference on Civil Rights"; Baldwin, *There is a Balm in Gilead*, 309; and King, *My Life with Martin Luther King, Jr.*, 274–75.

court injunction designed to co-opt the campaign there, and as a demonstration of the vitality of his leadership in the movement, King, Jr., who actually had no fear of the threat of arrest, jokingly responded: "Chuck, do I have to?" King, Jr. went on to joke "about how difficult it was even to shave in jail," and about "how as a pastor he was accustomed to having his things laid out for him."[111] A year later, when King, Jr. was released from the Birmingham jail, his staff members, thinking "that he should have a hero's welcome" in Atlanta, recommended using "a motorcade of Cadillacs." When informed of the plan, King, Jr. responded with raw humor, saying to his wife Coretta, "'Now, what would I look like coming back from jail in a Cadillac?" He went on to instruct his wife to "just drive our car to the airport, and I'll drive you home."[112] King, Jr. was equally humorous when speaking about his decision to launch a movement in a city such as Chicago during the winter of 1966. Forced to move to "three different hotels in a vain attempt to find warmth," he laughed and joked about "the hawk" and how rough it was on him and his staff.[113]

Even more serious matters that had to do with threats to King, Jr.'s personal well-being and life were not off-limits when it came to his humor. After King, Jr. was stabbed with a letter opener in Harlem in 1958 by Izola Curry, a forty-two-year-old deranged black woman, the police brought Curry into King, Jr.'s hospital room so he could identify her. Before King, Jr. could say anything, Curry said, "Yah, that's him. I'm going to report him to my lawyers." This struck King, Jr. "as being so funny," and "he smiled in spite of the terrible pain."[114] In the presence of his closest colleagues, King, Jr. even appeared to joke at times about his own death—a tendency they, for obvious reasons, never found funny.[115] "But that was the way he was all his life—playful—even to the very last day," wrote Coretta King. "In the

111. Branch, *Parting the Waters*, 614–15.
112. King, *My Life with Martin Luther King, Jr.*, 165; and Baldwin, *There is a Balm in Gilead*, 244–45 and 247.
113. McDonald, *Secretary to a King*, 93–94.
114. King, *My Life with Martin Luther King, Jr.*, 154–55.
115. Cotton, *If Your Back's Not Bent*, 263–64.

midst of the most serious times, Martin would bring fun into our lives with his ability to see humor in even the most difficult situations."[116]

King, Jr. never took himself and his struggles too seriously, and was capable of even self-deprecating humor. He joked about being whipped by his father up to age fifteen, about receiving too much credit for successes in the movement, about his fears and inadequacies, and also about his eating habits, his waistline, and even his "hard head."[117] It was the kind of self-deprecating humor that diffused critics. King, Jr. actually reached a point where he knew he could not live up to the image of perfection that so many of his admirers sought to bestow upon him, and so, he surrendered his entire life to a type of self-critical analysis that highlighted his finiteness while also lending itself to wit and humor.[118] King, Jr. spoke to this in a version of his sermon, "The Three Dimensions of a Complete Life," which he preached at the New Covenant Baptist Church in Chicago in April 1967, almost a year before his death. In that sermon, which drew lively responses and much laughter from the congregation, King, Jr. declared:

> I was not willing to accept myself. I was not willing to accept my tools and my limitations. But you know, in life we're called upon to do this. A Ford car trying to be a Cadillac is absurd, but if a Ford will accept itself as a Ford, *(All right)* it can do many things that a Cadillac could never do; It can get in parking spaces that a Cadillac can never get in. [*Laughter*] And in life some of us are Fords and some of us are Cadillacs. *(Yes)* Moses says in "Green Pastures," "Lord, I ain't much, but I is all I got." [*Laughter*] The principle of self-acceptance is a basic principle in life.[119]

Clearly, King, Jr.'s amazing capacity to joke about and laugh at himself was owing to a kind of unequivocal affirmation, acceptance, and celebration of his own individuality and personhood. He had much fun thinking and talking about himself because he had come to terms with his essential humanity. This also explains why King, Jr. was not

116. King, *My Life with Martin Luther King, Jr.*, 89 and 155; Baldwin, *There is a Balm in Gilead*, 306; and "'I Remember Martin,'" 38.
117. Reddick, *Crusader without Violence*, 53; Baldwin, *There is a Balm in Gilead*, 309; Carson, et al., eds., *King Papers*, IV, 227; and Carson, et al., eds., *King Papers*, V, 360.
118. David Garrow has offered rich insights into "King's intensely self-critical nature." See Garrow, *Bearing the Cross*, 587–88.
119. Carson and Holloran, eds., *A Knock at Midnight*, 124–25.

threatened, discomforted, or intimidated by others who delighted in making him the target of their own humor. Because he was widely projected in the image of "the black hero" in the 1960s, he naturally found a place in black comedy. The following anecdote from that period offers a certain perspective on the man who was known in some circles as "De Lawd":

> Two Negroes meet on a street corner in Atlanta, Georgia, and strike up a conversation.
> First speaker: "Boy, did you hear 'bout dey gonna move de Rock o' Gibraltar?"
> Second speaker: "Man, is you done loose you' mind? You know dey ain't nobody can move de Rock o'Gibraltar but God."
> First speaker: "Yeah, dey is gonna move it, too."
> Second speaker: "Well, who gonna move it?"
> First speaker: "Martin Luther King, dat's who."
> Second speaker: "Where he gonna put it?"[120]

King, Jr. was featured in the humor of some of the most well-known black and white comics in his day, including Moms Mabley and Alan King. Mabley told a lot of jokes portraying herself as a regular attendant at important conferences where she offered advice to US presidents and other world leaders, and King, Jr.'s name surfaced in one of her comic poems, "The Dreams of a Southern Governor." Here, Mabley described "the anguish of a bigoted politician who dreams that Martin Luther King has been elected President, that all of Congress was colored, that Negroes have taken over the government, and that the tables are now turned":

> I rushed over to the Capitol.
> And this is an honest fact:
> I started in the front door
> And Roy Wilkins made me go around to the back.[121]

Alan King, a white comedian, knew and spent time with Dr. King while

120. John A. Ricks, "'De Lawd' Descends and is Crucified: Martin Luther King, Jr., in Albany, Georgia," *Journal of Southwest Georgia History*, Vol. 2 (1984), 3–14; J. Mason Brewer, *American Negro Folklore* (New York: Quadrangle/The New York Times, 1968), 48; and Levine, *Black Culture and Black Consciousness*, 406–7.
121. See Levine, *Black Culture and Black Consciousness*, 364.

participating in fundraising efforts for the movement. At a benefit for King, Jr.'s SCLC in Harlem, New York, King delighted "the all-black audience" with a playful swipe at the civil rights leader who shared his last name. "Before I go any further," said the comedian King, "you should understand that you've been backing the wrong King. He wants to get you into Woolworth's. You stick with me, I'll get you into '21,'" which was quite suggestive coming from one who often played craps in Las Vegas. According to Dr. King's friend Harry Belafonte, who was also present that evening, "The crowd went crazy."[122]

Laughing at oneself is one way of being playful, and this was most certainly the case with Dr. King. His capacity for what might be called self-directed humor seemed at times almost inexhaustible. He often found both pleasure and relaxation by laughing at himself and others. He also experienced a much-needed release from the disappointments, anger, frustration, and stress that too often clouded his days.

C. Betcha Can't Jail Us All: Folk Wit, Humor, and the Movement

As Martin Luther King, Jr. studied the history of the black freedom struggle dating back to slavery, he discovered that his people had always employed wit and humor in order to survive and prosper in the racist society in which they found themselves. King, Jr. developed this sense as he reflected on the "familiar stereotypes of the Uncle Tom," the legend of the folk hero John Henry, and the adventures of Brer Rabbit as revealed in slave tales. "The extensive use of violence, ridicule, and distortion often required that the Negro develop skill in the pretense of self-deprecation," King, Jr. declared. "Frequently he played the fool to make a fool of his oppressor."[123] King, Jr. brought

---

122. Belafonte, *My Song*, 249.
123. King, "True Dignity," 7. Although King did not specifically mention Brer Rabbit in this piece, the drift of his discussion leaves little doubt that he knew about this colorful figure, which skillfully used wit and humor to gain the advantage over his bigger and more powerful foes, and about how the slaves lived vicariously through him. Don McKinney has an interesting essay in which he locates the roots of "the methods, ideals, and symbols" King exploited in the Birmingham campaign in "a moral heritage" that is embodied to a considerable degree "in black folklore." McKinney convincingly argues that King's Birmingham "protest was overtly moralistic in emphasizing freedom and the justice of equality and exhibited a methodological connection with the Brer Rabbit tales by relying on cunning and the 'translation of power' to achieve moral ends."

this and other insights to bear on his assessment of how large numbers of his people thought and behaved in the South during his time, especially in view of their own vulnerability and will to survive in the context of a white dominated society. A case in point was his account of an exchange between a Negro maid and her white mistress during the Montgomery bus boycott, the humorous thrust of which was, in his opinion, unmistakable:

> One old domestic, an influential matriarch to many young relatives in Montgomery, was asked by her wealthy employer, "Isn't this bus boycott terrible?" The old lady responded: "Yes, ma'am, it sure is. And I just told all my young'uns that this kind of thing is white folks' business and we just stay off the buses till they get this whole thing settled."[124]

Unable to express support for the boycott by direct and overt statement, the maid framed her response in terms that apparently escaped full detection by her mistress, and it offered clues into the power of both folk wit and the humor of absurdity. During southern civil rights campaigns, King, Jr. met many black common laborers, like this maid, who pretended to accept Jim Crow and its underlying beliefs and values while actually harboring resentment toward the whole system. Some supported the movement with small donations, by providing food for activists, and in other rather discreet ways while, at the same time, refusing, out of a fear of economic and political reprisals, to reveal their true character to their white bosses. It was out of this tendency toward caution, shrewdness, and deception that the cycle of trickster tales, focusing largely on Brer Rabbit, had developed generations earlier among slaves, and King, Jr. knew this. While his own appreciation for folk wit, humor, and laughter reflected his sense of that history and culture, it also owed much to his personal experiences with ordinary black folk who maneuvered and survived as

---

See Don S. McKinney, "Brer Rabbit and Brother Martin Luther King, Jr.: The Folktale Background of the Birmingham Protest," in *Journal of Religious Thought*, Vol. 46, no. 2 (Winter–Spring, 1989–1990), 42–52.

124. King, *Stride toward Freedom*, 79 and 82; and Carson, ed., *The Autobiography of Martin Luther King, Jr.*, 66.

best they could without exposing too much of themselves, and without allowing their spirits to be broken by their tormentors.[125]

These people were the very embodiment of the kind of wit and humor King, Jr. considered vital and necessary in the context of the civil rights struggle, and this is one of many reasons why he connected so well with them while also availing himself to their real life stories. King, Jr.'s appeal to and influence on them were never confined to merely a clever and wise use of nonviolent tactics. He was also known to employ sharp and ready wit and raw humor as he demonstrated his own resourcefulness in not only outthinking, outsmarting, and exploiting the gullibility of white opponents at all levels of society, but also, in easing fears and uneasiness among blacks who joined him in challenging the structures of white power and supremacy. This is precisely what happened in Birmingham in 1963 when King, Jr., "who usually hid his gifts for mimicry and funny stories from the public, skillfully used humor to defuse the crowd's nervousness at the prospect of facing" Bull Connor's "dirty tricks." Once Connor and his cronies realized that they could not prevent the forward march of peaceful protesters, King, Jr. reasoned, they would "have to say":

> "We're going to have to bring an end to our excesses for this can't stop these people. We tried to use water on them and we soon discovered that they were used to water for they were Methodists or Episcopalians or other denominations and they had to be sprinkled. And even those who hadn't been sprinkled happen to have been Baptists and not only did they stand up in the water, they went under the water." And dogs—well, I'll tell you, when I was growing up I was dog bitten for nothing, so I don't mind being bitten by a dog for standing up for freedom. And I was down there going to court the other day when we were in jail and they took us into City Hall for court under Brown. And I looked over there and saw a tank. A tank was sitting over there, and I didn't know what – and I said, "What is that?" Somebody said, "Well, that's Bull Connor's tank." And you know it's a white tank. Now, I want to say tonight that they can bring their dogs out, they can get his white tank, and our black faces will stand up before the white tank.[126]

125. King, "True Dignity," 1–10; King, Stride toward Freedom, 79; and Carson, ed., The Autobiography of Martin Luther King, Jr., 66.
126. Richard Lischer, The Preacher King: Martin Luther King Jr. and the Word that Moved America (New York: Oxford University Press, 1995), 247–48; and Martin Luther King, Jr., "Crisis and a Political

King, Jr. used the power of humor in this instance to help those around him to overcome the crippling effects of fear, and, as was always the case, it did not get "out of hand or become an end in itself." In this and other black Christian contexts in which he routinely operated, "laughter in the face of danger, like praise in a time of sorrow," represented "trust in God's authority over earthly rulers."[127] It also served as "a compensating mechanism" which enabled protesters to face white mob violence and brutality without backing down or striking back, and without succumbing ultimately to spiritual and emotional death.[128]

King, Jr. found that humor was an important and necessary way of bringing his people together to not only experience joy and laughter, but also, to understand their common plight and obligations, and this could not have been more important for one who valued human community as the highest ethical ideal. The culture within the movement was quite conducive to the galvanizing power of his brand of humor. King, Jr. enjoyed telling jokes and funny stories "that pointed out black people's ingenuity in dealing with difficult situations,"[129] and he did so to delight, unite, and inspire fellow activists at critical moments during the movement. Wherever and whenever he found himself among groups of his people—in churches, jail cells, on the streets, in the homes of unheralded foot soldiers—he engaged them with remarks and stories that were pleasantly humorous or jesting. King, Jr.'s humor enhanced his sociability, or his already remarkable ability to connect with people in times of struggle and disappointment, and he was able to develop close personal relationships while retaining the loyalty and affections of countless supporters of the civil rights

Rally in Alabama," unpublished version of a speech, Sixteenth Street Baptist Church, Birmingham, Alabama (3 May 1963), King Center Library and Archives, 2–4.

127. Lischer, *The Preacher King: Martin Luther King, Jr.*, 248; and King, "Crisis and a Political Rally in Alabama," 2–4.

128. This insight has benefitted enormously from Lawrence Levine's discussion of black humor as "a compensating mechanism," or as part of that creative energy that has always meant "emotional salvation." See Levine, *Black Culture and Black Consciousness*, 299. Levine also draws on Jessie Fauset, "The Gift of Laughter," in Locke, ed., *The New Negro*, 161–67. For further insight, also see McKinney, "Brer Rabbit and Brother Martin Luther King, Jr.," 48–52.

129. "'I Remember Martin,'" 40; King, *Stride toward Freedom*, 79 and 82; and Carson, ed., *The Autobiography of Martin Luther King, Jr.*, 66.

cause. The cases of King, Jr.'s wit and humor also constituted a much-needed antidote for the frustration and the low spirits that usually followed movement setbacks and failed civil rights campaigns.

Much of King, Jr.'s humor and laughter were directed at southern whites,[130] many of whom willfully and consistently sought to undermine, discredit, and even destroy all efforts for black freedom. As early as the Montgomery bus boycott, King, Jr. realized that he and other movement leaders could exploit the viciousness and thoughtlessness of white segregationists to the benefit of the movement, much as Brer Rabbit used his skills to outwit Brer Fox, Brer Bear, and the other bigger and more powerful animals to his advantage. There were many instances in which hate-filled whites became the very force by which the movement advanced. Not knowing how he and his associates would reach fifty thousand blacks in Montgomery with plans for the bus boycott in December 1955, for example, King, Jr. found the answer in an irate white woman who, after being given one of their leaflets by her black maid, telephoned the local newspaper, the *Montgomery Advertiser*, "to let the white community know what the blacks were up to." Consequently, the white press, determined to expose something it deemed discreditable, "made the contents of the leaflet a front-page story," thereby spreading the word for the protesters in a way that would have been impossible with only their own resources. "We laughed a lot about this," King, Jr.'s wife Coretta recalled, "and Martin later said that we owed them a great debt."[131] King, Jr. was equally humorous in giving credit to rabid segregationists such as Governors George C. Wallace of Alabama, Ross Barnett of Mississippi, and Orval Faubus of Arkansas—all of whom had been manipulated by movement activists into taking action that actually promoted rather than prohibited integration. "Maybe we pro-integrationists shouldn't be so hard on Governor Faubus after all," King, Jr. jokingly commented after the Little Rock public school crisis

---

130. Lawrence Levine contends that black humor has long "provided splendid and important opportunities to laugh at the whites who so profoundly affected the quality of the life black Americans lived. . . ." See Levine, *Black Culture and Black Consciousness*, 300, 305, 320, and 322.

131. King, *My Life with Martin Luther King, Jr.*, 104; and King, *Stride toward Freedom*, 49.

in 1957, "for, however ironical it may sound, he has done more to promote the cause of integration than almost any personality of this decade."[132]

King, Jr. was always eager to know about droll incidents and stories concerning the treatment of blacks by white southerners in courts and jails, for these accounts, perhaps more than anything else, revealed the sheer absurdity surrounding the entire system of Jim Crow. He never hesitated to share stories about some of the surprising and strangely amusing experiences he himself had while facing white juries or sitting in southern jails. He found it both amazing and oddly humorous that a southern jury of twelve white men found him not guilty after he had been indicted by a Montgomery grand jury "on a charge of falsifying his Alabama state income-tax returns for 1956 and 1958." "We had no idea that an all white jury of Montgomery, Alabama would ever think of acquitting Martin Luther King," he sarcastically declared.[133] An experience King, Jr. had while in jail in Birmingham in 1963 was also amusing in a rather quaint manner. Deeply puzzled as to why white policeman who had been so rude and disrespectful to him had quickly become more considerate and accommodating, King, Jr., after being told by his wife Coretta that President Kennedy had called them to make sure he was all right, smiled and remarked with a somewhat dry sense of humor: "So that's why everybody is suddenly being so polite. This is good to know."[134] Also during his stay in the Birmingham jail, King, Jr. talked calmly with the white wardens about the rightness of his cause as it related to bigotry and economic injustice, and after hearing them talk about "where they lived and how much they were earning," he said, in a tone that always provoked laughter when he shared the experience: "'Now, you know what? You ought to be marching with us. You're just as poor as Negroes.'"[135]

132. Martin Luther King, Jr., "Address at the National Bar Association," unpublished version, Milwaukee, Wisconsin (20 August 1959), King Center Library and Archives, 5; King, *My Life with Martin Luther King*, 217; and Carson, ed., *The Autobiography of Martin Luther King, Jr.*, 284 and 288–89.
133. King, *My Life with Martin Luther King, Jr.*, 169–71; and Carson, et al., eds., *King Papers*, V, 473. Taylor Branch is right in saying that "The laughter" in such instances "relieved an otherwise grim mood about racially skewered measures of Alabama justice." See Branch, *Parting the Waters*, 242.
134. King, *My Life with Martin Luther King, Jr.*, 211.
135. Carson and Holloran, eds., *A Knock at Midnight*, 179.

Amazingly, King, Jr. made fun and laughed a lot at the expense of white racist extremists who delighted in intimidating, verbally insulting, and physically assaulting blacks. The Ku Klux Klan's failed attempt to intimidate his people by marching in the black neighborhood after the Supreme Court declared bus segregation in Montgomery unconstitutional in 1956 really tickled King, Jr. He found it really laughable that blacks stood and "acted as though they were watching a circus parade." "We used to joke in those days about which of our friendly neighborhood grocers or dry cleaners was a Klansman or a member of the White Citizens Council," Coretta King reported, as she reflected on the violence of white bigots and their attempts to nullify court decisions striking down segregated public facilities.[136] The power of King, Jr.'s sense of humor became most evident after he was hit in the head by a Nazi leader while struggling for voting rights in Selma in 1965. When Dorothy Cotton asked if he was hurt, and as his aides scrambled to console him and to determine if he needed medical attention, King, Jr. brought calmness to the situation in his characteristically humorous style. "That fellow strikes a pretty hard blow,"[137] King, Jr. joked, a reaction that must have brought smiles and perhaps outright laughter from those around him. Cotton recalled that King, Jr. reacted in a similar fashion a year later in Chicago, after being hit by a brick thrown by a bigot during a march through a white neighborhood. With a chuckle, he told a journalist in the crowd: "Oh, I've been hit so many times that I'm immune to it."[138]

This was part of that indestructible quality that enabled King, Jr. to accept insults, blows, and the terror of receiving daily threats against his life without faltering or giving up. He saw the danger and the absurdity in such experiences, but he also saw the humor. Like generations of his forebears, he had the need to laugh at his enemies or adversaries. In more general terms, he appreciated this kind of humor

---

136. King, *My Life with Martin Luther King, Jr.*, 101 and 132.
137. Cotton, *If Your Back's Not Bent*, 235
138. Ibid., 249; James R. Ralph, Jr., *Northern Protest: Martin Luther King, Jr., Chicago, and the Civil Rights Movement* (Cambridge, MA: Harvard University Press, 1993), 123. King made the comment in a film documentary called "An Amazing Grace: Dr. Martin Luther King, Jr.," which covered parts of the Chicago Freedom Movement in the summer of 1966.

because it allowed him to laugh not only at white people, but also, at himself and the seemingly hopeless situation facing black people. Humor was his way of putting into proper perspective white people and the brutal and even sadistic nature of their racist practices.[139] This is what the black experience had always been about; namely, using humor and laughter in defining self and others, while also encountering, engaging, and rising above the ironies, contradictions, and painful realities of daily existence.[140] Whites would never have fully grasped the insights and humorous thrust in many of the stories, jokes, and anecdotes King, Jr. shared about life under the yoke of oppression.[141]

Even whites at the highest levels of this nation's political and governmental life did not escape the force of King, Jr.'s humor. It was most amusing to him that President Kennedy chose to take a walk with him in the Rose Garden to tell him that he was pressured by J. Edgar Hoover to put him under surveillance, "inferring that probably his own office was bugged, too."[142] Another humorous experience occurred during a meeting King, Jr. had with President Kennedy and other political and church officials after the great march on Washington

139. Lawrence Levine was especially useful in the development of this perspective. See Levine, *Black Culture and Black Consciousness*, 300, 320, and 322.
140. This study of King's wit, humor, and laughter has strengthened this author in two convictions. First, that there is a "close affinity between humor and philosophy," a position advanced by John Morreall and others. The nineteenth-century Danish existentialist philosopher Søren Kierkegaard held that "the comical is present wherever there is a contradiction, and wherever one is justified in ignoring the pain, because it is non-essential." I would change the last part of this statement to read: "wherever one is compelled to transcend the pain, because it can never have the last word in life." This, I think, more adequately defines what humor in the black experience is all about, and it also captures what James Weldon Johnson and Thomas Talley had in mind when they wrote about the power of transcendence embodied in black humor and laughter. The second conviction is that "the healing energy of playfulness and laughter" bears upon physical and psychological health in profound and enduring ways, as the pastoral psychologist and counselor Howard Clinebell has established in his works. See John Morreall, ed., *The Philosophy of Laughter and Humor* (Albany: State University of New York Press, 1987), 3 and 85; Levine, *Black Culture and Black Consciousness*, 299–300; and Howard Clinebell, *Well Being: A Personal Plan for Exploring and Enriching the Seven Dimensions of Life-Mind, Body, Spirit, Love, Work, Play, the Earth* (San Francisco: HarperCollins Publishers, 1992), 159.
141. For obvious reasons, King avoided the kind of ethnic jokes among blacks that traditionally targeted the Irish, Italians, Jews, and other white people. He was not a fan of ethnic humor in any form, undoubtedly because much of it was demeaning and insulting, though seldom so in a malicious way. King's humor was designed to uplift personhood, not to degrade it. He was a consistent personalist in this regard. See Levine, *Black Culture and Black Consciousness*, 301–10. For a rather short humorous account in which King highlighted the need to respect personhood over material things, see Carson and Holloran, eds., *A Knock at Midnight*, 150.
142. McDonald, *Secretary to a King*, 39–40.

in August 1963, in which the civil rights leader asked how former President Dwight Eisenhower might be persuaded through "a private moral appeal" to exert influence on Minority Leader Charles Halleck, "the most critical of the House Republicans," to support the passage of the impending civil rights legislation. "Chuckles broke out" when King, Jr. denied that he was willing to take on such a mission, suggesting instead that "some groups" should do this, especially since Ike happened "to be in the other denomination." There had to be some way to gain Eisenhower's support, King, Jr. quipped. "Isn't he a Democrat when he goes to church?"[143]

Many of King, Jr.'s witty comments about US presidents Dwight D. Eisenhower, John F. Kennedy, and Lyndon B. Johnson were made in closed SCLC staff meetings, when discussions turned to ways in which their administrations might be forced, on practical, political, and even moral grounds, to support the passage and enforcement of civil rights initiatives and legislation that increased racial integration.[144] Here, King, Jr.'s role mirrored and most certainly called to mind that of Brer Rabbit in the tales of William John Faulkner, at least in some ways. Like King, Jr., "Brer Rabbit's overwhelming concerns are ethical, his principle function that of forwarding the struggle for communal freedom" through his wit and ingenuity, "attributes hardly at variance with those that DuBois ascribed to the slave priest."[145]

143. Quoted from Branch, *Parting the Waters*, 885–86.
144. An example of this type of maneuvering on King and his staff's part is afforded in the film, "The Promised Land (1967-68)," from "The Eyes on the Prize Series." There King spoke about advancing the civil rights agenda, especially around the issues of poverty and Vietnam, by pitting President Johnson against the Congress. See "The Promised Land (1967-68)," directed by Jacqueline Shearer and Paul Stekler, originally aired (1990), from *Eyes on the Prize: America's Civil Rights Movement—DVD 7PK, AV Item, 7 DVD Set, Item No.: Eyes 700*.
145. For this insight, I am heavily indebted to the cultural historian Sterling Stuckey, who has noted that "In the Reverend Faulkner's tales, the religious leader is personified by Brer Rabbit in one tale after another, especially in those in which Brer Rabbit is the defender of the interests of the weak and defenseless." See Sterling Stuckey, *Slave Culture: Nationalist Theory and the Foundations of Black America* (New York: Oxford University Press, 1987), 256. The Faulkner tales, "Brer Tiger and the Big Wind" and "Brer Rabbit's Protest Meeting," are particularly relevant to this discussion. See William J. Faulkner, *The Days When the Animals Talked: Black American Folktales and How They Came to Be* (Chicago: Follett Publishing Company, 1977), 89–94 and 115–21. Also see McKinney, "Brer Rabbit and Brother Martin Luther King, Jr.," 48–52. On one occasion, King was intrigued by "a witty remark" made by a young male student during "a vigorous debate" concerning "the moral and practical soundness of nonviolence." "All I know is that, if rabbits could throw rocks," said the student with some sarcasm, "there would be fewer hunters in the

Some of King, Jr.'s humor actually questioned the claim that the Federal Bureau of Investigation (FBI), a governmental agency within the US Department of Justice, was effective in its activities as a criminal investigative organization and as a department of internal national intelligence. Convinced that J. Edgar Hoover and his associates were subjecting him to constant surveillance, King, Jr. often joked "with his colleagues about how any chance remark might be immortalized by one of the Bureau's hidden recorders."[146] "I remember when we were riding into the Black Belt [deep South]," recalled Fred Shuttlesworth, one of King, Jr.'s closest associates in Birmingham. "The FBI was trailing us to protect us. Martin said, 'the FBI are like federal Boy Scouts. They can't prevent anything, but they sure are great note takers. They'll write down how many blows you took before you fell.'"[147] When reacting to FBI charges against him and the civil rights movement, King, Jr. could be very funny. To the oft-repeated charge that he and his followers were communist-infiltrated and communist inspired, he insisted that "There are as many communists in this freedom movement as there are Eskimos in Florida."[148] When someone in the FBI was suspected of sending King, Jr. "a bizarre anonymous letter" and "a reel of audiotape" in January 1965, threatening to expose his immoralities and suggesting that he commit suicide, King, Jr. joined other SCLC staff members in prayer before making fun and laughing uproariously at what they all considered to be the gutter tactics of Hoover and his lily-white agency. Such amusing experiences were clearly indicative of how King, Jr. celebrated special moments despite the scrutiny of an FBI seemingly determined to destroy him and the movement he led.[149] For King, Jr., the FBI was merely representative

forest." See James M. Washington, ed., A Testament of Hope: The Essential Writings and Speeches of Martin Luther King, Jr. (New York: HarperCollins Publishers, 1991), 163.

146. See David J. Garrow, The FBI and Martin Luther King, Jr.: From "Solo" to Memphis (New York: W. W. Norton & Company, 1981), 218 and 307n38.

147. "'I Remember Martin,'" 40.

148. Quoted in Michael Friedly and David Gallen, Martin Luther King, Jr.: The FBI File (New York: Carroll & Graf Publishers, Inc., 1993), 41.

149. See Young, An Easy Burden, 327–31. Joseph Lowery, an SCLC staffer, recalled the rich humor and laughter that he and others shared with King on that occasion. See "The Johnson Tapes: Uncivil Liberties," Part II (Bethesda, MD: Discovery Channel Education, a Division of Discovery Communications, Inc., 2000).

of the kind of racism that was personalized, sanctioned, and institutionalized at all levels of white society, and his ability to joke about and laugh at this agency, which so many feared and respected, spoke volumes about his tendency to find humor in even the most difficult and unusual spaces.

King, Jr.'s closest aides and friends spent more time with him than anyone else during those tension-packed days of struggle, and his wit, humor, and laughter not only gave them a certain immunity against much of the bigotry and abuse they sustained, but also some reassurance that there was no need to worry about the future and the direction of the movement. Dorothy Cotton of SCLC's Citizenship Education Program scoffed at *Time Magazine's* description of King, Jr. as "humorless" in 1964, and insisted, instead, that he was often comical and "could be so playful, the life of the party." Noting that humor was part of that "intangible magnetic quality" that drew people to King, Jr. and put them at ease, Cotton reminisced:

> I still smile when I remember what fun Martin was; he could be really funny, even joking about some of the ridiculous ways that racism showed itself. For example, once when we were driving on a "people-to-people tour" recruiting and speaking, with four or five of us in the car, he said, laughing heartily, "I know how we can solve the race problem: we should get a law passed requiring everybody to marry someone of a different race!" I could see he was in his element when he had time to just hang out with us—his team and CEP soon-to-be "graduates." We always scheduled the "playtimes" in the afternoon. Dr. King was very gregarious and clearly enjoyed the relaxed atmosphere at our workshops.[150]

Humor and laughter accounted for much of King, Jr.'s amazing ability to connect with black people at all levels, whether they were children, youth, middle-aged, or elderly, and this was always evident to his colleagues. Staff members were the ones most often present when King, Jr. joked about most anything having to do with black

150. Cotton, *If You Back's Not Bent*, 142–43 and 188. Cotton's recollections are clearly supported by others who befriended and worked with King. SCLC associates variously described King as "funny," "playful," "fun-loving," "humorous," or as one who "was always in good humor" and "loved a good joke." See "'I Remember Martin,'" 33–34, 36, 38, and 40; Abernathy, *And the Walls Came Tumbling Down*, 468–69; Young, *An Easy Burden*, 328–29, 463–64, and 467; Young, *A Way Out of No Way*, 75 and 101; and Belafonte, *My Song*, 247.

people and the day-to-day rhythms of the struggle. According to King, Jr.'s ghostwriter Al Duckett, "Martin could tell everyday happenings in ways that would just make you roar with laughter because he had such a fantastic sense of humor."[151] Robert Williams, a childhood friend, schoolmate, and close aide of King, Jr., fully agreed. To illustrate the point, Williams, who was quite busy as a professor at Montgomery's Alabama State College at the time, recounted an incident involving King, Jr. and a student driver that Williams himself had designated to take King, Jr. "where he wanted to go." Referring to King, Jr. by his nickname, "Mike," Williams shared the rest of the humorous account in these terms:

> A short time later, they both came back to the school and Mike called me out of my class and asked how long before I'd be finished. I told him about an hour. He said he'd wait for me. I asked why couldn't the young man take him where he needed to go. He said: "This young man here nearly had 40 wrecks between here and my house (which was just four blocks away). So I'll wait for you." And he sat there until I finished my class.[152]

"Martin could also find fun in the stuffiest occasions," said Ralph Abernathy, as he reflected on a bit of King, Jr.'s humor in another academic setting in the northeast a few years later:

> I remember one day we were sitting on the stage at one of the great Ivy League schools, listening while the president was introducing me so I could introduce Martin to an auditorium jammed with students. As the president droned on, Martin leaned over and whispered to me, "Look at that man's shoes." I looked and saw that when the man rose up on his toes to make a point, he revealed that both of his soles had holes in them. Martin whispered again, quoting from "Amazing Grace": "It looks as if those shoes are saying, 'Through many dangers toils and snares I have already come'." At that moment the man ended his very serious introduction, and I had to walk to the podium, bent double with laughter, while Martin nodded soberly.[153]

---

151. Quoted in Garrow, *Bearing the Cross*, 550.
152. "'I Remember Martin,'" 40.
153. Abernathy, *And the Walls Came Tumbling Down*, 470; and Abernathy, "My Old Friend Martin," 6–7. King always took note of how people were dressed from head to toe, and was particularly interested in the shoes they wore. A very interesting observation about one who was seen by at least one close friend and associate as a little man with "*big feet*." See Belafonte, *My Song*, 296.

Much of King, Jr.'s humor came naturally, but he also learned from others since he loved to "hear stories about people that were humorous," and especially, stories that revealed black people's use of the keenest wit to survive in a hostile white world.[154] "He knew all of my jokes," said Abernathy of King, Jr., "and he wanted me to tell my jokes in the pulpit when we were together. Martin would always say, 'Ralph, tell the people that joke about so and so.'"[155] King, Jr. had this deep need to see people laugh, because he knew that this was one avenue into their hearts and souls. Abernathy recalled that this helped explain why women were so attracted to King, Jr.—"He could make them laugh." But there was always that greater purpose to King, Jr.'s wit and humor which never escaped Abernathy, Dorothy Cotton, Andrew Young, and others who worked with the civil rights leader. Abernathy put it best: "That kind of humor relaxed us in the midst of the tension and the frustration of the movement."[156]

The type of family fabric that existed within King, Jr.'s inner circle of colleagues was always conducive to cheerfulness, fun, and a lot of joking and laughter. Fun-filled and relaxed conversation was most common even after major civil rights events, and King, Jr. routinely and freely made fun of his colleagues' habits and weaknesses. Harry Belafonte noted that "even in the movement's darkest days, we still had room for humor."[157] This was most certainly the case on one occasion in early 1963, when King, Jr., according to Andrew Young, resorted to humor to lessen the strain, tension, or pressure his closest aides must have felt as they, reeling from SCLC's fiasco in Albany, Georgia, prepared for a campaign in Birmingham that offered little, if any, hope of a different outcome, especially at that point:

> Martin was great at turning fear into laughter. One night, as soon as it was apparent that we would be moving into Birmingham soon, he began to humorously speculate about who might have to give their life for

154. "'I Remember Martin,'" 40; and Baldwin Interview with Abernathy (7 May 1987).
155. Baldwin Interview with Abernathy (17 March 1987); Abernathy, *And the Walls Came Tumbling Down*, 468–70; and Baldwin, *There is a Balm in Gilead*, 304.
156. Abernathy, *And the Walls Came Tumbling Down*, 471; Baldwin Interview with Abernathy (17 March 1987); and Baldwin, *There is a Balm in Gilead*, 304.
157. See Young, *An Easy Burden*, 328; and Belafonte, *My Song*, 247.

freedom. Though we all knew that he was inevitably the prime target, he proceeded to go around the room and preach a brief satirical eulogy for each of us, emphasizing our individual foibles and foolishness. Before long, everybody was laughing and adding to the satirical commentary.[158]

Young knew of numerous occasions during which King, Jr. clowned in a similar manner before leading a campaign in the more segregated and dangerous parts of the South. Mindful of the relaxing and healing effects of this kind of humor, and of the positive energy derived from it, Young shared an equally funny account of how King, Jr. launched into one of his "mock eulogies" before he and his staff confronted vicious racists like Sheriff Jim Clark in Selma during the voting rights campaign in 1965:

Martin had a way of making fun out of any dangerous situation. He talked about going down to Selma. We knew the kind of people that were there. And he started preaching everybody's funeral. He was saying, "We were lucky in Birmingham, all of us got out alive." But some of us weren't going to make it out of Selma. And he'd go around the room sort of saying, "Well, Ralph, now if they get you...," and then he'd preach Ralph Abernathy's sermon for about five minutes. He just made fun of saying all the embarrassing things he could think of saying, pretending that he was preaching our eulogies and our funerals. That was the way that we dealt with the anxiety and the fear and the tension, by joking about it and laughing about it.[159]

King, Jr.'s good cheer in the face of difficulty and danger was most evident in the manner in which he turned even these gatherings into small celebrations. This was a vital part of what King, Jr. really appreciated in the realm of the private, for he could say and do things in the presence of his small cadre of friends and co-workers that he would not have felt comfortable saying and doing in public, and certainly not in the company of people who were not black, male, or clergy.[160] The FBI caught some of King, Jr.'s brand of intragroup humor

158. Young, A Way Out of No Way, 75. Also see Young, An Easy Burden, 194–95.
159. Quoted in Henry Hampton and Steve Fayer, Voices of Freedom: An Oral History of the Civil Rights Movement from the 1950s through the 1980s, with Sarah Flynn (New York: Bantam Books, 1990), 214–15.
160. Some sources have reported that King occasionally cursed, "told lewd jokes," and made "bawdy remarks" when meeting in privacy with the male preachers on the staff of SCLC. See Michael Eric Dyson, I May Not Get There with You: The True Martin Luther King, Jr. (New York: The Free Press, 2000),

on tape, as he joked around with Ralph Abernathy in a room at the Willard Hotel in Washington, DC, after the great march in August 1963. Vividly recalling King, Jr.'s exuberant spirit on that day, Andrew Young later mentioned that

> The only section of the tape that was in the least damaging to Martin was when he started teasing Ralph. Ralph had started complaining that he hadn't been allowed to speak at the march. Martin responded with, "Ralph, you had to be the head of an organization to speak. What we have to do is find you an organization that you can be the head of, so that on the next march, you can have the right to speak." And everybody present agreed that the one organization that Ralph was unquestionably the president of was the "National Association for the Advancement of Eating Chicken." Martin waxed eloquently, saying, "No one can challenge your preeminence, you would have no competition." And they all cracked on Ralph for about an hour. Everyone would think of something different to say about Ralph's organization. They laughed, big, deep, belly laughs, releasing all the tension of the day.[161]

This kind of "joking around" was always playful and affectionate in spirit, and it actually reinforced strong bonds between King, Jr., Abernathy, and others in the SCLC, whom King, Jr. affectionately called his "Ground Crew."[162] Although King, Jr. directed his humor at all of his closest comrades from time to time, most of his teasing and joking were at the expense of Abernathy, who was closer to him than anyone else in the movement. Amusing experiences that occurred when the two spent time in jail cells together came up on one occasion when King, Jr. was swapping stories with Harry Belafonte at his apartment in New York. "'Let me be sure to get arrested with people who don't snore,'" King "intoned," while casting a steady gaze toward Abernathy. Abernathy wildly protested the charge that he was a disruptive snorer. "King's eyes went wide with delight," and he "declared," undoubtedly with a look of surprise on his face: "You are *torture*. White folks ain't *invented* anything that can get to me like you do. *Anything* they want

177; Abernathy, *And the Walls Came Tumbling Down*, 436; Garrow, *Bearing the Cross*, 375; Baldwin Interview with Abernathy (17 March 1978); and Clayborne Carson, *Martin's Dream: My Journey and the Legacy of Martin Luther King, Jr.* (New York: Palgrave MacMillan, 2013), 117.
161. Young, *An Easy Burden*, 328–29.
162. McDonald, *Secretary to a King*, ix (foreword).

me to admit to, I will, if they'll just get you and your snoring out of my cell."[163] According to Belafonte, Abernathy's snoring sometimes brought roars of laughter when he and King chatted "at the end of the day" over mixed drinks:

> It wouldn't be long before we were laughing at something—like the way Ralph Abernathy, Martin's heavyset aide-de-camp, snored in that jail cell in Albany, Georgia, so loudly he kept Martin awake all night, so loudly that Martin was convinced it was Ralph's snoring that had driven their third cell mate, the poor local doctor, out of his wits. "Never again," Martin would say with Baptist fervor about sharing a room with Abernathy. "Never again, sweet Jesus."[164]

Because Belafonte and his wife Julie were so close to King, Jr., they were exposed to his humorous side in ways that only his preacher friends and aides knew so well. Julie had introduced King, Jr. "to the sherry," and he "kept up a running joke about how much he savored the nightcap of the most elegant New Yorkers."[165] Julie routinely brought out King, Jr.'s bottle of Harvey's Bristol Cream on those evenings when he showed up at the Belafonte's residence, and King, Jr. "would make a big deal of checking to see if anyone had drunk any since his last visit; he marked the level just to be sure."[166] Such evenings were usually devoted to moderate drinking and a lot of joking and laughter, but there were also moments when King, Jr. weighed in with thoughtful and provocative commentary around some issue or problem.

King, Jr. was, by some standards, the humorist of the civil rights movement, for he was more responsible than any other single person for creating, within the SCLC, a culture in which fun and laughter were not only tolerated, but expected.[167] He was funny and expected

163. Quoted in Branch, *Parting the Waters*, 706; and Baldwin Interview with Lee (9 July 1986).
164. The "poor, local doctor" mentioned here was William G. Anderson, the president of the Albany Movement while King and his SCLC were stationed there in 1961–62. Belafonte reported that Anderson "was overwhelmed by his imprisonment and appeared to be suffering a mental breakdown." "Martin feared the doctor," Belafonte added, "might not last much longer behind bars." See Belafonte, *My Song*, 244 and 247.
165. Branch, *Parting the Waters*, 706.
166. Belafonte, *My Song*, 247; and Branch, *Parting the Waters*, 706.
167. "'I Remember Martin,'" 34 and 38; and Abernathy, "My Old Friend Martin," 6–7. King's secretary, Dora McDonald referred to King as "the eloquent, funny, warm man," and she found it amazing

nothing less of those whom he befriended and worked with so closely. He seemingly never hesitated to make not only family members, but his closest friends and aides the butt of his occasional practical jokes. When experiencing an appetite for merry-making, King, Jr. was known to employ wordplay to trick Abernathy, Bernard Lee, and other close SCLC associates into saying something ludicrous. At other times, King, Jr. would simply disappear when Abernathy, Lee, Andrew Young, his brother, A. D., and others were hotly debating an issue and least expected it, as was the case when the question of what should be SCLC's approach to Vietnam came up in a meeting. Dorothy Cotton remembered that occasion:

> In one staff meeting Dr. King grew weary of the debate about the issue; he left the meeting and drove to my house. When he arrived there he was sort of giggly about the fact that he'd just left, not telling the team where he was going or why. But they knew. He was tired of the team's loud argument—mostly advising him what many supporters would say if he spoke out against the war. He did not come to my house to discuss the issue. His manner was almost childish. "They don't know where I am," he laughingly said to me.[168]

King, Jr.'s humor was a type of play that involved lifting the spirits and stimulating and refreshing the minds of those around him. Meetings filled with wholesome fun and laughter were what he associated with not only good fellowship and entertainment, but healing and healthy reinforcement at its best. This is part of what King, Jr. had in mind when he spoke, in January, 1960, about life's "transfiguring moments." "Often in life," he asserted, "we have those moments, transfiguring moments, that we are able to rise above the dull monotony of sameness and the miasma of everyday life and experience those periods of unutterable joy."[169] This is what endeared King, Jr. to those who shared so much of his life and commitment to freeing human beings. "There was a special kind of joy just being

that "Behind the public icon persona was a man of great wit and playfulness." She remembered that there was always a lot of laughter within the small circle of SCLC. See McDonald, *Secretary to a King*, 40, 78, 89–90, and 131.
168. Cotton, *If Your Back's Not Bent*, 250.
169. Carson, et. al., eds., *King Papers*, V, 351.

around him; we felt appreciated as both friends and staff," remarked Dorothy Cotton. "And he really was a lot of fun to be with." Referring mainly to the lingering memories that she and Andrew Young have of King, Jr., Cotton stated on another occasion that "We also laugh sometimes, remembering his antics and the joy it was to be with him, to work and struggle with him toward our freedom goals."[170]

King, Jr. was described by his friend Lawrence Reddick as "a big talker,"[171] and his rolling, mood-enhancing humor and peals of laughter convinced those closest to him in the movement that he was more often than not in a joyful and celebratory mood, despite his many personal trials and sufferings and the seemingly endless and daunting challenges before him. King, Jr. was arrested numerous times, constantly subjected to verbal and physical attack, often got bundles of hate mail, and sometimes received forty telephones calls a day threatening his life and the lives of his wife and children—experiences that would have broken the average person emotionally, and yet, he spent so much time teasing people, telling jokes, and laughing. There were times when feelings of guilt and depression surfaced, and understandably so, but he never faltered and was always open to having fun and celebrating life in the moment without worrying unnecessarily. Being deeply troubled and conflicted at times is part of being human, and no person escapes this entirely, but King, Jr. was not one who dwelled on or worried excessively about his own problems and misfortunes.[172] Such a tendency usually stems from an obsession

170. "'I Remember Martin,'" 34; and Cotton, *If Your Back's Not Bent*, 265.
171. Reddick, *Crusader without Violence*, 6.
172. Evidently, the testimony of many who were very close to King has not been taken seriously enough by all too many scholars and journalists who have written insightful and much-needed works on King, but they never really knew nor associated with King, and they seemingly suggest, on the basis of a careful manipulation of both written and oral sources, that King was an "intensely guilt-ridden" personality and a chronic worrier who essentially surrendered to "emotional trauma," "a growing pessimism," and "a deepening depression." The unanswered question that looms before us is how such a man could find so much time for teasing, joking, and laughter. See Lischer, *The Preacher King*, 167–72; Garrow, *Bearing the Cross*, 56 and 604; Branch, *Parting the Waters*, 702; David L. Chappell, *Waking from the Dream: The Struggle for Civil Rights in the Shadow of Martin Luther King, Jr.* (New York: Random House, 2014), 13, 187n12, and 188n26–27; Garrow, *The FBI and Martin Luther King, Jr.*, 216–18; Stewart Burns, *To the Mountaintop: Martin Luther King Jr.'s Sacred Mission to Save America, 1955-1968* (San Francisco: HarperCollins Publishers, Inc., 2004), 216, 260–61, 280, 287, 345–47, 355, 377–78, 394, 403, 406–7, 421–22, 427, and 429–30; Branch, *At Canaan's Edge*, 194–95, 216, and 734; and Burrow, "On Behind the Public Veil—Comments," 1–5.

with self, a problem King, Jr. never really had. Aside from his deep personal faith, humor was that ingredient that kept him from breaking under the weight of guilt and depression.[173] He was so strong, driven, resilient, and energetically focused, and humor was so intertwined into his daily routines until it is difficult to imagine him being sad or despondent for any significant period of time.[174] In short, King, Jr.'s humor reflected the indomitability of his own spirit, and it also symbolized the resilient and resolute spirit of a people who had learned to laugh in the face of adversity, hardship, and struggle. Rufus Burrow, Jr. has said this and much more in important references to King, Jr.'s cultural roots:

> If one does not have a clear sense of the black cultural, family, and church influences on King, it would be easy to conclude . . . that the pressure on King during those last two years of his life was such that he was nearly incapacitated a number of times during that period because of severe depression. And yet, when one has a sense of the real strength and encouragement that King drew from family, including his extended church family, the sense of relaxation that came from hearty conversation as he consumed his favorite soul food meals, the sense of calm that came from boyish horseplay with close friends (as occurred just hours before he was assassinated), the use that King made of humor and jokes, etc., one might well conclude that like any human being a person under such pressures would most assuredly experience moments of depression and despondency. However, this alone does not necessarily mean that King was incapacitated. Furthermore,

King's friend Lawrence Reddick said that King was "not at all a worrier or brooder." See Reddick, *Crusader without Violence*, 6; Friedly and Gallen, *Martin Luther King, Jr.*, 391; and Baldwin, *There is a Balm in Gilead*, 310.

173. This is clear from a reading of both King's statement on "Suffering and Faith" and the testimony of those who shared many of the most private moments with King. See Washington, ed., *A Testament of Hope*, 41–42; Friedly and Gallen, *Martin Luther King, Jr.*, 391; "'I Remember Martin,'" 33–34, 36, 38, and 40; Abernathy, "My Old Friend Martin," 6–7; and Baldwin Interview with Abernathy (17 March 1987). King said in his "Advice for Living" column in *Ebony* Magazine, in July, 1958, that "One of the things that a positive and healthy religious faith gives an individual is a sense of inner equilibrium which removes all basic worries." He added: "Religion does not say an individual will never confront a problem, or that he will never worry about anything; it simply says that if the individual is sufficiently committed to the way of religion, he will have something within that will cause him to transcend every worry situation with power and faith." Here King was obviously speaking out of that larger black experience to which he was heir, and there is every reason to believe that he would have commented similarly about humor and laughter. See Carson, et al., eds., *King Papers*, IV, 445.

174. Those closest to King recalled those times when he was depressed or frustrated, and they also speak of his amazing capacity to bounce back. Humor was very important here. See McDonald, *Secretary to a King*, 29, 82–83, 89–90, 97, and 131.

humor and jokes played such a central role in King's daily life that, more often than not, he was able to cope with whatever was thrown at him.[175]

Laughter was much more than a coping and compensating mechanism for King, Jr.; it was a critical part of his welfare and salvation. Laughter is always a testimony to the power of human endurance, especially for those who suffer and struggle daily under the heavy yoke of oppression. The explanation for why King, Jr. was so healthy, physically and emotionally,[176] lies in those empowering experiences of joking and laughing with people from different walks of life and in various contexts. For King, Jr., the experience was like going from the mountaintop back to the valley, which is how he frequently characterized what it meant to move from the company of the prestigious and powerful back to those quarters in the South in which ordinary people, despised, rejected, and victimized daily, found emotional balance, physical strength, and the power of no surrender in their faith and in their capacity to joke and laugh.[177]

Humor not only gave King, Jr. much of the equilibrium and stability he needed internally to survive and function without being

175. See Rufus Burrow, Jr., *Martin Luther King, Jr., and the Theology of Resistance* (Jefferson, NC: McFarland & Company, Inc., Publishers, 2015), 122; and Rufus Burrow, Jr., *A Child Shall Lead Them: Martin Luther King Jr., Young People, and the Movement* (Minneapolis: Fortress Press, 2014), 256–57. I made essentially these points in my earlier works on King, as far back as 1991, and Burrow is really the first scholar since that time to brilliantly explain why King never surrendered himself to despondency and what I call "a bleak, enervating pessimism." Burrow is quite right in saying that scholars who make so much of King's depression and how that affected him have not taken seriously "the black cultural studies genre in King studies." Moreover, they would do well to read works that explore the psychology of black people under oppression in the United States. See Baldwin, *There is a Balm in Gilead*, 33–35 and 304–10; and Lewis V. Baldwin and Amiri YaSin Al-Hadid, *Between Cross and Crescent: Christian and Muslim Perspectives on Malcolm and Martin* (Gainesville: University Press of Florida, 2002), 18–21. John Morreall's contention that "the person who faces life with a sense of humor has a calmer attitude and can view things more rationally" also has some relevance in the discussion of King's ability to confront the very worst daily while not breaking or faltering under the weight of guilt and depression. See Morreall, ed., *The Philosophy of Laughter and Humor*, 2. Harry Belafonte was amazed at King's "sense of calm," and he offers yet another explanation for King's resilience in the midst of life's pressures, setbacks, and hardships. Belafonte says that King "had a lot of conflicted feelings, but his sense of mission forced him to endure." See Belafonte, *My Song*, 149 and 298.

176. Lawrence Levine makes this point brilliantly throughout his discussion of black wit, humor, and laughter, and it applies very much to King. See especially, Levine, *Black Culture and Black Consciousness*, 299.

177. King, *My Life with Martin Luther King, Jr.*, 14; Baldwin Interview with Abernathy (17 March 1987); Baldwin Interview with Lee (9 July 1986).

overpowered physically and emotionally by life's challenges, difficulties, and seriousness, it also afforded him another frame of reference from which to better understand and explain the state of society and the world in an era of rapid social, political, and cultural transformation.[178] This accounted, in part, for King, Jr.'s deep respect and admiration for some of the most popular and celebrated comedians of his day, some of whom he studied almost with Socratic thoroughness. Moms Mabley and Dick Gregory figured prominently among his favorite black comics, but not always for the same reasons. Moms Mabley's humor was relevant as King, Jr. thought in terms of the need to cultivate self-pride and self-esteem, as his daughter, Yolanda once suggested:

> One of his favorite stories was something he picked up from the late comedienne Moms Mabley. There was a guy walking up the street with a processed "'do," you know, the '50s and '60s version of the curl look. Moms asks him, "Man, what is that you got on your head?" "Madame Walker," he says. Moms retorts, "You better tell Madame she better walk around them edges a little bit more." I don't think Daddy was fond of seeing men with "a 'do."[179]

King, Jr.'s point here in drawing on Moms was clear in light of his declaration, made repeatedly to his people, that "We need not process our hair to make it appear straight."[180] King, Jr. also found in Dick Gregory's humor reminders that his people should never be ashamed of their blackness, but he seemingly respected Gregory more because Gregory physically and financially supported civil rights demonstrations in Birmingham and other places.[181]

178. Morreall sees this as one of the virtues of a rich and vital humor, and I am heavily indebted to him for this idea. See Morreall, ed., *The Philosophy of Laughter and Humor*, 1–7 and 254.
179. "'I Remember Martin,'" 38.
180. King, *Where Do We Go from Here?*, 123.
181. King and Gregory actually became friends and participated together in civil rights activities and, on at least one occasion, appeared for an interview on racial disorders in major American cities. See Washington, ed., *A Testament of Hope*, 394–414; McDonald, *Secretary to a King*, 95; and Dick Gregory, *Write Me In!*, edited by James R. McGraw (New York: Bantam Books, Inc.,1968), 33. In one of his books, Gregory devoted the "Postscript" to "Dr. Martin Luther King's Last Message to America." See Richard Claxton Gregory, *No More Lies: The Myth and the Reality of American History* (New York: Harper & Row, Publishers, 1971), 337–45. Although King typically did not include comics among those "inspiring examples of Negroes who with determination" broke "through the shackles of circumstance" to "achieve excellence" in their field of endeavor, there is reason to

There was always that larger world of comedians that greatly stirred and enlightened King, Jr., even as he appreciated Moms, Gregory, and others who supremely embodied the power and uses of black humor. Bob Hope probably impressed King, Jr. as much as any black entertainer when it came to stand-up comedy and the rapid paced delivery of jokes. King, Jr. quoted Hope on numerous occasions when speaking about "the great world house," and more specifically, about how the "world in which we live is a world of geographical oneness" due to "modern scientific and technological revolutions." "Bob Hope has described this new jet-age that we live in as an age in which you'll be able to take a non-stop flight from Los Angeles, California to New York City," King, Jr. commented, "and if you happen to develop hiccups on taking off in Los Angeles you will hic in Los Angeles and cup in New York City." King, Jr. felt that Hope, "in a very humorous sense," was really making a profound point about humanity and the world, and he used Hope's words in advancing his view that the great challenge is for humankind to turn a world that is "geographically one" into a world that is also "spiritually one."[182] King, Jr. never had a problem using humor to convey certain truths about life and the universe, the interrelated and interdependent structure of reality, and the common destiny of humanity.

King, Jr.'s gift of wit, humor, and laughter never obscured the clarity and power of his ideas and message. In fact, one finds here critical evidence of his amazing capacity as a creative thinker, idealist, and optimist, and not some throwback to that "vacuous, happy-go-lucky, Sambo image" too long associated with black people whenever they

believe that he felt that they, like other artists, had a role to play in building black self-pride and esteem. See King, Where Do We Go from Here?, 126–27; and Carson, et al., eds., King Papers, IV, 402.

182. King often prefaced his comment by saying that "It is not common for a preacher to be quoting Bob Hope, but I think he has aptly described this jet age in which we live." He usually extended Hope's remark in saying that "If you take a flight from Tokyo, Japan, on Sunday morning, you will arrive in Seattle, Washington, on the preceding Saturday night. When your friends meet you at the airport and ask you when you left Tokyo, you will have to say, 'I left tomorrow'." See Carson, et al., eds., King Papers, IV, 78; King, Where Do We Go from Here?, 167–68; Washington, ed., A Testament of Hope, 138 and 209; Martin Luther King, Jr., "The Church on the Frontier of Racial Tension," unpublished version of a lecture, Southern Baptist Theological Seminary, Louisville, Kentucky (19 April 1961), King Center Library and Archives, 4; and Martin Luther King, Jr., "The American Dream," unpublished version of an address, Lincoln University, Oxford, Pennsylvania (6 June 1961), King Center Library and Archives, 11.

are free-spirited, fun-loving, and open to joyous humor and laughter.[183] Convinced that good-natured humor stimulated and revitalized the mind, King, Jr. told jokes, made witty comments, and laughed hard all of his life, and only seconds before he was assassinated at the Lorraine Motel in Memphis, on April 4, 1968, he was joking around and laughing with his brother, A. D., Ralph Abernathy, Samuel Billy Kyles, Jesse Jackson, and others.[184] That joyous buoyancy never really faded. King, Jr.'s wit, humor, and laughter were not only a vital part of that infectious energy he radiated and imparted to those around him, it also revealed so much about his mind, heart, and soul, and also, about his almost desperate search for a full life with all of its real joys and benefits.

---

183. Levine, *Black Culture and Black Consciousness*, 300. Joseph Boskin has provided one of the most perceptive treatments of the Sambo image and black humor. See Joseph Boskin, "The Complicity of Humor: The Life and Death of Sambo," in Morreall, ed., *The Philosophy of Laughter and Humor*, 250–62.
184. "'I Remember Martin,'" 38; King, *My Life with Martin Luther King, Jr.*, 292; King, *Daddy King*, 188–89; Young, *An Easy Burden*, 463–64; Young, *A Way Out of No Way*, 100–101; and Baldwin, *There is a Balm in Gilead*, 306–7.

7

"A Good Man, But Not a God"

Massive numbers of people nationwide and in other countries deify Martin Luther King, Jr. But I think now of what Andy said in a phone conversation with me recently: "Martin didn't need us to do that," to deify him. He needed us to help him." And we did.
    –Dorothy F. Cotton[1]

You don't need to go out this morning saying that Martin Luther King was a saint, oh no; I want you to know this morning that I am a sinner like all of God's children, but I want to be a good man, and I want to hear a voice saying to me one day, "I take you in and I bless you because you try. . . ."
    –Martin Luther King, Jr.[2]

Martin Luther King, Jr. is revered, canonized, and even cast in a messianic light in terms of his public legacy, and unfortunately, his basic and vivid "humanness" has gotten lost in the process.[3] His

---

1. Dorothy F. Cotton, *If Your Back's Not Bent: The Role of the Citizenship Education Program in the Civil Rights Movement* (New York: Atria Books, 2012), 265.
2. See Clayborne Carson and Peter Holloran, eds., *A Knock at Midnight: Inspiration from the Great Sermons of Reverend Martin Luther King, Jr.* (New York; Warner Books, Inc., 1998), 198–99; and David J. Garrow, *The FBI and Martin Luther King Jr.: From "Solo" to Memphis* (New York: W. W. Norton & Company, 1981), 219 and 308n40.
3. This point has been made in other works, such as Christine King Farris, *Through It All: Reflections on My Life, My Family, and My Faith* (New York: Atria Books, 2009), 126; and Michael Eric Dyson, *I May Not Get There with You: The True Martin Luther King, Jr.* (New York: The Free Press, 2000), ix. Ralph Abernathy, King's friend and closest associate, put it best in saying that what so many

biography functions in American history as more than simply the story of an individual life, and our annual celebrations of him have assumed ritualistic significance. The mythological status bestowed upon King, Jr. is highlighted by the tendency to look to him for answers to so many of the monumental social problems that still confront humanity in the twenty-first century. This is not really surprising in a culture in which we are perhaps too devoted to creating heroes and sheroes (Maya Angelou's word), and not committed enough to shaping and nurturing genuine, ordinary, and decent human beings.

King, Jr. was a great leader, but also, a regular human being. This is essentially how King, Jr. viewed himself—as merely a human being pressed by the demands of inner truth. He never wanted people to become a mass cult of personality centered on him.[4] This book is not so much about the great hero and iconic figure, but about the human being who lurked behind the public persona and the media spotlight. In other words, it focuses on not only King, Jr.'s personal hopes, doubts, and uncertainties, but also, on his delight in pleasant and passionate conversation, his humility and affinity to common people, his preference for the precious but ordinary things of life, his robust appetite for artfully prepared and delicious soul food meals, his enduring appreciation for music and dance, his cheerful and playful attitude and spirit, his abiding interest in games, sports, and sports heroes, and his amazing gift of wit, humor, and laughter. This is the person that most people never got to know, and that most people still do not know today. It is the person who enjoyed and celebrated life, but was never bigger than life. Although many spoke of King, Jr.'s larger-than-life personality, he never considered himself a larger-than-life person.

Although there is a biographical tone to *Behind the Public Veil*, it was

---

miss in King is "his humanity, warmth, and, above all, his unflagging capacity to have fun and to make everybody else join in." See Ralph David Abernathy, *And the Walls Came Tumbling Down: An Autobiography* (New York: Harper & Row, Publishers, 1989), 467; and Ralph David Abernathy, "My Old Friend Martin," *The Tennessean: USA Weekend*, Nashville, Tennessee (12–14 January 1990), 6.

4. Stewart Burns rightly suggests that this was happening long before King suffered martyrdom. See Stewart Burns, *To the Mountaintop: Martin Luther King Jr.'s Sacred Mission to Save America, 1955–1968* (San Francisco: HarperCollins Publishers, Inc., 2004), 171, 270, 276, 283, 287–88, 293, 330, and 434.

never meant to be a complete portrait of King, Jr.'s life. There are already numerous biographies of this phenomenal figure. The point here was to simply highlight ignored or trivialized sides of King, Jr.'s personality and life, thus allowing him to express his humanity as much as possible. What King, Jr. showed us about the grandeur of humanity, or humanity's potential for empathy, virtue, valor, and achievement, is not neglected, but so much of the accent is on what he revealed about the natural human tendencies and limitations that people so often share. The emerging portrait is that of a man who, despite great fame and achievements, was always approachable and affable—a man who allowed his own natural, genuine inclinations to guide him when dealing with people at all levels of society.

One would not be in error in calling this a book about culture, which is understandable in view of my many years of training, teaching, and scholarship as a cultural historian. I would describe it as a work that fits well into what Rufus Burrow, Jr. calls "the black cultural studies genre in King studies."[5] It is further confirmation of what I have tried to convey over more than thirty years of teaching and writing about King, Jr.—namely, that black cultural and religious sources are of pivotal importance in understanding his person, and also, his "life, thought, vision, and efforts to translate the ethical ideal of the beloved community into practical reality."[6] This is why I think that in studying King, Jr.'s most important formative influences, one must begin with his "Autobiography of Religious Development" (1950) before turning to versions of his "Pilgrimage to Nonviolence" (1958).[7] This book provides indisputable evidence for that claim.

While the stress in *Behind the Public Veil* is more on the private person than the public figure, the work shows that it is not always possible to neatly separate the two. This is understandable since every human

---

5. Rufus Burrow, Jr., *Martin Luther King, Jr., and the Theology of Resistance* (Jefferson, NC: McFarland & Company, Inc., 2015), 122.
6. Lewis V. Baldwin, *There is a Balm in Gilead: The Cultural Roots of Martin Luther King, Jr.* (Minneapolis: Fortress Press, 1991), 2.
7. See Clayborne Carson, et. al., eds., *The Papers of Martin Luther King, Jr., Volume I: Called to Serve, January 1929–June 1951* (Berkeley: University of California Press, 1992), 359–63; and Martin Luther King, Jr., *Stride toward Freedom: The Montgomery Story* (New York: Harper & Row, Publishers, 1958), 90–107.

being is, in some measure, a mixture of the private and the public persona. In his book, *The King God Didn't Save* (1970), John A. Williams wrote several chapters on both "The Private Man" and "The Public Man," and his treatment of King, Jr., in addition to what Richard Lischer, Stewart Burns, and others have written about the private King, Jr. and the public King, Jr., prove that the historical King, Jr. is virtually impossible to recognize and hold in view without some attention to both.[8] King, Jr. was a rare, complex mix of the private and the public persona, and he and those closest to him would have admitted this without hesitation. I became even more convinced of this while writing this book.

If there is one major lesson to be learned from *Behind the Public Veil*, it is that King, Jr. had an incredibly rich, complex, and meaningful life, over and beyond what he did and accomplished in the public sphere. He was *human* in the best sense of the word and, because of that authentic, and yet, profound "humanness," he had so much left to give this nation and the world.

---

8. John A. Williams, *The King God Didn't Save* (New York: Coward-McCann, Inc., 1970), 17–221; and Burns, *To the Mountaintop*, 253–54, 259–60, 264, and 346–47. Lischer reminds us that in the case of King, there was at times some "contradiction between the public mask and the private person," which is what being human is all about, but he never denies the importance of both in understanding King. See Richard Lischer, *The Preacher King: Martin Luther King Jr. and the Word that Moved America* (New York: Oxford University Press, 1995), 169.

Bibliography

Books and Manuscripts

Abernathy, Ralph D. *And the Walls Came Tumbling Down: An Autobiography.* New York: Harper & Row, Publishers, 1989.

"A History of Calvary Baptist Church," in *Program Booklet of the Calvary Baptist Church Centennial Celebration, 1879-1979.* Chester, PA: Linder Printing Company, 1979.

Ansbro, John J. *Martin Luther King, Jr.: The Making of a Mind.* Maryknoll, NY: Orbis Books, 1982.

Atlanta: A City of the Modern South. Compiled by The Works of the Writer's Program of The Works Project Administration in the State of Georgia. New York: Smith and Durrell, 1942.

Ayres, Alex, ed. *The Wisdom of Martin Luther King, Jr.: An A-to-Z Guide to the Ideas and Ideals of the Great Civil Rights Leader.* New York: Penguin Books USA, 1993.

Bagley, Edythe Scott. *Desert Rose: The Life and Legacy of Coretta Scott King.* Tuscaloosa: The University of Alabama Press, 2012.

Baldwin, Lewis V., ed. *"In a Single Garment of Destiny": A Global Vision of Justice—Martin Luther King, Jr.* Boston: Beacon Press, 2012.

———. *"Invisible" Strands in African Methodism: A History of the African Union Methodist Protestant and Union American Methodist Episcopal Churches, 1805-1980.* Metuchen, NJ: The American Theological Library Association and The Scarecrow Press, Inc., 1983.

———. *Never to Leave Us Alone: The Prayer Life of Martin Luther King Jr.* Minneapolis: Fortress Press, 2010.

_____. *There is a Balm in Gilead: The Cultural Roots of Martin Luther King, Jr.* Minneapolis: Fortress Press, 1991.

_____. *The Voice of Conscience: The Church in the Mind of Martin Luther King, Jr.* New York: Oxford University Press, 2010.

_____, ed. *"Thou, Dear God": Prayers that Open Hearts and Spirits—The Reverend Dr. Martin Luther King, Jr.* Boston: Beacon Press, 2012.

_____. *To Make the Wounded Whole: The Cultural Legacy of Martin Luther King, Jr.* Minneapolis: Fortress Press, 1992.

_____. *Toward the Beloved Community: Martin Luther King Jr. and South Africa.* Cleveland: Pilgrim Press, 1995.

_____ and Amiri Yasin Al-Hadid. *Between Cross and Crescent: Christian and Muslim Perspectives on Malcolm and Martin.* Gainesville: University Press of Florida, 2002.

_____ and Aprille V. Woodson. *Freedom is Never Free: A Biographical Portrait of E. D. Nixon, Sr.* Nashville, TN: United Parcel Service Branch, 1992.

_____ and Rufus Burrow, Jr., eds. *The Domestication of Martin Luther King Jr.: Clarence B. Jones, Right-Wing Conservatism, and the Manipulation of the King Legacy.* Eugene, OR: Cascade Books, 2013.

_____ and Paul R. Dekar, eds. *"In an Inescapable Network of Mutuality": Martin Luther King, Jr. and the Globalization of an Ethical Ideal.* Eugene, OR: Cascade Books, 2013.

_____ Rufus Burrow Jr., Barbara A. Holmes, and Susan Holmes Winfield, eds. *The Legacy of Martin Luther King, Jr.: The Boundaries of Law, Politics, and Religion.* Notre Dame, IN: University of Notre Dame Press, 2002.

Bartlett, John, *The Shorter Bartlett's Familiar Quotations: A Collection of Passages, Phrases, and Proverbs Traced to their Sources in Ancient and Modern Literature,* edited by Christopher Morley and Louella D. Everett. New York: Pocket Books, Inc., 1964.

Belafonte, Harry. *My Song: A Memoir,* with Michael Shnayerson. New York: Alfred A. Knopf, 2011.

Bennett, Lerone, Jr. *What Manner of Man: A Biography of Martin Luther King, Jr.* Chicago: Johnson Publishing Company, 1964.

Boddie, Charles E. *God's "Bad Boys": Eight Outstanding Black Preachers.* Valley Forge, PA: Judson Press, 1980.

Bradford, Sarah. *Harriet Tubman: The Moses of Her People*. 2nd edition. New York: Corinth Books, 1961; reprint, 1886.

Branch, Taylor. *At Canaan's Edge: America in the King Years, 1965–68*. New York: Simon & Schuster, 2006.

____. *Parting the Waters: America in the King Years, 1954–63*. New York: Simon and Schuster, 1988.

____. *Pillar of Fire: America in the King Years, 1963–65*. New York: Simon and Schuster, 1998.

Brewer, J. Mason. *American Negro Folklore*. New York: Quadrangle/The New York Times, 1968.

Burns, Stewart. *To the Mountaintop: Martin Luther King Jr.'s Sacred Mission to Save America, 1955–1968*. New York: HarperCollins Publishers, Inc., 2004.

Burrow, Rufus, Jr. *A Child Shall Lead Them: Martin Luther King Jr., Young People, and the Movement*. Minneapolis: Fortress Press, 2014.

____. *Extremist for Love: Martin Luther King Jr., Man of Ideas and Nonviolent Social Action*. Minneapolis: Fortress Press, 2014.

____. *God and Human Dignity: The Personalism, Theology, and Ethics of Martin Luther King, Jr.* Notre Dame, IN: University of Notre Dame Press, 2006.

____. *Martin Luther King, Jr., and the Theology of Resistance*. Jefferson, NC: McFarland & Company, Inc., Publishers, 2015.

Carawan, Guy and Carawan, Candie. *Sing for Freedom: The Story of the Civil Rights Movement through Its Songs*. Bethlehem, PA: Sing Out Corporation, 1990.

Carson, Clayborne. *Martin's Dream: My Journey and the Legacy of Martin Luther King, Jr.—A Memoir*. New York: Palgrave MacMillan, 2013.

____, ed. *The Autobiography of Martin Luther King, Jr.* New York: Warner Books, Inc., 1998.

____ and Peter Holloran, eds. *A Knock at Midnight: Inspiration from the Great Sermons of Reverend Martin Luther King, Jr.* New York: Warner Books, Inc., 1998.

____ and Kris Shepard, eds. *A Call to Conscience: The Landmark Speeches of Dr. Martin Luther King, Jr.* New York: Warner Books, Inc., 2001.

____, Ralph E. Luker, Penny A. Russell, and Louis R. Harlan, eds. *The Papers of Martin Luther King, Jr., Volume I: Called to Serve, January 1929-June 1951*. Berkeley: University of California Press, 1992.

_____, Ralph E. Luker, Penny A. Russell, Peter Holloran, and Louis R. Harlan, eds. *The Papers of Martin Luther King, Jr., Volume II: Rediscovering Precious Values, July 1951-November 1955.* Berkeley: University of California Press, 1994.

_____, Stewart Burns, Susan Carson, Peter Holloran, and Dana L. Powell H., eds. *The Papers of Martin Luther King, Jr., Volume III: Birth of a New Age, December 1955-December 1956.* Berkeley: University of California Press, 1997.

_____, Susan Carson, Adrienne Clay, Virginia Shadron, and Kieran Taylor, eds. *The Papers of Martin Luther King, Jr., Volume IV: Symbol of the Movement, January 1957-December 1958.* Berkeley: University of California Press, 2000.

_____, Tenisha Armstrong, Susan Carson, Adrienne Clay, and Kieran Taylor, eds. *The Papers of Martin Luther King, Jr., Volume V: Threshold of a New Decade, January 1959-December 1960.* Berkeley: University of California Press, 2005).

_____, Susan Carson, Susan Englander, Troy Jackson, and Gerald L. Smith, eds. *The Papers of Martin Luther King, Jr., Volume VI: Advocate of the Social Gospel, September 1948-March 1963.* Berkeley: University of California Press, 2007.

_____ and Tenisha Armstrong, eds. *The Papers of Martin Luther King, Jr., Volume VII: To Save the Soul of America, January 1961-August 1962.* Berkeley: University of California Press, 2015.

Carter, Sr., Lawrence E., ed. *Walking Integrity: Benjamin Elijah Mays, Mentor to Martin Luther King Jr.* Macon, GA: Mercer University Press, 1998.

Chappell, David L. *Inside Agitators: White Southerners in the Civil Rights Movement.* Baltimore: The John Hopkins University Press, 1994.

_____. *Waking from the Dream: The Struggle for Civil Rights in the Shadow of Martin Luther King, Jr.* New York: Random House, 2014.

Clark, Kenneth B. *King, Malcolm, Baldwin: Three Interviews.* Middletown, CT: Wesleyan University Press, 1985; originally published in 1963.

Clinebell, Howard. *Basic Types of Pastoral Care & Counseling: Resources for the Ministry of Healing and Growth.* Nashville: Abingdon Press, 2011.

_____. *Well Being: A Personal Plan for Exploring and Enriching the Seven Dimensions of Life—Mind, Body, Spirit, Love, Work, Play, the Earth.* New York: HarperCollins Publishers, Inc., 1992.

Collins, David R. *Not Only Dreamers: The Story of Martin Luther King, Sr. and Martin Luther King, Jr.* Elgin, IL: Brethren Press, 1986.

Cone, James H. *Martin & Malcolm & America: A Dream or a Nightmare*. Maryknoll, NY: Orbis Books, 1991.

Cooney, Patrick L. and Henry W. Powell. *The Life and Times of the Prophet Vernon Johns: Father of the Civil Rights Movement*. Unpublished Manuscript, 1998.

Cotton, Dorothy F. *If Your Back's Not Bent: The Role of the Citizenship Education Program in the Civil Rights Movement*. New York: Atria Books, 2012.

Courlander, Harold. *Negro Folk Music, U. S. A.* New York: Columbia University Press, 1963.

Cox, Harvey. *The Feast of Fools: A Theological Essay on Festivity and Fantasy*. New York: Harper & Row, Publishers, 1969.

Davis, Gerald L. *I Got the Word in Me and I Can Sing It, You Know*. Philadelphia: University of Pennsylvania Press, 1985.

Davis, Sammy, Jr. *Yes I Can: The Story of Sammy Davis, Jr.*, with Jane and Burt Boyar. New York: Pocket Books, 1965.

DeKorte, Juliann. *Ethel Waters: Finally Home*. Old Tappan, NJ: Fleming H. Revell Company, 1978.

Dixon, Christa K. *Negro Spirituals from Bible to Folk Song*. Philadelphia: Fortress Press, 1976.

Dollard, John. *Caste and Class in a Southern Town*. New York: Doubleday & Company, Inc., 1949.

Douglas, Charles Noel, comp. *Forty Thousand Sublime and Beautiful Thoughts: Gathered from the Roses, Clover Blossoms, Geraniums, Violets, Morning Glories, and Pansies of Literature*. New York: Louis Klopsch, 1904.

Douglass, Frederick. *Life and Times of Frederick Douglass*. Revised Edition. New York: The Crowell-Collier Publishing Company, 1962; reprint, 1892.

Downing, Frederick L. *To See the Promised Land: The Faith Pilgrimage of Martin Luther King, Jr.* Macon, GA: Mercer University Press, 1986.

DuBois, William E. B. *Dusk of Dawn: An Essay toward an Autobiography of a Race Concept*. New York: Schocken Books, 1971; originally published in 1940.

____. *The Souls of Black Folk in Three Negro Classics*. New York: Avon Books, 1965.

Dyson, Michael Eric. *I May Not Get There with You: The True Martin Luther King, Jr.* New York: The Free Press, 2000.

Egerton, John. *Southern Food: At Home, on the Road, in History*. New York: Alfred A. Knopf, Inc., 1987.

Evans, James H., Jr. *Playing: Christian Explorations of Daily Living.* Minneapolis: Fortress Press, 2010.

Evans, Zelia S. and J. T. Alexander, eds. *Dexter Avenue Baptist Church, 1877–1977: One Hundred Year History of a Famous Religious Institution.* Montgomery, AL: Dexter Avenue Baptist Church, 1978.

Fager, Charles E. *Selma, 1965: The March that Changed the South.* Boston: Beacon Press, 1985.

Farris, Christine King. *My Brother Martin: A Sister Remembers Growing Up with the Rev. Dr. Martin Luther King, Jr.* New York: Simon & Schuster Books for Young Readers, 2003.

____. *Through It All: Reflections on My Life, My Family, and My Faith.* New York: Atria Books, 2009.

Faulkner, William J. *The Days When the Animals Talked: Black American Folktales and How They Came to Be.* Chicago: Follett Publishing Company, 1977.

Fluker, Walter E. *They Looked for a City: A Comparative Analysis of the Ideal of Community in the Thought of Howard Thurman and Martin Luther King, Jr.* Lanham, MD: University Press of America, 1989.

Foner, Eric, ed. *America's Black Past: A Reader in Afro-American History.* New York: Harper & Row, Publishers, 1970.

Frazier, E. Franklin. *The Negro Family in the United States.* Chicago: The University of Chicago Press, 1968.

Freeman, Ronald L. *The Mule Train: A Journey of Hope Remembered.* Nashville: Rutledge Hill Press, 1998.

Friedly, Michael and Gallen, David. *Martin Luther King, Jr.: The FBI File.* New York: Carroll & Graf Publishers, Inc., 1993.

Garland, Phyl. *The Sound of Soul.* Chicago: Henry Regnery Company, 1969.

Garrow, David J. *Bearing the Cross: Martin Luther King, Jr., and the Southern Christian Leadership Conference.* New York: William Morrow and Company, Inc., 1986.

____. *The FBI and Martin Luther King, Jr.: From "Solo" to Memphis.* New York: W. W. Norton & Company, 1981.

Genovese, Eugene D. *The Southern Front: History and Politics in the Cultural War.* Columbia: University of Missouri Press, 1995.

Gitin, Maria. *This Bright Light of Ours: Stories from the Voting Rights Fight.* Tuscaloosa: The University of Alabama Press, 2014.

Graetz, Robert S. *A White Preacher's Message on Race and Reconciliation: Based on His Experiences Beginning with the Montgomery Bus Boycott*. Montgomery, AL: New South Books, 2006.

___. *Montgomery: A White Preacher's Memoir*. Minneapolis: Fortress Press, 1991.

Gregory, Dick. *Write Me In!*, edited by James R, McGraw. New York: Bantam Books, Inc., 1968.

Gregory, Richard Claxton. *No More Lies: The Myth and the Reality of American History*. New York: Harper & Row, Publishers, 1971.

Groos, Karl. *The Play of Man*. New York: D. Appleton, 1916.

Hampton, Henry and Steve Fayer. *Voices of Freedom: An Oral History of the Civil Rights Movement from the 1950s through the 1980s*, with Sarah Flynn. New York: Bantam Books, 1990.

Harris, Michael W. *The Rise of the Gospel Blues: The Music of Thomas A. Dorsey in the Urban Church*. New York: Oxford University Press, 1992.

Heilbut, Tony. *The Gospel Sound: Good News and Bad Times*. New York: Anchor Books/Anchor Press/Doubleday, 1975.

Helmer, Christine, ed. *The Global Luther: A Theologian for Modern Times*. Minneapolis: Fortress Press, 2009.

Hernton, Calvin C. *Sex and Racism in America*. New York: Grove Press, Inc., 1965.

Hester, William Hunter. *One Hundred and Five Years of Faith: A History of the Twelfth Baptist Church, 1840–1945*. Boston: Twelfth Baptist Church, 1946.

Hicks, Jr., H. Beecher *Images of the Black Preacher: The Man Nobody Knows*. Valley Forge, PA: Judson Press, 1977.

Honey, Michael K. *Going Down Jericho Road: The Memphis Strike, Martin Luther King's Last Crusade*. New York: W. W. Norton & Company, 2007.

Houser, George M. *No One Can Stop the Rain: Glimpses of Africa's Liberation Struggle*. New York: The Pilgrim Press, 1989.

Jackson, Jesse. *Make a Joyful Noise Unto the Lord: The Life of Mahalia Jackson, Queen of Gospel Singers*. New York: Dell Publishing Company, Inc., 1974.

Jackson, Joseph H. *A Story of Christian Activism: The History of the National Baptist Convention, USA, Inc*. Nashville, TN: Townsend Press, 1980.

Jackson, Troy. *Becoming King: Martin Luther King Jr. and the Making of a National Leader*. Lexington: The University Press of Kentucky, 2008.

Johnson, Clifton H., ed. *God Struck Me Dead: Voices of Ex-Slaves*, with a new

Introduction by Albert J. Raboteau. Cleveland: Pilgrim Press, 1993; originally published in 1969.

Johnson, James Weldon. *Along This Way: The Autobiography of James Weldon Johnson*. New York: Viking Press, 1933.

_____. *God's Trombones: Seven Negro Sermons in Verse*. New York: The Viking Press, 1977; originally published in 1927.

_____. *The Autobiography of an Ex-Colored Man*. New York: Alfred Knopf, 1927.

_____ and J. Rosamond Johnson. *The Books of American Negro Spirituals*. New York: Viking Press, 1953; originally published in 1925.

King, Bernice A. *Hard Questions, Heart Answers: Speeches and Sermons*. New York: Broadway Books, 1996.

King, Coretta Scott. *My Life with Martin Luther King, Jr*. New York: Henry Holt and Company, 1993; originally published in 1969.

King, Dexter Scott. *Growing Up King: An Intimate Memoir*, with Ralph Wiley. New York: Warner Books, Inc., 2003.

King, Martin Luther, Jr. *Strength to Love*. Philadelphia: Fortress Press, 1981; originally published in 1963.

_____. *Stride toward Freedom: The Montgomery Story*. New York: Harper & Row, Publishers, 1958.

_____. *The Measure of a Man*. Philadelphia: Fortress Press, 1988; originally published in 1959.

_____. *The Trumpet of Conscience*. San Francisco: Harper & Row, Publishers, 1987; originally published in 1967.

_____. *Where Do We Go from Here: Chaos or Community?* Boston: Beacon Press, 1968; originally published in 1967.

_____. *Why We Can't Wait*. New York: The New American Library, Inc., 1963.

King, Martin Luther, Sr. *Daddy King: An Autobiography*, with Clayton Riley. New York: William Morrow & Company, 1980.

King, Yolanda. *The Content of My Character*. Emmaus, PA: Rodale Press, 2002.

_____ and Wanda Marie. *Embracing Your Power in 30 Days: A Journey of Self Discovery and Personal Freedom*. Culver City, CA: Higher Ground Publications, 2005.

_____ and Elodia Tate. *Open My Eyes, Open My Soul: Celebrating Our Common Humanity*. New York: McGraw-Hill, 2004.

Lentz, Richard. *Symbols, the News Magazines, and Martin Luther King, Jr.* Baton Rouge: Louisiana State University Press, 1990.

Levine, Lawrence W. *Black Culture and Black Consciousness: Afro-American Folk Thought from Slavery to Freedom.* New York: Oxford University Press, 1978.

Lewis, David L. *King: A Critical Biography.* New York: Praeger Publishers, 1970.

Lincoln, C. Eric. *The Black Muslims in America.* Trenton, NJ: William B. Eerdmans Publishing Company and Africa World Press, Inc., 1994; originally published in 1961.

Ling, Peter. *Martin Luther King, Jr.* New York: Routledge, 2002.

Lischer, Richard. *The Preacher King: Martin Luther King Jr. and the Word that Moved America.* New York: Oxford University Press, 1995.

Locke, Alain, ed. *The New Negro: An Interpretation.* New York: Albert and Charles Boni, 1925.

Long, Michael G. *Martin Luther King Jr. on Creative Living.* St. Louis, MO: Chalice Press, 2004.

Martin Luther King Jr. 1929-1968: An Ebony Picture Biography. Chicago: Johnson Publishing Company, Inc., 1968.

Marty, Martin E. and Dean G. Pearman, eds., *New Theology No. 6: On Revolution and Non-Revolution, Violence and Non-Violence, Peace and Power.* New York: The Macmillan Company, 1972.

McDonald, Dora. *Secretary to a King: My Years with Martin Luther King, Jr., the Civil Rights Movement, and Beyond.* Montgomery, AL: New South Books, 2012.

McKnight, Gerald D. *The Last Crusade: Martin Luther King, Jr., the FBI, and the Poor People's Campaign.* Boulder, MO: Westview Press, 1998.

Medearis, Angela Shelf. *Dare to Dream: Coretta Scott King and the Civil Rights Movement,* illustrated by Anna Rich. New York: Puffin Books, 1994.

Meier, August and Elliot Rudwick, eds., *The Making of Black America: Essays in Negro Life and History.* 2 Vols. New York: Atheneum, 1974.

Mikell, Robert M. *Selma.* Huntsville, AL: Publishers Enterprise, Inc., 1965.

Miller, Keith D. *Voice of Deliverance: The Language of Martin Luther King, Jr., and Its Sources.* New York: The Free Press, 1992.

Miller, W. Jason. *Origins of the Dream: Hughes's Poetry and King's Rhetoric.* Gainesville: University Press of Florida, 2015.

Morreall, John, ed. *The Philosophy of Laughter and Humor.* Albany: State University of New York Press, 1987.

Muhammad, Elijah. *How to Eat to Live.* Chicago: Muhammad's Temple of Islam No. 2, 1972.

Oates, Stephen B. *Let the Trumpet Sound: The Life of Martin Luther King, Jr.* New York: Harper & Row, Publishers, 1982.

Program Booklet of the Calvary Baptist Church Centennial Celebration, 1879–1979. Chester, PA: Linder Printing Company, 1979.

Ralph, James R., Jr. *Northern Protest: Martin Luther King, Jr., Chicago, and the Civil Rights Movement.* Cambridge: Harvard University Press, 1993.

Reddick, Lawrence D. *Crusader without Violence: A Biography of Martin Luther King, Jr.* New York: Harper & Brothers, 1959.

Sanders, Cheryl J. *Empowerment Ethics for a Liberated People—A Path to African American Social Transformation.* Minneapolis: Fortress Press, 1995.

Silver, Murray M. *Daddy King & Me: Memories of the Forgotten Father of the Civil Rights Movement.* Savannah, GA: Continental Shelf Publishing, LLC, 2009.

Smiley, Tavis. *Death of a King: The Real Story of Dr. Martin Luther King Jr.'s Final Year*, with David Ritz. New York: Little, Brown, and Company, 2014.

Smith, Ervin. *The Ethics of Martin Luther King, Jr.* Lewiston, NY: The Edwin Mellen Press, 1981.

Smith, Kenneth L. and Ira G. Zepp, Jr. *Search for the Beloved Community: The Thinking of Martin Luther King, Jr.* Valley Forge, PA: Judson Press, 1974.

Songs of Zion: Supplemental Worship Resources, 12. Nashville: Abingdon Press, 1981.

Southern, Eileen. *The Music of Black Americans: A History.* Second Edition. New York: W. W. Norton & Company, Inc., 1983.

Spencer, Jon Michael. *Sacred Symphony: The Chanted Sermon of the Black Preacher.* Westport, CT: Greenwood Press, 1987.

Stuckey, Sterling. *Slave Culture: Nationalist Theory and the Foundations of Black America.* New York: Oxford University Press, 1987.

Talley, Thomas. *Negro Folk Rhymes.* Port Washington, NY: Kennikat Press, 1968; Originally published in 1922.

The Centennial Yearbook of the Calvary Baptist Church, 1879–1979. Chester, PA: Calvary Baptist Church, 1979.

The National Baptist Hymnal. Nashville: National Baptist Publishing Board, 1983.

Three-Fold Celebration Year: Souvenir Journal, Twelfth Baptist Church. Boston: Twelfth Baptist Church, May 1985.

Thurman, Howard. *Deep River and the Negro Spiritual Speaks of Life and Death.* Richmond, IN: Friends United Press, 1975.

____. *Jesus and the Disinherited.* Nashville: Abingdon Press, 1949.

Thurman, Michael, ed. *Voices from the Dexter Pulpit.* Montgomery, AL: New South Books, 2001.

Tribble, Sherman R. *Images of a Preacher: A Study of the Reverend Joseph Harrison Jackson.* Nashville, TN: Townsend Press, 2008.

Vaughn, Wally G. and Richard W. Wills, eds. *Reflections on Our Pastor: Dr. Martin Luther King, Jr., at Dexter Avenue Baptist Church, 1954-1960.* Dover, MA: The Majority Press, Inc., 1999.

Vivian, Octavia. *Coretta: The Story of Coretta Scott King.* Commemorative Edition. Minneapolis: Fortress Press, 2006.

Walker, Wyatt Tee. *"Somebody's Calling My Name": Black Sacred Music and Social Change.* Valley Forge, PA: Judson Press, 1979.

Washington, James M., ed. *A Testament of Hope: The Essential Writings and Speeches of Martin Luther King, Jr.* New York: HarperCollins Publishers, Inc., 1991; originally published in 1986.

____, ed. *I Have a Dream: Writings and Speeches that Changed the World.* New York: HarperCollins Publishers, 1992.

Watley, William D. *Roots of Resistance: The Nonviolent Ethic of Martin Luther King, Jr.* Valley Forge, PA: Judson Press, 1985.

Webb, Sheyann and Rachel West. *Selma, Lord, Selma: Childhood Memories of the Civil Rights Days.* As told to Frank Sikora. Tuscaloosa: The University of Alabama Press, 1997.

Williams, Donnie. *The Thunder of Angels: The Montgomery Bus Boycott and the People Who Broke the Back of Jim Crow,* with Wayne Greenhaw. Chicago: Lawrence Hill Books, 2006.

Williams, John A. *The King God Didn't Save.* New York: Coward-McCann, Inc., 1970.

Williams, Juan. *Eyes on the Prize: America's Civil Rights Years, 1954–1965.* New York: Viking Penguin, Inc., 1987.

Wiltshire, Susan Ford. *Public & Private in Vergil's Aeneid*. Amherst: The University of Massachusetts Press, 1989.

Young, Andrew. *An Easy Burden: The Civil Rights Movement and the Transformation of America*. New York: HarperCollins Publishers, Inc., 1996.

_____. *A Way Out of No Way: The Spiritual Memoirs of Andrew Young*. Nashville, TN: Thomas Nelson Publishers, 1994.

Journal and Magazine Articles

Baldwin, James. "The Dangerous Road before Martin Luther King, Jr." *Harper's Magazine*, 222 (February, 1961), 33–42.

Baldwin, Lewis V. "'A Home in Dat Rock': Afro-American Folk Sources and Slave Visions of Heaven and Hell." *JRT*, Vol. 41, no. 1 (Spring–Summer, 1984), 38–57.

_____. "A Reassessment of the Relationship Between Malcolm X and Martin Luther King, Jr." *The Western Journal of Black Studies*, Vol. 13, no.2 (September, 1989), 103–13.

_____. "Martin Luther King, Jr., the Black Church, and the Black Messianic Vision." *The Journal of the Interdenominational Theological Center*, Vol. 12, Nos. 1 and 2 (Fall, 1984/Spring, 1985), 93–108.

Britton, John H. "Women Stay in the Shadows, But Give Men Strength to Fight." *Jet*, Vol. XXV, no 17 (13 February 1964), 22–24.

Brown, Sterling A. "Negro Folk Expression." *Phylon*, Vol. 11, no. 4 (4th Quarter, 1950), 318–27.

Carson, Clayborne. "Martin Luther King, Jr.: The Crozer Years." *The Journal of Blacks in Higher Education*, no. 16 (Summer, 1997), 123–28.

_____. "Martin Luther King Jr.: The Morehouse Years." *The Journal of Blacks in Higher Education*, no. 15 (Spring, 1997), 121–25.

Dubaj, Katie J. "My Translucent Father." *Human Architecture: Journal of the Sociology of Self-Knowledge*, Vol. I, Issue 2 (2002), article 8.

Farris, Christine King. "The Young Martin: From Childhood through College." *Ebony*, Vol. XLI, no. 3 (January, 1986), 56–58.

Garber, Paul R. "Too Much Taming of Martin Luther King, Jr.?" *The Christian Century*, (5 June 1974), XCI, 616.

Harding, Vincent. "W. E. B. DuBois and the Black Messianic Vision." *Freedomways*, Vol. 9, no. 1 (Winter, 1969), 49–57.

"'I Remember Martin': People Close to the Late Civil Rights Leader Recall a Down-to-Earth and Humorous Man." *Ebony*, Vol. 39, no. 6 (April, 1984), 34, 36, 38, and 40.

Johnson, Robert E. "Daddy King's Own Book about His Tragedies." *Jet*, Vol. 59, no. 2 (25 September, 1980), 16.

King, Charles H. "Quest and Conflict: The Untold Story of the Power Struggle Between King and Jackson," *Negro Digest*, 16 (May, 1967), 6–10 and 71–79.

King, Martin Luther, Jr. "Advice for Living." *Ebony*, 13 (April, 1958), 104.

_____. "Advice for Living." *Ebony*, 13 (May, 1958), 112.

_____. "Honoring Dr. DuBois." *Freedomways*, Vol. 8, no. 2 (Spring, 1968), 104–11.

King, Martin Luther, Sr. "What Part Should Singing Play in Our Church Worship?," *Georgia Baptist* (1 March 1936).

McKinney, Don S. "Brer Rabbit and Brother Martin Luther King, Jr.: The Folktale Background of the Birmingham Protest." *JRT*, Vol. 46, no. 2 (Winter–Spring, 1989–1990), 42–52.

Nelson, Corinne. "New Books by African-American Authors." *The Collegian*, First Semester Super Issue (2002), 126.

Norment, Lynn. "New Generation of Kings Take Over." *Ebony*, Vol. L, no. 3 (January, 1995), 25–26, 28, 30, 32, and 34.

_____. "The King Family: Keepers of the Dream." *Ebony*, Vol. XLII, no. 3 (January, 1987), 25–26, 28, 30, 32, and 34.

Peters, William. "Our Weapon Is Love." *Redbook* (August, 1956), 42–43 and 71–73.

Ricks, John A. "'De Lawd' Descends and is Crucified: Martin Luther King, Jr., in Albany, Georgia." *Journal of Southwest Georgia History*, 2 (1984), 3–14.

Silver, Theodore. "Rev. M. L. King: Alabama Moses." *The American Negro*, I (June, 1956), 13–15.

West, Traci. "Gendered Legacies of Martin Luther King Jr.'s Leadership." *Theology Today*, Vol. 65, no 1 (2008), 41–56.

Newspaper Articles

Abernathy, Ralph D. "My Old Friend Martin." *The Tennessean: USA Weekend*, Nashville, Tennessee (12–14 January 1990).

Dirks, Lee E. "'The Essence is Love': The Theology of Martin Luther King, Jr." *National Observer* (30 December 1963).

"Funeral Notices." *Atlanta Daily World*, Atlanta, Georgia (19 May 1941).

"Funeral Wednesday." *Atlanta Daily World*, Atlanta, Georgia (20 May 1941).

Jones, Kirk Byron. "Old Chester, PA: Dr. Martin Luther King, Jr." *Delaware County Daily Times*, "Opinion and Commentary section" (16 January 1989).

King, Coretta Scott. "Empowering Women Will Benefit Nation." *The Tennessean*, Nashville, Tennessee (1 March 1988).

____. "U. S. Needs More Willing Women Participants in Foreign Policy." *The Tennessean*, Nashville, Tennessee (13 November 1990).

King, Martin Luther, Jr. "Hall of Famer." *New York Amsterdam News*, New York, New York (4 August 1963).

____. "The Negro Speaks—The Negro is the Most Glaring Evidence of White America's Hypocrisy." *St. Louis Post Dispatch* (25 August 1963).

____. "What the Nobel Prize Means to Me." *New York Amsterdam News* (28 November 1964).

Miller, Daryl. "King's Dream Endures Mixture of Music and Drama." *Los Angeles Times* (6 February 2000).

"Mrs. Williams to be Funeralized this Afternoon." *Atlanta Daily World*, Atlanta, Georgia (21 May 1941).

"Negro Pastor Urges King to Leave Town." *The Plain Dealer*, Cleveland Ohio (20 April 1967).

Patterson, Eugene. "Martin Luther King, Jr.: Where the Action Is?" *The Atlanta Constitution* (9 April 1967).

Poston, Ted. "Fighting Pastor: Martin Luther King, Jr." *New York Post*, New York, New York (8 April 1957).

"Rev. and Mrs. King Return to Atlanta." *Atlanta Daily World*, Atlanta, Georgia (7 July 1948).

"Rev. M. L. King, Jr. Guest Speaker for Cultural League." *Atlanta Daily World*, Atlanta, Georgia (11 July 1948).

Robinson, Jackie. "An Open Letter to Martin Luther King, Jr." *Chicago Defender* (13 May 1967).

———. "What I Think of Dr. Martin Luther King." *Chicago Defender*, Chicago, Illinois (1 July 1967).

Shelton, Robert. "Songs a Weapon in Rights Battle." *The New York Times* (20 August 1962).

Simon, Roger. "To Her, Rev. King was Simply Dad." *Chicago Tribune* (14 January 1985) and *Los Angeles Times* (14 January 1985).

Williams, Linda. "Molding Men: At Morehouse College, Middle Class Blacks are Taught to Lead," *The Wall Street Journal* (5 May 1987).

Web Sources and Online Articles

"Georgia Theresa Gilmore (2014). The Biography," accessed 22 May 2014, http://www.biography.com/people/georgia-gilmore-21392019.

Justice, Glen. "Remembering Mentor to a Generation of Young Black Preachers: Among His Interns was the Rev. Dr. Martin Luther King Jr.," posted 7 August 1994, http://articles.philly.com/1994-08-07/news/258416161oldest-black-church-senior-pastor-interns.

"MLK After 40 Years: A Fraternal Memoir," posted 26 January 2008, http://radioopensource.org/mlk-jr-after-40-years-a-fraternal-memoir/.

Dissertations

Goodloe, Marcus "Goodie." "Coalition of Conscience: An Assessment of Martin Luther King Jr.'s Leadership with Athletes and Entertainers During the Civil Rights Movement." PhD diss., Dallas Baptist University, 2011.

Yeakey, Lamont H. "The Montgomery, Alabama Bus Boycott, 1955–56." PhD diss., Columbia University, 1979.

Comments/Statements (unpublished)

Burrow, Rufus, Jr. "On *Behind the Public Veil*—Comments." (7 February 2015).

"Dr. King and Jackie Robinson Head Rebuilding for Burned Churches." SCLC Press Release (12 September 1962).

King, Martin Luther, Jr. "An Ambitious Dream Confronts Reality." Essay prepared For *Amsterdam News*, New York, New York (23 June 1965).

____. "Message for My People." Released to the Associated Press, New York City, New York (1 January 1966).

____. "Remarks at the Funeral of Armistead Phelps." Enid, Mississippi (12 June 1966).

____. "Statement Regarding Mahalia Jackson's Appearance in Atlanta." Atlanta, Georgia (26 November 1963).

____. "The Agenda for the Meeting of the SCLC." Richmond, Virginia (31 October 1958).

____. "True Dignity." (n.d.).

____ and Ralph D. Abernathy. "Why Our Prayer Vigil." Albany, Georgia (1962).

"Observe Human Rights Day December 10 by Answering this Appeal for Action Against Apartheid: International Sponsors." American Committee on Africa (July 1962).

"Remarks of Dr. Martin Luther King, Jr: *'EN GRÄNSLOS KVÄL PÅ OPERAN.'*" Stockholm, Sweden (31 March 1966).

The American Negro Leadership Conference on Africa: Resolution. Arden House, Columbia University, Harriman, New York (23–25 November 1962).

Interviews (unpublished)

A Private Interview with John Egerton, Nashville, Tennessee (27 June 1986).

A Private Interview with Bernard S. Lee, Washington, D. C. (9 July 1986).

A Private Interview with Reverend Ralph D. Abernathy, West Hunter Street Baptist Church, Atlanta, Georgia (17 March 1987).

A Private Interview with Reverend Ralph D. Abernathy, Wheat Street Baptist Church, Atlanta, Georgia (7 May 1987).

A Private Interview with Philip Lenud, Vanderbilt Divinity School, Nashville, Tennessee (7 April 1987).

A Private Interview with Emma Anderson, Chester, Pennsylvania (29 May 1987).

A Private Interview with Sara Richardson, Chester, Pennsylvania (29 May 1987).

A Private Interview with Reverend Michael E. Haynes, Twelfth Baptist Church, Boston, Massachusetts (25 June 1987).

A Private Interview with Reverend Robert S. Graetz, Cincinnati, Ohio (26 July 1988).

A Private Interview with George M. Houser, Pomona, New York (26 May 1993).

A Telephone Interview with David L. Baldwin (17 April 2015).

A Telephone Interview with James M. Lawson, Jr. (11 June 2013).

A Telephone Interview with Nelson Malden (15 March 2014).

A Telephone Interview with Nelson Malden (23 May 2014).

"Cassius Clay (Muhammad Ali) and Martin Luther King, Jr. Being Interviewed." Transcribed Document. Louisville, Kentucky (29 March 1967).

"Martin Luther King, Jr. Press Conference." An Interview, ABC, New York, New York (14 December 1967).

Letters and Emails (unpublished)

Anne Braden to Martin Luther King, Jr. (1 December 1962).

Email Message from Customer Service of Rodale Books to Lewis V. Baldwin (21 May 2015).

George M. Houser to Lewis V. Baldwin (9 October 1987).

Jackie Robinson to Martin Luther King, Jr. (9 October 1962).

Jackie Robinson to Martin Luther King, Jr. (10 April 1967).

James R. Wood to Mr. L. F. Palmer, dictated by Martin Luther King, Jr. (23 February 1961).

Joseph H. Jackson to Martin Luther King, Jr. (28 September 1955).

Martin Luther King, Jr. to Leroy Freeman (8 October 1962).

Martin Luther King, Jr. to Mahalia Jackson (10 January 1964).

Martin Luther King, Jr. to Mr. Robert Pobuda, Crowell School, Albion, Michigan (1 December 1960).

Martin Luther King, Jr. to Nat King Cole (18 July 1963).

Martin Luther King, Jr. to Sammy Davis, Jr. (28 March 1961).

Martin Luther King, Jr. to the Student Body of Jesse Crowell School, Albion, Michigan, (1 December 1960).

Muhammad Ali to Martin Luther King, Jr. (2 November 1967).

Nat King Cole to Martin Luther King, Jr. (25 June 1963).

Ralph McGill to Martin Luther King, Jr. (1 May 1967).

Wendell Foster to Martin Luther King, Jr. (10 April 1967).

Wyatt Tee Walker to Lewis V. Baldwin (30 April 2009).

Television Transcripts, Videotape Interviews, Recordings

"Face to Face: Dr. Martin Luther King, Jr. and John Freeman," U. K. (London?), Recorded from transmission and aired (29 October 1961).

King, Alberta. "Dr. Martin Luther King, Jr.: Birth to Twelve Years Old by His Mother," A Recording, Ebenezer Baptist Church, Atlanta, Georgia (18 January 1973).

King, Martin Luther, Jr. "Early Days." *The Voice of Greatness—Dr. Martin Luther King, Jr., 1929-1968: Excerpts from His Most Famous Speeches with the Clara Ward Singers.* London: Benash Record Company, Limited, 1971.

King, Martin Luther, Jr. "What is Man?" on "Sunday with Martin Luther King, Jr.," WAAF—AM, Chicago, Illinois (17 April 1966).

"Martin Luther King, Jr.: An Amazing Grace." 60 Minutes Videotape, 831V. Huntsville, Texas: Educational Video Network, Inc., n.d.

"Martin Luther King, Jr.: A Personal Portrait," a videotaped interview (Goldsboro, NC: Distributed by Carroll's Marketing and Management Service (1966–67).

"Martin Luther King, Jr., "Transcript of an Interview on the Merv Griffith Show." NBC sitcom, New York, New York (6 July 1967).

Robeson, Paul. *Songs of My People.* RCA Victor (recorded on 7 January 1926). LM–3292.

"The Johnson Tapes: Uncivil Liberties." Part II. Bethesda, MD: Discovery Channel Educational, a Division of Discovery Communications, Inc., 2000.

"The Promised Land 1967-68." Directed by Jacqueline Shearer and Paul Stekler. Originally aired 1990, from *Eyes on the Prize: America's Civil Rights Movement—DVD7PK, AV Item, 7 DVD Set, Item No.: Eyes 700.*

Special Citations

"Festival of Faith and Freedom 1962: Special Citation to Miss Mahalia Jackson." Bushnell Auditorium, Hartford, Connecticut (28 October 1962).

Coretta Scott King: "An Address at the National Conference on Civil Rights." Fisk University, Nashville, Tennessee (Speech; 5 April 1986).

Sermons of Dr. Martin Luther King, Jr.

"A Christian in a Revolutionary Age." (Fall, 1966).

"A Knock at Midnight." All Saints Church Los Angeles, California (25 June 1967).

"A Knock at Midnight." Canaan Baptist Church, New York, New York (24 March 1968).

"Answer to a Perplexing Question." Ebenezer Baptist Church, Atlanta, Georgia (3 March 1963).

"Discerning the Signs of History." Ebenezer Baptist Church, Atlanta, Georgia (15 November 1964).

"Dives and Lazarus." Atlanta, Georgia (10 March 1963).

"Guidelines for a Constructive Church." Ebenezer Baptist Church, Atlanta, Georgia (5 June 1966).

"Ingratitude." Ebenezer Baptist Church, Atlanta, Georgia (18 June 1967).

"Interruptions." Ebenezer Baptist Church, Atlanta, Georgia (21 January 1968).

"Is the Universe Friendly?" Ebenezer Baptist Church, Atlanta, Georgia (12 December 1965).

"Lost Sheep or the God of the Lost." (18 September 1966).

"Making the Best of a Bad Mess." Ebenezer Baptist Church, Atlanta, Georgia (24 April 1966).

"Moving to Another Mountain." Wesleyan University, Middletown, Connecticut (7 June 1964).

"My Call to Preach." American Baptist Convention (7 August 1959).

"New Wine in Old Bottles." Ebenezer Baptist Church, Atlanta, Georgia (2 January 1966).

"The Drum Major Instinct." Ebenezer Baptist Church, Atlanta, Georgia (4 February 1968).

"The Meaning of Hope." Dexter Avenue Baptist Church, Montgomery, Alabama (10 December 1967).

"The Prodigal Son." Ebenezer Baptist Church, Atlanta, Georgia (4 September 1966).

"Thou Fool." Mt. Pisgah Missionary Baptist Church, Chicago, Illinois (27 August 1967).

"Training Your Child in Love." Ebenezer Baptist Church, Atlanta, Georgia (8 May 1966).

"Transformed Nonconformist." Ebenezer Baptist Church, Atlanta, Georgia (16 January 1966).

"We Would See Jesus." Ebenezer Baptist Church, Atlanta, Georgia (7 May 1967).

"What a Mother Should Tell Her Child." Ebenezer Baptist Church, Atlanta, Georgia (12 May 1963).

"What is Man," on "Sunday with Martin Luther King, Jr." WAAF—AM, Chicago, Illinois (17 April 1966).

"Who are We?" Ebenezer Baptist Church, Atlanta, Georgia (5 February 1966).

Speeches of Dr. Martin Luther King, Jr.

"Address at a Mass Meeting." Clarksdale, Mississippi (19 March 1968).

"Address at a Mass Meeting." Maggie Street Baptist Church, Montgomery, Alabama (16 February 1968).

"Address at a Mass Meeting." St. James Baptist Church, Birmingham, Alabama (31 January 1966).

"Address at a Mass Meeting." Yazoo City, Mississippi (21 June 1966).

"Address at the Chicago Freedom Movement Rally." Soldier Field, Chicago, Illinois (10 July 1966).

"Address at the National Bar Association." Milwaukee, Wisconsin (20 August 1959).

"Address to the National Press Club." Washington, D. C. (19 July 1962).

"An Address at a Mass Meeting." Marks, Mississippi (19 March 1968).

"An Address at the Freedom Fund Report Dinner." 53rd Annual Convention of the NAACP, Atlanta, Georgia (5 July 1962).

"A Speech." Grenada, Mississippi (15 June 1966).

"Crisis and a Political Rally in Alabama." Sixteenth Street Baptist Church, Birmingham, Alabama (3 May 1963).

"Field of Education a Battleground." The United Federation of Teachers, New York, New York (14 March 1964).

"Prelude to Tomorrow." SCLC Operation Breadbasket Meeting, Chicago, Illinois (6 January 1968).

"Pre-Washington Campaign." Mississippi Leaders on the Washington Campaign, St. Thomas AME Church, Birmingham, Alabama (15 February 1968).

"Rally Speech on the Georgia Tour 'Pre-Washington Campaign.'" Albany, Georgia (22 March 1968).

"See You in Washington." SCLC Staff Retreat, Ebenezer Baptist Church, Atlanta, Georgia (17 January 1968).

"Speech at a Mass Meeting." Augusta, Georgia (22 March 1968).

"Speech at a Mass Meeting." Grenada, Mississippi (19 March 1968).

"Speech at a Mass Meeting." Macon, Georgia (22 March 1968).

"Speech at a Mass Meeting." Selma, Alabama (16 February 1968).

"Speech in Savannah." Savannah, Georgia (1 January 1961).

"Sleeping through a Revolution." Sheraton Hotel, Chicago, Illinois (10 December 1967).

"The Ballot." (17 July 1962).

"The Church on the Frontiers of Racial Tension." Gay Lectures, Southern Baptist Theological Seminary, Louisville, Kentucky (19 April 1961).

"The Crisis of Civil Rights." Operation Breadbasket Meeting, Chicago, Illinois (10 July 1967).

"The Dignity of Family Life." Abbott House, Westchester County, New York (29 October 1965).

"The Negro Family." University of Chicago, Chicago, Illinois (27 January 1966).

"Transforming a Neighborhood." The NATRA Convention, RCA Dinner, Atlanta, Georgia (10 August 1967).

"Why a Movement." (28 November 1967).

"Why We Must Go to Washington." SCLC Retreat, Ebenezer Baptist Church, Atlanta, Georgia (15 January 1968).

Index of Names